Documenting America
A Reader in United States History

Volume Two

from 1865 to the Present

Edited by
Leonard Pitt
California State University
Northridge, California

KENDALL/HUNT PUBLISHING COMPANY
2460 Kerper Boulevard P.O. Box 539 Dubuque, Iowa 52004-0539

To Dale, again.

Contents

Chapter Three: War

Chapter Four: Race

Chapter Five: Nationality and Religion

Chapter Eight: Environment

Preface

The historian Laurens Van Der Post faults "the popular habit of lifting history out of its proper context and bending it to the values of another age and day. In this way history is never allowed to be itself."

One way to let history be itself is to focus on original sources. This book, *Documenting America*, is designed to do just that—to help students think about the past as professional historians do—by analyzing evidence and forming their own judgments about what the evidence means. The documents presented here have a particular framework in that they grow out of important controversies that invite the reader to think about and pass judgment on the issues. Using them becomes a form of detective work, rather than a process of memorization.

Many students regard history as a vast mountain of facts waiting to be memorized (and repeated on examinations). But, to professionals, history is a process of asking questions about past events and sifting the evidence left over from those events in order to create coherent mental pictures of what happened. Many different interpretations are possible. In this sense, virtually anyone can be an historian.

There is a bonus in mastering this process. Most of the methods that historians employ to understand past events can also be used to make sense of the present.

The documents in this collection come from a variety of sources: public speeches, newspaper reports, essays, books, letters, song lyrics, congressional reports, journals, diaries, autobiographies, legal depositions, law codes, court decisions, etc. They contain the words of leaders, but also of ordinary people. In other words, they consist of the many types of sources that historians draw upon when reconstructing the past.

Of course in order to interpret documents, it is necessary to have as much background information as possible. To explain the meaning of documents one has to understand their context. *Documenting America* provides enough context in the headnotes to at least begin the analysis. A basic text book will contain valuable additional background and class lectures and discussions will bring to light other data. Additional information can be found in the *Dictionary of American Biography* and in the *Dictionary of American History*, and in books and articles available in many libraries.

Asking questions, as I have already suggested, is at the heart of the historical process. In the headnotes I have listed some questions you might want to explore. Other questions will occur to you that are at least as useful for understanding what was going on.

I have grouped related documents together to highlight recurrent patterns of change. The groupings themselves are important. *Documenting America* makes no attempt to cover all major events, as a basic textbook might. Instead, it provides sets of documents organized by major themes of American history. These themes are eight in number: wealth; power; war; race; nationality and religion; women and the family; community; and environment. Presenting the documents topically helps the reader to understand particular subjects in greater depth and to make more sense of them than if a simple chronological order were followed. Yet the time when things happened and the sequence of events are important, often vital, to historical interpretation, and the students should check the dates of various articles—and even create a chronological chart—to help reveal hidden relationships.

I hope you will enjoy the kind of detective work this book entails. To master the technique of interpretation may take time and patience, but the reactions of my own students suggest that students using this book will experience the satisfaction of making their own interpretations of history. You will be intrigued to discover that many people may read a document and come to different interpretations. And you will be amazed that your interpretation makes as much sense as anyone else's. You will realize also that an imaginative interpretation differs from wild guesswork.

Incidentally, this book has a companion volume that deals with the earlier part of our history. It is entitled *Documenting America: A Reader in United States History from Colonial Times to 1876,* and is issued by the same publisher.

As editor, I am very much interested in how this book will be used. I expect to change it as I receive information from readers. Please let me know how it works for you.

I wish to give grateful acknowledgement to two people who helped me greatly in the preparation of this work. My colleague, Ronald Schaffer, offered invaluable counsel in the picking of documents and the shaping of questions. My wife, Dale Pitt, gave general advice and performed extensive editorial work. Both should be exonerated, though, for any errors of fact or judgment that may appear here.

Leonard Pitt
February
1989

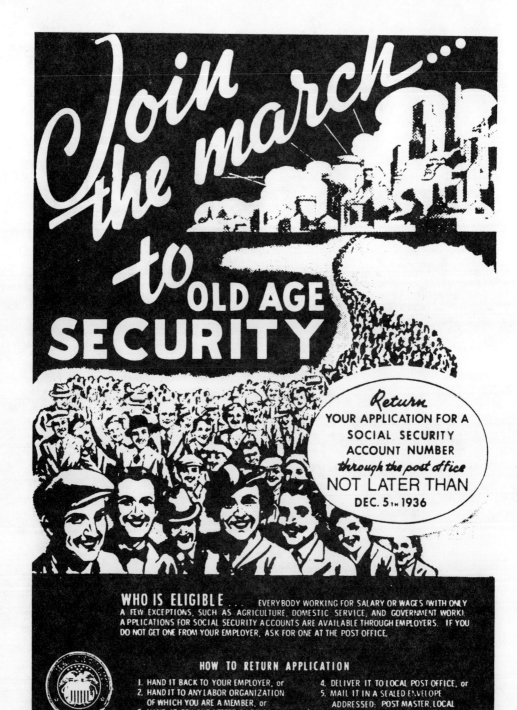

Chapter One: Wealth

1.1   The Gospel of Wealth

If anyone represented the American rags-to-riches ideal it was Andrew Carnegie (1835–1919). When he was twelve years old, he and his family—weavers displaced by power machinery—migrated from Scotland to the United States, where he rose from a child laborer to the richest man in the world. Carnegie built most of his fortune in the steel industry, mastering the industrial technology that was reshaping American society. He was a brilliant organizer and salesman, with a genius for integrating the parts of a giant business enterprise and selecting able managers to run it.

Carnegie's workers labored twelve hours a day, seven days a week, and, in some units, twenty-four hours straight every two weeks. Although he was not philosophically opposed to unions, his corporate managers crushed the steel workers' union at the Homestead, Pennsylvania plant by deploying three hundred private detectives and several thousand state troops.

But Carnegie felt it was wrong for the wealthy to devote themselves solely to amassing wealth. He believed they had an obligation to return some of their riches to society. He did so not by raising wages or lowering the cost of steel, or dribbling money to the poor and needy (which he thought would make them dependent on handouts). Instead, he developed a system of philanthropy that enabled him to control how his wealth would be distributed. During his lifetime he gave away $350,695,653 to erect library buildings, assist universities, promote international peace, develop the arts, and support other causes. At the time of his death in 1919, he left an estate of merely thirty million dollars.

In this essay, first published in 1889, Carnegie explains why, in a nation seemingly dedicated to equality, the growth of extremes in wealth and poverty is actually a virtue; and why people who want to even out such extremes are wasting their time.

Questions

How did Carnegie justify the concentration of wealth in the hands of a few? Is it, in your opinion, a sound argument?

Do very wealthy people tend to improve society, or was Carnegie an exception?

Should the richest segment have the right to shape society in the way they think best, or should it be done some other way? Do the wealthy have the best understanding of social needs?

Can you think of better ways of using such riches? Should Carnegie's workers have received higher wages even if that meant he would have had less to give away?

What does he mean by survival of the fittest? Carnegie talks about the law of competition; yet he and other captains of industry systematically destroyed competition in American industries. How do you explain this apparent contradiction?

Which people in America today tend to agree with Carnegie's ideas? Do you believe them? Explain.

The problem of our age is the proper administration of wealth, so that the ties of brotherhood may still bind together the rich and poor in harmonious relationship. The conditions of human life have not only been changed, but revolutionized, within the past few hundred years. In former days there was little difference between the dwelling, dress, food, and environment of the chief and those of his retainers. The Indians are to-day where civilized man then was. . . . The contrast between the palace of the millionaire and the cottage of the laborer with us to-day measures the change which has come with civilization.

This change, however, is not to be deplored, but welcomed as highly beneficial. It is well, nay, essential for the progress of the race, that the houses of some should be homes for all that is highest and best in literature and the arts, and for all the refinements of civilization, rather than that none should be so. Much better this great irregularity than universal squalor. . . . But whether the change be for good or ill, it is upon us, beyond our power to alter, and therefore to be accepted and made the best of. It is a waste of time to criticise the inevitable.

It is easy to see how the change has come. . . . Formerly articles were manu-

SOURCE: Andrew Carnegie, "Wealth," *North American Review*, 148 (June, 1889), 653–664.

factured at the domestic hearth or in small shops which formed part of the household. The master and his apprentices worked side by side, the latter living with the master, and therefore subject to the same conditions. When these apprentices rose to be masters, there was little or no change in their mode of life, and they, in turn, educated in the same routine succeeding apprentices. There was, substantially, social equality, and even political equality, for those engaged in industrial pursuits had then little or no political voice in the State.

But the inevitable result of such a mode of manufacture was crude articles at high prices. To-day the world obtains commodities of excellent quality at prices which even the generation preceding this would have deemed incredible. In the commercial world similar causes have produced similar results, and the race is benefited thereby. The poor enjoy what the rich could not before afford. What were the luxuries have become the necessaries of life. The laborer has now more comforts than the farmer had a few generations ago. The farmer has more luxuries than the landlord had, and is more richly clad and better housed. The landlord has books and pictures rarer, and appointments more artistic, than the King could then obtain.

The price we pay for this salutary change is, no doubt, great. We assemble thousands of operatives in the factory, in the mine, and in the counting-house, of whom the employer can know little or nothing, and to whom the employer is little better than a myth. All intercourse between them is at an end. Rigid Castes are formed, and, as usual, mutual ignorance breeds mutual distrust. Each Caste is without sympathy for the other, and ready to credit anything disparaging in regard to it. Under the law of competition, the employer of thousands is forced into the strictest economies, among which the rates paid to labor figure prominently, and often there is friction between the employer and the employed, between capital and labor, between rich and poor. Human society loses homogeneity.

The price which society pays for the law of competition, like the price it pays for cheap comforts and luxuries, is also great; but the advantages of this law are also greater still, for it is to this law that we owe our wonderful material development, which brings improved conditions in its train. . . . and while the law may be sometimes hard for the individual, it is best for the race, because it insures the survival of the fittest in every department. We accept and welcome, therefore, as conditions to which we must accommodate ourselves, great inequality of environment, the concentration of business, industrial and commercial, in the hands of a few, and the law of competition between these, as being not only beneficial, but essential for the future progress of the race. Having accepted these, it follows that there must be great scope for the exercise of special ability in the merchant and in the manufacturer who has to conduct affairs upon a great scale. That this talent for organization and management is rare among men is proved by the fact that it invariably secures for its

possessor enormous rewards, no matter where or under what laws or conditions. The experienced in affairs always rate the MAN whose services can be obtained as a partner as not only the first consideration, but such as to render the question of his capital scarcely worth considering, for such men soon create capital; while, without the special talent required, capital soon takes wings. Such men become interested in firms or corporations using millions; and estimating only simple interest to be made upon the capital invested, it is inevitable that their income must exceed their expenditures, and that they must accumulate wealth. . . .

Objections to the foundations upon which society is based are not in order, because the condition of the race is better with these than it has been with any others which have been tried. Of the effect of any new substitutes proposed we cannot be sure. The Socialist or Anarchist who seeks to overturn present conditions is to be regarded as attacking the foundation upon which civilization itself rests, for civilization took its start from the day that the capable, industrious workman said to his incompetent and lazy fellow, "If thou dost not sow, thou shalt not reap," and thus ended primitive Communism by separating the drones from the bees. One who studies this subject will soon be brought face to face with the conclusion that upon the sacredness of property civilization itself depends—the right of the laborer to his hundred dollars in the savings bank, and equally the legal right of the millionaire to his millions. To those who propose to substitute Communism for this intense Individualism the answer, therefore, is: The race has tried that. All progress from that barbarous day to the present time has resulted from its displacement. Not evil, but good, has come to the race from the accumulation of wealth by those who have the ability and energy that produce it. . . . We might as well urge the destruction of the highest existing type of man because he failed to reach our ideal as to favor the destruction of Individualism, Private Property, the Law of Accumulation of Wealth, and the Law of Competition; for these are the highest results of human experience, the soil in which society so far has produced the best fruit. Unequally or unjustly, perhaps, as these laws sometimes operate, and imperfect as they appear to the Idealist, they are, nevertheless, like the highest type of man, the best and most valuable of all that humanity has yet accomplished. . . .

. . . The question then arises,—and, if the foregoing be correct, it is the only question with which we have to deal,— What is the proper mode of administering wealth after the laws upon which civilization is founded have thrown it into the hands of the few? And it is of this great question that I believe I offer the true solution. It will be understood that *fortunes* are here spoken of, not moderate sums saved by many years of effort, the returns from which are required for the comfortable maintenance and education of families. This is not *wealth,* but only *competence,* which it should be the aim of all to acquire.

There are but three modes in which surplus wealth can be disposed of. It can be left to the families of the decedents; or it can be bequeathed for public purposes; or, finally, it can be administered during their lives by its possessors. Under the first and second modes most of the wealth of the world that has reached the few has hitherto been applied. Let us in turn consider each of these modes. The first is the most injudicious. In monarchical countries, the

estates and the greatest portion of the wealth are left to the first son, that the vanity of the parent may be gratified by the thought that his name and title are to descend to succeeding generations unimpaired. The condition of this class in Europe to-day teaches the futility of such hopes or ambitions. The successors have become impoverished through their follies or from the fall in the value of land. Even in Great Britain the strict law of entail has been found inadequate to maintain the status of an hereditary class. Its soil is rapidly passing into the hands of the stranger. Under republican institutions the division of property among the children is much fairer, but the question which forces itself upon thoughtful men in all lands is: Why should men leave great fortunes to their children? If this is done from affection, is it not misguided affection? Observation teaches that, generally speaking, it is not well for the children that they should be so burdened. Neither is it well for the state. Beyond providing for the wife and daughters moderate sources of income, and very moderate allowances indeed, if any, for the sons, men may well hesitate, for it is no longer questionable that great sums bequeathed oftener work more for the injury than for the good of the recipients. Wise men will soon conclude that, for the best interests of the members of their families and of the state, such bequests are an improper use of their means.

It is not suggested that men who have failed to educate their sons to earn a livelihood shall cast them adrift in poverty. If any man has been fit to rear his sons with a view to their living idle lives, or, what is highly commendable, has instilled in them the sentiment that they are in a position to labor for public ends without reference to pecuniary considerations, then, of course, the duty of the parent is to see that such are provided for *in moderation.* There are instances of millionaires' sons unspoiled by wealth, who, being rich, still perform great services in the community. Such are the very salt of the earth, as valuable as, unfortunately, they are rare; still it is not the exception, but the rule, that men must regard, and, looking at the usual result of enormous sums conferred upon legatees, the thoughtful man must shortly say, "I would as soon leave to my son a curse as the almighty dollar," and admit to himself that it is not the welfare of the children, but family pride, which inspires these enormous legacies.

As to the second mode, that of leaving wealth at death for public uses, it may be said that this is only a means for the disposal of wealth, provided a man is content to wait until he is dead before it becomes of much good in the world. Knowledge of the results of legacies bequeathed is not calculated to inspire the brightest hopes of much posthumous good being accomplished. The cases are not few in which the real object sought by the testator is not attained, nor are they few in which his real wishes are thwarted. In many cases the bequests are so used as to become only monuments of his folly. . . . Men who leave vast sums in this way may fairly be thought men who would not have left it at all, had they been able to take it with them. The memories of such cannot be held in grateful remembrance, for there is no grace in their gifts. It is not to be wondered at that such bequests seem so generally to lack the blessing. . . .

There remains, then, only one mode of using great fortunes; but in this we have the true antidote for the temporary unequal distribution of wealth, the reconciliation of the rich and the poor—a reign of harmony—another ideal, differing, indeed, from that of the Communist in requiring only the further evolution of existing conditions, not the total overthrow of our civilization. It is founded upon the present most intense individualism, and the race is prepared to put it in practice by degrees whenever it pleases. Under its sway we shall have an ideal state, in which the surplus wealth of the few will become, in the best sense, the property of the many, because administered for the common good, and this wealth, passing through the hands of the few, can be made a much more potent force for the elevation of our race than if it had been distributed in small sums to the people themselves. Even the poorest can be made to see this, and to agree that great sums gathered by some of their fellow-citizens and spent for public purposes, from which the masses reap the principal benefit, are more valuable to them than if scattered among them through the course of many years in trifling amounts. . . .

Poor and restricted are our opportunities in this life; narrow our horizon; our best work most imperfect, but rich men should be thankful for one inestimable boon. They have it in their power during their lives to busy themselves in organizing benefactions from which the masses of their fellows will derive lasting advantage, and thus dignify their own lives. The highest life is probably to be reached, not by such imitation of the life of Christ as Count Tolstoï gives us, but, while animated by Christ's spirit, by recognizing the changed conditions of this age, and adopting modes of expressing this spirit suitable to the changed conditions under which we live; still laboring for the good of our fellows, which was the essence of his life and teaching, but laboring in a different manner.

This, then, is held to be the duty of the man of Wealth: First, to set an example of modest, unostentatious living, shunning display or extravagance; to provide moderately for the legitimate wants of those dependent upon him; and after doing so to consider all surplus revenues which come to him simply as trust funds, which he is called upon to administer, and strictly bound as a matter of duty to administer in the manner which, in his judgment, is best calculated to produce the most beneficial results for the community—the man of wealth thus becoming the mere agent and trustee for his poorer brethren, bringing to their service his superior wisdom, experience, and ability to administer, doing for them better than they would or could do for themselves.

We are met here with the difficulty of determining what are moderate sums to leave to members of the family; what is modest, unostentatious living; what is the test of extravagance. There must be different standards for different conditions. The answer is that it is as impossible to name exact amounts or actions as it is to define good manners, good taste, or the rules of propriety; but, nevertheless, these are verities, well known although undefinable. Public sentiment is quick to know and to feel what offends these. So in the case of wealth. The rule in regard to good taste in the dress of men or women applies here. Whatever makes one conspicuous offends the canon. . . .

The best uses to which surplus wealth can be put have already been indicated. Those who would administer wisely must, indeed, be wise, for one of the serious obstacles to the improvement of our race is

indiscriminate charity. It were better for mankind that the millions of the rich were thrown into the sea than so spent as to encourage the slothful, the drunken, the unworthy. Of every thousand dollars spent in so called charity today, it is probable that $950 is unwisely spent; so spent, indeed, as to produce the very evils which it proposes to mitigate or cure. A wellknown writer of philosophic books admitted the other day that he had given a quarter of a dollar to a man who approached him as he was coming to visit the house of his friend. . . . the quarter-dollar given that night will probably work more injury than all the money which its thoughtless donor will ever be able to give in true charity will do good. He only gratified his own feelings, saved himself from annoyance,—and this was probably one of the most selfish and very worst actions of his life, for in all respects he is most worthy.

In bestowing charity, the main consideration should be to help those who will help themselves; to provide part of the means by which those who desire to improve may do so; to give those who desire to rise the aids by which they may rise; to assist, but rarely or never to do all. Neither the individual nor the race is improved by alms-giving. Those worthy of assistance, except in rare cases, seldom require assistance. The really valuable men of the race never do, except in cases of accident or sudden change. Every one has, of course, cases of individuals brought to his own knowledge where temporary assistance can do genuine good, and these he will not overlook. . . . He is the only true reformer who is as careful and as anxious not to aid the unworthy as he is to aid the worthy, and, perhaps, even more so, for in alms-giving more injury is probably done by rewarding vice than by relieving virtue.

The rich man is thus almost restricted to following the examples of Peter Cooper, Enoch Pratt of Baltimore, Mr. Pratt of Brooklyn, Senator Stanford, and others, who know that the best means of benefiting the community is to place within its reach the ladders upon which the aspiring can rise—parks, and means of recreation, by which men are helped in body and mind; works of art, certain to give pleasure and improve the public taste, and public institutions of various kinds, which will improve the general condition of the people;—in this manner returning their surplus wealth to the mass of their fellows in the forms best calculated to do them lasting good.

Thus is the problem of Rich and Poor to be solved. The laws of accumulation will be left free; the laws of distribution free. Individualism will continue, but the millionaire will be but a trustee for the poor; intrusted for a season with a great part of the increased wealth of the community, but administering it for the community far better than it could or would have done for itself. The best minds will thus have reached a stage in the development of the race in which it is clearly seen that there is no mode of disposing of surplus wealth creditable to thoughtful and earnest men into whose hands it flows save by using it year by year for the general good. This day already dawns. But a little while, and although, without incurring the pity of their fellows, men may die sharers in great business enterprises from which their capital cannot be or has not been withdrawn, and is left chiefly at death for public uses, yet the man who dies leaving behind him millions of available wealth, which was his to administer during life, will pass away "unwept, unhonored, and unsung," no matter to what uses he leaves the dross which he cannot take with him. Of such as these the public verdict will then be: "The man who dies thus rich dies disgraced."

Such, in my opinion, is the true Gospel concerning Wealth, obedience to which is destined some day to solve the problem of the Rich and the Poor, and to bring "Peace on earth, among men Good-Will."

1.2 The Generosity of Andrew Carnegie

Humor can be a devastating political and social weapon. Journalist Finley Peter Dunne (1867–1936) knew this when he created a newspaper column featuring a fictional character named "Mr. Dooley." The imaginary Mr. Dooley became a well-known commentator on the late nineteenth-century scene. He took the form of a Chicago Irish barman who usually expressed himself in dialogues with co-worker and straight-man, Malachi Hennessey. Delivering his sly wit in a strong Irish accent, Dooley managed to puncture many social and political balloons.

In the following dissertation, the saloon keeper takes a shot at one of Andrew Carnegie's most celebrated philanthropic projects, the Carnegie libraries. He implies that something be-

sides the love of humanity may have induced the great steel manufacturer to give away his millions.

Questions

What, according to Dooley/Dunne, was the unstated reason Carnegie gave away his fortune?

What, in your opinion, is the right way to deal with the poor and homeless, and what role should be played by individual volunteer workers, private philanthropy and government social services?

Are you aware of any current social commentators who use humor to make their points? Are they effective?

'Has Andhrew Carnaygie given ye a libry yet?' asked Mr. Dooley.

'Not that I know iv,' said Mr. Hennessy.

'He will,' said Mr. Dooley. 'Ye'll not escape him. Befure he dies he hopes to crowd a libry on ivry man, woman, an' child in th' counthry. He's given thim to cities, towns, villages, an' whistlin' stations. They're tearin' down gas-houses an' poor-houses to put up libries. Befure another year, ivry house in Pittsburg that ain't a blast-furnace will be a Carnaygie libry. In some places all th' buildin's is libries. If ye write him f'r an autygraft he sinds ye a libry. No beggar is iver turned impty-handed fr'm th' dure. Th' pan-handler knocks an' asts f'r a glass iv milk an' a roll. "No, sir," said Andhrew Carnaygie. "I will not pauperize this onworthy man. Nawthin' is worse f'r a beggar-man thin to make a pauper iv him. Yet it shall not be said iv me that I give nawthin' to th' poor. Saun-

ders, give him a libry, an' if he still insists on a roll tell him to roll th' libry. F'r I'm humorous as well as wise," he says.'

'Does he give th' books that go with it?' asked Mr. Hennessy.

'Books?' said Mr. Dooley. 'What ar-re ye talkin' about? D'ye know what a libry is? I suppose ye think it's a place where a man can go, haul down wan iv his fav'rite authors fr'm th' shelf, an' take a nap in it. That' not a Carnaygie libry. A Carnaygie libry is a large, brown-stone, impenethrible buildin' with th' name iv th' maker blown on th' dure. Libry, fr'm th' Greek wurruds, libus, a book an' ary, sildom,—sildom a book. A Carnaygie libry is archytechoor, not lithrachoor. Lithrachoor will be riprisinted. Th' most cillybrated dead authors will be honored be havin' their names painted on th' wall in distinguished comp'ny, as thus: Andhrew Carnaygie, Shakespeare; Andhrew Carnaygie, Byron; Andrew Carnaygie, Bobby Burns; Andhrew Carnaygie, an' so on. Ivry author is guaranteed a place next to pure readin' matther like a bakin' powdher advertise-

SOURCE: Finley Peter Dunne, "The Carnegie Libraries," *Dissertations by Mr. Dooley* (New York: Harper & Brothers, 1906), pp. 177–82.

mint, so that whin a man comes along that niver heerd iv Shakespeare he'll know he was somebody, because there he is on th' wall. That's th' dead authors. Th' live authors will stand outside an' wish they were dead.

'He's havin' gr-reat spoort with it. I r-read his speech th' other day, whin he laid th' corner-stone iv th' libry at Pianola, Ioway. Th' entire popylation iv this lithry cinter gathered to see an' hear him. There was th' postmaster an' his wife, th' blacksmith an' his fam'ly, the station agent, mine host iv th' Farmers' Exchange, an' some sthray live stock. "Ladies an' gintlemen," says he. "Modesty compels me to say nawthin' on this occasion, but I am not to be bulldozed," he says. "I can't tell ye how much pleasure I take in' disthributin' monymints to th' humble name around which has gathered so manny hon'rable associations with mesilf. I have been a very busy little man all me life, but I like hard wurruk, an' givin' away me money is th' hardest wurruk I iver did. It fairly makes me teeth ache to part with it. But there's wan consolation. I cheer mesilf with th' thought that no matther how much money I give it don't do anny particular person anny good. Th' worst thing ye can do f'r anny man is to do him good. I pass by th' organ-grinder on th' corner with a savage glare. I bate th' monkey on th' head whin he comes up smilin' to me window, an' hurl him down on his impecyoonyous owner. None iv me money goes into th' little tin cup. I cud kick a hospital, an' I lave Wall Sthreet to look afther th' widow an' th' orphan. Th' submerged tenth, thim that can't get hold iv a good chunk iv th' goods, I wud cut off fr'm th' rest iv th' wurruld an' prevint fr'm bearin' th' haughty name iv papa or th' still lovelier name iv ma. So far I've got on'y half me wish in this matther.

' "I don't want poverty an' crime to go on. I intind to stop it. But how? It's been holdin' its own f'r cinchries. Some iv th' gr-reatest iv former minds has undertook to prevint it an' has failed. They didn't know how. Modesty wud prevint me agin fr'm sayin' that I know how, but that' nayether here nor there. I do. Th' way to abolish poverty an' bust crime is to put up a brown-stone buildin' in ivry town in th' counthry with me name over it. That's th' way. I suppose th' raison it wasn't thried befure was that no man iver had such a name. 'Tis thrue me efforts is not apprecyated ivrywhere. I offer a city a libry, an' oftentimes it replies an' asks me f'r something to pay off th' school debt. I rayceive degraded pettyshuns fr'm so-called proud methropolises f'r a gas-house in place iv a libry. I pass thim by with scorn. All I ask iv a city in rayturn f'r a fifty-thousan'-dollar libry is that it shall raise wan millyon dollars to maintain th' buildin' an' keep me name shinny, an' if it won't do that much f'r lithrachoor, th' divvle take it, it's onworthy iv th' name iv an American city. What ivry community needs is taxes an' lithrachoor. I give thim both. Three cheers f'r a libry an' a bonded debt! Lithrachoor, taxation, an' Andhrew Carnaygie, wan an' insiprable, now an' foriver! They'se nawthin' so good as a good book. It's betther thin food; it's betther thin money. I have made money an' books, an' I like me books betther thin me money. Others don't, but I do. With these few wurruds I will conclude. . . ."

'All th' same, I like Andhrew Carnaygie. Him an' me ar-re agreed on that point. I like him because he ain't shamed to give publicly. Ye don't find him puttin' on false whiskers an' turnin' up his coat-collar whin he goes out to be benivolent. No sir. Ivry time he dhrops a dollar it makes a noise like a waither fallin' down-stairs with a tray iv dishes. He's givin' th' way we'd all like to give. I niver put annything in th' poor-box, but I wud if Father Kelly wud rig up like wan iv thim slot-machines, so that whin I stuck in a nickel me name wud appear over th' altar in red letthers. But whin I put a dollar in th' plate I get back about two yards an' hurl it so hard that th' good man turns around to see who done it. Do good be stealth, says I, but see that th' burglar-alarm is set. Anny benivolent money I hand out

I want to talk about me. Him that giveth to th' poor, they say, lindeth to th' Lord; but in these days we look f'r quick returns on our invistments. I like Andhrew Carnaygie, an', as he says, he puts his whole soul into th' wurruk.'

'What's he mane be that?' asked Mr. Hennessy.

'He manes,' said Mr. Dooley, 'that he's gin-rous. Ivry time he gives a libry he gives himsilf away in a speech.'

1.3 Who Made It From Rags to Riches?

Andrew Carnegie's success was so great that few other people could copy it. But there were many other success stories in the Gilded Age that seemed to encourage the hope that almost anyone could rise from rags to riches. The self-made man became a cult hero. He was often portrayed as a poor lad from a farm, small-town or immigrant background, who, at an early age, pulled himself up by his own bootstraps, and went to the big city to make his fortune. A recent study of industrial leaders in the 1870s tests some of these premises. Two scholars gathered information about several hundred leaders in textiles, railroads and steel. They traced their place of birth, fathers' occupations, levels of education and ages upon going to work. The results appears in the tables below. Note that a high proportion of these industrial leaders had fathers who were businessmen, came from a New England background, and were relatively old when they first went to work.

Questions

Do you find any surprises in the information on the chart? Can you draw a composite picture of an industrialist, using the information presented?

What significance is there in these findings compared to the rags-to-riches legend and myth? Should the information destroy or modify the myth of the self-made man? Does the myth continue today to any marked degree?

American Industrial Leaders of the 1870s in Textiles, Railroads and Steel

TABLE 1
Their Region of Birth

Birthplace	Textiles	Railroads	Steel	Total
	%	%	%	%
New England	90	39	24	51
Middle Atlantic	1	40	50	29
East North Central	1	4	7	4
South	1	6	1	3
West	..	1	..	1
U.S., Unspecified	..	..	4	2
United States	93	90	86	90
Foreign	7	10	14	10
Total cases (= 100%)	87	80	80	247

* These are census regions Combined in "South" are south Atlantic, south central, west south central, in "West" west north central, mountain, Pacific.

TABLE 2
Their Father's Occupation

Occupation	Textiles	Railroads	Steel	Total
	%	%	%	%
Businessman	57	49	48	51
Professional	7	16	16	13
Farmer	19	31	27	25
Public Official	2	4	..	3
Worker	15	..	11	8
Total cases (= 100%)	67	70	57	194

TABLE 3
The Highest Educational Level They Achieved

Education	Textiles	Railroads	Steel	Total
	%	%	%	%
Grammar School	25	22	43	30
High School	31	48	20	33
College	44	30	37	37
Total cases (= 100%)	59	64	60	183

SOURCE: Frances Gregory and Irene Neu, "The American Industrial Elite of the 1870s," in *Men in Business*, William Miller, ed. (Cambridge, Mass.: Harvard University Press, 1952), pp. 197, 202–203. Reprinted by permission of the publisher.

TABLE 4
Their Age on Going to Work

Age	Textiles	Railroads	Steel	Total
	%	%	%	%
15 or under	30	23	18	23
16–18	21	35	38	32
19 and over	49	42	44	45
Total cases (= 100%)	57	62	57	176

1.4   The Food Industry as Jungle

Upton Sinclair (1878–1968) was the most prolific radical writer of his time. He published over 100 works—novels, pamphlets, plays, and short stories—dealing with social problems, religion, war and peace, corruption, perversions of justice and economic inequality. Although a life-long socialist, he ran for governor of California in 1934 as an independent Democrat— and nearly won.

In his novel, The Jungle, *published in 1906, Sinclair hoped to reveal to middle-class readers the terrible living and working conditions of the immigrant working poor. By describing working conditions in a meat packing factory (see below), he seems to have affected the stomachs of his readers more than their minds. The book became the most famous American "muckraking novel" ever written.*

Questions

Do the events in these excerpts from The Jungle *seem plausible to you? Do you think Sinclair may have exaggerated to make his point? How did this novel affect public policy?*

Do you believe that the meat you eat today could be prepared under similar conditions? Explain your answer.

. . . It seemed as if every time you met a person from a new department, you heard of new swindles and new crimes. There was, for instance, a Lithuanian who was a cattle butcher for the plant where Marija had worked, which killed meat for canning only; and to hear this man describe the animals which came to his place would have been worth while for a Dante or a Zola. It seemed that they must have agencies all over the country, to hunt out old and crippled and diseased cattle to be canned. There were cattle which had been fed on "whisky-malt," the refuse of the breweries, and had become what the men called "steerly"—which means covered with boils. It was a nasty job killing these, for when you plunged your knife into them they would burst and splash foul-smelling stuff into your face; and when a man's sleeves were smeared with blood, and his hands steeped in it, how was he ever to wipe his face, or to clear his eyes so that he could see? It was stuff such as this that made the "embalmed beef" that had killed several times as many United States soldiers as all the bullets of the Spaniards; only the army beef, besides, was not fresh canned, it was old stuff that had been lying for years in the cellars.

Then one Sunday evening, Jurgis sat puffing his pipe by the kitchen stove, and talking with an old fellow whom Jonas had introduced, and who worked in the canning rooms at Durham's; and so Jurgis learned a few things about the great and only Durham canned goods, . . . And then there was "potted game" and "potted grouse," "potted ham," and "deviled ham"—de-vyled, as the men called it. "Devyled" ham was made out of the waste ends of smoked beef that were too small to

SOURCE: Upton Sinclair, *The Jungle* (New York, 1906), pp. 114–17, 160–62.

be sliced by the machines; and also tripe, dyed with chemicals so that it would not show white; and trimmings of hams and corned beef; and potatoes, skins and all; and finally the hard cartilaginous gullets of beef, after the tongues had been cut out. All this ingenious mixture was ground up and flavored with spices to make it taste like something. . . . men welcomed tuberculosis in the cattle they were feeding, because it made them fatten more quickly; and where they bought up all the old rancid butter left over in the grocery stores of a continent, and "oxidized" it by a forced-air process, to take away the odor, rechurned it with skim milk, and sold it in bricks in the cities! Up to a year or two ago it had been the custom to kill horses in the yards—ostensibly for fertilizer; but after long agitation the newspapers had been able to make the public realize that the horses were being canned. Now it was against the law to kill horses in Packingtown, and the law was really complied with—for the present, at any rate. . . .

There was another interesting set of statistics that a person might have gathered in Packingtown—those of the various afflictions of the workers. . . .

There were the men in the pickle rooms, for instance, where old Antanas had gotten his death; scarce a one of these that had not some spot of horror on his person. Let a man so much as scrape his finger pushing a truck in the pickle rooms, and he might have a sore that would put him out of the world; all the joints in his fingers might be eaten by the acid, one by one. Of the butchers and floorsmen, the beef-boners and trimmers, and all those who used knives, you could scarcely find a person who had the use of his thumb; time and time again the base of it had been slashed, till it was a mere lump of flesh against which the man pressed the knife to hold it. The hands of these men would be criss-crossed with cuts, until you could no longer pretend to count them or to trace them. They would have no nails,—they had worn them off pulling hides; their knuckles were swollen so that their fingers spread out like a fan. There were men who worked in the cooking rooms, in the midst of steam and sickening odors, by artificial light; in these rooms the germs of tuberculosis might live for two years, but the supply was renewed every hour. There were the beef-luggers, who carried two-hundred-pound quarters into the refrigerator-cars; a fearful kind of work, that began at four o'clock in the morning, and that wore out the most powerful men in a few years. There were those who worked in the chilling rooms, and whose special disease was rheumatism; the time limit that a man could work in the chilling rooms was said to be five years. There were the wool-pluckers, whose hands went to pieces even sooner than the hands of the pickle men; for the pelts of the sheep had to be painted with acid to loosen the wool, and then the pluckers had to pull out this wool with their bare hands, till the acid had eaten their fingers off. There were those who made the tins for the canned meat; and their hands, too, were a maze of cuts, and each cut represented a chance for blood poisoning. Some worked at the stamping machines, and it was very seldom that one could work long there at the pace that was set, and not give out and forget himself, and have a part of his hand chopped off. There were the "hoisters," as they were called, whose task it was to press the lever which lifted the dead cattle off the floor. They ran along upon a rafter, peering down through the damp and the steam; and as old Durham's architects had not built the killing room for the convenience of the hoisters, at every few feet they would have to stoop under a beam, say

four feet above the one they ran on; which got them into the habit of stooping, so that in a few years they would be walking like chimpanzees. Worst of any, however, were the fertilizer men, and those who served in the cooking rooms. These people could not be shown to the visitor,—for the odor of a fertilizer man would scare any ordinary visitor at a hundred yards, and as for the other men, who worked in tank rooms full of steam, and in some of which there were open vats near the level of the floor, their peculiar trouble was that they fell into the vats; and when they were fished out, there was never enough of them left to be worth exhibiting,—sometimes they would be overlooked for days, till all but the bones of them had gone out to the world as Durham's Pure Leaf Lard! . . .

Jonas had told them how the meat that was taken out of pickle would often be found sour, and how they would rub it up with soda to take away the smell, and sell it to be eaten on free-lunch counters; also of all the miracles of chemistry which they performed, giving to any sort of meat, fresh or salted, whole or chopped, any color and any flavor and any odor they chose. In the pickling of hams they had an ingenious apparatus, by which they saved time and increased the capacity of the plant—a machine consisting of a hollow needle attached to a pump; by plunging this needle into the meat and working with his foot, a man could fill a ham with pickle in a few seconds. And yet, in spite of this, there would be hams found spoiled, some of them with an odor so bad that a man could hardly bear to be in the room with them. To pump into these the packers had a second and much stronger pickle which destroyed the odor—a process known to the workers as "giving them thirty per cent." Also, after the hams had been smoked, there would be found some that had gone to the bad. Formerly these had been sold as "Number Three Grade," but later on some ingenious person had hit upon a new device, and now they would extract the bone, about which the bad part generally lay, and insert in the hole a white-hot iron. After this invention there was no longer Number One, Two, and Three Grade—there was only Number One Grade. . . .

It was only when the whole ham was spoiled that it came into the department of Elzbieta. Cut up by the two-thousand-revolutions-a-minute flyers, and mixed with half a ton of other meat, no odor that ever was in a ham could make any difference. There was never the least attention paid to what was cut up for sausage; there would come all the way back from Europe old sausage that had been rejected, and that was moldy and white—it would be dosed with borax and glycerine, and dumped into the hoppers, and made over again for home consumption. There would be meat that had tumbled out on the floor, in the dirt and sawdust, where the workers had tramped and spit uncounted billions of consumption germs. There would be meat stored in great piles in rooms; and the water from leaky roofs would drip over it, and thousands of rats would race about on it. It was too dark in these storage places to see well, but a man could run his hand over these piles of meat and sweep off handfuls of the dried dung of rats. These rats were nuisances, and the packers would put poisoned bread out for them; they would die, and then rats, bread, and meat would go into the hoppers together. This is no fairy story and no joke; the meat would be shoveled into carts, and the man who did the shoveling would not trouble to lift out a rat even when he saw one—there were things that went into the sausage in comparison with which a poisoned rat was a tidbit. There was no place for the men to wash their hands before they ate their dinner, and so they made a practice of washing them in the water that was to be ladled into the sausage. There were the butt-ends of smoked meat, and the scraps of corned beef, and all the odds and ends of the waste of the plants, that would be dumped into old barrels in the cellar and left there. Under the system of rigid economy which the packers enforced, there were some jobs that it only paid to do once in a long time, and among these was the cleaning out of the waste barrels. Every spring they did it; and in the barrels would be dirt and rust and old nails and stale water—and cartload after cartload of it would be taken up and dumped into the hoppers with fresh meat, and sent out to the public's breakfast. Some of it they would make into "smoked" sausage—but as the smoking took time, and was therefore expensive, they would call upon their chemistry department, and preserve it with borax and color it with gelatine to make it brown. All of their sausage came out of the same bowl, but when they came to wrap it they would stamp some of it "special," and for this they would charge two cents more a pound.

1.5 Working Conditions in Industry

In 1883, after a series of violent clashes between labor and capital, the U.S. Senate held hearings to learn what had brought about the strife. Supposedly, the hearings were intended to determine how the existing tariff laws worked. Did tariffs only increase the costs of finished goods for workers, or did they also improve job opportunities and encourage a higher standard of living? But the inquiry had a broad scope, and revealed a great deal about the true conditions of work and life in industrial America.

Partisan feeling about the tariff ran deep and strong in Congress, revealing a deep split on regional lines between the North and South. Senator Henry W. Blair of New Hamsphire chaired the hearings. He was fair-minded, and encouraged witnesses to speak their minds fully. Another prominent committee member was James Z. George of Mississippi. Although a conservative Southerner, he was a genuine friend of working people. Witnesses from all walks of life came forward voluntarily, including ordinary workers who customarily had no public voice.

One hearing witness was Robert D. Layton, a skilled axe-maker and the Grand Secretary of the Knights of Labor, the most important labor union in the country. In the excerpt of testimony below, he enlightens the senators as to the working and living conditions of industrial workers, especially those in coal and iron.

The legislative results of the hearings were meager: Congress formed the Bureau of Labor Statistics and passed a law restricting foreign contract labor. But Congress had established the important precedent of taking an interest in labor relations.

Questions

How did the life of the working class compare with that of the middle class and of the wealthy during the Gilded Age? Be specific. To what extent does Layton seem to reflect class consciousness? Is he portraying the life of radicals and rebels? What improvements does he appear to want?

What role should Congress play in regulating labor relations?

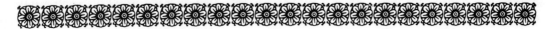

Sen. George: Can you tell us anything in regard to the physical conditions and surroundings of the working people, their food, their clothing, and whatever occurs to you pertaining to their mode of living?—A. There are differences, of course, in those respects, depending upon the amount of wages paid. The daily laborer perhaps lives more poorly than any of the others, has the least house room and the most illy-ventilated rooms, the least means of educating his children, and the least opportunity for society and other advantages. Then comes the coal miner, who receives more wages, but who generally lives in a little two-room house. These houses are built in long rows, not painted, with no grounds and no fences about the houses, and the men deal in the companies' stores, who tax them about all they can earn for their goods. . . .

Q. Don't you consider him a laborer?—A. Well, more skill enters into his occupation. . . .

Sen. Blair: As I am using the term laborer, it applies to all classes who perform manual work.

The Witness: It is all labor; but we usually divide it into skilled and unskilled labor. The work of the miner is skilled labor to a certain extent. I have seen the laborers along the Monongahela and the Allegheny Rivers, and down the Pan-Handle Railroad toward Wheeling, and in fact at all points on the roads leading out of Pittsburgh. The houses of those men as a rule consist, as I have said, of two rooms—one uptairs and the other downstairs. The houses are built in long rows without paint on the outside. The kitchen furniture consists generally of a stove and some dishes, a few chairs and a table. They have no carpets on the floors so far as I have seen. I am speaking now about the lower parts of the houses; I don't know about upstairs.

Sen. George: Is the kitchen in the lower room of the house or is it separate?—A. In the lower room. In many instances there are no cellars under the houses. If there were cellars the miners would be enabled to lay in a stock of supplies. . . . They are always frame houses. . . . Living as these people do in the coal regions, the children can run out and gather enough fuel to keep the houses warm, and I never knew any of them to suffer from cold. . . .

Q. The sleeping apartment is upstairs I suppose?—A. Yes, sir; but in some instances where the family is large it is downstairs in the kitchen. . . .

Sen. George: Is the kitchen also the sitting room of the family?—A. Yes, sir; it is the sitting room, kitchen, and parlor.

Q. And library?—A. And library . . . he generally can read.

Q. How are they supplied as to clothing?—A. Well, it is absolutely necessary for a miner to have two suits. The one that he wears when working in the mine is of the poorest quality, and usually very black and dirty, and then he has an ordinary suit of clothes besides.

Q. How are his wife and children clothed?—A. They are clad in the plainest possible garments, as a rule. . . . The wages may average $2.00 or $2.50 a day; but, dealing in these truck-stores, when the end of the month comes around he generally has very little lefft. I have known some of them to receive in actual money at the end of the month $.35 after the rent was taken out. . . .

Sen. Blair: What amount of rent?—A. All the way from $4 up to $8 or $9 a month. . . .

SOURCE: Testimony of Robert D. Layton, before the Senate Committee upon the Relations between Labor and Capital, 1883 (Washington, D.C., 1885), 4 vols.

Sen. George: What is the usual size of the lower room?—*A.* About 15 by 18 feet, or 18 by 20 feet. . . .

Q. How are they usually warmed, with a stove or with a fireplace?—*A.* Usually by a cook-stove.

Q. Is that the only heating apparatus they have?—*A.* Generally, I think. . . .

Sen. Blair: How are those people situated as to school privileges?—*A.* Usually the miner in the soft-coal regions, and I think in our hard-coal regions, too, puts his boys to work in the mine very young. I have observed boys of from eight to fourteen years of age working in the hard-coal region, and in the soft-coal mines boys of ten or twelve years of age are able to assist their parents materially in the mine, and unless the miner has a large number of them his boys are usually employed in that way helping their father. If there are only one or two boys in the family the father generally takes them into the mine with him. They go to school some, but their means of education is very limited.

Q. Is that because the father prefers that the boys should assist him in his work or because of a lack of school privileges?—*A.* The school privileges are generally good enough, but absolute necessity compels the father in many instances to take the child into the mine with him to assist in winning bread for the family.

Q. There is no compulsory school law in Pennsylvania, is there?—*A.* No, sir. . . .

Q. What are the personal habits of the miner generally as to economy or a disposition to save his wages?—*A.* . . . His desire may be to economize, but his opportunities for it are so poor that he seldom is able to accumulate any savings, let his desire for economy be ever so great.

Q. . . . Is there any other class of laborers in or about the mine whose wages are still lower than those of the miner?— *A.* Yes; but such work is usually done by young boys. Such work as driving the mules in the pit is done generally by the children of the miners. . . . When you leave the miner and go to the iron-worker, the man who works in the iron-mills, you find the social condition and surroundings somewhat improved. . . . The iron-worker has usually more room and better furniture, carpets, and so on, and his children are better clothed. . . . The iron-workers have the advantages of the markets in the large centers of industry, the cities, so that they can get a greater variety of food and are not confined, like the miners in isolated situations. . . . But if you go among the laborers employed in the iron-mills you will find them huddled together in tenement houses and no more comfortable than the miners.

Sen. George: Please state the distinction between the iron-worker and the laborer in the iron mills.—*A.* The laborer there performs the heavy work, the unskilled work, and waits upon the skilled worker, the iron-worker. The laborers receive from $1.00 to $1.25, or perhaps sometimes $1.75, a day. When we speak of a "laborer" in the iron-works, it is understood that we do not mean a man who performs any skilled labor. When you get above the laborer the men are designated by the character of the particular work in which they are engaged; they are called "rollers," "finishers," etc., and are skilled laborers. . . .

Q. To go back to the houses, you have described them as being in very close juxtaposition and very near the works. What grounds have they around them. . . ?—*A.* If there is any grass on the south side of Pittsburgh attached to a tenement house it is in a little box sitting on the windowsill. . . . I know numbers of houses where the backyard of each is not more than 8 feet by 10, and that is allowing more territory than many of the landlords do.

Q. What opportunities have the children under ten or twelve . . . ?—A. They are compelled to play on the streets. They have no other place. . . .

Q. They are exposed to danger, too, from carriages, wagons, and drays, I suppose?—A. Yes, sir; . . .

Q. What opportunities have men who live in these tenement houses and their families for recreation on Sundays and holidays? What resorts have they? Where do they go to? Do they stay in their houses, or do they go out into the country, or into the parks? . . . A. Well, usually they are tired and they stay at home. They may walk around sometimes on Sunday to see a friend, or they may go to church, but if they don't do that they stay at home and rest. . . .

Q. I have an idea that the life of a coal miner is very disagreeable. Now, why do men go into that business? . . .—A. . . . men are born to it; their fathers worked in the mines, and they began life in that way and never did anything else; they inherited it, as you may say. . . .

Sen. George: I had the idea that men were seduced into that sort of employment by extraordinarily remunerative wages?—A. The average miner's earnings, as I think will be shown to you, do not amount to more than $350 a year. That is the seductive compensation given to the miner for spending the greater portion of his life in utter darkness. In Pennsylvania the miners and other citizens had a law enacted at the last session of our general assembly prohibiting these . . . "pluck-me" stores . . . but our able constitutional lawyers, I believe, found holes in it, and the institutions continue. . . .

Sen. Blair: The effect of these "pluck-me" stores is, I suppose, to largely decrease the actual rate of wages received by the men, by reason of the higher prices that they are compelled to pay for everything they buy?—A. Yes, sir. I know a miner who told me that when flour was selling for $2.00 a sack in the city he was paying at one of these stores, eight miles from the city, $2.50 a sack. . . .

Q. Do the operators furnish everything?—A. Yes, sir; everything that the miners may need, their groceries, boots and shoes, calicoes, and everything of that kind. The "pluck-me" store is a general store. . . .

Q. Can you give us some instances of the obnoxious rules of which you speak?—A. Yes; one instance was on the part of a large firm of carriage manufacturers at Rochester, N.Y.—James Cunningham, Sons & Co. Just a year ago this month their men rebelled against certain rules that they had established in their works—rules degrading to human nature. For instance, the faucets in the water sinks were locked up, and when an employee wanted a drink of water he had to go to the foreman of his department and ask for a drink; the foreman went and unlocked the faucet and gave him a cupful of water, and whether that was enough to satisfy his thirst or not, it was all he got. When the men entered in the morning they were numbered by checks. A man lost his identity as a man and took a number like a prisoner in a penitentiary. The checks ran up to five hundred and something. If a man worked in the third or fourth story of the building . . . and if he was an old man . . . when the bell rang for dinner he was obliged to walk down several pairs of stairs, take off his check and then walk up stairs again to eat his dinner, and when he got done he had to walk down again and put on the check before the bell rang for afternoon work. In that way they knew just when a man came in or went out. Then, if a man was a piece-worker there, and got through his work at half past two or three o'clock, he was not permitted to leave the building until the regular time—six o'clock. No matter when he got through with his work, he had to stay there in dirt and discomfort, and could not go home or go out until six o'clock in the evening. Another obnoxious rule was that if a man was half or even quarter of a minute late he was shut out. They had a gate and it would be shut down upon a man even when he was going in, sometimes so quickly that he would hardly have time to draw his foot back to keep it from being crushed by the gate, and that man would be kept out until nine o'clock, so that he would make only three-quarters of a day's work. The rule was that the men had to be *in* the works before the whistle blew. . . .

Our miners almost universally complain of being cheated in the amount of coal that they take out. That is another cause of great aggravation and disturbance. In some mines, they dig and get pay for the "run of the bank"—that is, slack and lump and nut coal all go in together at so much a ton. In other mines the miners are paid for simply the lump coal; and all the rest is deducted. The men have to dig the other kinds for nothing, getting so much a bushel for the lump coal only. . . . As to wages, I presume there always has been, and to a certain extent always will be, a difference as long as self-interest controls . . . there is a large lack of confidence existing between the employers and the employed . . . the employed cen never get an advance in wages without either entering upon a strike, of longer or shorter duration, or at least threatening a strike. . . . We have known the employers to go on prospering, to grow richer and richer, to live in larger residences and travel more extensively, with their family expenditures constantly increasing, yet all the time, when approached for an increase of wages, they would declare that they were making nothing. . . .

Sen. George: The employee thinks, as I understand you, that his prosperity ought to increase with that of his employer?—*A.* He not only thinks so, but he absolutely knows that it should. . . .

1.6   Bread-and-Butter Unionism

In the late nineteenth century, labor organizers followed two basic models. One was the industry-wide union, open to both skilled and unskilled workers in a given industry. It was best represented by the Knights of Labor. Any manual laborer was eligible to join the Knights, including women, blacks and farmers. Many members were unskilled farm workers. The Knights were organized into large regional bodies, but not separate trades, for the K of L was not a trade union. Generally it opposed strikes. It fought for broad social reforms to bring about some sort of cooperative commonwealth that would replace capitalism.

The Knights of Labor flourished between 1878 and 1893. It suffered a decline as a result of the Haymarket riot in Chicago in 1886, when it was unfairly accused of fostering anarchistic violence. Its membership was then increasingly dominated by farmers rather than manual workers.

A second type of labor union then emerged. This was the trade union, organized more narrowly around the type of work performed and favoring the skilled workers over the unskilled. Trade unionism was soon exemplified by the organizations that formed the American Federation of Labor. The leading architect of the AFL was the cigar maker Samuel Gompers (1850–1924), an English-born Jew who migrated in 1863. Early in life Gompers had been a socialist, much influenced by Karl Marx. But after participating in a bitter strike in 1877, he grew convinced that labor should not seek broad social reforms, or the overthrow of the capitalist system. It should merely find a secure place within that system. Labor should sidestep excessive idealism or politics, and stick to bread-and-butter issues to increase wages, decrease working hours and improve working conditions. It should seek collective bargaining agreements by going on strike when necessary. Gompers' vision emerged as the dominant one for American labor by the first part of the twentieth century.

In 1883 (three years before being elected president of the AFL) Gompers voiced his concerns to the same Senate committee cited in the previous document. Part of the statement is reprinted below.

Questions

In light of what Gompers says, what is the main function of a labor union? Should unions be regarded as exercising a conservative or radical influence?

Why was the AFL more successful than the Knights in the long run?

Are these two models still represented in the labor movement today, and in what form? Consider the unions for auto workers, machinists, teachers, office workers, college professors, teamsters, farm workers, hospital workers, etc.

The Witness: What I wish to show is the condition of the cigar-makers at that period when there was no organization. When our organization commenced to emerge and reorganize throughout the country, the first year there were seventeen strikes in our trade, of which twelve or thirteen were successful. The rest were either lost or compromised. . . . In these last two years, . . . I am convinced that we have had over one hundred and sixty or one hundred and seventy strikes, and the strikes have been successful except in, perhaps, twenty instances, where they may have been lost or

SOURCE: Testimony of Samuel Gompers, before the Senate Committee upon the Relations between Labor and Capital, 1883.

compromised. . . . We have adopted a course of action which our experience has taught us, and that is, in certain periods of the year, when it is generally dull, not to strike for an advance of wages. Formerly, before the organization, men would probably strike for an advance of wages in the dull season, and be content that they were not reduced in the busy season. Our experience has taught us to adopt a different mode of action.

Sen. George: You strike now when business is active?—*A.* Yes, sir; and then, when we obtain an increase of wages when times are fair, our object is to endeavor to obtain fair wages during the dull season. . . . We have found that . . . it is entirely valueless to organize a union during a strike, and that it is little better than valueless to organize just immediately before a strike. We have found that if we are desirous of gaining anything in a strike, we must prepare in peace for the turbulent time which may come. And the Cigar-makers' International Union, of which I now speak especially, is an organization that has in its treasury between $130,000 and $150,000 ready to be concentrated within five days at any time at any given point. . . . That is, in the event of a strike at a given point . . . the unions throughout the entire country and Canada . . . forward their entire treasury if necessary, to be placed at the disposal of the organization that is in trouble. . . .

There is nothing in the labor movement that employers who have had unorganized laborers dread so much as organization; but organization alone will not do much unless the organization provides itself with a good fund, so that the operatives may be in a position, in the event of a struggle with their employers, to hold out. . . .

Modern industry evolves these organizations out of the existing conditions where there are two classes in society, one incessantly striving to obtain the labor of the other class for as little as possible, and to obtain the largest amount or number of hours of labor; and the members of the other class, being as individuals utterly helpless in a contest with their employers, naturally resort to combinations to improve their condition, and, in fact, they are forced by the conditions which surround them to organize for self-protection. Hence trades unions. Trades unions are not barbarous, nor are they the outgrowth of barbarism. On the contrary they are only possible where civilization exists. Trades unions cannot exist in China; they cannot exist in Russia. . . . But they have been formed successfully in this country, in Germany, in England, and they are gradually gaining strength in France. In Great Britain they are very strong; they have been forming there for fifty years, and they are still forming, and I think there is a great future for them yet in America. . . . A people may be educated, but to me it appears that the greatest amount of intelligence exists in that country or that state where the people are best able to defend their rights, and their liberties as against those who are desirous of undermining them. Trades unions are organizations that instill into men a higher motive-power and give them a higher goal to look to. . . . A man is sometimes reached by influences such as the church may hold out to him, but the conditions that will make him a better citizen and a more independent one are those that are evolved out of the trades union movement. . . .

Sen. Blair: The outside public, I think, very largely confound the conditions out of which the trades union grows or is formed, with the, to the general public mind, somewhat revolutionary ideas that are embraced under the names of socialism and communism. Before you get through, won't you let us understand to what extent the trades union is an outgrowth or an evolution of those ideas, and to what extent it stands apart from them and is based on different principles?—*A.* The trades unions are by no means an outgrowth of socialistic or communistic ideas or principles, but the socialistic and communistic notions are evolved from some of the trades unions' movements. As to the question of the principles of communism or socialism prevailing in trades unions, there are a number of men who connect themselves as workingmen with the trades unions who may have socialistic convictions, yet who never gave them currency. . . . On the other hand, there are men—not so numerous now as they have been in the past—who are endeavoring to conquer the trades-union movement and subordinate it to those doctrines, and in a measure, in a few such organizations that condition of things exists, but by no means does it exist in the largest, most powerful, and best organized trades unions. . . .

Sen. George: You state, then, that the trades unions generally are not propagandists of socialistic views?—*A.* They are not. On the contrary, the endeavors of which I have spoken, made by certain persons to conquer the trades unions in certain cases, are resisted by the trades unionists; in the first place for the trades unions' sake, and even persons who have these convictions perhaps equally as strong as the others will yet subordinate them entirely to the good to be received directly through the trades unions. . . .

Q. Do you think the trades unions have impeded or advanced the spread of socialistic views?—*A.* I believe that the existence of the trades-union movement, more especially where the unionists are better organized, has evoked a spirit and a demand for reform, but has held in check the more radical elements in society. . . .

1.7 Unions and Personal Liberty

Forcing an American to join an organization against his or her will runs contrary to a strong tradition of personal liberty. Employers have often raised this point in fighting unions. It was undemocratic and un-American, they charged, to establish a closed shop and force a worker to belong to a union. By the same token, those who pressed the case for unions have asserted that the closed shop and compulsory union membership are essential to unionism and fully compatible with democratic objectives. This debate has gone on for generations.

In the selections that follow the issue is addressed by Dudley Taylor, general counsel for the Chicago employers association (1914); Clarence S. Darrow, the most outstanding labor and criminal attorney of his time (1915); Finley Peter Dunne, a social critic (1914); Walter P. Reuther, head of the auto workers union (1953); and Sen. Barry Goldwater, a conservative Republican from Arizona (1953). Dunne speaks through fictional Irish American characters named Mr. Dooley and Mr. Hennessey in a Chicago saloon (see also Document 1.2).

Questions

What is the meaning of "open shop" and "closed shop?" Are the employers really interested in personal liberty, or do they have something else in mind? Do the labor advocates really believe in personal liberty?

In your opinion, is there a fundamental conflict between unionism and personal liberty? What other pro- and anti-union arguments have been used over the years?

Dudley Taylor —

. . . I do feel this, that a labor organization ought to be in a position to merit the confidence of the public and of employers, for that matter, and ought not to rely upon coercion. But what do we see? We see members of labor unions who do not dare to go to the meetings of their union and raise their voice in protest. We continually read in the newspapers of this city how some man has been assaulted and possibly kicked downstairs for presuming to say something in a labor union meeting. I have talked with the members of labor unions regarding violence and graft—good, decent, respectable fellows—and I have said, "Why don't you have a house cleaning; why don't you go down there and why don't you take some of your people down there and open up these things and

find out and be decent?" You simply get a smile from those fellows if they have one in their system. They don't dare do it. They are coerced into the union; they are coerced to do as the union directs, and we see the evidence of it every day. Some trouble is experienced somewhere in this city; a man goes around and perhaps whistles, blows a tin whistle, or snaps his fingers and the men go on a strike. Why? The chances are they don't know anything about it; the chances are they are opposed to it, because for the time being it takes their living from them or a considerable part of their living, but they have no choice or option but to obey. If those men were not coerced; if they were in fear of violence that would not be the case.

I say that the labor unions as organized today, generally speaking, are thriving on coercion. It should not be so; it should be voluntary. This matter of the closed-shop proposition ought to be a voluntary proposition. The employer ought to be able to look at the contract and look over the union—the officers of the union—judging something of the past history, and say, I will be a lot better off doing business with your union; I want it in my business, and enter into the closed-shop agreement voluntarily, if he wishes to do so, and not to be compelled and coerced to do it and have

SOURCES: From the testimony of Dudley Taylor, July 22, 1914, U.S. Congress, Senate, *Final Report and Testimony Submitted to Congress by the Commission on Industrial Relations*, 64th Cong., 1st sess., Senate Doc. 415 (Washington, U.S. Government Printing Office, 1916), IV, 3237–3238; testimony of Clarence Darrow, May 18, ibid., 1915, XI, 10805–10806; Finley Peter Dunne, "Mr. Dooley on the Open Shop," in *Literary Digest*, LXVII (November 27, 1920), 19; testimony of Walter P. Reuther, U.S. Congress, Senate, Committee on Labor and Public Welfare, *Hearings, Taft-Hartley Act Revisions*, 83d Cong., 1st sess., 1953, Part 1, pp. 409–410, 415–417.

the members coerced and compelled to go into the union and stay in the union and do as the union officers say. That is, in my judgment, un-American and wrong. . . .

Clarence S. Darrow —

. . . Of course, there is a lot of nonsense talked about [the union shop]. They talk about the inalienable right of a man to work; he has no such right; no one has a right to work, and the man who stands for the open shop does not care for anybody's rights to work, except the nonunion man, and they only care for him because they can use him. If a man has any constitutional right to work he ought to have some legal way of getting work. If the Constitution is going to guarantee the right to work, it ought to guarantee some place to work, and there is no such thing. . . .

The workingman spends a good share of his waking moments in a shop. He does not need to invite a nonunion man into his house if he does not want to, and probably won't, and he is under no more obligation to work with him in a factory if he does not want to. If a Presbyterian does not want to work with a Catholic, he may be narrow and bigoted, but he does not have to. Of course, a union man has a direct reason for it; he believes and he understands and feels that the nonunion man is working against the interests of his class; that the only way a workingman can get anything is by collective bargaining, and by saying, "If you don't give us a raise, not only I will quit but we will all quit and tie up your business"; that is the only way he can do it. One man quitting out of 50,000 is nothing, or even ten men or one hundred men, but if they all quit, so they can do with the employer what the employer does with you, when he discharges you, then they can

bargain and there is no other kind of bargaining but collective bargaining.

The nonunion man comes along and says, "I will take your place." He is not loyal to the union, and the union man regards him as a traitor to his class, and he won't work with him, and he has a perfect right to refuse to work with him.

There is no such thing as the open shop, really. There is a union shop and a nonunion shop. Everybody that believes in the open shop disbelieves in the union shop, whatever they say; and I do not say that unions are perfect, they are not. The people that work with them know that better than anybody else. They are just doing the best they can with the job they have, which is a hard one, and with the material they have, which is not perfect. In many instances they are brutal, and have to be, and it is generally like the law, and works individual hardship here and there, but it is one of the necessary things in the industrial world, and the fight is between those who believe in unions and those who disbelieve in them. Those who disbelieve in them say they believe in the open shop; but the open shop is simply a back door to put the union man out.

Finley Peter Dunne —

"What's all this that's in the papers about the open shop?" asked Mr. Hennessey.

"Why, don't ye know?" said Mr. Dooley. "Really, I'm surprised at yer ignorance, Hinnissey. What is th' open shop? Sure, 'tis where they kape the doors open to accommodate th' constant stream av' min comin' in t' take jobs cheaper than th' min what has th' jobs. 'Tis like this, Hinnissey; Suppose wan av these freeborn citizens is workin' in an open shop f'r th' princely wage av wan large iron dollar a day av tin hour. Along comes anither son-av-gun and he sez t' th' boss, "Oi think Oi could handle th' job nicely f'r ninety cints." "Sure," sez th' boss, and th' wan dollar man gets out into th' crool woruld t' exercise hiz inalienable roights as a freeborn American citizen an' scab on some other poor devil. An' so it goes on, Hinnissey. An' who gits th' benefit? Thrue, it saves th' boss money, but he don't care no more f'r money thin he does f'r his right eye. It's all principle wid him. He hates t' see men robbed av their indipindence. They must have their indipindence, regardless av anything else."

"But," said Mr. Hennessey, "those open-shop min ye menshun say they are f'r unions if properly conducted."

"Shure," said Mr. Dooley, "if properly conducted. An' there we are: an' how would they have them conducted? No strikes, no rules, no contracts, no scales, hardly iny wages, an' dam' few mimbers."

Walter P. Reuther v. Senator Barry Goldwater —

. . . We think, you see, that the union is an attempt to extend the democratic processes in the industrial community; that organized society is based upon the principle that within the framework of a given society the people who make up that society have to work out rules and regulations to govern the relationship of one to the other. . . .

The union performs some very important and essential functions. We handle grievances. We handle the grievances of all the workers. We have umpire machinery. The unions pay for the umpire machinery. When he hands down a decision, all the workers get the benefits. We have legal services. All the workers get the benefit of the cases we may process in unemploy-

ment compensation. All the workers get the benefit because we establish precedents; we work out basic policies. We have a medical department. We work on health problems. We work on occupational diseases. All the workers get the benefit of these.

Since all the workers in the industrial community get the benefits of these services performed by the union, made possible by the union, we believe that since all the workers share in the services all the workers ought to share in the cost of providing those services. . . .

Mr. REUTHER. It is government by majority rule, and what is wrong with that? We fought the Revolutionary War around a very fundamental principle, and we were right: Around the idea of taxation without representation.

This is the other side of that coin. This is the matter of representation without taxation. One principle is as sound as the other, because if it is wrong to be taxed without representation, it is wrong to have representation without taxation.

Since all the workers in the industrial community have a right to vote democratically in determining whether our union is going to be the bargaining agency, we cannot get sole bargaining rights unless a majority of the workers support us at the National Labor Relations Board. So having gotten majority support, we then represent the machinery by which the workers in the industrial community govern themselves and have their work done. They all get the benefits of that machinery; they ought all to pay the taxes which make that machinery possible. . . .

Senator Goldwater. . . .

I am very much interested in Mr. Reuther's development of the closed shop and the union shop. There is only one question in this whole field in my mind. What about the man who just does not want to belong to a union?

Mr. Reuther. Well, if a fellow works in a General Motors plant and does not want to belong to a union, he does not have to work there.

Senator Goldwater. But suppose he wants to work there?

Mr. Reuther. If you want to live in a certain community and you want the benefits of the work of that community, you have to pay taxes in that community. If you do not, you do not have to live in that community. That is the freedom of choice. The only check is that it has to be a democratic choice, decision; it has to be a majority democratic decision.

Inside of the industrial community, General Motors has 400,000 employees. How can a complex industrial society like ours work out machinery within this industrial community to meet these problems unless it can be done by a democratic decision of the people involved?

Senator Goldwater. I get down to the individual who does not want to belong to a union. Let us extend your thinking a little bit further. Take the matter of churches. Certainly churches benefit everybody. Yet we all do not support churches. Should we include laws to tax everybody to support churches in the community? . . .

It gets down to that, and that is, in my mind, the only question: What about the individual?

Mr. Reuther. The UAW-CIO, for example, to use a specific case, are certified as the sole collective bargaining agent. We represent every General Motors worker in our units. No church represents all the people in the community. You are dealing with an entirely different kind of thing.

The church is a fraternal religious organization that you can choose to belong to or choose not to belong to; but our unions are the sole bargaining agent under the law. We represent every General Motors Worker. When we process a grievance, every General Motors worker gets the benefit of that. If we have a case that goes to the court on some workmen's compensation case, that sets a principle, and every GM worker gets the benefit of that protection that we want. If we have our doctors go in and check on the dust in a foundry or the fumes in a factory plant and we take corrective steps to protect the health of the workers, every worker in that plant gets the benefit of that.

The church does not perform that kind of function in the community. The church deals with the spiritual values. You can either choose to get them or you can choose not to get them.

But we are by law the agency by which all workers in a given factory take care of their industrial problems. In other words, we really are like a government within that factory, within that industrial community. If you are going to have a government within the industrial community, you have a right to insist that it is a democratic government; you have a right to insist that the workers who make up the industrial citizens in that industrial community have a right to elect their officers democratically, have a right to make democratic majority decisions. But having made the democratic majority decisions, the people in the minority are obligated to go along with the majority just as they are when you vote taxes for schools in your community. What is the difference? It is the same principle. . . .

1.8 The Impact of the Great Depression

For about twelve years, from 1929 to 1941, Americans suffered through the Great Depression. Its impact was persistent and widespread, extending for wage workers and sharecroppers, ranchers and teachers, bankers and entrepreneurs. They experienced joblessness, hunger and lower income. They lost farms, homes and dreams of a better future. The depression led to "hunger riots," political upheaval and institutional change, but not to revolution.

Among the sources that record the economic collapse of the 1930s and how it affected daily life are newspaper accounts, congressional testimony and oral history reminiscences. Several such items follow: news reports of a hunger riot (from the New York Times, *1931); testimony describing the desperate plight of farmers and ranchers (Oscar Ameringer, 1932); a newspaper profile of an unemployed engineer (Langland Heinz, 1932); an oral account of a man who served in the Civilian Conservation Corps (Blackie Gold), and a second oral account by a black Texas sharecropper (Emma Tiller). These last two reminiscences are from Studs Terkel's revealing collection of interviews, entitled* Hard Times: An Oral History of the Great Depression *(1970).*

Questions

What seemed to be in the minds of the rioters? With such widespread and severe economic dislocation, why didn't riots evolve into full-scale political rebellion?

According to Ameringer, some parts of the country enjoyed plentiful harvests of grain, fruit and vegetables, while others saw thousands of people going hungry? Why was there such tragic poverty amid plenty? Why had the food supply broken down, and what policy changes would have been needed to correct the problem?

Ironically, engineer Heinz had a professional career much like that of President Hoover. What might the two men have said to each other if they had met?

Why did Gold seem to enjoy life during the depression, and why would he hide his experiences from his children? (Have any older members of your family discussed their experiences in the 1930s?)

What does Tiller's account reveal about black-white relations in rural Texas during the depression?

Newspaper Account —

OKLAHOMA CITY, Jan. 20 (AP).—A crowd of men and women, shouting that they were hungry and jobless, raided a grocery store near the City Hall today. Twenty-six of tte men were arrested. Scores loitered near the city jail following the arrests, but kept well out of range of fire hose made ready for use in case of another disturbance.

The police tonight broke up a second meeting of about one hundred unemployed men and arrested Francis Owens, alleged head of the "Oklahoma City Unemployed Council," who was accused of instigating the raid.

Before the grocery was entered, a delegation of unemployed, led by Owens, had demanded of City Manager E. M. Fry that the authorities furnish immediate relief. Owens rejected a request by Mr. Fry for the names and addresses of the "Unemployed Council," said to number 2,500 men and women, both whites and Negroes.

The raiders disregarded efforts of H. A. Shaw, the store manager, to quiet them.

"It is too late to bargain with us," the leaders shouted, as they stripped the shelves.

The police hastily assembled emergency squads and dispersed the crowd numbering 500, with tear gas. Only those who were trapped in the wrecked store were arrested. Five women among them were released. The windows of the store were smashed as the raiders attempted to flee.

John Simmons was held on a charge of assault after he had leaped on the back of Lee Mullenix, a policeman, when the officer attempted to enter the crowded store.

Floyd Phillips was charged with inciting a riot. The police said he was one of the speakers who harangued the crowd at the City Hall before they began a parade that ended at the store.

Oscar Ameringer —

During the last three months I have visited, as I have said, some 20 States of this wonderfully rich and beautiful country. Here are some of the things I heard and saw: In the State of Washington I was told that the forest fires raging in that region all summer and fall were caused by unemployed timber workers and bankrupt farmers in an endeavor to earn a few honest dollars as fire fighters. The last thing I saw on the night I left Seattle was numbers of women searching for scraps of food in the refuse piles of the principal market of that city. A number of Montana citizens told me of thousands of bushels of wheat left in the fields uncut on account of its low price that hardly paid for the harvesting. In Oregon I saw thousands of bushels of apples rotting in the orchards. Only absolute flawless apples were still salable, at from 40 to 50 cents a box containing 200 apples. At the same time, there are millions of children who, on account of the poverty of their parents, will not eat one apple this winter.

While I was in Oregon the Portland Oregonian bemoaned the fact that thousands of ewes were killed by the sheep raisers because they did not bring enough in the market to pay the freight on them. And while Oregon sheep raisers fed mutton to the buzzards, I saw men picking for meat

SOURCES: The Ameringer item is from *Unemployment in the United States,* hearings before a subcommittee or the committee on Labor, House of Representatives, 72nd Cong., 1 sess., on H.R. 206, 1932), pp. 98–99 and 100–101. The hunger riots item is from *New York Times,* Jan. 21 and Feb. 26, 1931. The Heinz story is from *New York Times,* May 4, 1932. The Gold and Tiller accounts are from Studs Terkel, *Hard Times: An Oral History of the Great Depression* (New York: Random House, 1970), reprinted by permission of the publisher.

scraps in the garbage cans in the cities of New York and Chicago. I talked to one man in a restaurant in Chicago. He told me of his experience in raising sheep. He said that he had killed 3,000 sheep this fall and thrown them down the canyon, because it cost $1.10 to ship a sheep, and then he would get less than a dollar for it. He said he could not afford to feed the sheep, and he would not let them starve, so he just cut their throats and threw them down the canyon.

The roads of the West and Southwest teem with hungry hitchhikers. The camp fires of the homeless are seen along every railroad track. I saw men, women, and children walking over the hard roads. Most of them were tenant farmers who had lost their all in the late slump in wheat and cotton. Between Clarksville and Russellville, Ark., I picked up a family. The woman was hugging a dead chicken under a ragged coat. When I asked her where she had procured the fowl, first she told me she had found it dead in the road, and then added in grim humor, "They promised me a chicken in the pot, and now I got mine."

In Oklahoma, Texas, Arkansas, and Louisiana I saw untold bales of cotton rotting in the fields because the cotton pickers could not keep body and soul together on 35 cents paid for picking 100 pounds. The farmers cooperatives who loaned the money to the planters to make the crops allowed the planters $5 a bale. That means 1,500 pounds of seed cotton for the picking of it, which was in the neighborhood of 35 cents a pound. A good picker can pick about 200 pounds of cotton a day, so that the 70 cents would not provide enough pork and beans to keep the picker in the field, so that there is fine staple cotton rotting down there by the hundreds and thousands of tons.

As a result of this appalling overproduction on the one side and the staggering underconsumption on the other side, 70 percent of the farmers of Oklahoma were unable to pay the interests on their mortgages. Last week one of the largest and oldest mortgage companies in that State went into the hands of the receiver. In that and other States we have now the interesting spectacle of farmers losing their farms by foreclosure and mortgage companies losing their recouped holdings by tax sales.

The farmers are being pauperized by the poverty of industrial populations and the industrial populations are being pauperized by the poverty of the farmers. Neither has the money to buy the product of the other, hence we have overproduction and underconsumption at the same time and in the same country. . . .

I do not say we are going to have a revolution on hand within the next year or two, perhaps never. I hope we may not have such; but the danger is here. That is the feeling of our people—as reflected in the letters I have read. I have met these people virtually every day all over the country. There is a feeling among the masses generally that something is radically wrong. They are despairing of political action. They say the only thing you do in Washington is to take money from the pockets of the poor and put it into the pockets of the rich. They say that this Government is a conspiracy against the common people to enrich the already rich. I hear such remarks every day.

I never pass a hitch hiker without inviting him in and talking to him. Bankers even are talking about that. They are talking in irrational tones. You have more Bolshevism among the bankers to-day than the hod carriers, I think. It is a terrible situation, and I think something should be done and done immediately.

Langlan Heinz —

A heavily bearded man in a faded brown suit, who said he was a graduate of the University of Colorado and had held responsible positions as a civil engineer in this country, China, Panama and the jungles of Venezuela, was arraigned yesterday on a charge of vagrancy in Flatbush Court, where he told such a dramatic and straightforward story of his experiences that he held the attention of the crowded courtroom for nearly an hour. Magistrate Eilperin adjourned the case until Friday so that a thorough investigation could be made.

The defendant said he was Langlan Heinz, 44 years old. He was arrested at 4 A.M. by a policeman who found him sleeping on an improvised cot in a vacant lot near Flatbush Avenue, between Fillmore Avenue and Avenue R, Brooklyn. Heinz said he had made this lot his home for forty-six days.

In a well-modulated voice, Heinz began the recital of his experiences by saying that he was born in Dodge City, Kan., had received his early schooling there and then had entered the University of Colorado from which he was graduated with a Bachelor of Science degree in 1911. He worked in various parts of the country as a civil engineer until 1921, when he came to New York City and worked for the city for seven years as a structural draftsman.

In 1929, Heinz said, he went to Shanghai where he worked as a draftsman for ten months at $450 a month. Most of his earnings he sent to his mother, who is living

. . . [in] Los Angeles, Cal. When the Shanghai job was finished, Heinz continued, he went to Panama, where he got occasional employment, and then worked for an oil company in Maturin, Venezuela.

While at Maturin Heinz was sent into the jungle territory but contracted fever after a few months and was idle for a long period. When he recovered he went back to Trinidad and then, his money almost depleted, worked his way by ship back to Los Angeles and to his mother's home. After several months in California he sailed for Cairo, Egypt, in December, 1930, but lost his passport en route and was not allowed to land.

He next went to Naples where he worked for ten months in a wine factory and learned the Italian language. On New Year's Day, 1932, he landed in this country at Jersey City. He said he remembered that he had left about $1,000 worth of tools in the office in which he had worked for the city and stayed at a hotel in Manhattan during his attempts to find them. He was unsuccessful, however, and when his savings were used up he left the hotel and started walking the streets.

A month and a half ago he made the Brooklyn lot his home. Firemen at a firehouse near by gave him occasional shower baths, he said, and housewives and school children in the neighborhood gave him food. Each day he went to the Brooklyn waterfront in an effort to obtain employment on some outgoing ship.

Heinz, who substantiated his story from time to time with names and dates, said he had two brothers and two sisters living in different parts of the country. One brother, he said, was a member of the Board of Education in Los Angeles.

Blackie Gold —

Whatever I have, I'm very thankful for. I've never brought up the Depression to my children. Never in my life. Why should I? What I had to do, what I had to do without, I never tell 'em what I went through, there's no reason for it. They don't have to know from bad times. All they know is the life they've had and the future that they're gonna have.

All I know is my children are well-behaved. If I say something to my daughters, it's "Yes, sir," "No, sir." I know where my kids are at all times. And I don't have no worries about them being a beatnik.

I've built my own home. I almost have no mortgage. I have a daughter who's graduating college, and my daughter did not have to work, for me to put her through college. At the age of sixteen, I gave her a car, that was her gift. She's graduating college now: I'll give her a new one.

We had to go out and beg for coal, buy bread that's two, three days old. My dad died when I was an infant. I went to an orphan home for fellas. Stood there till I was seventeen years old. I came out into the big wide world, and my mother who was trying to raise my six older brothers and sisters, couldn't afford another mouth to feed. So I enlisted in the Civilian Conservation Corps. The CCC. This was about 1937.

I was at CCC's for six months, I came home for fifteen days, looked around for work, and I couldn't make $30 a month, so I enlisted back in the CCC's and went to Michigan. I spent another six months there planting trees and building forests. And came out. But still no money to be made. So back in the CCC's again. From there I went to Boise, Idaho, and was attached to the forest rangers. Spent four and a half months fighting forest fires.

These big trees you see along the highways—all these big forests were all built by the CCC. We went along plain barren ground. There were no trees. We just dug trenches and kept planting trees. You could plant about a hundred an hour.

I really enjoyed it. I had three wonderful square meals a day. No matter what they put on the table, we ate and were glad to get it. Nobody ever turned down food. They sure made a man out of ya, because you learned that everybody here was equal. There was nobody better than another in the CCC's. We never had any race riots. Couple of colored guys there, they minded their business; we minded ours.

I came out of there, enlisted in the navy. I spent five and a half years in the United States Navy. It was the most wonderful experience I've ever had. Three wonderful meals a day and my taxes paid for. I had security.

I came up the hard way, was never in jail, never picked up and whatever I've done, I have myself to thank for. No matter how many people were on relief in those days, you never heard of any marches. The biggest stealing would be by a guy go by a fruit store and steal a potato. But you never heard of a guy breaking a window. In the Thirties, the crimes were a hundred percent less than they are now. If a guy wants to work, there's no reason for being poor. There's no reason for being dirty. Soap and water'll clean anybody. Anybody that's free and white in a wonderful country like these United States never had any wants, never.

In the days of the CCC's, if the fella wouldn't take a bath, we'd give 'im what we call a brushing. We'd take this fella, and we'd take a big scrub brush and we'd give 'em a bath, and we'd open up every pore, and these pores would get infected. That's all he needed was one bath. I imagine we gave a hundred of 'em. A guy'd come in, he'd stink, ten guys would get him in the shower, and we'd take a GI brush. If a guy come in, he wanted to look like a hill-billy—no reflection on the boys from the South—but if he wanted to look like the backwoods, we'd cut his hair off. Yeah, we'd keep him clean. . . .

Emma Tiller —

In 1929, me and my husband were share-croppers. We made a crop that year, the owner takin' all of the crop.

This horrible way of livin' with almost nothin' lasted up until Roosevelt.

I picked cotton. We weren't getting but thirty-five cents a hundred, but I was able to make it. 'Cause I also worked people's homes, where they give you old clothes and shoes.

At this time, I worked in private homes a lot and when the white people kill hogs, they always get the Negroes to help. The cleanin' of the insides and clean up the mess afterwards. And then they would give you a lot of scraps. . . .

In 1934, in this Texas town, the farmers was all out of food. The government gave us a slip, where you could pick up food. For a week, they had people who would come and stand in line, and they couldn't get waited on. This was a small town, mostly white. Only five of us in that line were Ne-groes, the rest was white. We would stand all day and wait and wait and wait. And get nothin' or if you did, it was spoiled meat.

We'd been standin' there two days, when these three men walked in. They had three shotguns and a belt of shells. They said, lookin' up and down that line, "You all just take it easy. Today we'll see that

everybody goes home, they have food." Three white men.

One of 'em goes to the counter, lays his slip down and says he wants meat. He had brought some back that was spoiled. He said to the boss, "Would you give this meat for your dog?" So he got good meat. He just stood there. So the next person gets waited on. It was a Negro man. He picked up the meat the white man brought back. So the white guy said, "Don't take that. I'm gonna take it for my dog." So the boss said, "I'm gonna call the police."

So the other reaches across the counter and catches this guy by the tie and chokes him. The Negro man had to cut the tie so the man wouldn't choke to death. When he got up his eyes was leakin' water. The other two with guns was standin' there quietly. So he said, "Can I wait on you gentlemen?" And they said, "We've been here for three days. And we've watched these people fall like flies in the hot sun, and they go home and come back the next day and no food. Today we purpose to see that everybody in line gets their food and then we gonna get out." They didn't point the guns directly at him. They just pointed 'em at the ceiling. They said, "No foolin' around, no reachin' for the telephone. Wait on the people. We're gonna stand here until every person out there is waited on. When you gets them all served, serve us."

The man tried to get the phone off the counter. One of the guys said, "I hope you don't force me to use the gun, because we have no intentions of getting nobody but you. And I wouldn't miss you. It wouldn't do you any good to call the police, because we stop 'em at the door. Everybody's gonna get food today." And everybody did.

The Government sent two men out there to find out why the trouble. They found out this man and a couple others had rented a huge warehouse and was stackin' that food and sellin' it. The food that was supposed to be issued to these people. These three men was sent to the pen.

When the WPA came in, we soon got to work. The people, their own selves, as they would get jobs on WPA, they quit goin' to the relief station. They just didn't want the food. They'd go in and say, "You know, this is my last week, 'cause I go to work next week." The Negro and white would do this, and it sort of simmered down until the only people who were on relief were people who were disabled. Or families where there weren't no man or no one to go out and work on the WPA. . . .

1.9 The Concentration of Wealth

Supporters of the "Reagan Revolution" claimed that the administration of Ronald Reagan had markedly improved the economic standing of Americans. The argument, repeated time and again during the elections of 1984 and 1988, was that most people were better off economically under Reagan than they had been under liberal Democratic leadership. In 1988, the Democratic staff of the Joint Economic Committee of the Congress produced a brief report challenging at least one part of this assumption. The subject was "The Concentration of Wealth in the United States." The research compared the ownership of homes, autos, furnishings, appliances and bank accounts in this country in 1963 and 1983, and it showed that wealth had lately become greatly concentrated. The rich were richer and the lower classes were poorer. The top one half of one percent of the wealthy—"the super rich"—accounted for more than 35 percent of the net wealth in the United States.

Portions of the report are included below, including narrative comments, a table and three charts. Footnotes are omitted.

Questions

Is the evidence used in this study persuasive? What are the main conclusions? What message can you draw from the charts?

Compare and contrast the assumptions of John Adams and Thomas Jefferson, quoted below, with those of Andrew Carnegie cited in document 1.1.

Are there serious dangers in an excessive concentration of wealth in the hands of a few? How has wealth concentration affected our country in the past, for example in the Gilded Age or the 1920s?

If the report makes sense, what, if anything, can be done about the problem? Discuss the methods available in a democracy—tax reforms, housing subsidies, low-income loans, etc.—that could create a more equitable distribution of wealth.

Wealth can be defined as stored-up purchasing power. It can be measured by the value of what could be purchased if all of a family's debts were paid off and the remaining assets turned into cash. The amount of wealth that a family has in any given year is determined by the value which changing markets place upon the various assets which the family holds. . . .

. . . The Commerce Department reports on national income and personal and disposable personal income, the Census Bureau on median family income, the Agriculture Department on farm income, and the Bureau of Labor Statistics (BLS), with its various professional, household, and establishment surveys, can define income right down to monthly changes in average hourly earnings. . . . There are no regular reports on wealth-holding in this country; unlike income, our understanding of wealth—its nature and distribution—is much more limited. . . .

Only twice has the Federal Government attempted comparable and comprehensive surveys of wealth which could provide a much greater, and firsthand, base of information about the concentration of wealth. The first Survey of Financial Characteristics of Consumers was conducted under the supervision of the Federal Reserve Board in 1963. In 1983, a second survey was sponsored by the "Fed", the Department of Health and Human Services, the Comptroller of the Currency, and other government agencies. Both were conducted for the Fed by the Survey Research Center of the University of Michigan.

SOURCE: The Democratic Staff of the Joint Economic Committee of the U.S. Congress, "The Concentration of Wealth in th United States: Trends in the Distribution of Wealth among American Families" (Washington, D.C., July 1988).

This staff study analyzes the new 1983 survey data, and shows the types of assets held by American families, the distribution of wealth, and how that distribution has changed over time. For the first time, the 1963 and 1983 data are presented on a comparable basis to show the percentage of wealth held by the super rich, the very rich, the rich, and all other American families.

The forms of wealth held by most Americans are rather limited. They include homes, automobiles, furnishings, appliances, and a little money in checking and savings accounts. Only a small minority of families owns corporate stock or commercial real estate, and even fewer families will ever own a corporate or municipal bond or a Treasury bill.

In the aggregate, American families owned about $12 trillion in gross assets in the spring of 1983 when the Survey of Consumer Finances was conducted. Their net worth totaled nearly $10.6 trillion in holdings ranging from real estate through IRA's to business assets. . . .

What is the source of wealth? The American work ethic is only part of the answer. Hard work and saving out of income appear to account for about a third of today's wealth. Part comes from inheritance and the inevitable working of the axiom that money makes money. A considerable part of the change in wealth between 1963 and 1983 resulted from market revaluations of accumulated wealth. The most widely publicized revaluations are those of the stock market, but real estate appreciation also brought revaluations of the most commonly held asset of significant size for most families, the house in which they live. For most families, the value of their house is higher the longer they have lived in it.

But the nature of the asset that is the family home illustrates the difference between wealth and great wealth. Except for money that may be raised by second mortgages on that part of a home that has been paid off, family residences, of necessity, are not an available asset for most families. They cannot be turned into liquid cash without rendering the family homeless. By contrast, in richer families, the proportion of wealth tied up in illiquid assets like homes is likely to be much lower; a much larger share is disposable wealth, which can be put to work to make more wealth.

This paper analyzes 1983 data as it relates to the distribution of wealth among American families and trends concerning that distribution. . . .

Among those who have been concerned about the concentration of wealth were several of our founding fathers. According to John Adams, "the balance of power in a society accompanies the balance of property and land. . . . If the multitude," he wrote, "is possessed of the balance of real estate, the multitude will have the balance of power and, in that case, the multitude will take care of the liberty, virtue, and interest of the multitude in all acts of government."

Thomas Jefferson, writing from France to James Madison, noted that "property of this country (France) is absolutely concentrated in very few hands" with grave consequences for French society. He concluded that "legislators cannot invent too many devices for subdividing property" to ensure the democratic and productive capacities of a nation.

The concentration of wealth in a few hands also is believed by some to affect the functioning of free markets. Individuals with greater wealth have a capacity to have greater impact on the demand and supply

of goods, services, and instruments of wealth-holding. That impact can be used to further increase their wealth, which inevitably leads to fundamental alterations in the nature of the market. . . .

. . . John Kenneth Galbraith has argued that one cause of the Great Depression was a concentration of wealth that became so great that the general public could no longer afford to buy the abundant products generated by the economy of 1929.

Whether one shares all or none of these concerns, knowledge concerning the distribution of national wealth can provide considerable insight into the nature of our society. . . .

The distribution of these assets among the population was remarkably uneven in 1983. The population was divided into four basic groups for the purpose of analyzing distribution. The top 0.5 percent of households are categorized as the "super rich," the next 0.5 percent of households are categorized as the "very rich," the next 9 percent—or those households that rank between the 90th and 99th percentile in wealth-holding—are categorized at the "rich," and, finally, the bottom 90 percent are simply referred to as "everybody else."

The most striking result from the survey data is the extraordinary amount of national wealth held by the top half of 1 percent of families. These super rich households accounted for more than 35 percent of net wealth and 32 percent of gross wealth. If the equity in personal residences from net wealth is excluded, the top half of 1 percent of households owned more than 45 percent of the privately held wealth of this country.

These households appeared to have a very strong grip on the Nation's businesses. They owned 58 percent of unincorporated businesses and 46.5 percent of all personally owned corporate stock. They also held 77 percent of the value of trusts and 62 percent of state and local bonds.

In 1983, there were 420,000 super rich households. The least any of these households held in net assets was more than $2.5 million. The most wealthy were worth hundreds of times that amount. On average, this group held net assets of $8.9 million.

The next richest 420,000 households, or the second half of the top 1 percent of wealth-holders, were decidedly less well off than the top half of the top 1 percent. These very rich families held net assets ranging from $1.4 million to $2.5 million. They owned 7 percent of the Nation's net wealth, or about one-fifth as much as the 420,000 super rich families. Their business holdings included slightly more than 8 percent of the unincorporated business assets of the Nation and nearly 14 percent of the personally held corporate stock. When their business holdings are combined with those of super rich families, 66 percent of unincorporated businesses and 60 perent of personally held corporate stock are in the hands of the top 1 percent of all households.

Our so-called rich families, those between the 90th and 99th percentile of wealth-holding, had net assets that ranged from $206,000 to $1.4 million. This group is made up of a little more than 7.5 million households. These households held another 30 percent of the total wealth owned by American families, which included 27 percent of unincorporated business interests and 29 percent of personally held corporate stock. Families in this group were, on average, about one-twentieth as well off

as the super rich, less than a quarter as well off as the very rich, but more than 10 times as well off as everybody else. When the assets of the rich were combined with those of the very rich and super rich, 71.8 percent of the net wealth of American families was owned by this top 10 percent of families. This included almost 94 percent of unincorporated business assets and nearly 90 percent of all personally held stock.

The remaining 90 percent of American families owned only about 28 percent of the Nation's wealth held by families, and most of that was tied up in the equity of family homes. If home equities were subtracted from net assets, the bottom 90 percent of American families would hold only 16.5 percent of the remaining family-owned wealth of this country. . . .

The distribution of wealth among American families changed remarkably during the 20 years. The wealthiest one-half of 1 percent increased their share of wealth-holding from 25.4 percent to 35.1 percent, or by 38 percent. This increased share came at the expense of each of the other three groups. . . . The very rich (the second half of the top percent) saw their share drop from 7.35 percent to 6.75 percent, or by 8 percent. The rich (those between the 90th and 99th percentile) dropped from a little over 32 percent to just under 30 percent, or by 7 percent. Everybody else (the bottom 90 percent) dropped from an almost 35 percent share of the Nation's wealth in 1963 to just over 28 percent in 1983. That constituted almost a 20 percent drop in the share of national wealth held by the lower 90 percent of American families. . . .

Table
Growth in Family Wealth Between 1963 and 1983
(1983 Dollars)

	Super Rich Upper 1/2%		Very Rich 2nd 1/2%		Rich 90 to 99th %		Everyone Else 0 to 90th %		All Households 100%	
	1963	1983	1963	1983	1963	1983	1963	1983	1963	1983
Real Estate	120.5	821.8	53.5	226.6	485.0	1584.2	1231.2	2729.7	1890.2	5362.3
Home (Gross)	42.0	189.1	26.9	111.7	283.5	950.3	1123.9	2334.4	1476.3	3585.5
Other (Gross)	77.9	632.7	27.2	114.9	201.5	633.9	107.3	395.3	413.9	1776.8
Corporate Stock	347.0	456.6	99.3	132.2	209.2	287.7	58.3	105.2	713.8	981.7
Bonds	64.1	143.6	7.7	24.6	43..9	129.5	49.0	31.9	164.7	329.6
Savings Bonds	4.5	4.0	1.3	0.7	35.9	7.1	42.0	17.1	83.6	28.9
Other Federal Bonds	17.9	32.2	1.3	4.4	1.9	50.9	0.3	6.3	21.5	93.8
State and Local Bonds	35.2	101.6	2.2	13.2	3.2	45.0	0.0	3.9	40.7	163.7
Corporate Bonds	6.4	5.8	2.9	6.3	2.9	26.5	6.7	4.6	18.9	43.2
Checking Accounts	13.8	12.0	4.2	8.3	22.4	32.0	36.2	63.5	76.6	115.8
Savings Accounts	23.4	4.0	10.3	0.7	127.5	7.1	176.5	177.4	337.7	189.2
Certificates of Deposit		20.6		23.1		150.2		191.8		385.7
Money Market and Call Accounts		46.5		19.3		97.7		102.3		265.8
IRA's and Keogh		21.1		10.5		64.3		46.7		142.6
Trusts	153.8	378.4	3.8	24.5	10.6	64.9	5.8	23.8	174.0	491.6
Business Assets (Net)	260.5	1904.9	79.8	263.2	354.3	897.6	214.0	206.3	908.6	3272.0
Management Interest		1753.2		224.3		746.8		178.8		2903.1
Non-Management Interest		151.7		38.9		150.8		27.5		368.9
Insurance Cash Surrender Value	13.1	16.9	5.1	9.1	43.2	54.2	94.8	180.6	156.3	260.8
Land Contracts	12.8	15.6	22.7	2.8	30.1	38.2	17.3	54.6	83.0	111.2
Miscellaneous	11.2	25.9	8.3	17.8	23.4	40.5	17.0	73.7	59.9	157.9
Gross Assets	1020.1	3867.9	294.7	762.7	1349.7	3448.1	1900.1	3987.5	4564.6	12066.2
Debt	37.5	153.8	10.6	48.4	101.9	278.9	550.1	997.9	700.0	1479.0
Consumer Debt		31.2		17.4		60.1		218.4		327.1
Real Estate Debt		122.6		31.0		218.8		779.5		1151.9
Net Worth	982.6	3714.1	284.2	714.3	1247.8	3169.2	1350.0	2989.6	3864.6	10587.2
Net Worth as % of Total Net Worth	25.4%	35.1%	7.4%	6.7%	32.3%	29.9%	34.9%	28.2%	100.0%	100.0%
Gross Assets Minus Home Value	978.1	3678.8	267.8	651.0	1066.2	2497.8	776.3	1653.1	3088.4	8480.7
Gross Assets Minus Home Value As a % of Total Gross Assets	31.7%	43.4%	8.7%	7.7%	34.5%	29.5%	25.1%	19.5%	100.0%	100.0%

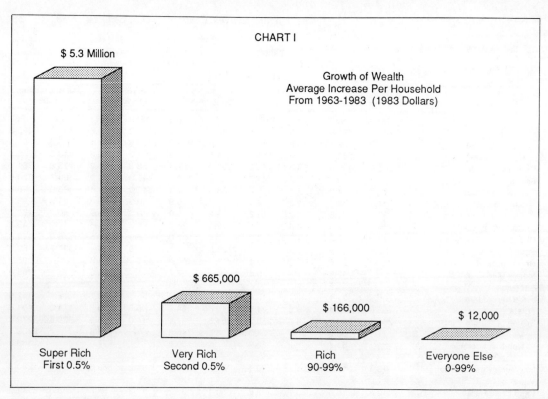

CHART I

Growth of Wealth
Average Increase Per Household
From 1963-1983 (1983 Dollars)

$ 5.3 Million

$ 665,000

$ 166,000

$ 12,000

Super Rich
First 0.5%

Very Rich
Second 0.5%

Rich
90-99%

Everyone Else
0-99%

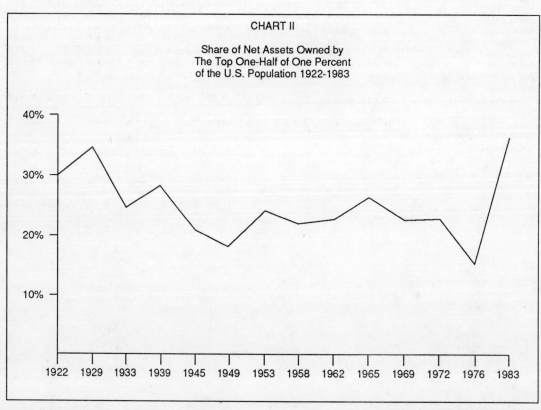

CHART II

Share of Net Assets Owned by
The Top One-Half of One Percent
of the U.S. Population 1922-1983

40%

30%

20%

10%

1922 1929 1933 1939 1945 1949 1953 1958 1962 1965 1969 1972 1976 1983

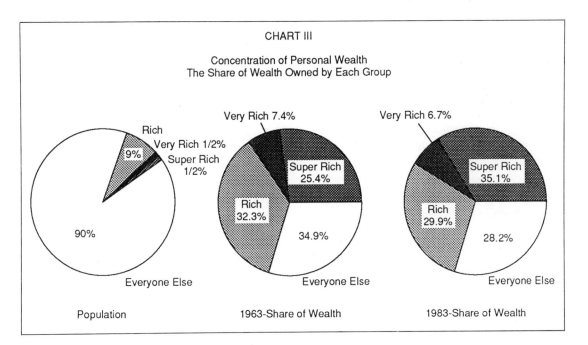

CHART III

Concentration of Personal Wealth
The Share of Wealth Owned by Each Group

Population

Rich
9%
Very Rich 1/2%
Super Rich
1/2%
90%
Everyone Else

1963-Share of Wealth

Very Rich 7.4%
Super Rich
25.4%
Rich
32.3%
34.9%
Everyone Else

1983-Share of Wealth

Very Rich 6.7%
Super Rich
35.1%
Rich
29.9%
28.2%
Everyone Else

1.10   The Reagan Revolution

After eight years as President, Ronald Reagan left office with the highest personal approval rating since Franklin D. Roosevelt. By the same token, even many of those who liked him personally disagreed with him on policy. His critics accused him of avoiding pressing problems such as race relations, a growing body of homelessness and a ballooning national debt.

The most militant conservatives gave Ronald Reagan a mixed report card. They believed he hadn't fought hard enough for key social issues such as allowing prayer in the schoools, providing aid to parochial schools, and ending public support for abortions. (Nor were the conservatives altogether happy with his handling of the Soviet Union. In his haste to negotiate the intermediate nuclear forces treaty with the Soviets, he seemed to forget his vow to fight the "evil empire" to the bitter end.) In other ways—in attacking government expenditures for domestic programs and deregulating of banking and other industries—his leadership as a conservative seemed more successful. Advocates talked approvingly of a "Reagan Revolution."

At all times, Reagan remained a champion of the cause of conservatism. In an address to the Conservative Political Action Conference in 1988, he reaffirmed his commitments and pointed to various successes. He was especially proud of his war against government bureaucracy and support for the private economic sector. He stressed the economic advances made by average Americans during his term of office. He pointed to declining inflation, rising yearly *income and average wages, tax reform, improvements in employment, and in opportunities for women and minorities. He also emphasized his commitment to improvements in the judiciary. One topic he avoided was the national debt.*

Questions

How well did Reagan serve the conservatives during his term of office? How well did he serve the nation? To what extent are his critics correct about the issues he avoided? What significance do you find in his not discussing the national debt?

What is a good working definition of conservatism? Historically, who have been the most important American conservatives? What is the meaning of the term "Reagan Revolution"? Is it possible to lead a revolution and remain a conservative?

It's great to be here, and I thank you. [*Applause*] No, please. It's great to be here tonight, and I'm delighted to see so many old friends. And now let's get right to it. . . .

A couple of weeks ago, I talked about the state of our Union, and tonight I'd like to talk about something that I think in many ways is synonymous: the state of our movement. During the past year, plenty of questions have been asked about the conservative movement by some people who were surprised to find out back in 1980 that there was such a thing. I mean a powerful new political movement capable of running a victorious national campaign based on an unabashed appeal to the American people for conservative ideas and principles. . . .

And right now some of the Potomac seers are saying we conservatives are tired;

SOURCE: Ronald Reagan, "Remarks at the Annual Conservative Political Action Conference Dinner," February 11, 1988, *Public Papers of the Presidents, Administration of Ronald Reagan* (Washington, D.C., 1988).

or they're saying we don't have a candidate, that we don't know what to do with ourselves this year. I even hear some of those candidates in the other party saying how easy it's going to be to win the Presidency for their liberal agenda, because they can run on—of all things—this administration's economic record [*Laughter*]. . . .

Well, my fellow conservatives, I think that's exactly what this year is about . . . letting the liberals in Washington discover, once again, the lesson they refuse to learn, letting them know just how big our election year will be—because of booming economic growth and individual opportunity—and how big an election year ball and chain they've given themselves with a 7-year record of opposition to the real record, but most of all, letting them know that the real friends of the conservative movement aren't those entrenched in the Capital City for 50 years. . . . I'm talking about those who, if the case is aggressively put before them, will vote for limited government, family values, and a tough, strong foreign policy every single time. I'm talking about those believers in common sense and sound values, your friends and mine, the American people.

You see, those who underestimate the conservative movement are the same people who always underestimate the American people. Take the latest instance. As I mentioned, in recent months some people . . . have actually taken on themselves of proving to the American people that they've been worse off under this administration than they were back in the Carter years of the seventies.

Now, I agree with you; this takes some doing. [*Laughter*] How do they manage it? Well, you see, any statistical comparison of the two recent administrations would start with 1977 to 1981 as the budget years of the last administration and 1981 to 1987 as the pertinent years for this one. Now, that sounds reasonable enough. But our opponents have a new approach, one that would have embarrassed even the emperor's tailors.

They take the year 1977, go up to 1983, and then they stop. So, you see, not only do 1984 and 1985 not get counted in their data base, but they include in this administration's economic record 4 years of the last Democratic administration. . . .

But the truth is otherwise, because under the last administration real per capita disposable income rose at only 1-percent annual rate, only half the 2-percent rate of increase under this administration—a gain that has totaled 12.4 percent in 6 years. Under the last administration, median family income declined 6.8 percent, while under this administration, it went up 9.1 percent. Or take real after-tax labor income per hour. If you use the approach adopted by our liberal critics, you see a 4½ percent decline. But the truth is that that figure fell

8½ percent under the last administration and we turned this around and accounted for an 8.9-percent increase.

Under the last administration, the average weekly wage went down an incredible 10 percent in real terms, which accounted for the worst drop in postwar history. Here again, we've stopped the decline, and that's not to mention what all this has meant in terms of opportunity for women, for blacks, and minorities—the very groups our opponents say they most want to help.

Well, since the recovery began, 70 percent of the new jobs have been translated into opportunities for women; and black and other minority employment has risen twice as fast as all other groups. Minority family income has also increased at a rate over 40 percent faster than other groups. In addition, since 1983, 2.9 million people have climbed out of poverty, and the poverty rate has declined at the fastest rate in more than 10 years.

So, think for a moment on what these statistics mean and the kind of political nerve and desperation it takes to try to sell the American people on the idea that in the 1980's they never had it so bad. The truth is we're in the 63d month of this nonstop expansion. Real gross national product growth for 1987 was 3.8 percent, defying the pessimists and even exceeding our own forecast—which was criticized as being too rosy at the time—by more than one-half percent. Inflation is down from 13½-percent in 1980 to only around 4 percent or less this year. And there's over 15 million new jobs.

So, believe me, I welcome this approach by the opposition. And I promise you every time they use it I'll just tell the story of a friend of mine who was asked to a costume ball a short time ago. He slapped some egg on his face and went as a liberal economist. [*Laughter*]. . . .

The American people know what limited government, tax cuts, deregulation, and the move towards privitization have meant: It's meant the largest peacetime expansion in our history. And I can guarantee you they won't want to throw that away for a return to budgets beholden to the liberal special interests.

No, I think the economic record of conservatives in power is going to speak for itself. . . .

And so, I say to you tonight that the vision and record that we will take aggressively to the American people this November is a vision that all Americans—except a few on the left—share; a vision of a nation that believes in the heroism of ordinary people living ordinary lives; of tough courts and safe streets; of a drug free America where schools teach honesty, respect, love of learning and, yes, love of country; a vision of a land where families can grow in love and safety and where dreams are made with opportunity. This is the vision. This is the record. This is the agenda for victory this year.

Well, that's the record then on the economy and the social issues. . . .

. . . I intend to campaign vigorously for whoever our nominee is, and tonight I ask each of you to join me in this important crusade. Let's ask the American people to replenish our mandate. Let's tell them if they want 4 more years of economic progress and the march of world freedom they must help us this year—help us settle the matter before lunchtime, help make 1988 the year of the Waterloo liberal. I just have to add here, when you look at the figures overall, that they have the nerve even to still be out there and campaigning. [*Laughter*]. . . .

Back when the war on poverty began, which poverty won—[*laughter*]—from 1965 to 1980—in those 15 years, the Federal budget increased to five times what it had been in '65. And the deficit increased to 38 times what it had been just 15 years before. It's built-in. It's structural. And you and I need to get representatives not only in the executive branch but out there in the Legislature so that we can change that structure that is so built-in and that threatens us with so much harm.

Well, I've gone on too long for all of you here, but I couldn't resist, because you're the troops. You're out there on the frontier of freedom. One young soldier over there in Korea, one of our men, saluted me when I visited there and very proudly said, "Mr. President, we're on the frontier of freedom." Well, so are you.

Thank you. God bless you all.

Chapter Two: Power

2.1 The Impeachment of Andrew Johnson

The Constitution provides that federal officials "shall be removed from Office on Impeachment for, and Conviction of, Treason, Bribery, or other high Crimes and Misdemeanors." The House of Representatives hands down a bill of impeachment and the Senate uses that bill to try the accused. In 1868, Andrew Johnson became the first President to be subjected to impeachment proceedings. (The second was Richard Nixon in 1974—see below, document 2.10.) The combative Johnson quarrelled with the Congress over Reconstruction policy. The contest took an ugly turn after the election of 1866, when many of Johnson's friends were defeated despite his active support. The Congress, now dominated by Radical Republicans, was anxious to impose its will on the South despite the President's intervention. Congress passed the Tenure of Office Act to prohibit the President from removing any civil officer without the consent of the Senate. When Johnson tried to remove from his Cabinet Secretary of War Edwin M. Stanton, a staunch Radical Republican, the battle reached a showdown.

The House handed down articles of impeachment (excerpted below) and Johnson stood trial. In addition to the Stanton matter, Congress cited Johnson for attempting to undermine the Army's chain of command in the occupation of the South. It also cited him for attempting to bring public ridicule against the Congress. After a stormy proceeding the Senate acquitted Johnson by one vote. Stanton resigned and was appointed by President Grant to the Supreme Court, but he died before he could serve.

The impeachment was a struggle over how the South should be ruled and what rights the blacks should have. But it also was a power struggle between two branches of government. Had Congress toppled Johnson, the office of the presidency might have been permanently damaged and the balance of power altered. Congress might have begun to resemble the English or French Parliament, with the speaker of the House having a more dominant role in the government than the President.

Questions

Was the impeachment proceeding fair, or was the Congress too overbearing? Why did members of the Senate balk at the way it was conducted? Was the battle substantive or merely symbolic?

Had Johnson been removed, what precedent might this have set for later battles between Congress and the President? How might it have affected the course of Reconstruction?

IN THE HOUSE OF REPRESENTATIVES,
UNITED STATES,
March 2, 1868.

ARTICLES EXHIBITED BY THE HOUSE OF REPRESENTATIVES OF THE UNITED STATES, IN THE NAME OF THEMSELVES AND ALL THE PEOPLE OF THE UNITED STATES, AGAINST ANDREW JOHNSON, PRESIDENT OF THE UNITED STATES, IN MAINTENANCE AND SUPPORT OF THEIR IMPEACHMENT AGAINST HIM FOR HIGH CRIMES AND MISDEMEANORS IN OFFICE.

ARTICLE I. That said Andrew Johnson, President of the United States, on the 21st day of February, A.D. 1868, at Washington, in the District of Columbia, unmindful of the high duties of his office, of his oath of office, and of the requirement of the Constitution that he should take care that the laws be faithfully executed, did unlawfully and in violation of the Constitution and laws of the United States issue an order in writing for the removal of Edwin M. Stanton from the office of Secretary for the Department of War, said Edwin M. Stanton having been theretofore duly appointed and commissioned, by and with the advice and consent of the Senate of the United States, as such Secretary; and said Andrew Johnson, President of the United States, on the 12th day of August, A.D. 1867, and during the recess of said Senate having suspended by his order Edwin M. Stanton from said office, and within twenty days after the first day of the next meeting of said Senate—that is to say, on the 12th day of December, in the year last aforesaid—having reported to said Senate such suspension, with the evidence and reasons for his action in the case and the name of the person designated to perform the duties of

SOURCE: Richardson, ed., *Messages and Papers of the Presidents*, Vol. VI, p. 709 ff.

such office temporarily until the next meeting of the Senate; and said Senate thereafterwards, on the 13th day of January, A.D. 1868, having duly considered the evidence and reasons reported by said Andrew Johnson for said suspension, and having refused to concur in said suspension, whereby and by force of the provisions of an act entitled "An act regulating the tenure of certain civil offices, passed March 2, 1867, said Edwin M. Stanton did forthwith resume the functions of his office, whereof the said Andrew Johnson had then and there due notice; and said Edwin M. Stanton, by reason of the premises, on said 21st day of February, being lawfully entitled to hold said office of Secretary for the Department of War; which said order for the removal of said Edwin M. Stanton is in substance as follows: that is to say:

EXECUTIVE MANSION,
Washington, D.C., February 21, 1868.
HON. EDWIN M. STANTON,
Washington, D.C.

SIR: By virtue of the power and authority vested in me as President by the Constitution and laws of the United States, you are hereby removed from office as Secretary for the Department of War, and your functions as such will terminate upon the receipt of this communication.

You will transfer to Brevet Major-General Lorenzo Thomas, Adjutant-General of the Army, who has this day been authorized and empowered to act as Secretary of War *ad interim*, all records, books, papers, and other public property now in your custody and charge.

Respectfully, yours,
ANDREW JOHNSON

which order was unlawfully issued with intent then and there to violate the act entitled "An act regulating the tenure of certain civil offices," passed March 2, 1867 . . . whereby said Andrew Johnson, President of the United States, did then and there commit and was guilty of a high misdemeanor in office.

ART. II. That on said 21st day of February, A.D. 1868, at Washington, in the District of Columbia, said Andrew Johnson, President of the United States, . . . did, with intent to violate the Constitution of the United States and the act aforesaid, issue and deliver to one Lorenzo Thomas a letter of authority in substance as follows; that is to say:

> EXECUTIVE MANSION,
> *Washington, D.C., February 21, 1868.*
> Brevet Major-General
> Lorenzo Thomas,
> *Adjutant-General United States Army,*
> *Washington, D.C.*
> SIR: The Hon. Edwin M. Stanton having been this day removed from office as Secretary for the Department of War, you are hereby authorized and empowered to act as Secretary of War *ad interim,* and will immediately enter upon the discharge of the duties pertaining to that office.
>
> Mr. Stanton has been instructed to transfer to you all the records, books, papers, and other public property now in his custody and charge.
> Respectfully, yours,
> ANDREW JOHNSON

then and there being no vacancy in said office of Secretary for the Department of War; whereby said Andrew Johnson, President of the United States, did then and there commit and was guilty of a high misdemeanor in office.

ART. III. That said Andrew Johnson, President of the United States, on the 21st day of February, A.D. 1868, at Washington, in the District of Columbia, did commit and was guilty of a high misdemeanor in office

in this, that without authority of law, while the Senate of the United States was then and there in session, he did appoint one Lorenzo Thomas to be Secretary for the Department of War *ad interim,* without the advice and consent of the Senate, and with intent to violate the Constitution of the United States. . . .

ART. IV. That said Andrew Johnson, President of the United States, . . . did unlawfully conspire wth one Lorenzo Thomas, and with other persons to the House of Representatives unknown with intent, by intimidation and threats, unlawfully to hinder and prevent Edwin M. Stanton, then and there the Secretary for the Department of War, . . . from holding said office of Secretary for the Department of War, contrary to and in violation of the Constitution of the United States and of the provisions of an act entitled "An act to define and punish certain conspiracies," approved July 31, 1861; . . .

ART. V. That said Andrew Johnson, President of the United States, . . . did unlawfully conspire with one Lorenzo Thomas, and with other persons to the House of Representatives unknown to prevent and hinder the execution of an act entitled "An act regulating the tenure of certain civil offices," passed March 2, 1867. . . .

ART. VI. That said Andrew Johnson, President of the United States . . . did unlawfully conspire with one Lorenzo Thomas by force to seize, take, and possess the property of the United States in the Department of War and then and there in the custody and charge of Edwin M. Stanton, Secretary for said Department, contrary to the provisions of an act entitled "An act to define and punish certain conspiracies," approved July 31, 1861, and with intent to violate and disregard an act entitled "An act regulating the tenure of certain civil offices," passed March 2, 1867; . . .

ART. VIII. That said Andrew Johnson, President of the United States . . . with intent unlawfully to control the disbursement of the moneys appropriated for the military service and for the Department of War, . . . did unlawfully, and in violation of the Constitution of the United States, and without the advice and consent of the Senate of the United States, . . . there being no vacancy in the office of Secretary for the Department of War, and with intent to violate and disregard the act aforesaid, then and there issue and deliver to one Lorenzo Thomas a letter of authority, . . .

ART. IX. That said Andrew Johnson, President of the United States, on the 22d day of February, A.D. 1868, . . . in disregard of the Constitution and the laws of the United States duly enacted, as Commander in Chief of the Army of the United States, did bring before himself then and there William H. Emory, a major-general by brevet in the Army of the United States, actually in command of the Department of Washington and the military forces thereof, and did then and there, as such Commander in Chief, declare to and instruct said Emory that part of a law of the United States, passed March 2, 1867, entitled "An Act making appropriations for the support of the Army for the year ending June 30, 1868, and for other purposes," especially the second section thereof, which provides, among other things, that "all orders and instructions relating to military operations issued by the President or Secretary of War shall be issued through the General of the Army, and in case of his inability through the next in rank," was unconstitutional . . . with intent thereby to induce said Emory, in his official capacity as commander of the Department of Washington, to violate the provisions of said act and to take and receive, act upon, and obey such orders as he, the said Andrew Johnson, might make and give, and which should not be issued through the General of the Army of the United States, according to the provisions of said act, . . .

ART. X. That said Andrew Johnson, President of the United States, unmindful of the high duties of his office and the dignity and proprieties thereof, and of the harmony and courtesies which ought to exist and be maintained between the executive and legislative branches of the Government of the United States, . . . did attempt to bring into disgrace, ridicule, hatred, contempt, and reproach the Congress of the United States and the several branches thereof, to impair and destroy the regard and respect of all the good people of the United States for the Congress. . . .

2.2   The Farmers' Rebellion

Beginning in the depression of the 1870s, American farmers became agitated about the disadvantages of commercial agriculture and began to organize politically. By the 1890s, many of them were so convinced that the Republican and Democratic parties were indifferent to their problems that they formed their own national political organization, the People's party, soon to be known as "the Populists." In 1892 the Populists ran a Union veteran for president and a Confederate veteran for vice president, as well as candidates for Congress and various state legislatures. They drew most of their support from farmers and miners in the West and South, but also had the support of the Knights of Labor and the Prohibitionist party.

The Populist platform of 1892 is a detailed statement of their position. The first part lists all of their grievances, and the second part details their solutions. They demand government intervention and partial government ownership of the means of production. In the 1892 balloting they won about 8.5 percent of the vote and made a second run in 1896, with William Jennings Bryan as their standard bearer. This was the climax of the farmers' political rebellion.

Questions

Summarize the grievances of the rebellious farmers who started the People's party. How justified were they?

Some Americans, like Andrew Carnegie, felt that America was dividing into classes of rich and poor, and that this was desirable in the long run. What did the Populists think about this?

If Populists believed that all the branches of government had been captured by the rich, why did they expect to use government to solve their problems? Why did they want an initiative and a referendum, and why were they so eager to use silver as well as gold as currency in the United States?

Since most Populists were farmers, why did they favor an eight-hour day and attack the hiring of private detectives who were being used against industrial workers?

How did the Populisit platform influence the Progressives and other reformers of the twentieth century?

Some contemporaries (as well as historians) believe the Populists were deluded and their economic ideas were foolish. What do you think about those ideas and about the Populists' analysis of America in the 1890s?

Preamble

The conditions which surround us best justify our co-operation; we meet in the midst of a nation brought to the verge of moral, political, and material ruin. Corruption dominates the ballot-box, the Legislatures, the Congress, and touches even the ermine of the bench. The people are demoralized; most of the States have been compelled to isolate the voters at the polling places to prevent universal intimidation and bribery. The newspapers are largely subsidized or muzzled, public opinion silenced, business prostrated, homes covered with mortgages, labor impoverished, and the land concentrating in the hands of capitalists. The urban workmen are denied the right to organize for self-protection, imported pauperized labor beats down their wages, a hireling standing army, unrecognized by our laws, is established to shoot them down, and they are rapidly degenerating into European conditions. The fruits of the toil of millions are boldly stolen to build up colossal fortunes for a few, unprecedented in the history of mankind; and the possessors of these, in turn, despise the Republic and endanger liberty. From the same prolific womb of governmental injustice we breed the two great classes—tramps and millionaires.

The national power to create money is appropriated to enrich bond-holders; a vast public debt payable in legal-tender currency has been funded into gold-bearing bonds, thereby adding millions to the burdens of the people.

Silver, which has been accepted as coin since the dawn of history, has been demonetized to add to the purchasing power of gold by decreasing the value of all forms of property as well as human labor, and the supply of currency is purposely abridged to fatten usurers, bankrupt enterprise, and enslave industry. A vast conspiracy against mankind has been organized on two continents, and it is rapidly taking possession of the world. If not met and overthrown at once it forebodes terrible social convulsions, the destruction of civilization or the establishment of an absolute despotism.

We have witnessed for more than a quarter of a century the struggles of the two great political parties for power and plunder, while grievous wrongs have been inflicted upon the suffering people. We charge that the controlling influences

dominating both these parties have permitted the existing dreadful conditions to develop without serious effort to prevent or restrain them. Neither do they now promise us any substantial reform. They have agreed together to ignore, in the coming campaign every issue but one. They propose to drown the outcries of a plundered people with the uproar of a sham battle over the tariff, so that capitalists, corporations, national banks, rings, trusts, watered stock, the demonetization of silver and the oppressions of the usurers may all be lost sight of. They propose to sacrifice our homes, lives, and children on the altar of mammon; to destroy the multitude in order to secure corruption funds from the millionaires.

Assembled on the anniversary of the birthday of the nation, and filled with the spirit of the grand general and chief who established our independence, we seek to restore the government of the Republic to the hands of the "plain people," with which class it originated. We assert our purposes to be identical with the purposes of the National Constitution; to form a more perfect union and establish justice, insure domestic tranquility, provide for the common defense, promote the general welfare, and secure the blessings of liberty for ourselves and our posterity.

We declare that this Republic can only endure as a free government while built upon the love of the people for each other and for the nation; that it cannot be pinned together by bayonets; that the Civil War is over, and that every passion and resentment which grew out of it must die with it, and that we must be in fact, as we are in name, one united brotherhood of free men.

Our country finds itself confronted by conditions for which there is no precedent in the history of the world; our annual agricultural productions amount to billions of dollars in value, which must, within a few weeks or months, be exchanged for billions of dollars' worth of commodities consumed in their production; the existing currency supply is wholly inadequate to make this exchange; the results are falling prices, the formation of combines and rings, the impoverishment of the producing class. We pledge ourselves that if given power we will labor to correct these evils by wise and reasonable legislation, in accordance with the terms of our platform.

We believe that the power of government—in other words, of the people—should be expanded (as in the case of the postal service) as rapidly and as far as the good sense of an intelligent people and the teachings of experience shall justify, to the end that oppression, injustice, and poverty shall eventually cease in the land.

While our sympathies as a party of reform are naturally upon the side of every proposition which will tend to make men intelligent, virtuous, and temperate, we nevertheless regard these questions, important as they are, as secondary to the great issues now pressing for solution, and upon which not only our individual prosperity but the very existence of free institutions depend; and we ask all men to first help us to determine whether we are to have a republic to administer before we differ as to the conditions upon which it is to be administered, believing that the forces of reform this day organized will never cease to move forward until every wrong is righted and equal rights and equal privileges securely established for all the men and women of this country.

Platform

We declare, therefore—

First.—That the union of the labor forces of the United States this day consummated shall be permanent and perpetual; may its spirit enter into all hearts for the salvation of the Republic and the uplifting of mankind.

Second.—Wealth belongs to him who creates it, and every dollar taken from industry without an equivalent is robbery. "If any will not work, neither shall he eat." The interests of rural and civil labor are the same; their enemies are identical.

Third.—We believe that the time has come when the railroad corporations will either own the people or the people must own the railroads; and should the government enter upon the work of owning and managing all railroads, we should favor an amendment to the constitution by which all persons engaged in the government service shall be placed under a civil-service regulation of the most rigid character, so as to prevent the increase of the power of the national administration by the use of such additional government employees.

Finance.—We demand a national currency, safe, sound, and flexible issued by the general government only, a full legal tender for all debts, public and private, and that without the use of banking corporations; a just, equitable, and efficient means of distribution direct to the people, at a tax not to exceed 2 percent, per annum, to be provided as set forth in the sub-treasury plan of the Farmers' Alliance, or a better system; also by payments in discharge of its obligations for public improvements.

1. We demand free and unlimited coinage of silver and gold at the present legal ratio of 16 to 1.
2. We demand that the amount of circulating medium be speedily increased to not less than $50 per capita.
3. We demand a graduated income tax.
4. We believe that the money of the country should be kept as much as possible in the hands of the people, and hence we demand that all State and national revenues shall be limited to the necessary expenses of the government, economically and honestly administered.
5. We demand that postal savings banks be established by the government for the safe deposit of the earnings of the people and to facilitate exchange.

Transportation.—Transportation being a means of exchange and a public necessity, the government should own and operate the railroads in the interest of the people. The telegraph and telephone, like the post-office system, being a necessity for the transmission of news, should be owned and operated by the government in the interest of the people.

Land.—The land, including all the natural sources of wealth, is the heritage of the people, and should not be monopolized for speculative purposes, and alien ownership of land should be prohibited. All land now held by railroads and other corporations in excess of their actual needs, and all lands now owned by aliens should be reclaimed by the government and held for actual settlers only.

Expression of Sentiments

Your Commitee on Platform and Resolutions beg leave unanimously to report the following:

Whereas, Other questions have been presented for our consideration, we hereby submit the following not as a part of the Platform of the Peoples Party, but as resolutions expressive of the sentiment of this Convention.

1. Resolved, That we demand a free ballot and a fair count in all elections, and pledge ourselves to secure it to every legal voter without Federal intervention, through the adoption by the States of the unperverted Australian or secret ballot system.
2. Resolved, That the revenue derived from a graduated income tax should be applied to the reduction of the burden of taxation now levied upon the domestic industries of this country.
3. Resolved, That we pledge our support to fair and liberal pensions to ex-Union soldiers and sailors.
4. Resolved, That we condemn the fallacy of protecting American labor under the present system, which opens our ports to the pauper and criminal classes of the world and crowds out our wage-earners; and we denounce the present ineffective laws against contract labor, and demand the further restriction of undesirable immigration.
5. Resolved, That we cordially sympathize with the efforts of organized workingmen to shorten the hours of labor, and demand a rigid enforcement of the existing eight-hour law on Government work, and ask that a penalty clause be added to the said law.
6. Resolved, That we regard the maintenance of a large standing army of mercenaries, known as the Pinkerton system, as a menace to our liberties, and we demand its abolition; and we condemn the recent invasion ot the Territory of Wyoming by the hired

assassins of plutocracy, assisted by federal officers.

7. Resolved, That we commend to the favorable consideration of the people and the reform press the legislative system known as the initiative and referendum.

8. Resolved, That we favor a constitutional provision limiting the office of President and Vice-President to one term, and providing for the election of Senators of the United States by a direct vote of the people.

9. Resolved, That we oppose any subsidy or national aid to any private corporation for any purpose.

10. Resolved, That this convention sympathizes with the Knights of Labor and their righteous contest with the tyrannical combine of clothing manufacturers of Rochester, and declare it to be a duty of all who hate tyranny and oppression to refuse to purchase the goods made by the said manufacturers, or to patronize any merchants who sell such goods.

2.3 Exposing Standard Oil

Henry Demarest Lloyd was the first journalist to indict a giant corporation in print. His target was the Standard Oil Corporation, founded and controlled by John D. Rockefeller. In 1881 he published an exposé in The Atlantic Monthly *magazine showing how the petroleum corporation, working hand-in-glove with the railroads, had conspired secretly to own or control most of the petroleum production in the U.S. This was the start of a series of sensational "muckraking" articles on monopolies. Many who read the exposés by Lloyd and others (see also Document 1.4), concluded that the trusts had grown too rich and powerful for the good of the nation, and that something had to be done about them.*

Lloyd's researches convinced him that the "Lords of Industry" had seized control of the American economy. If true competition had ever been possible, Lloyd thought, it was no longer so. Indeed, he believed that laissez-faire *had probably been a mistaken dogma from the moment it was first characterized in 1776 by the English political economist, Adam Smith, in his epochal work,* The Wealth of Nations.

Questions

How, according to Lloyd, did Rockefeller conspire with the railroads to dominate the petroleum industry?

Since the nation had benefited greatly from corporate enterprises like Rockefeller's, should it not have graciously accepted the disadvantages that the trusts produced? What was wrong with monopoly power?

What role does monopoly power play today? Is pure free enterprise really attainable? Is it necesary, or desirable, for government to step in to regulate free enterprise?

When Commodore Vanderbilt began [in] the world he had nothing, and there were no steamboats or railroads. He was thirty-five years old when the first locomotive was put into use in America. When he died, railroads had become the greatest force in modern industry, and Vanderbilt was the richest man of Europe or America, and the largest owner of railroads in the world. . . . The history is not yet finished, but the railroads owe on stocks and bonds $4,6000,000,000—more than twice our national debt, . . . and [they] tax the people annually $490,000,000—one and a half-times more than the government's revenue last year. . . . More than any other class, our railroad men have developed the country, and tried its institutions. . . .

Our treatment of "the railroad problem" will show the quality and calibre of our political sense. It will go far in foreshadowing the future lines of our social and political growth. It may indicate whether the American democracy, like all the democratic experiments which have preceded it, is to become extinct because the people had not wit enough or virtue enough to make the common good supreme. . . .

Kerosene has become, by its cheapness, the people's light the world over. In the United States we used 220,000,000 gallons of petroleum last year. It has come into

such demand abroad that . . . after articles of food, this country has but one export, cotton, more valuable than petroleum. . . . In the United States, in the cities as well as the country, petroleum is the general illuminator. . . .

Very few of the forty millions of people in the United States who burn kerosene know that its production, manufacture, and export, its price at home and aboard, have been controlled for years by a single corporation—the Standard Oil Company. This company began in a partnership, in the early years of the Civil War, between Samuel Andrews and John Rockefeller in Cleveland. Rockefeller had been a bookkeeper in some interior town in Ohio, and had afterwards made a few thousand dollars by keeping a flour store in Cleveland. Andrews had been a day laborer in refineries, and so poor that his wife took in sewing. He found a way of refining by which more kerosene could be got out of a barrel of petroleum than by any other method, and set up for himself a ten-barrel still in Cleveland, by which he cleared $500 in six months. Andrews' still and Rockefeller's savings have grown into the Standard Oil Company. It has a capital, nominally $3,500,000, but really much more, on which it divides among its stockholders every year millions of dollars of profits. . . .

The four quarters of the globe are partitioned among the members of the Standard combinations. . . . The Standard

SOURCE: Henry Demarest Lloyd, "Story of a Great Monopoly," *The Atlantic Monthly* (March 1881), XLVII, 317–34.

produces only one fiftieth or sixtieth of our petroleum, but dictates the price of all, and refines nine tenths. . . . There is not today a merchant in Chicago, or in any other city in the New England, Western, or Southern States, dealing in kerosene, whose prices are not fixed for him by the Standard. . . . Nobody knows how many millions Rockefeller is worth. Current gossip . . . puts his income last year at a figure second only . . . to that of Vanderbilt. . . .

Their great business capacity would have insured the managers of the Standard success, but the means by which they achieved monopoly was by conspiracy with the railroads. Mr. Simon Sterne, counsel for the merchants of New York in the New York investigation, declared that the relations of the railroads to the Standard exhibited "the most shameless perversion of the duties of a common carrier to private ends that has taken place in the history of the world." The Standard killed its rivals, in brief, by getting the great trunk lines to refuse to give them transportation. Commodore Vanderbilt is reported to have said that there was but one man—Rockefeller—who could dictate to him. Whether or not Vanderbilt said it, Rockefeller did it. The Standard has done everything with the Pennsylvania legislature, except refine it. . . .

The contract is in print by which the Pennslvania Railroad agreed with the Standard, under the name of the South Improvement Company, to double the freights on oil to everybody, but to repay the Standard one dollar for every barrel of oil it shipped, and one dollar for every barrel any of its competitors shipped. . . . Vanderbilt . . . has given the Standard special rates and privileges. He has paid it back in rebates millions of dollars, which have enabled it to crush out all competitors. . . .

. . . [T]he public rate for transporting crude oil was $1.40 a barrel, but the Standard paid only eighty-eight and a half cents, and finally but ten cents. . . . The rebates given the Standard extend to nearly every State in the Union. These rebates are about equal to the average value of the oil at the wells. The railroads of the United States virtually give the Standard its raw material free. . . .

. . . There was apparently no trick the Standard would not play. It delivered its competitors inferior oils when they had ordered the high-priced article out of which alone they could manufacture the fancy brands their customers called for. . . . Hundreds and thousands of men have been ruined by these acts of the Standard and the railroads. . . . Mr. Alexander, of Cleveland, tells how he was informed by Rockefeller, of the Standard, that if he would not sell out he should be crushed out. . . .

Today, in every part of the United States, people who burn kerosene are paying the Standard Oil Company a tax on every gallon amounting to several times its original cost to that concern. . . . A family that uses a gallon of kerosene a day pays a yearly tribute to the Standard of $32, the income from $800 in four per cents. . . .

It is the railroads that have bred the millionaires who are now buying newspapers, and getting up corners in wheat, corn, and cotton, and are making railroad consolidations that stretch across the continent. By the same tactics that the railroads have used to build up the Standard, they can give other combinations of capitalists the control of the wheat, lumber, cotton, or any other product of the United States. . . .

One mind invented the locomotive, established the railroad, and discovered the law of this new force. All railroad history has been a vindication of George Stephenson's saying that where combination was possible competition was impossible. Today, wherever in this country there is a group of railroads doing business at a common point, you will find a pool. These pools are nothing more mysterious than combinations to prevent competition. . . .

These pools must be either dispersed . . . or controlled. . . . The cat must be killed or belled. In either case, it must be confronted by a power greater than itself. . . . In less than the ordinary span of a life-time, our railroads have brought upon us the worst labor disturbance, the greatest of monopolies, and the most formidable combination of money and brains that ever overshadowed a state. The time has come to face the fact that the forces of capital and industry have outgrown the forces of our government. . . .

2.4 The First Antitrust Law

Out of the exposés of journalists—and the clamor of angry farmers, entrepreneurs, laborers and middle-class citizens—came the first federal legislation controlling the new economic giants. The first big corporations targeted by Congress for control were the railroads. A conservative bipartisan Congress passed the Interstate Commerce Commission Act of 1887. It established the first federal regulatory agency, a model for all the others to come. The new ICC law set up a five-member commission to hear complaints and look at the records of private rail corporations. But the Commission lacked the authority actually to fix rates and was forced to rely on the courts for "cease and desist orders." In fact, the ICC was totally ineffectual for the first twenty years of its life. Only during the Progressive era did Congress amend the law and give the Commission a sharper set of teeth.

The same political outcry that produced the ICC led to the first legislation controlling the industrial monopolies. In 1890, the U.S. Congress passed the Sherman Anti-Trust Law. It declared illegal any contract, combination or conspiracy that restrained trade or commerce, and it provided for fines, prison terms, and damage suits against people who violated that law. (See excerpt below).

For ten years the Sherman Act was practically a dead letter. The federal government seldom invoked it—except against labor unions to break strikes. The Attorney General attempted to prosecute a few corporations, but if the judiciary interpreted the Act literally, it would condemn countless American companies for engaging in anti-competitive activities. It would have punished some of the nation's largest corporations for what had become their normal behavior, and possibly even imprisoned their managers. This would have revolutionized the American economic system, something that the conservatives who staffed the nation's courts were not inclined to do. In The United States v. E. C. Knight, *in 1985, the U.S. Supreme Court effectively nullified the Act. Eventually, in 1911, the Supreme Court tried to solve this problem by ruling that only activities the courts deemed "unreasonable" violated the Sherman law.*

The antitrust movement gained further ground during the Progressive era. Under the Clayton Antitrust Act of 1914, loopholes in the Sherman Act were eliminated and the use of the anti-trust laws against labor unions curtailed.

Questions

Summarize in your own words the provisions of the Sherman Act. Why did political conservatives agree to pass this legislation? What consequences did they fear if they failed to do so?

In the early twentieth century, new regulatory agencies were established to deal with business excesses and older ones strengthened; in recent decades the trend has been toward deregulation, for example, in airlines and banking. How effectively have regulatory agencies worked, and why was there a reaction against them? Are weaker or stronger regulatory agencies needed today?

Antitrust laws were weakly enforced in the 1920s and strongly enforced in the 1930s. How strongly are they enforced today?

An Act To protect trade and commerce against unlawful restraints and monopolies. . . .

Be it enacted

Sec. 1. Every contract, combination in the form of trust or otherwise, or conspiracy, in restraint of trade or commerce among the several States, or with foreign nations, is hereby declared to be illegal. Every person who shall make any such contract or engage in any such combination or conspiracy, shall be deemed guilty of a misdemeanor, and, on conviction thereof, shall be punished by fine not exceeding five thousand dollars, or by imprisonment not exceeding one year, or by both said punishments, in the discretion of the court.

Sec. 2. Every person who shall monopolize, or attempt to monopolize, or combine or conspire with any other person or persons, to monopolize any part of the trade or commerce among the several States, or with foreign nations, shall be deemed guilty of a misdemeanor. . . .

Sec. 3. Every contract, combination in form of trust or otherwise, or conspiracy, in restraint of trade or commerce in any Territory of the United States or of the District of Columbia, or in restraint of trade or commerce between any such Territory and another, or between any such Territory or Territories and any State or States or the District of Columbia, or with foreign nations, or between the District of Columbia and any State or States or foreign nations, is hereby declared illegal. Every person who shall make any such contract or engage in any such combination or conspiracy, shall be deemed guilty of a misdemeanor. . . .

Sec. 4. The several circuit courts of the United States are hereby invested with ju-

Source: *U.S. Statutes at Large*, XXIV, 397 ff.; XXVI, 209.

risdiction to prevent and restrain violations of this act; and it shall be the duty of the several district attorneys of the United States, in their respective districts, under the direction of the Attorney-General, to institute proceedings in equity to prevent and restrain such violations. . . .

SEC. 5. Whenever it shall appear to the court before which any proceeding under Section four of this act may be pending, that the ends of justice require that other parties should be brought before the court, the court may cause them to be summoned, whether they reside in the district in which the court is held or not; and subpoenas to that end may be served in any district by the marshal thereof.

SEC. 6. Any property owned under any contract or by any contract or by any combination, or pursuant to any conspiracy (and being the subject thereof) mentioned in section one of this act, and being in the course of transportation from one State to another, or to a foreign country, shall be forfeited to the United States, and may be seized and condemned by like proceedings as those provided by law for the forfeiture, seizure, and condemnation of property imported into the United States contrary to law.

SEC. 7. Any person who shall be injured in his business or property by any other person or corporation by reason of anything forbidden or declared to be unlawful by this act, may sue therefor in any circuit court of the United States in the district in which the defendant resides or is found without respect to the amount in controversy, and shall recover threefold the damages by him sustained, and the costs of suit, including a reasonable attorney's fee.

SEC. 8. That the word "person," or "persons," wherever used in this act shall be deemed to include corporations and associations existing under or authorized by the laws of either the United States, the laws of any of the Territories, the laws of any State, or the laws of any foreign country.

2.5 Presidential Trust Bashing

As the concentration of wealth and power by the trusts continued virtually unchecked, public resentment grew. In the early decades of the century, two of the most important leaders of the Progressive movement, Theodore Roosevelt and Woodrow Wilson, were forced to face the trust issue.

The Republican Roosevelt found a way to control giant companies and calm public fears of plutocracy without affecting American capitalism. By threatening to prosecute particular corporations under the Sherman Act and by actually moving against a few of them, he hoped to force the great barons of industry and finance to consult with his administration before they destroyed their competition. In 1907 he explained his position in his seventh annual message to Congress, excerpted below.

Five years later, Roosevelt, who had acquired the reputation of a "trust buster," ran for president as the candidate of the Progressive or Bull Moose party. His opponents were the

Republican candidate, former president William Howard Taft, and a Democrat, Woodrow Wilson, governor of New Jersey.

Wilson argued that Roosevelt's method of regulating large industrial combinations would only benefit the trust themselves and in the end would hurt the country and American business itself. In campaign speeches (like the two excerpted here) he offered another approach.

Questions

Compare and contrast Roosevelt's and Wilson's proposed methods for dealing with the trusts. What does Roosevelt think about ending business combinations? Which man had the more realistic view of the problems posed by large corporations? Did Roosevelt deserve his reputation as a "trust buster"?

Why does Wilson feel it is a mistake to have government try to control large corporations through regulation? What does he say about the effects of anti-competitive practices on American companies and their willingness to adopt new technology?

Wilson seems to think there is something wrong with Americans developing a "generation of employees." Do you find anything wrong with being an employee? What alternative was he thinking of?

In your opinion, do very large businesses, including banks, dominate the nation's economy and government? If so, what is wrong with that? What, if anything, should be done about large business combinations in our own times?

Could a candidate publicly say today what Wilson and Roosevelt said in these excerpts and still stand a chance of becoming president?

Theodore Roosevelt, Dec. 3, 1907 —

In my Message to the Congress on December 5, 1905, I said:

"In our industrial and social system the interests of all men are so closely intertwined that in the immense majority of cases a straight-dealing man, who by his efficiency, by his ingenuity and industry,

benefits himself, must also benefit others. Normally, the man of great productive capacity who becomes rich by guiding the labor of many other men does so by enabling them to produce more than they could produce without his guidance; and both he and they share in the benefit, which comes also to the public at large. The superficial fact that the sharing may be unequal must never blind us to the underlying fact that there is this sharing, and that the benefit comes in some degree to each man concerned. Normally, the wage-

SOURCES: Woodrow Wilson, "A Speech from a Rear Platform in Elk Point, South Dakota," Sept. 17, 1912; Theodore Roosevelt, "Seventh Annual Message," Dec. 3, 1907.

worker, the man of small means, and the average consumer, as well as the average producer, are all alike helped by making conditions such that the man of exceptional business ability receives an exceptional reward for his ability. Something can be done by legislation to help the general prosperity; but no such help of a permanently beneficial character can be given to the less able and less fortunate save as the results of a policy which shall inure to the advantage of all industrious and efficient people who act decently; and this is only another way of saying that any benefit which comes to the less able and less fortunate must of necessity come even more to the more able and more fortunate. If, therefore, the less fortunate man is moved by envy of his more fortunate brother to strike at the conditions under which they have both, though unequally, prospered, the result will assuredly be that while damage may come to the one struck at, it will visit with an even heavier load the one who strikes the blow. Taken as a whole, we must all go up or go down together.

"Yet while not merely admitting, but insisting upon this, it is also true that where there is no governmental restraint or supervision some of the exceptional men use their energies, not in ways that are for the common good, but in ways which tell against this common good. The fortunes amassed through corporate organizations are now so large, and vest such power in those that wield them, as to make it a matter of necessity to give to the sovereign—that is, to the Government, which represents the people as a whole—some effective power of supervision over their corporate use. In order to insure a healthy social and industrial life, every big corporation should be held responsible by, and be accountable to, some sovereign strong enough to control its conduct. I am in no sense hostile to corporations. This is an age of combination, and any effort to prevent all combination will be not only useless, but in the end vicious, because of the contempt for law which the failure to enforce law inevitably produces. We should, moreover, recognize in cordial and ample fashion the immense good effected by corporate agencies in a country such as ours, and the wealth of intellect, energy, and fidelity devoted to their service, and therefore normally to the service of the public, by their officers and directors. The corporation has come to stay, just as the trade union has come to stay. Each can do and has done great good. Each should be favored so long as it does good. But each should be sharply checked where it acts against law and justice.

. . . Only the National Government can in thoroughgoing fashion exercise the needed control. This does not mean that there should be any extension of Federal authority, for such authority already exists under the Constitution in amplest and most far-reaching form; but it does mean that there should be an extension of Federal activity. This is not advocating centralization. It is merely looking facts in the face, and realizing that centralization in business has already come and can not be avoided or undone, and that the public at large can only protect itself from certain evil effects of this business centralization by providing better methods for the exercise of control through the authority already centralized in the National Government by the Constitution itself. . . .

. . . In my Message to the Congress a year ago, in speaking of the antitrust laws, I said:

"The actual working of our laws has shown that the effort to prohibit all combination, good or bad, is noxious where it is not ineffective. Combination of capital, like combination of labor, is a necessary element in our present industrial system. It is not possible completely to prevent it; and if it were possible, such complete prevention would do damage to the body politic. What we need is not vainly to try to prevent all combination, but to secure such rigorous and adequate control and supervision of the combinations as to prevent their injuring the public, or existing in such forms as inevitably to threaten injury. . . . It is unfortunate that our present laws should forbid all combinations instead of sharply discriminating between those combinations which do evil.

Woodrow Wilson, Sept. 17, 1912 —

Are you satisfied that the gates of opportunity are just as wide open to the youngsters, to your sons, as they used to be? Do you think that the channels for independent action in this country are as wide open as they used to be? Do you feel easy about the way in which your governments are controlled? I will tell you one proof that you don't feel easy. There is one thing that political parties dare not do now. They do not dare to put corporation lawyers up for office, particularly lawyers who have been the advisers of railway corporations. Now I used to be a lawyer myself before I repented, and I don't see anything dishonest in giving legal advice to a railway company. I do not see anything dishonorable in being the adviser of any great corporation. They have a right to know what the law is. They have a right, if they pay for it, to get the best legal advice obtainable. Then why is it you don't want to elect corporation lawyers to office? . . . You must be under the impression . . . that

the corporations are having a bigger voice in the government of this country than you are, and that you don't want to put their particular advisers in control of the government. Just another way of saying that you don't like the way in which your governments are controlled by special interests. Don't you feel that somebody is holding you off at arm's length and saying: "Yes, at election time we have to come around and consult you. We have got to let you vote. But after you have voted, we have arranged it. We will see to it that the things are done which the big interests bring about, but you are not classified as one of the big interests."

The government of this country, therefore, is not as accessible to the people of this country as it ought to be, and what I want to ask you men, particularly who are going to vote on the fifth of November, is this: How are you going to get next to your own government, and who is going to deliver you from these situations? Now there are two programs: The Democratic program is this, to see to it that competition is so regulated that the big fellow cannot put the little fellow out of business, for he has been putting the little fellow out of business for the last half generation. Whereas the program of the third party is to take these big fellows that have been putting the little fellow out of business and regulate them, saying, "That is all right, you have put the other fellows out of business, but we are not going to put the little fellows back where you destroyed them, but we are going to adopt you and say, you run the business of the country, but run it the way we tell you to run it."

Now you may like that program, and that is the choice you have got to make between a program which will prevent the little fellow from being crushed, and a program which will take the big fellow and have the business of the country run through him, under government regulations; notwithstanding the fact that he has built up his business by watered stock, on which you have got to pay interest, just as long as he does business and is permitted to do business. . . .

If the government is to tell big businessmen how to run their business, then don't you see the big businessmen have to get closer to the government than they are now? Don't you see they have to capture the government in order not to be restrained too much by it? Got to capture the government—they have already captured it. Are you going to invite the fellows inside to stay inside? They don't have to get there. They are there. Are you going to own your own premises, or are you not? That is your choice. . . .

Woodrow Wilson, Sept. 25, 1912 —

The Government of the United States at present is a mere foster child of the special interests. . . .

Now, I, for my part, don't want to belong to a nation, and take leave prettily to believe that I do not belong to a nation, that needs to be taken care of by guardians. I want to belong to a nation, and I am proud that I do belong to a nation, that knows how to take care of itself. If I thought that the American people were reckless, were ignorant, were vindictive, do you suppose I would want to put the government in their hands? But the beauty of democracy is that when you are reckless you destroy your own established conditions of life. When you are vindictive, you wreak your vengeance upon yourself, and that the whole stability of democratic policy rests upon the fact that every interest is every

man's interest. If it were not so, there could be no community; if it were not so, there could be no cooperation; if it were not so, there could be no renewal. And that to my mind is the most important part of the whole matter. For what I am anxious about, ladies and gentlemen, is the conditions which the next generation will find, for the present generation finds this—that if, for example, you add to the reputation of America for ingenuity by originating a great invention, a great industrial invention, a singular thing happens to you. If you want, let us say, a million dollars to build your plant and advertise your product and employ your agents and make a market for it, where are you going to get the million dollars? Because the minute you apply for the million dollars, this proposition is put to you: "This invention will interfere with the established processes and market control of certain great industries. We are already financing those industries. Their securities are in our hands. We will lend you the money if you will make an arrangement with those industries and go in with them. If you will not, then you can't have the money." I am generalizing the statement, but I could particularize it. I could tell you instances where exactly that thing happened. And by the combinations of great industries, processes are not only being standardized, but they are being kept at a single point of development and efficiency of operation. The increase of the power to produce in proportion to the cost of production is not studied in America as it used to be studied, because if you don't have to improve your processes in order to excel a competitor (if you are human, you aren't going to improve your processes) and if you can prevent the competitor from coming into the field, then you can sit at your leisure and behind this wall of protection which prevents the brains of any foreigner competing with you, you can rest at your ease for a whole generation.

And so I say that I want to see those conditions created which will permit this: Let a man begin his business on never so small a scale and let him be safe in beginning it on a small scale. He is not safe now, because if he enters a field where a great combination has established a market, that great combination will undersell him in his local market, which is his only market, making its necessary profits in other parts of the country until he is killed off. And

enterprise after enterprise is nipped in its infancy by the monopolistic control of our industrial markets. So that America is about to see another generation which must be a generation of employees unless it makes up its mind to be a generation of masters. The great militant, fighting, triumphant America is a nation of officers, a nation of men who are their own masters, a nation of men who will originate their own processes of industry and of life. And we shall never see the day, I confidently predict, when America will allow itself to be employed and patronized and taken care of.

2.6 Socialism and Individualism

Today, the United States is the only industrial nation lacking a viable socialist movement. But such a movement existed early in the century, and it appealed to people from many walks of life—workers, farmers, professionals and intellectuals—who hoped to erase the ills of urban and industrial life under capitalism.

The most famous American literary figure drawn to socialism was Jack London (1876–1916), the author of The Call of the Wild *(1903), a classic animal adventure story, and* The Iron Heel *(1908), a novel describing life under a fascist dictatorship. Sailor, ranch-hand and bohemian, London was a restless, romantic and contradictory figure. He had difficulty reconciling his socialist principle with his love of material comfort, and his interest in organized politics with his wild personal adventurism. (He also had recurrent bouts of alcoholism.)*

In 1905, London wrote the essay, "How I Became a Socialist," reprinted below. It first appeared in a book entitled The War of the Classes.

As a rule, American socialists favored peaceful and democratic means of achieving their goals. The 1912 platform of the Socialist Party of America, the major socialist political organization, is also reprinted. It is important to realize that this document belongs to an era before the Bolshevik Revolution in Russia in 1917. The Socialist standard-bearer in the 1912 presidential election was labor leader Eugene V. Debs. Debs, who once declared, "I am for socialism because I am for humanity," ran against Democrat Woodrow Wilson, Republican William H. Taft, and Progressive Theodore Roosevelt. He polled six percent of the total vote.

The Socialist platform is founded on class consciousness but also on a belief that the transition to "the cooperative commonwealth" would be peaceful. Although much of it resembles that of the Progressive party, the very last paragraph puts the Socialists in a camp by themselves.

Questions

What is a workable definition of socialism?

What experiences brought London along the path from individualism to socialism? Is his explanation plausible?

Which segments of society would have favored the 1912 Socialist platform? Are you surprised at anything you read? How much of this platform would appeal to a Jack London, and why? Why didn't socialism of this type become more popular in this country?

How does the Socialist platform compare with the Populist platform in 1892 and the Progressive position in 1912? Consider especially the "industrial demands" and "political demands" stated in the document.

What has been the fate of American socialism in more recent years?

Jack London —

It is quite fair to say that I became a Socialist in a fashion somewhat similar to the way in which the Teutonic pagans became Christians—it was hammered into me. Not only was I not looking for Socialism at the time of my conversion, but I was fighting it. I was very young and callow, did not know much of anything, and though I had never even heard of a school called "Individualism," I sang the paean of the strong with all my heart.

This was because I was strong myself. By strong I mean that I had good health and hard muscles, both of which possessions are easily accounted for. I had lived my childhood on California ranches, my boyhood hustling newspapers on the streets of a healthy Western city, and my youth on the ozone-laden waters of San Francisco Bay and the Pacific Ocean. I loved life in

SOURCES: Jack London, "How I Became a Socialist," *War of the Classes* (1905); Socialist Party, *Proceedings of the National Convention of the Socialist Party, 1912* (Chicago, 1912), pp. 196–98.

the open, and I toiled in the open at the hardest kinds of work. Learning no trade, but drifting along from job to job, I looked on the world and called it good, every bit of it. Let me repeat, this optimism was because I was healthy and strong, bothered with neither aches nor weaknesses, never turned down by the boss because I did not look fit, able always to get a job at shovelling coal, sailorizing, or manual labor of some sort.

And because of all this, exulting in my young life, able to hold my own at work or fight, I was a rampant individualist. It was very natural. I was a winner. Wherefore I called the game, as I saw it played, or thought I saw it played, a very proper game for MEN. To be a MAN was to write man in large capitals on my heart. To adventure like a man, and fight like a man, and do a man's work (even for a boy's pay)—these were things that reached right in and gripped hold of me as no other thing could. And I looked ahead into long vistas of a hazy and interminable future, into which, playing what I conceived to be MAN'S game, I should continue to travel with un-failing health, without accidents, and with muscles ever vigorous. As I say, this future was interminable. I could see myself only raging through life without end like one of Nietzsche's *blond beasts,* lustfully roving and conquering by sheer superiority and strength.

As for the unfortunates, the sick, and ailing, and old, and maimed, I must con-fess I hardly thought of them at all, save that I vaguely felt that they, barring acci-dents, could be as good as I if they wanted to real hard, and could work just as well. Accidents? Well, they represented FATE, also spelled out in capitals, and there was no getting around FATE. Napoleon had had an accident at Waterloo, but that did not dampen my desire to be another and later Napoleon. Further, the optimism bred of a stomach which could digest scrap iron and a body which flourished on hardships did not permit me to consider accidents as even remotely related to my glorious per-sonality.

I hope I have made it clear that I was proud to be one of Nature's strong-armed noblemen. The dignity of labor was to me the most impressive thing in the world. Without having read Carlyle, or Kipling, I formulated a gospel of work which put theirs in the shade. Work was everything. It was sanctification and salvation. The pride I took in a hard day's work well done would be inconceivable to you. It is almost inconceivable to me as I look back upon it. I was as faithful a wage slave as ever cap-italist exploited. To shirk or malinger on the man who paid me my wages was a sin, first, against myself, and second, against him. I considered it a crime second only to treason and just about as bad.

In short, my joyous individualism was dominated by the orthodox bourgeois ethics. I read the bourgeois papers, lis-tened to the bourgeois preachers, and shouted at the sonorous platitudes of the bourgeois politicians. And I doubt not, if other events had not changed my career, that I should have evolved into a profes-sonal strike-breaker, (one of President Eliot's American heroes), and had my head and my earning power irrevocably smashed by a club in the hands of some militant trades-unionist.

Just about this time, returning from a seven months' voyage before the mast, and just turned eighteen, I took it into my head to go tramping. On rods and blind bag-gages I fought my way from the open West, where men bulked big and the job hunted the man, to the congested labor centres of the East, where men were small potatoes and hunted the job for all they were worth. And on this new *blond-beast* adventure I found myself looking upon life from a new and totally different angle. I had dropped down from the proletariat into what soci-ologists love to call the "submerged tenth," and I was startled to discover the way in which that submerged tenth was re-cruited.

I found there all sorts of men, many of whom had once been as good as myself and just as *blond-beastly;* sailor-men, soldier-men, labor-men, all wrenched and dis-torted and twisted out of shape by toil and hardship and accident, and cast adrift by their masters like so many old horses. I battered on the drag [panhandled] and slammed back gates [begged at backdoors] with them, or shivered with them in box cars and city parks, listening the while to life-histories which began under auspices as fair as mine, with digestions and bodies equal to and better than mine, and which ended there before my eyes in the sham-bles at the bottom of the Social Pit.

And as I listened my brain began to work. The woman of the streets and the man of the gutter drew very close to me. I saw the picture of the Social Pit as vividly as though it were a concrete thing, and at the bottom of the Pit I saw them, myself above them, not far, and hanging on to the slippery wall by main strength and sweat. And I confess a terror seized me. What when my strength failed? when I should be unable to work shoulder to shoulder with the strong men who were as yet babes unborn? And there and then I swore a great oath. It ran something like this: *All my days I have worked hard with my body, and according to the number of days I have worked, by just that much am I nearer the bottom of the Pit. I shall climb out of the Pit, but not by the muscles of my body shall I climb out. I shall do no more hard work, and may God strike me dead if I do another day's hard work with my body more than I absolutely have to do.* And I have been busy ever since running away from hard work.

Incidentally, while tramping some ten thousand miles through the United States and Canada, I strayed into Niagara Falls, was nabbed by a fee-hunting constable, denied the right to plead guilty or not guilty, sentenced out of hand to thirty days' imprisonment for having no fixed abode and no visible means of support, handcuffed and chained to a bunch of men similarly circumstanced, carted down country to Buffalo, registered at the Erie County Penitentiary, had my head clipped and my budding mustache shaved, was dressed in convict stripes, compulsorily vaccinated by a medical student who practised on such as we, made to march the lock-step, and put to work under the eyes of guards armed with Winchester rifles—all for adventuring in *blond-beastly* fashion. Concerning

further details deponent sayeth not, though he may hint that some of his plethoric national patriotism simmered down and leaked out of the bottom of his soul somewhere—at least, since that experience he finds that he cares more for men and women and little children than for imaginary geographical lines.

To return to my conversion. I think it is apparent that my rampant individualism was pretty effectively hammered out of me, and something else as effectively hammered in. But, just as I had been an individualist without knowing it, I was not a Socialist without knowing it, withal, an unscientific one. I had been reborn, but not renamed, and I was running around to find out what manner of thing I was. I ran back to California and opened the books. I do not remember which ones I opened first. It is an important detail anyway. I was already It, whatever It was, and by aid of the books I discovered that It was a Socialist. Since that day I have opened many books, but no economic argument, no lucid demonstration of the logic and inevitableness of Socialism affects me as profoundly and convincingly as I was affected on the day when I first saw the walls of the Social Pit rise around me and felt myself slipping down, down, into the shambles at the bottom.

The Socialist Platform —
Working Program

As measures calculated to strengthen the working class in its fight for the realization of its ultimate aim, the cooperative commonwealth, and to increase its power of resistance to capitalist oppression, we advance and pledge ourselves and our elected officers to the following program:

Collective Ownership

a. The collective ownership and democratic management of railroads, wire and wireless telegraphs and telephones, express services, steamboat lines and all other social means of transportation and communication and of all large-scale industries.

b. The immediate acquirement by the municipalities, the states or the federal government, of all grain elevators, stockyards, storage warehouses, and other distributing agencies, in order to reduce the present extortionate cost of living.

c. The extension of the public domain to include mines, quarries, oil wells, forests, and water power.

d. The further conservation and development of natural resources for the use and benefit of all the people:

1. By scientific forestation and timber protection.
2. By the reclamation of arid and swamp tracts.
3. By the storage of flood waters and the utilization of water power.
4. By the stoppage of the present extravagant waste of the soil and of the products of mines and oil wells.
5. By the development of highway and waterway systems.

e. The collective ownership of land wherever practicable, and in cases where such ownership is impracticable, the appropriation by taxation of the annual rental value of all land held for speculation or exploitation.

f. The collective ownership and democratic management of the banking and currency system.

Unemployment

a. The immediate government relief of the unemployed by the extension of all useful public works. All persons employed on such works to be engaged directly by the government under a workday of not more than eight hours and at not less than the prevailing union wages. The government also to establish employment bureaus; to lend money to states and municipalities without interest for the purpose of carrying on public works, and to take such other measures within its power as will lessen the widespread misery of the workers caused by the misrule of the capitalist class.

Industrial Demands

The conservation of human resources, particularly of the lives and well being of the workers and their families:

a. By shortening of the workday in keeping with the increased productiveness of machinery.

b. By securing to every worker a rest period of not less than a day and a half in each week.

c. By securing a more effective inspection of workshops, factories and mines.

d. By forbidding the employment of children under sixteen years of age.

e. By the co-operative organization of the industries in the federal penitentiaries for the benefit of the convicts and their dependents.

f. By forbidding the interstate transportation of the products of child labor, of convict labor and of all uninspected factories and mines.

g. By abolishing the profit system in government work and substituting either the direct hire of labor or the awarding of contracts to co-operative groups of workers.

h. By establishing minimum wage scales.

i. By abolishing official charity and substituting a non-contributory system of old-age pensions, a general system of insurance by the State of all its members against unemployment and invalidism and a system of compulsory insurance by employers of their workers, without cost to the latter, against industrial diseases accidents and death.

Political Demands

a. The absolute freedom of press, speech and assembly.

b. The adoption of a graduated income tax, the increase of the rates of the present corporation tax and the extension of inheritance taxes graduated in proportion to the value of the estate and to nearness of kin—the proceeds of these taxes to be employed in the socialization of industry.

c. The abolition of the monopoly ownership of patents and the substitution of collective ownership, with direct awards to inventors by premiums or royalties.

d. Unrestricted and equal suffrage for men and women.

e. The adoption of the initiative, referendum and recall and of proportional representation, nationally as well as locally.

f. The abolition of the Senate and of the veto power of the President.

g. The election of the President and of the Vice-President by the direct vote of the people.

h. The abolition of the power usurped by the Supreme Court of the United States to pass upon the constitutionality of the legislation enacted by Congress. National laws to be repealed only by act of Congress or by a referendum vote of the whole people.

i. The abolition of the present restrictions upon the amendment of the constitution so that instrument may be made amendable by a majority of the voters in a majority of the States.

j. The granting of the right of suffrage in the District of Columbia with representation in Congress and a democratic form of municipal government for purely local affairs.

k. The extension of democratic government to all United States territories.

l. The enactment of further measures for general education and particularly for vocational education in useful pursuits. The Bureau of Education to be made a Department.

m. The enactment of further measures for the conservation of health. The creation of an independent bureau of health, with such restrictions as will secure full liberty to all schools of practice.

n. The separation of the present Bureau of Labor from the Department of Commerce and its elevation to the rank of a department.

o. Abolition of all federal district courts and the United States circuit courts of appeals. State courts to have jurisdiction in all cases arising between citizens of the several states and foreign corporations. The election of all judges for short terms.

p. The immediate curbing of the power of the courts to issue injunctions.

q. The free administration of the law.

r. The calling of a convention for the revision of the constitution of the United States.

Such measures of relief as we may be able to force from capitalism are but a preparation of the workers to seize the whole powers of government, in order that they may thereby lay hold of the whole system of socialized industry and thus come to their rightful inheritance.

2.7   Court Reform or Presidential Dictatorship

The power struggle between the President and the Supreme Court is an old one. Whenever the high court has resisted their policies, strong presidents have gone on the offensive. Jefferson, Jackson, Lincoln, Theodore Roosevelt and Franklin D. Roosevelt each had their confrontations.

The most blatant contest in modern times involved FDR in the 1930s. The President felt greatly frustrated when the Supreme Court struck down parts of the National Industrial Recovery Act of 1933. FDR considered that law to be the keystone of the New Deal. He began to fear that the justices would also cripple the Social Security Act and the Wagner Act, an important labor law, thus laying waste his efforts to cope with the Great Depression.

In 1936, while basking in the afterglow of a solid election victory, FDR undertook a vigorous campaign to bring new blood into the federal judiciary. He sent a bill to Congress proposing that, for every federal judge who refused to retire after age 70, he could appoint another, up to a maximum of six new Supreme Court judges and forty-four new judges in lower courts. The old conservatives would either back the liberal minority or be outvoted by them.

But FDR's frontal attack on the courts in 1937 outraged many people. He was accused of seeking a presidential dictatorship. Although a masterful politician, in this instance he badly misread the political signs. To make matters worse he refused to take good advice. In Congress, the bloom was already off the New Deal. For 168 days Congress did little else but debate this matter, further draining the President's political capital. The press was almost uniformly against him. The public would not buy his "court-packing" plan. FDR finally threw in the towel and withdrew his proposal.

And yet, the older justices soon began changing their minds. The Court started supporting New Deal legislation by votes of 5 to 4. And several justices retired, allowing FDR to make new appointments. Thus he was able, in a more acceptable way, to protect his reforms.

The documents presented below illustrate the court-packing controversy. In the first, FDR presents his plan to the public in a radio address of March 9, 1937. The second is a negative recommendation from the Senate Judiciary Committee in 1937, after FDR sent his measure to Congress.

Questions

What arguments did Roosevelt use to support his plan? What are the Senate's counter-arguments?

What is the proper course for a President whose entire program is opposed by the courts? Should the Supreme Court be influenced by public opinion?

What other major controversies have occurred since the 1930s that have involved strife between the Court and a President?

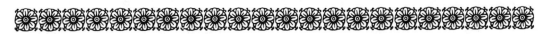

Franklin Delano Roosevelt —

Tonight, sitting at my desk in the White House, I make my first radio report to the people in my second term of office.

I am reminded of that evening in March four years ago, when I made my first radio report to you. We were then in the midst of the great banking crisis. . . .

In 1933 you and I knew that we must never let our economic system get completely out of joint again—that we could not afford to take the risk of another great depression.

We also became convinced that the only way to avoid a repetition of those dark days was to have a government with power to prevent and to cure the abuses and the inequalities which had thrown that system out of joint.

We then began a program of remedying those abuses and inequalities—to give balance and stability to our economic system— to make it bombproof against the causes of 1929.

Today we are only part way through that program—and recovery is speeding up to a point where the dangers of 1929 are again becoming possible, not this week or month perhaps, but within a year or two.

National laws are needed to complete that program. Individual or local or State effort alone cannot protect us in 1937 any better than 10 years ago. . . .

The American people have learned from the depressions. For in the last three national elections an overwhelming majority of them voted a mandate that the Congress and the President begin the task of providing that protection—not after long years of debate, but now.

The courts, however, have cast doubts on the ability of the elected Congress to protect us against catastrophe by meeting squarely our modern social and economic conditions.

We are at a crisis in our ability to proceed with that protection. It is a quiet crisis. There are no lines of depositors outside closed banks. But to the farsighted it is far-reaching in its possibilities of injury to America.

I want to talk with you very simply about the need for present action in this crisis—the need to meet the unanswered challenge of one-third of a nation ill-nourished, ill-clad, ill-housed. . . .

. . . The Court has more and more often and more and more boldly asserted a power

SOURCE: Franklin D. Roosevelt, *Reorganizing the Federal Judiciary,* 9 March 1937, in *Senate Reports,* 75th Congress, 1st sess., 5 Jan.–21 Aug. 1937, vol. I, pp. 41–44; Report no. 711, "Reorganization of the Federal Judiciary," pp. 1, 9–23. NO PERMISSION REQUIRED.

to veto laws passed by the Congress and State legislatures in complete disregard of this original limitation.

In the last four years the sound rule of giving statutes the benefit of all reasonable doubt has been cast aside. The Court has been acting not as a judicial body, but as a policy-making body.

When the Congress has sought to stabilize national agriculture, to improve the conditions of labor, to safeguard business against unfair competition, to protect our national resources, and in many other ways to serve our clearly national needs, the majority of the Court has been assuming the power to pass on the wisdom of these acts of the Congress—and to approve or disapprove the public policy written into these laws. . . .

The Court in addition to the proper use of its judicial functions has improperly set itself up as a third House of the Congress—a superlegislature, as one of the Justices has called it—reading into the Constitution words and implications which are not there, and which were never intended to be there.

We have, therefore, reached the point as a Nation where we must take action to save the Constitution from the Court and the Court from itself. We must find a way to take an appeal from the Supreme Court to the Constitution itself. We want a Supreme Court which will do justice under the Constitution—not over it. In our courts we want a government of laws and not of men.

I want—as all Americans want—an independent judiciary as proposed by the framers of the Constitution. That means a Supreme Court that will enforce the Constitution as written—that will refuse to amend the Constitution by the arbitrary

exercise of judicial power—amendment by judicial say-so. It does not mean a judiciary so independent that it can deny the existence of facts universally recognized. . . .

What is my proposal? It is simply this: Whenever a judge or justice of any Federal Court has reached the age of seventy and does not avail himself of the opportunity to retire on a pension, a new member shall be appointed by the President then in office, with the approval, as required by the Constitution, of the Senate of the United States.

That plan has two chief purposes. By bringing into the judicial system a steady and continuing stream of new and younger blood, I hope, first, to make the administration of all Federal justice speedier and therefore less costly; secondly, to bring to the decision of social and economic problems younger men who have had personal experience and contact with modern facts and circumstances under which average men have to live and work. This plan will save our National Constitution from hardening of the judicial arteries. . . .

Those opposing this plan have sought to arouse prejudice and fear by crying that I am seeking to 'pack' the Supreme Court and that a baneful precedent will be established.

What do they mean by the words 'packing the Court'?

Let me answer this question with a bluntness that will end all honest misunderstanding of my purposes.

If by that phrase 'packing the Court' it is charged that I wish to place on the bench spineless puppets who would disregard the law and would decide specific cases as I wished them to be decided. I make this answer: That no President fit for his office would appoint, and no Senate of honorable men fit for their office would confirm, that kind of appointees to the Supreme Court.

But if by that phrase the charge is made that I would appoint and the Senate would confirm Justices worthy to sit beside present members of the Court who understand those modern conditions; that I will appoint Justices who will not undertake to override the judgment of the Congress on legislative policy: that I will appoint Justices who will act as Justices and not as legislators—if the appointment of such Justices can be called 'packing the Courts'—then I say that I, and with me the vast majority of the American people, favor doing just that thing—now. . . .

Like all lawyers, like all Americans, I regret the necessity of this controversy. But the welfare of the United States, and indeed of the Constitution itself, is what we all must think about first. Our difficulty with the Court today rises not from the Court as an institution but from human beings within it. But we cannot yield our constitutional destiny to the personal judgment of a few men who, being fearful of the future, would deny us the necessary means of dealing with the present.

This plan of mine is no attack on the Court; it seeks to restore the Court to its rightful and historic place in our system of constitutional government and to have it resume its high task of building anew on the Constitution 'a system of living law.' . . .

Committee on the Judiciary—

The Committee on the Judiciary, to whom was referred the bill (S. 1392) to reorganize the judicial branch of the Government after full consideration, having unanimously amended the measure, hereby report the bill adversely with the recommendation that it do not pass. . . .

The committee recommends that the measure be rejected for the following primary reasons:

I. The bill does not accomplish any one of the objectives for which it was originally offered.

II. It applies force to the judiciary and in its initial and ultimate effect would undermine the independence of the courts.

III. It violates all precedents in the history of our Government and would in itself be a dangerous precedent for the future.

IV. The theory of the bill is in direct violation of the spirit of the American Constitution and its employment would permit alteration of the Constitution without the people's consent or approval; it undermines the protection our constitutional system gives to minorities and is subversive of the rights of individuals.

V. It tends to centralize the Federal district judiciary by the power of assigning judges from one district to another at will.

VI. It tends to expand political control over the judicial department by adding to the powers of the legislative and executive departments respecting the judiciary.

This measure was sent to the Congress by the President on Feb. 5, 1937, with a message (appendix A) setting forth the objectives sought to be attained.

It should be pointed out here that a substantial portion of the message was devoted to a discussion of the evils of conflicting decisions by inferior courts on constitutional questions and to the alleged abuse of the power of injunction by some of the Federal courts. These matters, however, have no bearing on the bill before us, for it contains neither a line nor a sentence dealing with either of those problems.

Nothing in this measure attempts to control, regulate, or prohibit the power of any Federal court to pass upon the constitutionality of any law—State or National.

Nothing in this measure attempts to control, regulate, or prohibit the issuance of injunctions by any court, in any case, whether or not the Government is a party to it.

If it were to be conceded that there is need of reform in these respects, it must be understood that this bill does not deal with these problems. . . .

2.8   The Military-Industrial Complex

In his Farewell Address on January 17, 1961, President Dwight Eisenhower warned the nation of the dangers of the "military-industrial complex." It is ironic that a former five-star general, an advocate of strong military defense, and a public figure best known for his bland style would leave with such a dramatic and unexpected parting shot.

Since then the military-industrial complex has been under close public scrutiny. Critics of the complex have pointed out that general and defense contractors have forged an unholy alliance, that the production of war goods has led to bloated profits, and that worthy peacetime objectives have been starved to feed military budgets.

While many people disagreed with the beloved "Ike," they were reluctant to say so publicly. Not so Senator Barry Goldwater, the conservative Arizona Republican, who looked approvingly on the benefits of the military-industrial complex. Below is a portion of Eisenhower's Farewell Address and an opposing piece by Goldwater in 1969, from the Congressional Record.

Questions

What exactly is the "military-industrial complex" and does it include elements other than the military and corporate establishments? What evidence is there that the nation has not heeded Eisenhower's advice? Have his predictions about a loss of liberty proven true? If General Eisenhower was right, what can stop or reverse the trend?

According to Goldwater what benefits and disadvantages result from the complex? Which man is closer to the truth, in your opinion?

Dwight D. Eisenhower —

My fellow Americans:

Three days from now, after half a century, in the service of our country, I shall lay down the responsibilities of office as, in traditional and solemn ceremony, the authority of the Presidency is vested in my successor. . . .

We now stand ten years past the midpoint of a century that has witnessed four major wars among great nations. Three of them involved our own country. Despite these holocausts, America is today the strongest, the most influential and most productive nation in the world. Understandably proud of this pre-eminence we yet realize that America's leadership and prestige depend, not merely upon our unmatched material progress, riches and military strength, but on how we use our power in the interests of world peace and human betterment.

Throughout America's adventure in free government, our basic purposes have been to keep the peace; to foster progress in human achievement, and to enhance liberty, dignity and integrity among people and among nations. To strive for less would be unworthy of a free and religious people. Any failure traceable to arrogance, or our lack of comprehension or readiness to sacrifice would inflict upon us grievous hurt both at home and abroad.

Progress toward these noble goals is persistently threatened by the conflict now engulfing the world. It commands our whole attention, absorbs our very beings.

SOURCES: Dwight D. Eisenhower, "Farewell Radio and Television Address to the American People, January 17, 1961," in Eisenhower, *Public Papers of the Presidents of the United States, 1960–61* Washington, D.C.: Government Printing Office, 1961), 1037–39; Barry Goldwater in *Congressional Record*, Ninety-first Congress, 1st sess., pp. 3719–21.

We face a hostile ideology—global in scope, atheistic in character, ruthless in purpose, and insidious in method. Unhappily the danger it poses promises to be of indefinite duration. To meet it successfully, there is called for, not so much the emotional and transitory sacrifices of crisis, but rather those which enable us to carry forward steadily, surely, and without complaint the burdens of a prolonged and complex struggle—with liberty the stake. Only thus shall we remain, despite every provocation, on our charted course toward permanent peace and human betterment. . . .

A vital element in keeping the peace is our military establishment. Our arms must be mighty, ready for instant action, so that no potential aggressor may be tempted to risk his own destruction.

Our military organization today bears little relation to that known by any of my predecessors in peacetime, or indeed by the fighting men of World War II or Korea.

Until the latest of our world conflicts, the United States had no armaments industry. American makers of plowshares could, with time and as required, make swords as well. But now we can no longer risk emergency improvisation of national defense; we have been compelled to create a permanent armaments industry of vast proportions. Added to this, three and a half million men and women are directly engaged in the defense establishment. We annually spend on military security more than the net income of all United States corporations.

This conjunction of an immense military establishment and a large arms industry is new in the American experience. The total influence—economic, political, even spiritual—is felt in every city, every statehouse, every office of the federal government. We recognize the imperative need for this development. Yet we must not fail to comprehend its grave implications. Our toil, resources, and livelihood are all involved; so is the very structure of our society.

In the councils of government, we must guard against the acquisition of unwarranted influence, whether sought or unsought, by the military-industrial complex. The potential for the disastrous rise of misplaced power exists and will persist.

We must never let the weight of this combination endanger our liberties or democratic processes. We should take nothing for granted. Only an alert and knowledgeable citizenry can compel the proper meshing of the huge industrial and military machinery of defense with our peaceful methods and goals, so that security and liberty may prosper together.

Akin to, and largely responsible for the sweeping changes in our industrial-military posture, has been the technological revolution during recent decades.

In this revolution, research has become central; it also becomes more formalized, complex, and costly. A steadily increasing share is conducted for, by, or at the direction of, the federal government. . . .

The prospect of domination of the nation's scholars by federal employment, project allocations, and the power of money is ever present—and is gravely to be regarded.

Yet, in holding scientific research and discovery in respect, as we should, we must also be alert to the equal and opposite danger that public policy could itself become the captive of a scientific-technological elite.

It is the task of statesmanship to mold, to balance, and to integrate these and other forces, new and old, within the principles of our democratic system—ever aiming toward the supreme goals of our free society.

Another factor in maintaining balance involves the element of time. As we peer into society's future, we—you and I, and our government—must avoid the impulse to live only for today, plundering, for our own ease and convenience, the precious resources of tomorrow. We cannot mortgage the material assets of our grandchildren without risking the loss also of their political and spiritual heritage. We want democracy to survive for all generations to come, not to become the insolvent phantom of tomorrow.

Down the long lane of the history yet to be written America knows that this world of ours, ever growing smaller, must avoid becoming a community of dreadful fear and hate, and be, instead, a proud confederation of mutual trust and respect.

Such a confederation must be one of equals. The weakest must come to the conference table with the same confidence as do we, protected as we are by our moral, economic, and military strength. That table, though scarred by many past frustrations, cannot be abandoned for the certain agony of the battlefield.

Disarmament, with mutual honor and confidence, is a continuing imperative. Together we must learn how to compose differences, not with arms, but with intellect and decent purpose. Because this need is so sharp and apparent I confess that I lay down my official responsibilities in this field with a definite sense of disappointment. As one who has witnessed the horror and the lingering sadness of war—as one who knows that another war could utterly destroy this civilization which has been so slowly and painfully built over thousands of years—I wish I could say tonight that a lasting peace is in sight.

Happily, I can say that war has been avoided. Steady progress toward our ultimate goal has been made. But, so much remains to be done. As a private citizen, I shall never cease to do what little I can to help the world advance along that road. . . .

Barry Goldwater—

I believe it is long past the time when questions relating fundamentally to the defense of this nation should be placed in their proper perspective. Let us take the military-industrial complex and examine it closely. What it amounts to is that we have a big Military Establishment, and we have a big industrial plant which helps to supply that establishment. This apparently constitutes a complex. If so, I certainly can find nothing to criticize but much to be thankful for in its existence.

Ask yourselves, for example, why we have a large, expensive Military Establishment and why we have a large and capable defense industry. The answer is simply this: We have huge worldwide responsibilities. We face tremendous challenges. In short, we urgently require both a big defense establishment and a big industrial capacity. Both are essential to our safety and to the preservation of freedom in a world fraught with totalitarian aggression. Merely because our huge responsibilities necessitate the existence of a military-industrial complex does not automatically make that complex something we must fear or feel ashamed of. You might consider where we would be in any negotiations which might be entered into with the Soviet Union if we did not have a big mil-

itary backed by a big industrial complex to support our arguments. . . .

What would the critics of the military-industrial complex have us do? Would they have us ignore the fact that progress occurs in the field of national defense as well as in the field of social sciences? Do they want us to turn back the clock, disband our Military Establishment, and do away with our defense-related industrial capacity? Mr. President, do these critics of what they term a military-industrial complex really want to default on our worldwide responsibilities, turn our back on aggression and slavery, and develop a national policy of selfish isolation?

Rather than deploring the existence of a military-industrial complex, I say we should thank heaven for it. That complex gives us our protective shield. It is the bubble under which our nation thrives and prospers. It is the armor which is unfortunately required in a world divided. For all those who complain about the military-industrial complex, I ask this question: "What would you replace it with? Would you have the Government do it?" Well, our Government has tried it in the past, and failed—dismally so.

What is more, I believe it is fair to inquire whether the name presently applied is inclusive enough. Consider the large number of scientists who contributed all of the fundamental research necessary to develop and build nuclear weapons and other products of today's defense industries. Viewing this, should not we call it the "scientific-military-industrial complex?" By the same token, do not forget the amount of research that has gone on in our colleges and universities in support of our defense-related projects. Maybe we should call it an "educational-scientific-military-industrial complex." Then, of course, the vast financing that goes into this effort certainly makes the economic community an integral part of any such complex. Now we have a name that runs like this: "An economic-educational-scientific-military-industrial complex. . . ."

Many of the problems that are being encountered in the area of national defense today stem not so much from a military-industrial complex as they do from the mistakes and miscalculations of a "civilian complex" or perhaps I should say a "civilian-computer-complex." My reference here, of course, is to the Pentagon hierarchy of young civilians—often referred to as the "whiz kids"—which was erected during the McNamara era in the questionable name of "cost effectiveness." And this complex, Mr. President, was built in some measure to shut out the military voice in a large area of defense policy decision making.

I suggest that the military-industrial complex is not the all-powerful structure that our liberal friends would have us believe. Certainly nobody can deny that this combination took a drubbing at the hands of Mr. McNamara and his civilian cadres during the last 8 years. . . . If the military-industrial complex had been the irresistible giant its critics describe, we would certainly today be better equipped. We would undoubtedly have a nuclear-powered Navy adequate to the challenge presented by the Soviet naval might. We would certainly have in the air—and not just on a drawing board—a manned, carry-on bomber. We would never have encountered the kind of shortages which cropped up in every area of the military as a result of the demands from Vietnam. There would have been no shortage of military helicopters. There would have been no shortage of trained helicopter pilots. There would have been no need to use outdated and faulty equipment. No concern ever would have arisen over whether our supply of bombs was sufficient to the task in Southeast Asia.

In conclusion, Mr. President, I want to point out that a very strong case can be made for the need for a more powerful military-industrial complex than we have had during the past eight years. At the very least, I wish to say that the employment practices of industries doing business with the Pentagon—practices which lead them to hire the most knowledgeable men to do their work—are no cause for shock. Nor are these practices dangerous to the American people.

I have great faith in the civilian leaders of our Government and of our military services. I have no desire to see the voice of the military become all-powerful or even dominant in our national affairs. But I do believe that the military viewpoint must always be heard in the highest councils of our Government in all matters directly affecting the protection and security of our nation.

2.9 Student Radicalism in the 1960s

The emergence of student radicalism in the 1960s stunned the nation. Students in the 1950s, the era of McCarthyism and Eisenhower prosperity, were dubbed politically passive. The new mood of radicalism manifested itself in civil rights demonstrations, opposition to the

Vietnam War, demands for reform within universities, and environmental activism. Part of it resulted from the moral passion of young people struggling for racial and economic justice. Part of it was based on the romantic visions of people who professed a "counter-culture." Part of it grew from the belief that universities represent open enquiry. In any case, this wave of student radicalism lasted well into the 1970s.

A pivotal point in the emergence of the new student movement was a meeting of Students for a Democratic Society at Port Huron, Michigan in June 1962. The SDS considered itself the leading edge of a New Left, and was dedicated to a major reform of society. It soon figured strongly in many radical demonstrations around the century. The major author of the 58-page "Port Huron Statement" was a 21-year-old University of Michigan undergraduate, Tom Hayden. (He would remain in the public eye as a defendant in the trial of the so-called "Chicago Seven," a husband of film star Jane Fonda, and a mainstream member of the California legislature.)

In setting forth the concerns of radical students, the statement tried to move beyond the tired slogans and agendas of liberals, socialists and communists. It called for the formation of a New Left. It coined a phrase, "participatory democracy," and it looked to the university for leadership. The introduction, plus a few other excerpts from the Port Huron Statement, follow.

Questions

What do the authors of the statement mean by "participatory democracy?" What did they expect of the New Left? How, according to SDS, should the nation's economic system work? What changes did they hope to bring about in the university? Were any of these expectations realized?

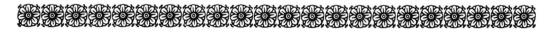

Introduction: Agenda for a Generation

We are people of this generation, bred in at least modest comfort, housed now in universities, looking uncomfortably to the world we inherit.

When we were kids the United States was the wealthiest and strongest country in the world; the only one with the atom bomb, the least scarred by modern war. . . . Many of us began maturing in complacency.

As we grew, however, our comfort was penetrated by events too troubling to dismiss. First, the permeating and victimizing fact of human degradation, symbolized by the Southern struggle against racial bigotry, compelled most of us from silence to activism. Second, the enclosing fact of the Cold War, symbolized by the presence of the Bomb, brought awareness

SOURCE: Tom Hayden et al., *Port Huron Statement*, mimeographed (n.p. Students for a Democratic Society, 1962).

that we ourselves, and our friends, and millions of abstract "others" we knew more directly because of our common peril, might die at any time. . . .

We witnessed, and continue to witness, other paradoxes. With nuclear energy whole cities can easily be powered, yet the dominant nation-states seem more likely to unleash destruction greater than that incurred in all wars of human history. Although our own technology is destoying old and creating new forms of social organization, men still tolerate meaningless work and idleness. While two-thirds of mankind suffers undernourishment, our own upper classes revel amidst superfluous abundance. Although world population is expected to double in forty years, the nations still tolerate anarchy as a major principle of international conduct and uncontrolled exploitation governs the sapping of the earth's physical resources. Although mankind desperately needs revolutionary leadership, America rests in national stalemate, its goals ambiguous and tradition-bound instead of informed and clear, its democratic system apathetic and manipulated rather than "of, by, and for the people." . . . The worldwide outbreak of revolution against colonialism and imperialism, the entrenchment of totalitarian states, the menace of war, overpopulation, international disorder, supertechnology— these trends were testing the tenacity of our own commitment to democracy and freedom and our abilities to visualize their application to a world in upheaval.

Our work is guided by the sense that we may be the last generation in the experiment with living. But we are a minority— the vast majority of our people regard the temporary equilibriums of our society and world as eternally-functional parts. In this is perhaps the outstanding paradox: we

ourselves are imbued with urgency, yet the message of our society is that there is no viable alternative to the present. . . .

Some would have us believe that Americans feel contentment amidst prosperity—but might it not better be called a glaze above deeply-felt anxieties about their role in the new world? And if these anxieties produce a developed influence to human affairs, do they not as well produce a yearning to believe there *is* an alternative to the present, that something *can* be done to change circumstances in the school, the workplaces, the bureaucracies, the government? It is to this latter yearning, at once the spark and engine of change, that we direct our present appeal. The search for truly democratic alternatives to the present, and a commitment to social experimentation with them, is a worthy and fulfilling human enterprise, one which moves us and, we hope, others today. . . .

Values

Unlike youth in other countries we are used to moral leadership being exercised and moral dimensions being clarified by our elders. But today, for us, not even the liberal and socialist preachments of the past seem adequate to the forms of the present. . . . It has been said that our liberal and socialist predecessors were plagued by vision without program, while our own generation is plagued by program without vision. . . .

Theoretic chaos has replaced the idealistic thinking of old—and, unable to reconstitute theoretic order, men have condemned idealism itself. Doubt has replaced hopefulness—and men act out a defeatism that is labelled realistic. The decline of utopia and hope is in fact one of the defining features of social life today. The reasons are various: the dreams of the older left were perverted by Stalinism and never recreated; the congressional stalemate makes men narrow their view of the possible; the specialization of human activity leaves little room for sweeping thought; the horrors of the twentieth century, symbolized in the gas-ovens and concentration camps and atom bombs, have blasted hopefulness. To be idealistic is to be considered apocalyptic, deluded. To have no serious aspirations, on the contrary, is to be "toughminded." . . . .

Men have unrealized potential for self-cultivation, self-direction, self-understanding, and creativity. It is this potential that we regard as crucial and to which we appeal, not to the human potentiality for violence, unreason, and submission to authority. The goal of man and society should be human independence. . . .

This kind of independence does not mean egotistic individualism—the object is not to have one's way so much as it is to have a way that is one's own. Nor do we deify man—we merely have faith in his potential.

Human relationships should involve fraternity and honesty. Human interdependence is contemporary fact. . . .

We would replace power rooted in possesion, privilege, or circumstance by power and uniqueness rooted in love, reflectiveness, reason, and creativity. As a *social system* we seek the establishment of a democracy of individual participation, governed by two central aims: that the individual share in those social decisions determining the quality and direction of his life; that society be organized to encourage independence in men and provide the media for their common participation.

In a participatory democracy, the political life would be based in several root principles:

that decision-making of basic social consequence be carried on by public groupings;

that politics be seen positively, as the art of collectively creating an acceptable pattern of social relations;

that politics has the function of bringing people out of isolation and into community, thus being a necessary, though not sufficient, means of finding meaning in personal life;

that the political order should serve to clarify problems in a way instrumental to their solution; it should provide outlets for the expression of personal grievance and aspiration; opposing views should be organized so as to illuminate choices and facilitate the attainment of goals; channels should be commonly available to relate men to knowledge and to power so that private problems—from bad recreation facilities to personal alienation—are formulated as general issues.

The economic sphere would have as its basis the principles:

that work should involve incentives worthier than money or survival. It should be educative, not stultifying; creative, not mechanical; self-directed, not manipulated, encouraging independence, a respect for others, a sense of dignity and a willingness to accept social responsibility, since it is this experience that has crucial influence on habits, perceptions and individual ethics;

that the economic experience is so personally decisive that the in-

dividual must share in its full determination;
    that the economy itself is of such
social importance that its major resources and means of production
should be open to democratic participation and subject to democratic
social regulation.

Like the politcal and economic ones,
major social institutions—cultural, educational, rehabilitative, and others—should
be generally organized with the well-being
and dignity of man as the essential measure of success. . . .

It is imperative that the means of violence be abolished and the institutions—
local, national, international—that encourage nonviolence as a condition of conflict be developed.

These are our central values, in skeletal
form. It remains vital to understand their
denial or attainment in the context of the
modern world.

The Students

In the last few years, thousands of
American students demonstrated that they
at least felt the urgency of the times. They
moved actively and directly against racial
injustices, the threat of war, violations of
individual rights of conscience and, less
frequently, against economic manipula-
tion. They succeeded in restoring a small
measure of controversy to the campuses
after the stillness of the McCarthy
period. . . .

If student movements for change are still
rarities on the campus scene, what is commonplace there? . . .

Almost no students value activity as citizens. Passive in public, they are hardly
more idealistic in arranging their private
lives: . . .

Apathy toward apathy begets a privately constructed universe, a place of sys-

tematic study schedules, two nights each
week for beer, a girl or two, and early marriage; a framework infused with personality, warmth, and under control, no matter
how unsatisfying otherwise. . . .

Politics Without Politics

The American political system is not the
democratic model of which its glorifiers
speak. In actuality it frustrates democracy
by confusing the individual citizen, para-
lyzing policy discussion, and consoli-
dating the irresponsible power of military
and business interests.

A crucial feature of the political apparatus in America is that greater differences
are harbored within each major party than
the differences existing between them. Instead of two parties presenting distinctive
and significant differences of approach,
what dominates the system is a natural in-
terlocking of Democrats from Southern
states with the more conservative elements of the Republican party. . . .

The party overlap, however, is not the
only structural antagonist of democracy in
politics. First, the localized nature of the
party system does not encourage discussion of national and international issues:
thus problems are not raised by and for
people, and political representatives usually are unfettered from any responsibilities to the general public except those
regarding parochial matters. Second, whole
constituencies are divested of the full political power they might have: many Negroes in the South are prevented from
voting, migrant workers are disenfran-
chised by various residence requirements,
some urban and suburban dwellers are vic-
timized by gerrymandering, and poor
people are too often without the power to
obtain political representation. Third, the
focus of political attention is significantly

distorted by the enormous lobby force, composed predominantly of business interests, spending hundreds of millions each year in an attempt to conform facts about productivity, agriculture, defense, and social services, to the wants of private economic groupings. . . .

A most alarming fact is that few, if any, politicians are calling for changes in these conditions. . . . Their speeches and campaign actions are banal, based on a degrading conception of what people want to hear. They respond not to dialogue, but to pressure: and knowing this, the ordinary citizen sees even greater inclination to shun the political sphere. The politician is usually a trumpeter to "citizenship" and "service to the nation," but since he is unwilling to seriously rearrange power relationships, his trumpeters only increase apathy by creating no outlets. Much of the time the call to "service" is justified not in idealistic terms, but in the crasser terms of "defending the free world from communism"—thus making future idealistic impulses harder to justify in anything but Cold War terms.

In such a setting of status quo politics, where most if not all government activity is rationalized in Cold War anti-communist terms, it is somewhat natural that discontented, super-patriotic groups would emerge through political channels and explain their ultra-conservatism as the best means of Victory over Communism. . . . But actually "anti-communism" becomes an umbrella by which to protest liberalism, internationalism, welfarism, the active civil rights and labor movements.

The University and Social Change

We believe that the universities are an overlooked seat of influence.

First, the university is located in a permanent position of social influence. Its educational function makes it indispensable and automatically makes it a crucial institution in the formation of social attitudes. Second, in an unbelievably complicated world, it is the central institution for organizing, evaluating, and transmitting knowledge. Third, the extent to which academic resources presently are used to buttress immoral social practice is revealed first, by the extent to which defense contracts make the universities engineers of the arms race. . . . But these social uses of the universities' resources also demonstrate the unchangeable reliance by men of power on the men and storehouses of knowledge: this makes the university functionally tied to society in new ways, revealing new potentials, new levers for change. Fourth, the university is the only mainstream institution that is open to participation by individuals of nearly any viewpoint. . . . Social relevance, the accessibility to knowledge, and internal openness—these together make the university a potential base and agency in a movement of social change.

1. Any new left in America must be, in large measure, a left with real intellectual skills, committed to deliberativeness, honesty, reflection as working tools. The university permits the political life to be an adjunct to the academic one, and action to be informed by reason.
2. A new left must be distributed in significant social roles throughout the country. The universities are distributed in such a manner.
3. A new left must consist of younger people who matured in the post-war world, and partially be directed to the recruitment of younger people. The

university is an obvious beginning point.

4. A new left must include liberals and socialists, the former for their relevance, the latter for their sense of thoroughgoing reforms in the system. The university is a more sensible place than a political party for these two traditions to begin to discuss their differences and look for political synthesis.

5. A new left must start controversy across the land, if national policies and national apathy are to be reversed. The ideal university is a community of controversy, within itself and in its effects on communities beyond.

6. A new left must transform modern complexity into issues that can be understood and felt close-up by every human being. It must give form to the feelings of helplessness and indifference, so that people may see the political, social, and economic sources of their private troubles and organize to change society. . . .

To turn these possibilities into realities will involve national efforts at university reform by an alliance of students and faculty. They must wrest control of the educational process from the administrative bureaucracy. They must make fraternal and functional contact with allies in labor, civil rights, and other liberal forces outside the campus. They must import major public issues into the curriculum—research and teaching on problems of war and peace is an outstanding example. They must make debate and controversy, not dull pedantic cant, the common style for educational life. They must consciously build a base for their assault upon the loci of power.

As students for a democratic society, we are committed to stimulating this kind of social movement, this kind of vision and program in campus and community across the country. If we appear to seek the unattainable, as it has been said, then let it be known that we do so to avoid the unimaginable.

2.10 Is the President Above the Law?

Richard Nixon once said, "It is quite obvious that there are certain inherently governmental actions which if undertaken by the sovereign in protection of the interest of the nation's security are lawful but which if undertaken by private persons are not. (Los Angeles Times, *March 12, 1976)." Nixon was not the first president to be accused of placing himself above the law, but he was the first one in modern times to be subject to impeachment proceedings for acting on that assumption.*

Nixon's troubles resulted from his involvement in the Watergate break-in of June 1972, the most sensational political scandal of the century. Burglars were caught in the offices of the Democratic National Committee in the Watergate apartment complex in the nation's capital. They were trying to tap the phone and steal documents that might be used in "dirty tricks" against political enemies. The burglars had close ties to high officials in the Republican party and the White House.

The President was never officially charged with prior knowledge of the break-in, but rather of attempting to cover up the deed. In 1973 impeachment proceedings against Nixon began in the House of Representatives. The charges also included the accusation that he used the FBI and Internal Revenue Service illegally, and failed to turn over documents needed by the House. In 1974, the Supreme Court ordered the President to hand over tape recordings that implicated him in the coverup (including the one cited below). The House Judiciary Committee, by a sizeable majority, voted to impeach the President on grounds of obstruction of justice, abuse of power, and refusal to obey a congressional subpoena to release his tapes.

Nixon resigned rather than stand trial. He was officially pardoned by Gerald Ford, the man he appointed as his successor. Several top officials of his administration were later convicted for their roles in the coverup and served prison terms.

Three documents on Nixon's administration follow. One is a memo from E. Howard Hunt, a former CIA official and "dirty tricks" specialist, to Charles W. Colson, special counsel to the President, dated July 28, 1971. It proposes ways of smearing Daniel Ellsberg, the Department of Defense analyst who has leaked the secret Pentagon Papers to the press. A second item is a selection from a transcript describing a White House meeting of June 23, 1972, when top advisor Haldeman first informs the President of the break-in. A third is a presidential address in 1973 when Nixon presents what he says is a "full" account of the Watergate events.

Questions

Under our Constitition, can the government legally undertake operations of the sort that Hunt had in mind against Ellsberg? Explain.

In your opinion, are there any circumstances when the President can overthrow the constitutional checks against tyranny? What are the rights of "the sovereign" in acting to defend national security? What constitutes a threat to national security?

Compare the dialogue in the transcripts with the account Nixon presents in his public address. How do they differ?

Compare the evidence and charges brought against Nixon with those brought against Andrew Johnson in 1868 (Document 2.1). Was the scope of the charges against Nixon narrower and therefore more fair?

Howard Hunt—

SUBJECT: Neutralization of Ellsberg

I am proposing a skeletal operations plan aimed at building a file on Ellsberg that will contain all available overt, covert and derogatory information. This basic tool is essential in determining how to destroy his public image and credibility.

Items:

Obtain all overt press material on Ellsberg and continue its collection;

Request CIA to perform a covert psychological assessment/evaluation on Ellsberg;

Interview Ellsberg's first wife;

Interview Ellsberg's Saigon contacts: the restaurant owner, Nicolai, and his mistress whom Ellsberg coveted;

Request CIA, FBI, and CIC for their *full* holdings on Ellsberg;

Examine Ellsberg personnel files at ISA (Pentagon) and the Rand Corporation, *including clearance materials*;

Obtain Ellsberg's files from his psychiatric analyst;

Inventory Ellsberg's ISA and Rand colleagues; determine where they are, and whether any might be approachable.

I realize that, as a practical nurse, not all the foregoing items can be accomplished; even so, they represent desiderata.

White House Transcript —

HALDEMAN: Now, on the investigation, you know the Democratic break-in thing, we're back in the problem area because the FBI is not under control, because [Director Patrick] Gray doesn't exactly know how to control it and they have—their investigation is now leading into some productive areas. . . . They've been able to trace the money—not through the money itself—but through the bank sources—the banker. And it goes in some directions we don't

want it to go. Ah, also there have been some [other] things—like an informant came in off the street to the FBI in Miami who was a photographer or has a friend who is a photographer who developed some films through this guy [Bernard] Barker and the films had pictures of Democratic National Committee letterhead documents and things. So it's things like that that are filtering in. [Attorney General John] Mitchell came up with yesterday, and [Presidential Counsel] John Dean analyzed very carefully last night and concludes, concurs now with Mitchell's recommendation that the only way to solve this, and we're set up beautifully to do it . . . is for us to have [CIA Assistant Director Vernon] Walters call Pat Gray and just say, "Stay to hell out of this—this is ah, [our] business here. We don't want you to go any further on it." That's not an unusual development, and ah, that would take care of it.

PRESIDENT: What about Pat Gray—you mean Pat Gray doesn't want to?

HALDEMAN: Pat does want to. He doesn't know how to, and he doesn't have any basis for doing it. Given this, he will then have the basis. He'll call [FBI Assistant Director] Mark Felt in, and the two of them—and Mark Felt wants to cooperate because he's ambitious—

PRESIDENT: Yeah.

HALDEMAN: He'll call him in and say, "We've got the signal from across the river to pull the hold on this." And what will fit rather well because the FBI agents who are working the case, at this point, feel that's what it is.

PRESIDENT: This is CIA? They've traced the money? Who'd they trace it to?

HALDEMAN: Well they've traced it to a name, but they haven't gotten to the guy yet.

PRESIDENT: Would it be somebody here?

HALDEMAN: Ken Dahlberg.

PRESIDENT: Who the hell is Ken Dahlberg?

HALDEMAN: He gave $25,000 in Minnesota and, ah, the check went directly to this guy Barker.

PRESIDENT: It isn't from the Committee though, from [Finance Chairman Maurice] Stans?

HALDEMAN: Yeah. It is. It's directly traceable and there's some more through some Texas people that went to the Mexican bank which can also be traced to the Mexican bank—they'll get their names today.

PRESIDENT: Well, I mean, there's no way—I'm just thinking if they don't cooperate, what do they say? That they were approached by the Cubans? That's what Dahlberg has to say, the Texans too.

HALDEMAN: Well, if they will. But then we're relying on more and more people all the time. That's the problem and they'll [i.e., the FBI] stop if we could take this other route.

PRESIDENT: All right.

HALDEMAN: And you seem to think the thing to do is get them to stop?

PRESIDENT: Right, fine.

HALDEMAN: They [Mitchell and Dean] say the only way to do that is from White House instructions. And it's got to be to [CIA Director Richard] Helms and to—ah, what's his name. . . . ? Walters.

PRESIDENT: Walters.

HALDEMAN: And the proposal would be that [presidential adviser John] Ehrlichman and I call them in, and say, ah—

PRESIDENT: All right, fine. How do you call him in—I mean you just—well, we protected Helms from one hell of a lot of things.

HALDEMAN: That's what Ehrlichman says.

PRESIDENT: Of course; this [Howard] Hunt [business.] That will uncover a lot of things. You open that scab there's a hell of a lot of things and we just feel that it would be very detrimental to have this thing go any further. This involves these Cubans, Hunt, and a lot of hanky-panky that, we have nothing to do with ourselves. Well what the hell, did Mitchell know about this?

HALDEMAN: I think so. I don't think he knew the details, but I think he knew.

PRESIDENT: He didn't know how it was going to be handled though—with Dahlberg and the Texans and so forth? Well who was the asshole that did? Is it [G. Gordon] Liddy? Is that the fellow? He must be a little nuts!

HALDEMAN: He is.

PRESIDENT: I mean he just isn't well screwed on is he? Is that the problem?

HALDEMAN: No, but he was under pressure, apparently, to get more information, and as he got more pressure, he pushed the people harder.

PRESIDENT: Pressure from Mitchell?

HALDEMAN: Apparently. . . .

PRESIDENT: All right, fine, I understand it all. We won't second-guess Mitchell and the rest. Thank God it wasn't [special counsel Charles] Colson.

HALDEMAN: The FBI interviewed Colson yesterday. They determined that would be a good thing to do. To have him take an interrogation which he did, and the FBI guys working the case concluded that there were one or two possibilities—one, that this was a White House (they don't think that there is anything at the Election Committee) they think it was either a White House operation and they had some obscure reasons for it—non-political, or it was a—Cuban [operation] and [involved] the CIA. And after their interrogation of Colson yesterday, they concluded it was not the White House, but are now convinced it is a CIA thing, so the CIA turnoff would—

PRESIDENT: Well, not sure of their analysis, I'm not going to get that involved. I'm (unintelligible).

HALDEMAN: No, sir, we don't want you to.

PRESIDENT: You call them in.

HALDEMAN: Good deal.

PRESIDENT: Play it tough. That's the way they play it and that's the way we are going to play it. . . .

Meeting 2 (1:04–1:13 P.M.)

PRESIDENT: O.K. . . . Just say (unintelligible) very bad to have this fellow Hunt, ah, he knows too damned much. . . . If it gets out that this is all involved, the Cuba thing, it would be a fiasco. It would make the CIA look bad, it's going to make Hunt look bad, and it is likely to blow the whole Bay of Pigs thing which we think would be very unfortunate—both for CIA, and for the country, at this time, and for American foreign policy. Just tell him to lay off. Don't you [think so]?

HALDEMAN: Yep. That's the basis to do it on. Just leave it at that. . . .

Richard Nixon—

I want to talk to you tonight from my heart on a subject of deep concern to every American.

In recent months, members of my Administration and officials of the Committee for the Re-election of the President—including some of my closest friends

and most trusted aides—have been charged with involvement in what has come to be known as the Watergate affair. These include charges of illegal activity during and preceding the 1972 Presidential election and charges that responsible officials participated in efforts to cover up that illegal activity.

The inevitable result of these charges has been to raise serious questions about the integrity of the White House itself. Tonight I wish to address those questions.

Last June 16, while I was in Florida trying to get a few days' rest after my visit to Moscow, I first learned from news reports of the Watergate break-in. I was appalled at this senseless, illegal action, and I was shocked to learn that employees of the Re-election Commitee were apparently among those guilty. I immediately ordered an investigation by appropriate government authorities. On September 15, as you will recall, indictments were brought against seven defendants in the case.

As the investigation went forward, I repeatedly asked those conducting the investigation whether there was any reason to believe that members of my Administration were in any way involved. I received repeated assurances that there were not. Because of these continuing reassurances—because I believed the reports I was getting, because I had faith in the persons from whom I was getting them—I discounted the stories in the press that appeared to implicate members of my Administration or other officials of the campaign committee.

Until March of this year, I remained convinced that the denials were true and that the charges of involvement by members of the White House staff were false. The comments I made during this period, and the comments made by my Press Secretary on my behalf, were based on the information provided to us at the time we made those comments. However, new information then came to me which persuaded me that there was a real possibility that some of these charges were true, and suggesting further that there had been an effort to conceal the facts both from the public, from you, and from me.

As a result, on March 21, I personally assumed the responsibility for coordinating intensive new inquiries into the matter, and I personally ordered those conducting the investigations to get all the facts and to report them directly to me, here in this office.

I again ordered that all persons in the Government or at the Re-election Committee should cooperate fully with the FBI, the prosecutors and the Grand Jury. I also ordered that anyone who refused to cooperate in telling the truth would be asked to resign from government service. And, with ground rules adopted that would preserve the basic constitutional separation of powers between the Congress and the Presidency, I directed that members of the White House staff should appear and testify voluntarily under oath before the Senate Committee investigating Watergate.

I was determined that we should get to the bottom of the matter, and that the truth should be fully brought out—no matter who was involved. . . .

Today, in one of the most difficult decisions of my Presidency, I accepted the resignation of two of my closest associates in the White House—Bob Haldeman, John Ehrlichman—two of the finest public servants it has been my privilege to know.

I want to stress that in accepting these resignations, I mean to leave no implica-

tion whatever of personal wrongdoing on their part, and I leave no implication tonight of implication on the part of others who have been charged in this matter. . . .

Because Attorney General Kleindienst—though a distinguished public servant, my personal friend for 20 years, with no personal involvement whatever in this matter—has been a close personal and professional associate of some of those who are involved in this case, he and I both felt that it was also necessary to name a new Attorney General.

The Counsel to the President, John Dean, has also resigned.

As the new Attorney General, I have today named Elliot Richardson, a man of unimpeachable integrity and rigorously high principle. I have directed him to do everything necessary to ensure that the Department of Justice has the confidence and trust of every law abiding person in this country.

I have given him absolute authority to make all decisions bearing upon the prosecution of the Watergate case and related matters. I have instructed him that if he should consider it appropriate, he has the authority to name a special supervising prosecutor for matters arising out of the case. . . .

Looking back at the history of this case, two questions arise:

How could it have happened?

Who is to blame?

Political commentators have correctly observed that during my 27 years in politics, I have always previously insisted on running my own campaigns for office.

But 1972 presented a very different situation. In both domestic and foreign policy, 1972 was a year of crucially important decisions, of intense negotiations, of vital new directions, particularly in working toward the goal which has been my overriding concern throughout my political career—the goal of bringing peace to America and peace to the world.

That is why I decided, as the 1972 campaign approached, that the Presidency should come first and politics second. To the maximum extent possible, therefore, I sought to delegate campaign operations, and to remove the day-to-day campaign decisions from the President's office and from the White House. I also, as you recall, severely limited the number of my own campaign appearances.

Who, then, is to blame for what happened in this case?

For specific criminal action by specific individuals, those who committed those actions, must, of course, bear the liability and pay the penalty.

For the fact that alleged improper actions took place within the White House or within my campaign organization, the easiest course would be for me to blame those to whom I delegated the responsibility to run the campaign. But that would be a cowardly thing to do.

I will not place the blame on subordinates—on people whose zeal exceeded their judgment, and who may have done wrong in a cause they deeply believed to be right.

In any organization, the man at the top must bear the responsibility. That responsibility, therefore, belongs here, in this office. I accept that. And I pledge to you tonight, from this office, that I will do everything in my power to ensure that the guilty are brought to justice, and that such abuses are purged from our political processes in the years to come, long after I have left this office. . . .

. . . I love America. I deeply believe that America is the hope of the world, and I know that in the quality and wisdom of the leadership America gives lies the only hope for millions of people all over the world, that they can live their lives in peace and freedom. We must be worthy of that hope, in every sense of the word. Tonight, I ask for your prayers to help me in everything that I do throughout the days of my Presidency to be worthy of their hopes and of yours.

God bless America and God bless each and every one of you.

Chapter Three: War

3.1 On Sea Power

Alfred T. Mahan (1840–1914) viewed the world as a kind of jungle where nations strug-gled for economic advantages and physical survival. A navy admiral and historian, he had written the single most influential book on naval theory of modern time. It was called, The Influence of Sea Power Upon History, 1660–1783. *The key to success for nations like the United States lay, Mahan argued, in a strong navy. He pressed for the building of a fleet of offensive ships driven by coal-fired steam engines, an enlarged merchant marine, and new naval bases (and colonial territories) to support the fleet. Theodore (and Franklin) Roosevelt and the leaders of Germany, Japan and England read Admiral Mahan's works with great interest, finding in them support for naval expansion programs.*

Questions

What does Mahan mean when he says that Americans must look outward? How would American interest in foreign trade affect the kind of navy it needs? What danger does he see for America in someone building a canal through the isthmus of Central America? Would you say his fears were justified?

According to Mahan, where would the United States need bases to protect the areas vital to its interest (as Mahan envisions those interests)? How would the U.S. acquire them and what would their acquisition mean for its relations with other countries that wished to expand their own naval power? Would following Mahan's suggestions increase or decrease the chance of war?

What did his ideas imply for America's relations with inhabitants of areas he felt the U.S. had to control?

To affirm the importance of distant markets, and the relation to them of our own immense powers of production, implies logically the recognition of the link that joins the products and the markets,—that is, the carrying trade. . . . Further, . . . the acknowledgment . . . carries with it a view

SOURCE: From A. T. Mahan, *The Interests of America in Sea Power* (Boston, 1897).

of the relations of the United States to the world radically distinct from the simple idea of self-suffcingness. We shall not follow far this line of thought before there will dawn the realization of America's unique position, facing the older worlds of the East and West. . . .

The opening of a canal through the Central American Isthmus, . . . by modifying the direction of trade routes, will induce a great increase of commercial activity and carrying trade throughout the Caribbean Sea. . . . This now comparatively deserted nook of the ocean will become, like the Red Sea, a great thoroughfare of shipping, and will attract, as never before in our day, the interest and ambition of maritime nations. Every position in that sea will have enhanced commercial and military value, and the canal itself will have become a strategic center of the most vital importance. . . . It will be a link between the two oceans; but . . . the use, unless most carefully guarded by treaties, will belong wholly to the beligerent which controls the sea by its naval power. In case of war, the United States will . . . be impotent, as against any of the great maritime powers, to control the Central American canal. Militarily speaking, and having reference to European complications only, the piercing of the Isthmus is nothing but a disaster to the United States, in the present state of her military and naval preparation. It is especially dangerous to the Pacific coast; but the increased exposure of one part of our seaboard reacts unfavorably upon the whole military situation. . . .

The United States is woefully unready, not only in fact but in purpose to assert in the Caribbean and Central America a weight of influence proportioned to the extent of her interest. We have not the navy, and what is worse, we are not willing to have the navy, that will weigh seriously in any disputes with those nations whose interests will conflict there with our own. We have not, and we are not anxious to provide, the defense of the seaboard which will leave the navy free for its work at sea. We have not, but many other powers have, positions, either within or on the borders of the Caribbean, which not only possess great natural advantages for the control of that sea, but have received and are receiving that artificial strength of fortification and armament which will make them practically inexpungable. . . . That which I deplore . . . is that the nation neither has nor cares to have its sea frontier so defended, and its navy of such power, as shall suffice, with the advantages of our position, to weigh seriously when inevitable discussions arise . . . about the Caribbean Sea or the canal. Is the United States, for instance, prepared to allow Germany to acquire the Dutch stronghold of Curacao, fronting the Atlantic outlet of both the proposed canals of Panama and Nicaragua? Is she prepared to acquiesce in any foreign power purchasing from Haiti a naval station on the Windward Passage, through which pass our steamer routes to the Isthmus? Would she acquiesce in a foreign protectorate over the Sandwich Islands, the great central station . . . on our lines of communication with both Australia and China? . . .

Yet, were our sea frontier as strong as it now is weak, passive self-defense, whether in trade or war, would be but a poor policy, so long as this world continues to be one of struggle and vicissitude. All around us now is strife; "the struggle of life," "the race of life," are phrases so familiar that we do not feel their significance till we stop to think about them.

. . . Are our people, however, so unaggressive that they are likely not to want their own way in matters where their interests turn on points of disputed right, or so little sensitive as to submit quietly to encroachment by others, in quarters where they long have considered their own influence should prevail?

Our self-imposed isolation in the matter of markets, and the decline of our shipping interest in the last thirty years, have coincided singularly with an actual remoteness of this continent from the life of the rest of the world. The writer has before him a map of the North and South Atlantic oceans, showing the direction of the principal trade routes and the proportion of tonnage passing over each; and it is curious to note what deserted regions, comparatively, are the Gulf of Mexico, the Caribbean Sea, and the adjoining countries and islands. . . . The significance is unmistakable; Europe has now little mercantile interest in the Caribbean Sea.

When the Isthmus is pierced, this isolation will pass away, and with it the indifference of foreign nations. From wheresoever they come and whithersoever they afterward go, all ships that use the canal will pass through the Caribbean. Whatever the effect produced upon the prosperity of the adjacent continent and islands by the thousand wants attendant upon maritime activity, around such a focus of trade will center large commercial and political interests. To protect and develop its own, each nation will seek points of support and means of influence in a quarter where the United States always has been jealously sensitive to the intrusion of European powers. The precise value of the Monroe Doctrine is understood very loosely by most Americans, but the effect of the familiar phrase has been to develop a national sensitiveness, which is a more frequent cause of war than material interests; and over disputes caused by such feelings there will preside none of the calming influence due to the moral authority of international law, with its recognized principles. . . .

Whether they will or no, Americans must now begin to look outward. The growing production of the country demands it. An increasing volume of public sentiment demands it. The position of the United States, between the two Old Worlds and the two great oceans, makes the same claim, which will soon be strengthend by the creation of the new link joining the Atlantic and Pacific. The tendency will be maintained and increased by the growth of the European colonies in the Pacific, by the advancing civilization of Japan, and by the rapid peopling of our Pacific states with men who have all the aggressive spirit of the advanced line of national progress.

3.2   The Roosevelt Corollary

In his annual messages to Congress in 1904 and 1905, President Theodore Roosevelt proclaimed what became known as the Roosevelt Corollary to the Monroe Doctrine. The original Monroe Doctrine, a statement of U.S. foreign policy issued by Pres. James Monroe in 1823, arose out of U.S. concerns about European claims to the Northwest and to Latin America. Roosevelt's statement, excerpted below, is taken from his 1904 message. At that time his immediate concern was the threat of European intervention in the affairs of the Dominican Republic.

Questions

What was the original message of the Monroe Doctrine, and how did Roosevelt enlarge upon it?

Look especially at the passage which begins with "Chronic wrongdoing" and ends with " . . . an international police power." What does it mean in ordinary English? Why do you suppose Roosevelt decided to state those ideas in the language he used? How would a patriotic American of Roosevelt's time have felt about the Roosevelt Corollary? How might a patriotic citizen of a Latin-American nation have reacted to it?

Does the United States follow the Roosevelt Corollary today? Should it?

. . . It is not true that the United States feels any land hunger or entertains any projects as regards the other nations of the Western Hemisphere save such as are for their welfare. All that this country desires is to see the neighboring countries stable, orderly, and prosperous. Any country whose people conduct themselves well can count upon our hearty friendship. If a nation shows that it knows how to act with reasonable efficiency and decency in social and political matters, if it keeps order and pays its obligations, it need fear no interference from the United States. Chronic wrongdoing, or an impotence which results in a general loosening of the ties of civilized society, may in America, as elsewhere, ultimately require intervention by some civilized nation, and in the Western Hemisphere the adherence of the United States to the Monroe Doctrine may force the United States, however reluctantly, in flagrant cases of such wrongdoing or impotence, to the exercise of an international police power. If every country washed by the Caribbean Sea would show the progress in stable and just civilization which with the aid of the Platt amendment Cuba has shown since our troops left the island, and which so many of the republics in both Americas are constantly and brilliantly showing, all question of interference by this Nation with their affairs would be at an end. Our interests and those of our southern neighbors are in reality identical. They have great natural riches, and if within their borders the reign of law and justice obtains, prosperity is sure to come to them. While they thus obey the primary laws of civilized society they may rest assured that they will be treated by us in a spirit of cordial and helpful sympathy. We would interfere with them only in the last resort, and then only if it became evident that their inability or unwillingness to do justice at home and abroad had violated the rights of the United States or had invited foreign aggression to the detriment of the entire body of American nations. It is a mere truism to say that every nation, whether in America or anywhere else,

SOURCE: *Messages and Papers of the Presidents.* Vol. XIV, p. 6923 ff.

which desires to maintain its freedom, its independence, most ultimately realize that the right of such independence can not be separated from the responsibility of making good use of it.

3.3 The Tampico Incident

On April 9, 1914, officers of the Mexican government arrested several sailors from an American gunboat in Tampico, scene of recent fighting between pro- and anti-government factions. The Mexican Revolution was then in progress. President Woodrow Wilson intensely disliked the current President of Mexico, Victoriano Huerta, partly because Huerta had come to power over the dead bodies of the previous president and vice president of Mexico. He refused to recognize Huerta's government.

American historians tend to feel that Wilson disliked the diplomacy of power and economic influence that he had inherited from Theodore Roosevelt and William Howard Taft, and preferred instead to conduct a missionary diplomacy aimed at bringing democracy to other peoples. "I am going to teach the South American republics to elect good men!" he had said the previous fall.

For the sailor's arrest, the American naval commander in the area, Rear Admiral Henry T. Mayo, demanded an apology and a twenty-one gun salute to the American flag. The Mexican government refused. President Wilson then asked Congress for authority to retaliate. Congress granted it on April 22, one day after an American force had landed in Vera Cruz, rather than Tampico. Almost everybody expected that another full-scale war between the two nations was about to begin. (The U.S. had administered a humiliating defeat on Mexico in 1846–47 and took from Mexico over a third of her territory.) U.S. troops seized the customs house and prevented a German ship from delivering a load of munitions to Huerta's government. Not for seven months did American occupation forces withdraw from Mexico.

Questions

Why did Wilson take this action? What reasons does he present to the Congress? Does he seem sincere? Does Wilson's address to Congress support the interpretation of American historians stated above?

Does the approach of a German munitions ship to Vera Cruz suggest another possible reason for landing American troops there rather than at the port where the arrest took place? In light of the history of the Mexican War in the 1840s, what do you suppose would have happened to Huerta's government during this time of revolutionary upheaval if it had apologized to the U.S. and delivered a salute to the American flag?

Gentlemen of the Congress:

It is my duty to call your attention to a situation which has arisen in our dealings with General Victoriano Huerta at Mexico City which calls for action, and to ask your advice and cooperation in acting upon it. On the 9th of April a paymaster of the U.S.S. *Dolphin* landed at the Iturbide Bridge landing at Tampico with a whaleboat and boat's crew to take off certain supplies needed by his ship, and while engaged in loading the boat was arrested by an officer and squad of men of the army of General Huerta. . . . Admiral Mayo regarded the arrest as so serious an affront that he was not satisfied with the apologies offered, but demanded that the flag of the United States be saluted with special ceremony by the military commander of the port.

The incident can not be regarded as a trivial one, especially as two of the men arrested were taken from the boat itself—that is to say, from the territory of the United States—but had it stood by itself it might have been attributed to the ignorance or arrogance of a single officer. Unfortunately, it was not an isolated case. A series of incidents have recently occurred which can not but create the impression that the representatives of General Huerta were willing to go out of their way to show disregard for the dignity and rights of this Government and felt perfectly safe in doing what they pleased, making free to show in many ways their irritation and contempt. . . .

The manifest danger of such a situation was that such offenses might grow from bad to worse until something happened of so gross and intolerable a sort as to lead directly and inevitably to armed conflict. It was necessary that the apologies of General Huerta and his representatives should go much further, that they should be such as to attract the attention of the whole population to their significance, and such as to impress upon General Huerta himself the necessity of seeing to it that no further occasion for explanations and professed regrets should arise. I, therefore, felt it my duty to sustain Admiral Mayo in the whole of his demand and to insist that the flag of the United States should be saluted in such a way as to indicate a new spirit and attitude on the part of the Huertistas.

Such a salute, General Huerta has refused, and I have come to ask your approval and support in the course I now propose to pursue.

The Government can, I earnestly hope, in no circumstances be forced into war with the people of Mexico. Mexico is torn by civil strife. If we are to accept the tests of its own constitution, it has no government. General Huerta has set his power up in the City of Mexico, such as it is, without right and by methods for which there can be no justification. Only part of the country is under his control. If armed conflict should unhappily come as a result of his attitude of personal resentment toward this Government, we should be fighting only General Huerta and those who adhere to him and give him their support, and our object would be only to restore to the people of the distracted Republic the opportunity to set up again their own laws and their own government.

But I earnestly hope that war is not now in question. I believe I speak for the American people when I say that we do not desire to control in any degree the affairs of our sister Republic. Our feeling for the people of Mexico is one of deep and genuine friendship, and every thing that we have so far done or refrained from doing has proceeded from our desire to help

SOURCE: *American State Papers, Foreign Relations of the United States*, 1914, p. 474

them, not to hinder or embarrass them. We would not wish even to exercise the good offices of friendship without their welcome and consent. The people of Mexico are entitled to settle their own domestic affairs in their own way, and we sincerely desire to respect their right. The present situation need have none of the grave implications of interference if we deal with it promptly, firmly, and wisely.

No doubt I could do what is necessary in the circumstances to enforce respect for our Government without recourse to the Congress, and yet not exceed my constitutional powers as President; but I do not wish to act in a manner possibly of so grave consequence except in close conference and cooperation with both the Senate and House. I, therefore, come to ask your approval that I should use the armed forces of the United States in such ways and to such an extent as may be necessary to obtain from General Huerta and his adherents the fullest recognition of the rights and dignity of the United States, even amidst the distressing conditions now unhappily obtaining in Mexico.

There can in what we do be no thought of aggression or of selfish aggrandizement. We seek to maintain the dignity and authority of the United States only because we wish always to keep our great influence unimpaired for the uses of liberty, both in the United States and wherever else it may be employed for the benefit of mankind.

3.4 The Occupation of Haiti

United States military forces occupied Haiti more or less regularly for two decades beginning in 1915. At stake was our interest in Caribbean raw materials and shipping.

A recent revolution had left the Republic of Haiti with a very unstable government. U.S. Secretary of State William Jennings Bryan especially wished to safeguard American financial interests in Haiti, including investments in the Haitian national bank and railroad. Complicating matters further, Germany and France, now at war with one another, had taken considerable interest in Haiti. They lent its shaky regime money and seemed to have designs on the Môle of St. Nicholas, a fort overlooking the Windward Passage, a strait between Cuba and Haiti, that was used by ships passing to and from the newly opened Panama Canal.

The following three documents concern the period from 1915 to 1923. The first is a telegram drafted by Secretary Bryan and State Department counselor Robert Lansing and approved by President Woodrow Wilson. It was sent to the American minister in Haiti on December 12, 1914, and declares the conditions under which the United States would recognize the new government of Haiti.

In the second document, Lansing provides a rationale for U.S. occupation of Haiti in a letter to Woodrow Wilson, dated August 3, 1915. In the third document, written in 1923, Lansing (who was now Secretary of State) comments on whether the United States should allow self-government to the black inhabitants of the Virgin Islands which the U.S. had bought from Denmark in 1917.

Questions

In the first document, what do Bryan and Lansing mean when they say that the Haitian government has to meet its obligations to outside nations? What are these "obligations," and what might happen if Haiti failed to meet them? Why did the authors put this passage in the document?

In the second document, what does Lansing's letter tell you about Wilson's actual reasons for sending the marines to Vera Cruz (Document 3.3)? What light does it throw on the President's statement to Congress after the Tampico incident? Does Lansing appear to think that Wilson wanted the American people to be fully informed about the interventions in Mexico and Haiti? Should the administration have told the American people its actual reasons for sending American troops to those countries or should it have devised explanations which, while not true, sounded plausible and appealing?

In the third document, did Lansing believe that the Haitians, who were black, could govern themselves? Since he was a co-author of the first document, what do you make of the statement in that document about self-government in Haiti? What part do you think racism may have played in U.S. relations in Latin America? Do you feel it plays any role today?

After reviewing these three documents and the Roosevelt Corollary (Document 3.2), what attitude would you say the American government in those days held toward the American people? Can Americans ever properly judge their government's handling of foreign affairs if the government lies to them? What are the disadvantages of telling them the truth?

William Jennings Bryan and Robert Lansing, December 12, 1914 —

[What Haiti needs is] . . . a government capable of maintaining order and meeting the country's obligations to outside nations. Such a government is impossible however unless it rests upon the consent of the governed and gives expression to the will of the people. It will be necessary, therefore, for us to have information as to the fiscal standing and general plans of the government and as to its attitude toward foreigners of other nations, including its attitude on subjects relating to the Môle of St. Nicholas.

Robert Lansing to President Wilson, August 3, 1915 —

We have no excuse of reprisal as we had at Vera Cruz, to take over the city government and administer the offices. There would appear to me to be but one reason that could be given for doing so, and that is the humane duty of furnishing means to relieve the famine situation. If our naval authorities should take over the collection of customs on imports and exports these might be expended on the ground of dire necessity for the relief of the starving people.

Lansing, 1923 —

The experience of Liberia and Haiti show [sic] that the African race are devoid of any capacity for political organization and lack genius for government. Unquestionably there is in them an inherent tendency to revert to savagery and to cast aside the shackles of civilization which are irksome to their physical nature.

3.5 Entering the Great War

On April 2, 1917 Woodrow Wilson asked Congress for a declaration of war against Germany, and Congress obliged. Wilson and his administration had attempted to keep the United States out of World War I, but this had become increasingly difficult. He and most members of his administration favored the Allied cause. America was one of the world's chief sources of money, food, raw materials, and weapons. Since the British fleet blockaded Europe, the United States supplied the Allies exclusively.

Germany used submarines to block shipments to the Allies. Since these fragile, slow-moving vessels were most protected and deadliest when they fired torpedoes below water, they often sank their prey without warning. Sometimes they killed American passengers, as in the 1915 attack on the Lusitania. *The U.S. threatened to retaliate for attacks against American property and lives, and for a while Germany backed down. But at the end of 1916, with the war stalemated, German officials decided to resume unrestricted submarine warfare. They gambled that even if the U.S. entered to war, German U-boats could choke off supplies from America to England and France, forcing the Allies to settle the war on Germany's terms.*

Other incidents influenced America's entry into the war, including a German offer to restore to Mexico territories that the U.S. had seized during the Mexican-American War—if Mexico joined with Germany in fighting the United States. Still, the resumption of unrestricted submarine warfare in 1917 was the immediate cause of Wilson's address to Congress excerpted below.

Questions

What reasons does Wilson present for entering the war? Would a policy of armed neutrality, which the President rejected, have worked? Can Wilson's stated objectives be achieved through war? Is it wise to urge a nation like ours to fight for altruistic and unselfish reasons rather than for territorial or commercial gain, or national security?

When Wilson speaks of making the world safe for democracy and the priv- ilege of people everywhere to choose their own way of life, does he seem to be thinking of countries like Haiti, Mexico and Cuba?

Why does Wilson distinguish between the German government and the German people? Is there a conflict between his call to fight without rancor, and his intent to use all the power and resources of the United States to bring Germany to terms?

Would you have voted for this declaration of war?

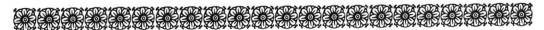

I have called the Congress into extraor- dinary session because there are serious, very serious, choices of policy to be made, and made immediately, which it was nei- ther right nor constitutionally permissible that I should assume the responsibility of making.

On the third of February last I officially laid before you the extraordinary an- nouncement of the Imperial German Gov- ernment that on and after the first day of February it was its purpose to put aside all restraints of law or of humanity and use its submarines to sink every vessel that sought to approach either the ports of Great Britain and Ireland or the western coasts of Europe or any of the ports controlled by the ene- mies of Germany within the Mediterra- nean. That had seemed to be the object of the German submarine warfare earlier in the war, but since April of last year the Im- perial Government had somewhat re- strained the commanders of its undersea craft in conformity with its promise then given to us that passenger boats should not

Source: Address delivered at a Joint Session of the Two Houses of Congress, April 2, 1917, U.S. 65th Congress, 1st sess., *Senate Doc.* 5.

be sunk and that due warning would be given to all other vessels which its sub- marines might seek to destroy, when no resistance was offered or escape attempted, and care taken that their crews were given at least a fair chance to save their lives in their open boats. . . . The new policy has swept every restriction aside. Vessels of every kind, whatever their flag, their char- acter, their cargo, their destination, their errand, have been ruthlessly sent to the bottom without warning and without thought of help or mercy for those on board, the vessels of friendly neutrals along with those of belligerents. Even hospital ships and ships carrying relief to the sorely bereaved and stricken people of Belgium, though the latter were provided with safe conduct through the proscribed areas by the German Government itself and were distinguished by unmistakable marks of identity, have been sunk with the same reckless lack of compassion or of principle.

I was for a little while unable to believe that such things would in fact be done by any government that had hitherto sub- scribed to the humane practices of civi- lized nations. International law had its origin in the attempt to set up some law which would be respected and observed upon the seas, where no nation had right of dominion and where lay the free highways of the world. . . . I am not now thinking of the loss of property involved, immense and serious as that is, but only of the wanton and wholesale destruction of the lives of non-combatants, men, women, and children, engaged in pursuits which have always, even in the darkest periods of modern history, been deemed innocent and legitimate. Property can be paid for; the lives of peaceful and innocent people cannot be. The present German submarine warfarer against commerce is a warfare against mankind.

It is a war against all nations. American ships have been sunk, American lives taken, in ways which it has stirred us very deeply to learn of, but the ships and people of other neutral and friendly nations have been sunk and overwhelmed in the waters in the same way. There has been no discrimination. The challenge is to all mankind. . . .

When I addressed the Congress on the twenty-sixth of February last I thought that it would suffice to assert our neutral rights with arms, our right to use the seas against unlawful interference, our right to keep our people safe against unlawful violence. But armed neutrality, it now appears, is impracticable. Because submarines are in effect outlaws when used as the German submarines have been used against merchant shipping, it is impossible to defend ships against their attacks as the law of nations has assumed that merchantmen would defend themselves against privateers or cruisers, visible craft giving chase upon the open sea. It is common prudence in such circumstances, grim necessity indeed, to endeavor to destroy them before they have shown their own intention. They

must be dealt with upon sight, if dealt with at all. The German Government denies the right of neutrals to use arms at all within the areas of the sea which it has proscribed, even in the defense of rights which no modern publicist has ever before questioned their right to defend. The intimation is conveyed that the armed guards which we have placed on our merchant ships will be treated as beyond the pale of law and subject to be dealt with as pirates would be. Armed neutrality is ineffectual enough at best; in such circumstances and in the face of such pretensions it is worse than ineffectual: it is likely only to produce what it was meant to prevent; it is practically certain to draw us into the war without either the rights or the effectiveness of belligerents. There is one choice we cannot make, we are incapable of making: we will not choose the path of submission. . . .

With a profound sense of the solemn and even tragical character of the step I am taking and of the grave responsibilities which it involves, but in unhesitating obedience to what I deem my constitutional duty, I advise that the Congress declare the recent course of the Imperial German Government to be in fact nothing less than war against the government and people of the United States; that it formally accept the status of belligerent which has thus been thrust upon it; and that it take immediate steps not only to put the country in a more thorough state of defense but also to exert all its power and employ all its resources to bring the Government of the German Empire to terms and end the war.

What this will involve is clear. It will involve the utmost practicable cooperation in counsel and action with the governments now at war with Germany, and, as incident to that, the extension to those governments of the most liberal financial credits, in order that our resources may so far as possible be added to theirs. It will involve the organization and mobilization of all the material resources of the country to supply the materials of war and serve the incidental needs of the Nation in the most abundant and yet the most economical and efficient way possible. It will involve the immediate full equipment of the navy in all respects but particularly in supplying it with the best means of dealing with the enemy's submarines. It will involve the immediate addition to the armed forces of the United States already provided for by law in case of war at least five hundred thousand men, who should, in my opinion, be chosen upon the principle of universal liability to service, and also the authorization of subsequent additional increments of equal force so soon as they may be needed and can be handled in training. It will involve also, of course, the granting of adequate credits to the Government, sustained, I hope, so far as they can equitably be sustained by the present generation, by well conceived taxation. . . .

. . . I have exactly the same things in mind now that I had in mind when I addressed the Senate on the twenty-second of January last; the same that I had in mind when I addressed the Congress on the third of February and on the twenty-sixth of February. Our object now, as then, is to vindicate the principles of peace and justice in the life of the world as against selfish and autocratic power and to set up amongst the really free and self-governed peoples of the world such a concert of purpose and of action as will henceforth insure the observance of those principles. Neutrality is no longer feasible or desirable where the peace of the world is involved and the freedom of its peoples, and the menace to that peace and freedom lies in the existence of autocratic governments backed by organized force which is controlled wholly by their will, not by the will of their people. We have seen the last of neutrality in such circumstances. . . .

We have no quarrel with the German people. We have no feeling towards them but one of sympathy and friendship. It was not upon their impulse that their government acted in entering this war. It was not with their previous knowledge or approval. It was a war determined upon as wars used to be determined upon in the old, unhappy days when peoples were nowhere consulted by their rulers and wars were provoked and waged in the interest of dynasties or of little groups of ambitious men who were accustomed to use their fellow men as pawns and tools. . . .

. . . We are now about to accept gauge of battle with this natural foe to liberty and shall, if necessary, spend the whole force of the nation to check and nullify its pretensions and its power. We are glad, now that we see the facts with no veil of false pretense about them, to fight thus for the ultimate peace of the world and for the liberation of its peoples, the German peoples included: for the rights of nations great and small and the privilege of men everywhere to choose their way of life and of obedience. The world must be made safe for democracy. Its peace must be planted upon the tested foundations of political liberty. We have no selfish ends to serve. We desire no conquest, no dominion. We seek no indemnities for ourselves, no material compensation for the sacrifices we shall freely make. We are but one of the champions of the rights of mankind. We shall be satisfied when those rights have been made as secure as the faith and the freedom of nations can make them.

Just because we fight without rancor and without selfish object, seeking nothing for ourselves but what we shall wish to share with all free peoples, we shall, I feel confident, conduct our operations as belligerents without passion and ourselves observe with proud punctilio the principles of right and of fair play we profess to be fighting for.

I have said nothing of the Governments allied with the Imperial Government of Germany because they have not made war upon us or challenged us to defend our right and our honor. The Austro-Hungarian Government has, indeed, avowed its unqualified indorsement and acceptance of the reckless and lawless submarine warfare adopted now without disguise by the Imperial German Government . . . but that Government has not actually engaged in warfare against citizens of the United States on the seas, and I take the liberty, for the present at least, of postponing a discussion of our relations with the authorities at Vienna. We enter this war only where we are clearly forced into it because there are no other means of defending our rights. . . .

. . . We are, let me say again, the sincere friends of the German people, and shall desire nothing so much as the early reestablishment of intimate relations of mutual advantage between us,—however hard it may be for them, for the time being, to believe that this is spoken from our hearts. We have borne with their present Government through all these bitter months because of that friendship,—exercising a patience and forbearance which would otherwise have been impossible. We shall, happily, still have an opportunity to prove that friendship in our daily attitude and actions towards the millions of men and women of German birth and native sympathy who live amongst us and share our life, and we shall be proud to prove it towards all who are in fact loyal to their neighbors and to the Government in the hour of test. They are, most of them, as true and loyal Americans as if they had never known any other fealty or allegiance. They will be prompt to stand with us in rebuking and restraining the few who may be of a different mind and purpose. If there should be disloyalty, it will be dealt with with a firm hand of stern repression; but, if it lifts its head at all, it will lift it only here and there and without countenance except from a lawless and malignant few.

It is a distressing and oppressive duty, Gentlemen of the Congress, which I have performed in thus addressing you. There are, it may be, many months of fiery trial and sacrifice ahead of us. It is a fearful thing to lead this great peaceful people into war, into the most terrible and disastrous of all wars, civilization itself seeming to be in the balance. But the right is more precious than peace, and we shall fight for the things which we have always carried nearest our hearts,—for democracy, for the right of those who submit to authority to have a voice in their own Governments, for the rights and liberties of small nations, for a universal dominion of right by such a concert of free peoples as shall bring peace and safety to all nations and make the world itself at last free. To such a task we can dedicate our lives and our fortunes, everything that we are and everything that we have, with the pride of those who know that the day has come when America is privileged to spend her blood and her might for the principles that gave her birth and happiness and the peace which she has treasured. God helping her, she can do no other.

3.6 On the Brink in 1940

The following pair of documents from the files of the U.S. Army War Plans Division were originally classified SECRET. *They describe the reactions of key U.S. government people to the activities of the Axis powers—Germany, Italy, and Japan—at the very moment of the German conquest of France. The first document, dated 22 May 1940, involves national strategic decisions; the second, also from May 1940, is a memo from General George C. Marshall, Chief of Staff of the United States Army, to the War Plans Division. Other people mentioned in the documents are President Franklin D. Roosevelt; Admiral Harold R. Stark, Chief of Naval Operations; and Sumner Welles, who represented the Department of State. "MBR" is Colonel Matthew B. Ridgway of the War Plans Division. The 180th Meridian is approximately 1200 nautical miles west of Honolulu, Hawaii.*

Questions

Do you think the documents actually represent what these top government officials believed. Why? What did they seem to expect the Axis powers to do and when? What do the words "imminently probable" mean? Did the American leaders mentioned in the documents think the United States was adequately prepared to face the Axis? Are the main concerns of those leaders economic, humanitarian, or strategic? How can you tell? Is it likely that Roosevelt and his chief advisors had other reasons for opposing Axis activities that are not mentioned in these documents?

Do the documents suggest the U.S. might have entered the Second World War even if Japan had not attacked? Explain.

Memorandum on National Strategic Decisions, May 22, 1940 —

Further imminently probable complications of today's situation are:

    a. Nazi-inspired revolution in Brazil.

    b. Widespread disorders with attacks on U.S. citizens in Mexico and raids along our southern border.

    c. Japanese hostilities against the United States in the Far East.

    d. Decisive Allied defeat, followed by German aggression in the Western Hemisphere.

    e. All combined.

We have vital interests in three general areas: a. The Far East. b. South America. c. Europe.

SOURCES: Memorandum, "National Strategic Decisions," 22 May 1940, WPD 4175-7; and Memorandum from G. C. Marshall, Chief of Staff, 23 May 1940, WPD 4175-10, National Archives.

There should be an immediate decision as to what major military operations we must be prepared to conduct.

It is not practicable to send forces to the Far East, to Europe, and to South America all at once, nor can we do so to a combination of any two of these areas without dangerous dispersion of force.

We cannot conduct major operations either in the Far East or in Europe due both to lack of means at present and because of the resultant abandonment of the United States interest in the area to which we do not send forces.

It would appear that conditions now developing limit us for at least a year, more or less, to the conduct of offensive-defensive operations in defense of the Western Hemisphere and of our own vital interests; such limited offensive operations in Mexico as the situation may require; possible protective occupation of European possessions in the Western Hemisphere; and the defense of Continental United States and its overseas possessions East of the 180th Meridian.

This appears to be the maximum effort of which we are capable today.

Intelligent, practical planning and later successful action, require an early decision regarding these matters:

1st-as to what we are *not* going to do.
2nd-as to what we *must prepare* to do.

Note for the Record 23 May 1940. Mr. Welles read this memo in Gen. Marshall's presence this day and expressed his complete agreement with every word of it. MBR

George C. Marshall, May 23, 1940 —

In a discussion with the President yesterday afternoon, and with Mr. Sumner Welles this morning, the memorandum prepared yesterday on the subject 'National Strategic Decisions', I found the President in general agreement, also Admiral Stark, and specifically Mr. Welles. They [all felt that we must not concern ourselves beyond the 180 meridian, and that we must concentrate on the South American situation.] All were in comparative agreement with the proposal which I make to have cruisers, with marines aboard, in certain South American ports on the East Coast, to be available to support the existing governments in the event of an attempted Nazi overthrow. . . .

3.7 Appeasing Japan

After the fall of France in 1940, Japanese forces moved into northern Indochina, an area previously controlled by the French. Although the United States government was extremely disturbed by this event, and by the war Japan had been waging for years against China, it continued to allow shipments of several kinds of strategic materials to Japan. On July 21 Japan signed an agreement with the government of occupied France allowing Japanese forces to use air and naval bases in southern Indochina. Japan could then threaten vital shipping routes and parts of the British and Dutch empires, as well as American positions in the Philippines. On the 24th Japanese troops occupied southern Indochina. The next day, the White House issued a radio bulletin (see Document below) in which President Roosevelt explained why his administration had allowed war materials such as oil to be sent to Japan while Americans were being compelled to limit their consumption of gasoline.

On July 26, Roosevelt froze Japanese assets in the United States, closed all United States ports to Japanese vessels, and embargoed the sale of American oil products to Japan. Great Britain and the Netherlands government-in-exile followed suit.

Questions

Considering what Roosevelt said on July 25, what do you think he expected Japan to do?

Does his explanation of why the U.S. hadn't cut off Japan's oil supply earlier seem plausible?

Why did Roosevelt feel it was necessary to prevent a war in the South Pacific? Do you believe he was right? How did U.S. policy in the South Pacific affect Europe?

. . . Now the answer is a very simple one. There is a world war going on, and has been for some time—nearly two years. One of our efforts, from the very beginning, was to prevent the spread of that world war in certain areas where it hadn't started. One of those areas is a place called the Pacific Ocean—one of the largest areas of the earth. There happened to be a place in the South Pacific where we had to get a lot of things—rubber—tin—and so forth and so on—down in the Dutch East Indies, the Straits Settlements, and Indochina. And we had to help get the Australian surplus of meat and wheat, and corn, for England.

It was very essential from our own selfish point of view of defense to prevent a war from starting in the South Pacific. So our foreign policy was—trying to stop a war from breaking out down there. At the same time, from the point of view of even France at that time—of course France still had her head above water—we wanted to keep that line of supplies from Australia and New Zealand going to the Near East—all their troops, all their supplies that they have maintained in Syria, North Africa and Palestine. So it was essential for Great Britain that we try to keep the peace down there in the South Pacific.

All right. And now here is a nation called Japan. Whether they had at that time aggressive purposes to enlarge their empire southward, they didn't have any oil of their own up in the north. Now if we cut the oil off, they probably would have gone down to the Dutch East Indies a year ago, and you would have had war.

3.8   War Warnings, 1941

Some historians, and Franklin Roosevelt's critics, have argued that the administration knew the Pearl Harbor attack was coming and purposely placed American warships there as a lure to induce the Japanese to attack American soil, thereby forcing the United States into war with the Axis. Other scholars contend that this is hindsight reasoning that selects out bits of information indicating where and when the Japanese were going to attack, while ignoring contrary information. Another theory claims that Roosevelt knew he was risking war, and felt it was necessary to take the risk, but was himself surprised when the Japanese audaciously attacked the American Pacific fleet.

It is now clear that conditions verged on war in November, 1941. American cryptographers had broken the Japanese diplomatic code, allowing American officials to know what the government in Tokyo was telling its emissaries in Washington. United States officials knew on November 22, 1941 that the Japanese intended to take some drastic steps if its conflicts with the U.S., Britain and the Netherlands were not resolved within a week. The action, it later turned out, consisted of Japanese attacks on British and Dutch possessions and on American planes, warships and military installations in the Philippines and Hawaii. The Chief of Naval Operations warned his commanders on November 24th, including the commander at Pearl Harbor, that the chances of a favorable settlement with Japan were doubtful and that a "surprise aggressive movement in any direction including attack on Philippines or Guam" was possible.

On the 27th, Chief of Staff George C. Marshall sent a telegram to the Army Commander in Hawaii. It included the information reprinted below.

Questions

In light of General Marshall's message, was the Japanese assault on Pearl Harbor on December 7, 1941, an "unprovoked" attack, as Roosevelt told the nation the following day?

If you were the President and had received Marshall's telegram, what would you have done?

Negotiations with Japan appear to be terminated to all practical purposes with only the barest possibilities that the Japanese Government might come back and offer to continue Period Japanese future action unpredictable but hostile action possible at any moment Period If hostilities cannot comma repeat cannot comma be avoided the United States desires that Japan commit the first overt act Period. . . .

3.9 Dropping the Atomic Bombs

The decision by President Harry S. Truman to drop atomic bombs on Japan in August 1945 was one of the most momentous decisions made by any leader in modern times. The two bombs obliterated the Japanese cities of Hiroshima and Nagasaki, killing hundreds of thousands of people. It also sparked an international debate about military strategy, diplomacy and public morality that reverberates to this day.

Truman defended his decision to use the bombs as a means of saving American lives and shortening the war. But several arguments have been raised in refutation. One is that Japan was militarily so near total collapse that extreme measures need not have been taken. General Eisenhower was among those who counselled against using the bomb for this reason. Another asserts that the bomb was used to impress the Soviets with U.S. strength on the eve of their coming into the war in the Pacific. The danger was that they might otherwise attempt to dictate terms against Japan at the war's end. Still another argument claims that the use of such a horrible weapon on innocent civilians placed us morally in the same camp as our military enemies, Germany and Japan. Critics add that the bomb could have been used in a demonstration drop on an unoccupied part of Japan before being unleashed over densely occupied cities.

Henry L. Stimson (1867–1950), Secretary of War for five years under Presidents Roosevelt and Truman, was the civilian official most intimately concerned with developing the bomb since 1941. In the selection that follows, Stimson presents a memorandum that he showed Truman when the new chief executive took office, and offers further commentary justifying the decision to use the bomb.

Questions

Stimson refers to "my chief purpose" in recommending use of the weapon. What might have been his other purposes, such as sending a message to Russia about American strength?

In your opinion, should the bomb have been used at all? Would it have been desirable to make a demonstration of the bomb on unoccupied territory, before using it on urban targets?

In your opinion, was the decision to drop the bombs on Japanese cities justifiable? Defend your answer. Can you think of arguments not mentioned in the article?

Since the U.S. shared the atomic secret with Great Britain, should it also have shared it with the Soviets, who were also our wartime allies? If the U.S. had not used the atom bomb on Japanese cities, how might it have affected Soviet policy toward us during the Cold War?

If Japan was as weak as Stimson said it was, why didn't the U.S. simply tighten the naval blockade and let it wither on the vine, instead of invading it or destroying its cities from the air?

On March 15, 1945, I had my last talk with President Roosevelt. . . .

I did not see Franklin Roosevelt again. The next time I went to the White House to discuss atomic energy was April 25, 1945, and I went to explain the nature of the problem to a man whose only previous knowledge of our activities was that of a Senator who had loyally accepted our assurance that the matter must be kept a secret from him. . . .

I discussed with him the whole history of the project. . . . I also discussed with President Truman the broader aspects of the subject, and the memorandum which I used in this discussion is again a fair sample of the state of our thinking at the time.

Memorandum Discussed with President Truman
April 25, 1945

1. *Within four months we shall in all probability have completed the most terrible weapon ever known in human history, one bomb of which could destroy a whole city.*

2. *Although we have shared its development with the U.K., physically the U.S. is at present in the position of controlling the re-*

Source: From Henry L. Stimson, "The Decision to Use the Atomic Bomb," appeared in *Harper's Magazine* (February, 1947), pp. 97–107, and later in a book by Stimson and McGeorge Bundy, *On Active Service in Peace & War*, copyright 1947 by Henry L. Stimson. [Reprinted by permission of Harper & Row, Publishers, and Hutchinson Publishing Group, Ltd., British publishers. Footnotes omitted.]

sources with which to construct and use it and no other nation could reach this position for some years. . . .

b. Although its construction under present methods requires great scientific and industrial effort and raw materials, which are temporarily mainly within the possession and knowledge of U.S. and U.K., it is extremely probable that much easier and cheaper methods of production will be discovered by scientists in the future. . . .

5. *The world in its present state of moral advancement compared with its technical development would be eventually at the mercy of such a weapon. In other words, modern civilization might be completely destroyed.*

6. *. . . Both inside any particular country and between the nations of the world, the control of this weapon will undoubtedly be a matter of the greatest difficulty and would involve such thoroughgoing rights of inspection and internal controls as we have never heretofore contemplated.*

7. *Furthermore. . . . our leadership in the war and in the development of this weapon has placed a certain moral responsibility upon us which we cannot shirk without very serious responsibility for any disaster to civilization which it would further.*

8. *On the other hand, if the problem of the proper use of this weapon can be solved, we would have the opportunity to bring the world into a pattern in which the peace of the world and our civilization can be saved.*

9. *As stated in General Groves' report, steps under way looking towards the establishment of*

a select committee of particular qualifications for recommending action to the executive and legislative branches of our government when secrecy is no longer in full effect. The committee would also recommend the actions to be taken by the War Department prior to that time in anticipation of the postwar problems. All recommendations would of course be first submitted to the President.

The next step in our preparations was the appointment of the committee referred to in paragraph (9) above. This committee, which was known as the Interim Committee, was charged with the function of advising the President on the various questions raised by our apparently imminent success in developing an atomic weapon. . . .

The discussions of the committee ranged over the whole field of atomic energy, in its political, military, and scientific aspects. . . . The committee's work included the drafting of the statements which were published immediately after the first bombs were dropped, the drafting of a bill for the domestic control of atomic energy, and recommendations looking toward the international control of atomic energy. The Interim Committee was assisted in its work by a Scientific Panel whose members were the following: Dr. A. H. Compton, Dr. Enrico Fermi, Dr. E. O. Lawrence, and Dr. J. R. Oppenheimer. All four were nuclear physicists of the first rank; all four had held positions of great importance in the atomic project from its inception. At a meeting with the Interim Committee and the Scientific Panel on May 31, 1945, I urged all those present to feel free to express themselves on any phase of the subject, scientific or political. Both General Marshall and I at this meeting expressed the view that atomic energy could not be considered simply in terms of military weapons but must also be considered in terms of a new relationship of man to the universe.

On June 1, after its discussions with the Scientific Panel, the Interim Committee unanimously adopted the following recommendations:

1. The bomb should be used against Japan as soon as possible.
2. It should be used on a dual target—that is, a military installation or war plant surrounded by or adjacent to houses and other buildings most susceptible to damage, and
3. It should be used without prior warning [of the nature of the weapon]. One member of the committee, Mr. Bard, later changed his view and dissented from recommendation.

In reaching these conclusions the Interim Committee carefully considered such alternatives as a detailed advance warning or a demonstration in some uninhabited area. Both of these suggestions were discarded as impractical. They were not regarded as likely to be effective in compelling a surrender of Japan, and both of them involved serious risks. Even the New Mexico test would not give final proof that any given bomb was certain to explode when dropped from an airplane. . . . Furthermore, we had no bombs to waste. It was vital that a sufficient effect be quickly obtained with the few we had. . . .

. . . The ultimate responsibility for the recommendation to the President rested upon me, and I have no desire to veil it. The conclusions of the committee were similar to my own, although I reached mine independently. . . .

The facts upon which my reasoning was based and steps were taken to carry it out now follow.

U.S. Policy Toward Japan in July 1945

The principle political, social, and military objective of the United States in the summer of 1945 was the prompt and complete surrender of Japan. . . .

Japan, in July 1945, had been seriously weakened by our increasingly violent attacks. It was known to us that she had gone so far as to make tentative proposals to the Soviet government, hoping to use the Russians as mediators in a negotiated peace. . . . If she should persist in her fight to the end, she had still a great military force.

In the middle of July 1945, the intelligence section of the War Department General Staff estimated Japanese military strength. . . . The total strength of the Japanese Army was estimated at about 5,000,000 men. These estimates later proved to be in very close agreement with official Japanese figures.

The Japanese Army was in much better condition than the Japanese Navy and Air Force. . . . As we understood it in July, there was a very strong possibility that the Japanese government might determine upon resistance to the end, in all the areas of the Far East under its control. In such an event the Allies would be faced with the enormous task of destroying an armed force of five million men and five thousand suicide aircraft, belonging to a race which had already amply demonstrated its ability to fight literally to the death.

The strategic plans of our armed forces for the defeat of Japan, as they stood in July, had been prepared without reliance upon the atomic bomb, which had not yet been tested in New Mexico. We were planning an intensified sea and air blockade. . . . followed in turn by an invasion of the main island on Honshu in the spring of 1946. The total U.S. military and naval force involved in this grand design was of the order of 5,000,000 men; if all those indirectly concerned are included, it was larger still. . . .

. . . I was informed that such operations might be expected to cost over a million casualties, to American forces alone. Additional large losses might be expected among our allies, and, of course, if our campaign were successful and if we could judge by previous experience, enemy casualties would be much larger than our own. . . .

. . . I wrote a memorandum for the President, on July 2, which I believe fairly represents the thinking of the American government as it finally took shape in action. This memorandum was prepared after discussion and general agreement with Joseph C. Grew, Acting Secretary of State, and Secretary of the Navy Forrestal, and when I discussed it with the President, he expressed his general approval.

Memorandum for the President
July 2, 1945

Proposed Program for Japan

1. The plans of operation up to and including the first landing have been authorized and the preparations for the operation are now actually going on. . . .

2. There is reason to believe that the operation for the occupation of Japan following the landing may be a very long, costly, and arduous struggle on our part. . . .

3. If we once land on one of the main islands and begin a forceful occupation of Japan, we shall probably have cast the die of last ditch resistance. The Japanese are highly patriotic and certainly susceptible to calls for fanatical resistance to repel an invasion. Once started in actual invasion, we shall in my opinion have to go through with an even more bitter finish fight than in Germany. . . .

4. A question then comes: Is there any alternative to such a forceful occupation of Japan which will secure for us the equivalent of an unconditional surrender of her forces and a permanent destruction of her power again to strike an aggressive blow at the "peace of the Pacific"? I am inclined to think that there is enough such chance to make it well worthwhile our giving them a warning of what is to come and a definite opportunity to capitulate. . . .

We have the following enormously favorable factors on our side—factors much weightier than those we had against Germany:

Japan has no allies.

Her navy is nearly destroyed and she is vulnerable to a surface and underwater blockade which can deprive her of sufficient food and supplies for her population.

She is terribly vulnerable to our concentrated air attack. . . .

She has against her not only the Anglo-American forces but the rising forces of China and the ominous threat of Russia.

We have inexhaustible and untouched industrial resources. . . .

We have great moral superiority through being the victim of her first sneak attack.

. . . I believe Japan is susceptible to reason in such a crisis. . . . She has within the past century shown herself to possess extremely intelligent people, capable in an unprecedentedly short time of adopting not only the complicated technique of Occidental civilization but to a substantial extent their culture and their political and social ideas. Her advance in all these respects during the short period of sixty or seventy years has been one of the most astounding feats of national progress in history—a leap from the isolated feudalism of centuries into the position of one of the six or seven great powers of the world. . . .

My own opinion is in her favor on the two points involved in this question:

a. I think the Japanese nation has the mental intelligence and versatile capacity in such a crisis to recognize the folly of a fight to the finish and

to accept the proffer of what will amount to an unconditional surrender; and

b. I think she has within her population enough liberal leaders (although now submerged by the terrorists) to be depended upon for her reconstruction as a responsible member of the family of nations. I think she is better in this respect than Germany was. . . .

On the other hand, I think that the attempt to exterminate her armies and her population by gunfire or other means will tend to produce a fusion of race solidity and antipathy which has no analogy in the case of Germany. We have a national interest in creating, if possible, a condition wherein the Japanese nation may live as a peaceful and useful member of the future Pacific community.

5. It is therefore my conclusion that a carefully timed warning be given to Japan by the chief representatives of the United States, Great Britain, China, and, if then a belligerent, Russia by calling upon Japan to surrender and permit the occupation of her country in order to insure its complete demilitarization for the sake of the future peace.

This warning should contain the following elements:

The varied and overwhelming character of the force we are about to bring to bear on the islands.

The inevitability and completeness of the destruction which the full application of this force will entail.

The determination of the Allies to destroy permanently all authority and influence of those who have deceived and misled the country into embarking on world conquest.

The determination of the Allies to limit Japanese sovereignty to her main islands and to render them powerless to mount and support another war.

The disavowal of any attempt to extirpate the Japanese as a race or to destroy them as a nation.

A statement of our readiness, once her economy is purged of its militaristic influence, to permit the Japanese to maintain such industries, particularly of a light consumer character, as offer no threat of aggression against their neighbors, but which can produce a sustaining economy, and. . . . in accordance with our now established foreign trade policy, in due course to enter into mutually advantageous trade relations with her.

The withdrawal from their country as soon as the above objectives of the Allies are accomplished, and. . . . we should add that we do not exclude a constitutional monarchy under her present dynasty, it would substantially add to the chances of acceptance.

6. Success of course will depend on the potency of the warning which we give her. . . . For that reason the warning must be tendered before the actual invasion has occurred and while the impending destruction, though clear beyond peradventure, has not yet reduced her to fanatical despair. If Russia is a part of the threat, the Russian attack, if actual, must not have progressed too far. Our own bombing should be confined to military objectives as far as possible.

It is important to emphasize the double character of the suggested warning. It was designed to promise destruction if Japan resisted, and hope, if she surrendered.

It will be noted that the atomic bomb is not mentioned in this memorandum. On grounds of secrecy the bomb was never mentioned except when absolutely necessary, and furthermore, it had not yet been tested. It was of course well forward in our minds, as the memorandum was written and discussed, that the bomb would be the best possible sanction if our warning were rejected. . . .

My chief purpose was to end the war in victory with the least possible cost in the lives of the men in the armies which I had helped to raise. In the light of the alternatives which, on a fair estimate, were open to us believe that no man, in our position and subject to our responsibilities, holding in his hands a weapon of such possibilities for accomplishing this purpose and saving those lives, could have failed to use it and afterwards looked his countrymen in the face.

As I read over what I have written, I am aware that much of it, in this year of peace, may have a harsh and unfeeling sound. . . . The face of war is the face of death; death is an inevitable part of every order that a wartime leader gives. The decision to use the atomic bomb was a decision that brought death to over a hundred thousand Japanese. No explanation can change that fact and I do not wish to gloss it over. But this deliberate, premeditated destruction was our least abhorrent choice. . . .

In the last great action of the Second World War we were given final proof that war is death. War in the twentieth century has grown steadily more barbarous, more destructive, more debased in all its aspects. Now, with the release of atomic energy, man's ability to destroy himself is very nearly complete. The bombs dropped on Hiroshima and Nagasaki ended a war. They also made it wholly clear that we must never have another war. This is the lesson men and leaders everywhere must learn, and I believe that when they learn it they will find a way to lasting peace. There is no other choice.

3.10 Cold War and Containment

The long-simmering hostility between the United States and the Soviet Union, partially submerged while they were Allies fighting the Axis, turned into the Cold War after 1945. As the Soviet Union occupied or took indirect control of countries on its border, the American government feared that the Russians wanted to subvert capitalist countries, break up American power, and perhaps spread revolution to the United States. Some Americans wanted to respond by rolling the Soviet Union back to its prewar borders. Another group, including George Kennan of the State Department, who had served in Moscow during World War II, proposed to contain Soviet expansion. Kennan's views, which first appeared anonymously in a 1947 article, "The Sources of Soviet Conduct," eventually became the basis for American policy.

Questions

Does Kennan consider the Russians trustworthy? What does he see as the causes of Soviet hostility toward capitalism? Does he believe that a Soviet attack on the U.S. is imminent? What are Kennan's proposals for stopping the spread of communism? Are there any parallels between what the Soviets wanted to do to the United States and what Kennan wanted to do to the Soviet Union?

In view of what has happened since 1947, and considering that the United States was then the only country with the atomic bomb, would it have been better for America to have gone to war with the U.S.S.R. at that time, or at least to have threatened an atomic war if the Russians did not give up Eastern Europe?

What is the current status of the Cold War?

. . . [We] are going to continue for a long time to find the Russians difficult to deal with. [This] does not mean that they should be considered as embarked upon a do-or-die program to overthrow our society by a given date. The theory of the inevitability of the eventual fall of capitalism has the fortunate connotation that there is no hurry

about it. The forces of progress can take their time in preparing the final *coup de grâce*. Meanwhile, what is vital is that the "Socialist fatherland"—that oasis of power which has been already won for Socialism in the person of the Soviet Union—should be cherished and defended by all good Communists at home and abroad, its fortunes promoted, its enemies badgered and confounded. The promotion of premature, "adventuristic" revolutionary projects

SOURCE: [George Kennan], "The Sources of Soviet Conduct," *Foreign Affairs* (July, 1947).

abroad which might embarrass Soviet power in any way would be an inexcusable, even a counter-revolutionary act. The cause of Socialism is the support and promotion of Soviet power, as defined in Moscow.

This brings us to the second of the concepts important to contemporary Soviet outlook. That is the infallibility of the Kremlin. The Soviet concept of power, which permits no focal points of organization outside the Party itself, requires that the Party leadership remain in theory the sole repository of truth. For if truth were to be found elsewhere, there would be justification for its expression in organized activity. But it is precisely that which the Kremlin cannot and will not permit.

The leadership of the Communist Party is therefore always right, and has been always right ever since in 1929 Stalin formalized his personal power by announcing the decisions of the Politburo were being taken unanimously.

On the principle of infallibility there rests the iron discipline of the Communist Party. In fact, the two concepts are mutually self-supporting. Perfect discipline requires recognition of infallibility. Infallibility requires the observance of discipline. And the two together go far to determine the behaviorism of the entire Soviet apparatus of power. But their effect cannot be understood unless a third factor be taken into account: namely, the fact that the leadership is at liberty to put forward for tactical purposes any particular thesis which it finds useful to the cause at any particular moment and to require the faithful and unquestioning acceptance of that thesis by the members of the movement as a whole. This means that truth is not a constant but is actually created, for all intents and purposes, by the Soviet leaders themselves. It may vary from week

to week, from month to month. It is nothing absolute and immutable—nothing which flows from objective reality. It is only the most recent manifestation of the wisdom of those in whom the ultimate wisdom is supposed to reside, because they represent the logic of history. The accumulative effect of these factors is to give to the whole subordinate apparatus of Soviet power an unshakable stubbornness and steadfastness in its orientation. This orientation can be changed at will by the Kremlin but by no other power. Once a given party line has been laid down on a given issue of current policy, the whole Soviet governmental machine, including the mechanism of diplomacy, moves inexorably along the prescribed path, like a persistent toy automobile wound up and headed in a given direction, stopping only when it meets with some unanswerable force. The individuals who are the components of this machine are unamenable to argument or reason which comes to them from outside sources. Their whole training has taught them to mistrust and discount the glib persuasiveness of the outside world. Like the white dog before the phonograph, they hear only the "master's voice." And if they are to be called off from the purposes last dictated to them, it is the master who must call them off. Thus the foreign representative cannot hope that his words will make any impression on them. The most that he can hope is that they will be transmitted to those at the top, who are capable of changing the party line. But even those are not likely to be swayed by any normal logic in the words of the bourgeois representative. Since there can be no appeal to common purposes, there can be no appeal to common mental approaches. For this reason, facts speak louder than words to the ears of the Kremlin; and words carry the greatest weight when they have the ring of reflecting, or being backed up by, facts of unchallengeable validity.

But we have seen that the Kremlin is under no ideological compulsion to accomplish its purposes in a hurry. . . . these precepts are fortified by the lessons of Russian history: of centuries of obscure battles between nomadic forces over the stretches of a vast unfortified plain. Here caution, circumspection, flexibility and deception are the valuable qualities; and their value finds natural appreciation in the Russian or the oriental mind. Thus the Kremlin has no compunction about retreating in the face of superior force. And being under the compulsion of no timetable, it does not get panicky under the necessity for such retreat. . . . if it finds unassailable barriers in its path, it accepts these philosophically and accommodates itself to them. The main thing is that there should always be pressure, unceasing constant pressure, toward the desire goal. There is no trace of any feeling in Soviet psychology that that goal must be reached at any given time.

These considerations make Soviet diplomacy at once easier and more difficult to deal with than the diplomacy of individual aggressive leaders like Napoleon and Hitler. On the one hand it is more sensitive to contrary force, more ready to yield on individual sectors of the diplomatic front when that force is felt to be too strong, and thus more rational in the logic and rhetoric of power. On the other hand it cannot be easily defeated or discouraged by a single victory on the part of its opponents. And the patient persistence by which it is animated means that it can be effectively countered not by sporadic acts which represent the momentary whims of democratic opinion but only by intelligent long-range policies on the part of Russia's adversaries—policies no less steady in their

purpose, and no less variegated and resourceful in their application, than those of the Soviet Union itself.

In these circumstances it is clear that the main element of any United States policy toward the Soviet Union must be that of a long-term, patient but firm and vigilant containment of Russian expansive tendencies. It is important to note, however, that such a policy has nothing to do with outward histrionics: with threats or blustering or superfluous gestures of outward "toughness." While the Kremlin is basically flexible in its reaction to political realities, it is by no means unamenable to considerations of prestige. Like almost any other government, it can be placed by tactless and threatening gestures in a position where it cannot afford to yield even though this might be dictated by its sense of realism. The Russian leaders are keen judges of human psychology, and as such they are highly conscious that loss of temper and of self-control is never a source of strength in political affairs. They are quick to exploit such evidences of weakness. For these reasons, it is a *sine qua non* of successful dealing with Russia that the foreign government in question should remain at all times cool and collected and that its demands on Russian policy should be put forward in such a manner as to leave the way open for a compliance not too detrimental to Russian prestige.

III

In the light of the above, it will be clearly seen that the Soviet pressure against the free institutions of the western world is something that can be contained by the adroit and vigilant application of counterforce at a series of constantly shifting geographical and political points, corresponding to the shifts and manoeuvres of Soviet policy, but which cannot be charmed or talked out of existence. . . .

. . . [T]he future of Soviet power may not be by any means as secure as Russian capacity for self-delusion would make it appear to the men in the Kremlin. That they can keep power themselves, they have demonstrated. That they can quietly and easily turn it over to others remains to be proved. Meanwhile, the hardships of their rule and the vicissitudes of international life have taken a heavy tool of the strength and hopes of the great people on whom their power rests. It is curious to note that the ideological power of Soviet authority is strongest today in areas beyond the frontiers of Russia, beyond the reach of its police power. . . . And who can say with assurance that the strong light still cast by the Kremlin on the dissatisfied peoples of the western world is not the powerful afterglow of a constellation which is in actuality on the wane? This cannot be proved. And it cannot be disproved. But the possibility remains (and in the opinion of this writer it is a strong one) that Soviet power, like the capitalist world of its conception, bears within it the seeds of its own decay, and that the sprouting of these seeds is well advanced.

IV

It is clear that the United States cannot expect in the foreseeable future to enjoy political intimacy with the Soviet regime. It must continue to regard the Soviet Union as a rival, not a partner, in the political arena. It must continue to expect that Soviet policies will reflect no abstract love of peace and stability, no real faith in the possibility of a permanent happy coexistence of the Socialist and capitalist worlds, but

rather a cautious, persistent pressure toward the disruption and weakening of all rival influence and rival power.

Balanced against this are the facts that Russia, as opposed to the western world in general, is still by far the weaker party, that Soviet policy is highly flexible, and that Soviet society may well contain deficiencies which will eventually weaken its own total potential. This would of itself warrant the United States entering with reasonable confidence upon a policy of firm containment, designed to confront the Russians with unalterable counter-force at every point where they show signs of encroaching upon the interests of a peaceful and stable world.

But in actuality the possibilities for American policy are by no means limited to holding the line and hoping for the best. It is entirely possible for the United States to influence by its actions the internal developments, both within Russia and throughout the international Communist movement, by which Russian policy is largely determined. This is not only a question of the modest measure of informational activity which this government can conduct in the Soviet Union and elsewhere, although that, too, is important. It is rather a question of the degree to which the United States can create among the peoples of the world generally the impression of a country which knows what it wants, which is coping successfully with the problems of its internal life and with the responsibilities of a World Power, and which has a spiritual vitality capable of holding its own among the major ideological currents of the time. To the extent that such an impression can be created and maintained, the aims of Russian Communism must appear sterile and quixotic, the hopes and enthusiasm of Moscow's supporters must wane, and added strain must be imposed on the Kremlin's foreign policies. For the palsied decrepitude of the capitalist world is the keystone of Communist philosophy. Even the failure of the United States to experience the early economic depression which the ravens of the Red Square have been predicting with such complacent confidence since hostilities ceased would have deep and important repercussions throughout the Communist world. . . .

It would be an exaggeration to say that American behavior unassisted and alone could exercise a power of life and death over the Communist movement and bring about the early fall of Soviet power in Russia. But the United States has it in its power to increase enormously the strains under which Soviet policy must operate, to force upon the Kremlin a far greater degree of moderation and circumspection than it

has had to observe in recent years, and in this way to promote tendencies which must eventually find their outlet in either the break-up or the gradual mellowing of Soviet power. For no mystical, Messianic movement—and particularly not that of the Kremlin—can face frustration indefinitely without eventually adjusting itself in one way or another to the logic of that state of affairs.

Thus the decision will really fall in large measure in this country itself. The issue of Soviet-American relations is in essence a test of the overall worth of the United States as a nation among nations. To avoid destruction the United States need only measure up to its own best traditions and prove itself worthy of preservation as a great nation.

Surely, there was never a fairer test of national quality than this.

3.11   Investigating Loyalty

The Cold War generated tremendous fear and anxiety inside the United States. Not only did Americans fear Soviet activities overseas, but they also believed that the Russians were using the American Communist Party to subvert the nation internally.

The American government fostered these fears for three major reasons. First, it was necessary to persuade the public that their former friendly ally in the struggle against Nazi Germany was now a dangerous enemy. Second, the Republican Party recognized that one way to score gains against the Democrats, dominant in national politics since 1932, was to charge that they were soft on Communism. This forced the Democrats to prove that they did not tolerate Communists and were running an administration free of subversives. One way of achieving this was to initiate loyalty investigations of government employees. Third, demagogues such as Senator Joseph R. McCarthy of Wisconsin realized that they could attain enormous publicity and power by attributing Communist successes overseas to an internal conspiracy led by some of the country's most prominent citizens.

Two documents follow that indicate how the loyalty program worked. The first is an excerpt from President Truman's loyalty order of March 1947. The second is an excerpt from a government loyalty hearing. A State Department employee was discharged for security reasons and asked for the reasons so that he could defend himself. The Loyalty Board representative replied as indicated. The document demonstrates the type of questions asked and suggests the sort of behavior that was considered suspect.

Questions

As you read the following documents, consider how you might have defended yourself in a loyalty investigation. What were the probable reasons for the questions that were asked, and how would you have responded? There were severe penalties for answering falsely or refusing to reply, including loss of a job and, in some cases, fines and imprisonment. What do you think your response might have been if a friend or neighbor were charged with disloyalty?

What does it mean to be loyal, and what does it mean to be disloyal? How should the U.S. have dealt with foreign agents operating within its government?

Truman's Loyalty Order of March 1947 —

There shall be a loyalty investigation of every person entering the civilian employment of any department or agency of the Executive Branch of the Federal Government. . . .

An officer or employee who is charged with being disloyal shall have a right to an administrative hearing before a loyalty board in the employing department or agency. He may appear before such board personally, accompanied by counsel or representative of his own choosing, and present evidence on his own behalf, through witnesses or by affidavit. . . .

The officer or employee shall be served with a written notice of such hearing in sufficient time, and shall be informed therein for the nature of the charges against

him in sufficient detail, so that he will be enabled to prepare his defense. The charges shall be stated as specifically and completely as, in the discretion of the employing department or agency, security considerations permit, . . .

[T]he investigative agency may refuse to disclose the names of confidential informants. . . .

Loyalty Hearing Transcripts —

Board Member: Well, we realize the difficulty you are in. . . . on the other hand, I'd suggest that you might think back over your own career and perhaps in your own mind delve into some of the factors that have gone into your career which you think might have been subject to question and see what they are and see whether you'd like to explain or make any statement with regard to any of them. . . .

Board Member: Did you ever act as an organizer for the Communist Party or attempt to recruit others?

Employee: No.

Board Member: [It] has been corroborated, checked and verified.

Employee's Attorney: By whom?

Board Member: I can't tell you. . . . We don't even know who the accuser is. . . .

Board Member: Did you ever hear any political discussions at [blank]'s home? . . .

Board Member: Are your friends and associates intelligent, clever? . . .

Board Member: Have you ever had Negroes in your home? . . .

Board Member: There is a suspicion in the record that you are in sympathy with the underprivileged. Is this true?

Board Member: When did you become a member of the Communist Party? . . .

Employee: I never became a member of the Communist Party. . . .

Board Member: If you are, as you say, a loyal American, why do you persist in denying that you were a member of the Communist Party? . . .

3.12 The American Presence in Vietnam

From the 1950s through the 1970s, the United States stationed troops in Southeast Asia to oppose armed revolution by Communist-led forces in Laos, Cambodia, and particularly northern Vietnam. By the late 1960s, over half a million American GIs were fighting in Indochina. This huge military presence occasioned a bitter public debate about our reasons for being in Vietnam. Were we there for strategic, diplomatic, economic or other reasons? The debate reached a critical level in 1971 with the release of the "Pentagon Papers," secret documents given to the press by Daniel Ellsberg, a government war planner who had become an opponent of U.S. involvement in Vietnam. The Pentagon Papers consisted of parts of a forty-three volume history of the Vietnam War prepared by the Defense Department. The report contained the four documents excerpted below.

The first item is from a 1954 study by the U.S. Joint Chiefs of Staff to President Eisenhower on possible U.S. military intervention in Indochina. In 1954, as the Vietminh were about to overcome the French Army, France asked the United States to intervene with troops and possible nuclear weapons. The United States had been supplying the French in Indochina for years. President Eisenhower submitted the problem to the Joint Chiefs of Staff who responded, in part as indicated.

The second item dates from 1961. At the 1954 Geneva Conference it was agreed to split Vietnam into two zones, North Vietnam, controlled by the Vietminh, and South Vietnam, controlled by a government friendly to France and the United States. The two sections were to be united through national elections in 1956. These elections never took place, partly because the United States and its South Vietnamese ally believed the winner would be Ho Chi Minh, the Communist leader of the Vietminh. Each side began to violate the Geneva agreement by sending military forces into the other's zone. The Vietminh supported revolutionary cells in South Vietnam under a local organization called the National Liberation Front and referred to by the Americans and South Vietnamese as the Vietcong. The South Vietnamese government had great difficulty stopping the growth of the Vietcong. In 1961 President Kennedy sent Secretary of State Dean Rusk and Secretary of Defense, Robert S. McNamara to investigate the problem. They returned with a report excerpted below.

The third item is a "Plan of Action for South Vietnam," September 3, 1964, attributed to Assistant Secretary of Defense John T. McNaughton. During the Kennedy Administration, and after Kennedy's assassination, during the administration of Lyndon B. Johnson, the United States tried to defeat the National Liberation Front by pacifying South Vietnam. Pacification, an old technique used to deal with peoples such as Native Americans and the inhabitants of Central American and Caribbean countries, blended force with rewards for cooperation. In Vietnam, the local government attempted to concentrate the civilian population in zones where they could be separated from the guerrillas. At the same time, American military and civilian workers tried to improve living conditions for the Vietnamese, reducing their incentive to join the Communist-led revolution. McNaughton describes what happened to the pacification program, evaluates the situation in South Vietnam, and proposes actions for the United States.

The fourth item, dated March 24, 1965, is another memo from McNaughton, giving the Defense Department's reason for America's presence in Vietnam. A few weeks before President Johnson ordered a large increase in the number of American troops fighting in Vietnam, ostensibly to help a friendly nation resist aggression from the north and to make sure America's word was respected in the world, McNaughton prepared another gloomy memorandum.

Questions

In the first document, if the Joint Chiefs were right, why did the United States fight the longest war in its history in Indochina?

In the second document Rusk and McNamara say that the loss of South Vietnam to Communism would destroy SEATO (the South East Asia Treaty Organization) and undermine the credibility of American commitments elsewhere. Where is "elsewhere"? Since Kennedy substantially increased the number of American military "advisors" in Vietnam, was the U.S. beginning to fight the Vietnam war to preserve its credibility?

In the third document, what does McNaughton mean by his references to "images," "scenario," and "audiences"? Why does he worry about keeping the sit-

uation under control? Look closely at the paragraph labeled "actions." Why does McNaughton want to provoke the North Vietnamese into giving the United States an excuse to escalate? Do you see any similarity between this document and the war warning issued by General Marshall before Japan attacked Pearl Harbor?

In the fourth document, do you accept McNaughton's reasons for America's military presence in Vietnam? Do you think they are justified? What do you believe were the most important reasons for the U.S. presence?

Joint Chiefs of Staff, 1954 —

The Joint Chiefs of Staff desire to point out their belief that, from the point of view of the United States, with reference to the Far East as a whole, *Indochina is devoid of decisive military objectives and the allocation of more than token* U.S. armed forces *in Indochina would be a serious diversion of* limited U.S. capability.

Dean Rusk and Robert S. McNamara, 1961 —

1. *United States National Interests in South Vietnam.*

The deteriorating situation in South Vietnam requires attention to the nature and scope of United States national interests in that country. The loss of South Vietnam to Communism would involve the transfer of a nation of 20 million people from the free world to the Communist bloc. The loss of South Vietnam would make

SOURCE: *The Pentagon Papers.*

pointless any further discussion about the importance of Southeast Asia to the free world; we would have to face the near certainty that the remainder of Southeast Asia and Indonesia would move to a complete accommodation with Communism, if not formal incorporation within the Communist bloc. The United States, as a member of SEATO, has commitments with respect to South Vietnam under the Protocol to the SEATO Treaty. Additionally, in a formal statement at the conclusion session of the 1954 Geneva Conference, the United States representative stated that the United States "would view any renewal of the aggression . . . with grave concern and as seriously threatening international peace and security."

The loss of South Vietnam to Communism would not only destroy SEATO but would undermine the credibility of American commitments elsewhere. Further, loss of South Vietnam would stimulate bitter domestic controversies in the United States and would be seized upon by extreme elements to divide the country and harass the Administration.

John T. McNaughton, September 3, 1964 — *

1. Analysis of the present situation. The situation in South Vietnam is deteriorating. Even before the government sank into confusion last week, the course of the war in South Vietnam had been downward, with Viet Cong incidents increasing in number and intensity and military actions become larger and more successful, and with less and less territory meaningfully under the control of the government. Successful ambushes had demonstrated an unwillingness of the population even in what were thought to be pacified areas to run the risk of informing on the Viet Cong. War weariness was apparent. The crisis of the end of August—especially since the competing forces have left the government largely "faceless" and have damaged the government's ability to manage the pacification program—promises to lead to further and more rapid deterioration. . . . The objective of the United States is to reverse the present downward trend. Failing that, the alternative objective is to emerge from the situation with as good an image as possible in US, allied and enemy eyes.

2. Inside South Vietnam. We must in any event keep hard at work inside South Vietnam. This means, inter alia, immediate action:

(a) to press the presently visible leaders to get a real government in operation;

(b) to prevent extensive personnel changes down the line;

(c) to see that lines of authority for carrying out the pacification program are clear.

New initiatives might include action:

(d) to establish a US Naval base, perhaps at Danang;

(e) to embark on a major effort to pacify one province adjacent to Saigon.

A separate analysis is being made of a proposal:

(f) to enlarge significantly the US military role in the pacification program inside South Vietnam—e.g., large numbers of US special forces, divisions of regular combat troops, US air, etc., to "interlard" with or to take over functions of geographical areas from the South Vietnamese armed forces. . . .

3. Outside the borders of South Vietnam. There is a chance that the downward trend can be reversed—or a new situation created offering new opportunities, or at least a convincing demonstration made of the great costs and risks incurred by a country which commits aggression against an ally of ours—if the following course of action is followed. The course of action is made up of actions outside the borders of South Vietnam designed to put increasing pressure on North Vietnam but designed also both to create as little risk as possible of the kind of military action which would be difficult to justify to the American public and to preserve where possible the option to have no US military action at all. . . .

Actions. The actions, in addition to present continuing "extra-territorial" actions (US U-2 recce of DRV, US jet recce of Laos, T-28 activity in Laos), would be by way of an orchestration of three classes of actions, all designed to meet these five desiderata—(1) from the US, GVN and hopefully allied points of view, they should be

*Explanation of abbreviations for the fourth document: recce = reconnaissance; U-2 = a high altitude reconnaissance plane; DRV = North Vietnam or North Vietnamese government; T-28 = a small aircraft; desiderata = what we desire to occur; GVN = South Vietnamese Government; escalate = raise the level of fighting.

legitimate things to do under the circumstances, (2) they should cause apprehension, ideally increasing apprehension, in the DRV, (3) they should be likely at some point to provoke a military DRV response, (4) the provoked response should be likely to provide good grounds for us to escalate if we wished, and (5) the timing and crescendo should be under our control, with the scenario capable of being turned off at any time. . . .

4. Actions of opportunity. While the above course of action is being pursued, we should watch for other DRV actions which would justify (words illegible). Among such DRV actions might be the following:

a. Downing of US recee or US rescue aircraft in Laos (likely by AA, unlikely by MIG).

b. MIG action in Laos or South Vietnam (unlikely).

c. Mining of Saigon Harbor (unlikely).

d. VC attacks on South Vietnamese POL storage, RR bridge, etc. (dramatic incident required).

e. VC attacks (e.g., by mortars) on, or take-over of, air fields on which US aircraft are deployed (likely).

f. Some barbaric act of terrorism which inflames US and world opinion (unlikely). . . .

6. Chances to resolve the situation. Throughout the scenario, we should be alert to chances to resolve the situation:

a. To back the DRV down, so South Vietnam can be pacified.

b. To evolve a tolerable settlement.

I. Explicit settlement (e.g., via a bargaining-from-strength conference, etc.).

II. Tacit settlement (e.g., via piecemeal live-and-let-live Vietnamese "settle-

ments," a de facto "writing off" of indefensible portions of SVN, etc.).

c. If worst comes and South Vietnam disintegrates or their behavior becomes abominable, to "disown" South Vietnam, hopefully leaving the image of "a patient who died despite the extraordinary efforts of a good doctor."

7. Special considerations during next two months. The relevant "audiences" of US actions are the Communists (who must feel strong pressures), the South Vietnamese (whose morale must be buoyed), our allies (who must trust us as "underwriters"), and the US public (which must support our risk-taking with US lives and prestige). During the next two months, because of the lack of "rebuttal time" before election to justify particular actions which may be distorted to the US public, we must act with special care—signalling to the DRV that initiatives are being taken, to the GVN that we are behaving energetically despite the restraints of our political season, and to the US public that we are behaving with good purpose and restraint.

John T. McNaughton, March 24, 1965 —

1. US aims:

70%—To avoid a humiliating US defeat (to our reputation as a guarantor).

20%—To keep SVN (and the adjacent) territory from Chinese hands.

10%—To permit the people of SVN to enjoy a better, freer way of life.

ALSO—To emerge from crisis without unacceptable taint from methods used.

NOT—To "help a friend," although it would be hard to stay in if asked out.

Chapter Four: Race

4.1 Black Codes

After slavery ended, Southern states were forced to develop new laws governing the civil status of newly freed blacks. They tended to update the "black codes" that had formerly regulated the conduct of free blacks under slavery. These laws closely controlled social and economic relations between the races. The Mississippi black code of 1865 (excerpted below) was fairly typical. In reviewing such codes, the Republican-dominated U.S. Congress concluded that the South was merely trying to reintroduce slavery through the back door.

Questions

What subjects does the Mississippi code cover? Why does it pay so much attention to wages, contracts and terms of labor? Look at III. Sec. 7 regarding vagrancy, and IV. Sec. 5 of the penal laws. What would happen to blacks who failed to pay fines or taxes?

Which of these laws would be most objectionable to black people? In what ways did these laws represent an improvement, for blacks, over their status under slavery? How would a white plantation owner defend them? Do these laws justify the decision of the Radical Republican majority in Congress to impose military rule on the South in March, 1867?

I. Civil Rights of Freedmen in Mississippi

Sec. 1. *Be it enacted, . . .* That all freedmen, free negroes, and mulattoes may sue and be sued, implead and be impleaded, in all the courts of law and equity of this State, and may acquire personal property, and choses in action, by descent or purchase, and may dispose of the same in the same manner and to the same extent that white persons may: *Provided,* That the provisions of this section shall not be so

SOURCE: *Laws of Mississippi,* 1865, pp. 86, 90, 165.

construed as to allow any freedman, free negro, or mulatto to rent or lease any lands or tenements except in incorporated cities or towns, in which places the corporate authorities shall control the same. . . .

Sec. 3. . . . All freedmen, free negroes, or mulattoes who do now and have herebefore lived and cohabited together as husband and wife shall be taken and held in law as legally married, and the issue shall be taken and held as legitimate for all purposes; that it shall not be lawful for any freedman, free negro, or mulatto to intermarry with any white person; nor for any white person to intermarry with any freedman, free negro, or mulatto; and any person who shall so intermarry, shall be deemed guilty of felony, and on conviction thereof shall be confined in the State penitentiary for life; and those shall be deemed freedmen, free negroes, and mulattoes who are of pure negro blood, and those descended from a negro to the third generation, inclusive, though one ancestor in each generation may have been a white person.

Sec. 4. . . . In addition to cases in which freedmen, free negroes, and mulattoes are now by law competent witnesses, freedmen, free negroes, or mulattoes shall be competent in civil cases, when a party or parties to the suit, either plaintiff or plaintiffs, defendant or defendants, and a white person or white persons, is or are the opposing party or parties, plaintiff or plaintiffs, defendant or defendants. They shall also be competent witnesses in all criminal prosecutions where the crime charged is alleged to have been committed by a white person upon or against the person or property of a freedman, free negro, or mulatto: *Provided,* that in all cases said witnesses shall be examined in open court, on the stand; except, however, they may be examined before the grand jury, and shall in all cases be subject to the rules and tests of the common law as to competency and credibility. . . .

Sec. 6. . . . All contracts for labor made with freedmen, free negroes, and mulattoes for a longer period than one month shall be in writing, and in duplicate, attested and read to said freedman, free negro, or mulatto by a beat, city or county officer, or two disinterested white persons of the county in which the labor is to be performed, of which each party shall have one; and said contracts shall be taken and held as entire contracts, and if the laborer shall quit the service of the employer before the expiration of his term of service, without good cause, he shall forfeit his wages for that year up to the time of quitting.

Sec. 7. . . . Every civil officer shall, and every person may, arrest and carry back to his or her legal employer any freedman, free negro, or mulatto who shall have quit the service of his or her employer before the expiration of his or her term of service without good cause; and said officer and person shall be entitled to receive for arresting and carrying back every deserting employe aforesaid the sum of five dollars, and ten cents per mile from the place of arrest to the place of delivery; and the same shall be paid by the employer, and held as a set-off for so much against the wages of said deserting employe: *Provided,* that said arrested party, after being so returned, may appeal to the justice of the peace or member of the board of police of the county, who, on notice to the alleged employer, shall try summarily whether said appellant is legally employed by the alleged employer, and has good cause to quit said employer; either party shall have the right of appeal to the county court, pending which the alleged deserter shall be remanded to the alleged employer or otherwise disposed of, as shall be right and just; and the decision of the county court shall be final. . . .

II. Mississippi Apprentice Law

Sec. 1. . . . It shall be the duty of all sheriffs, justices of the peace, and other civil officers of the several counties in this State, to report . . . all freedmen, free negroes, and mulattoes, under the age of eighteen, in their respective counties, beats or districts, who are orphans, or whose parent or parents have not the means or who refuse to provide for and support said minors; and thereupon it shall be the duty of said probate court to order the clerk of said court to apprentice said minors to some competent and suitable person, on such terms as the court may direct. . . .

Sec. 3. . . . In the management and control of said apprentice, said master or mistress shall have the power to inflict such moderate corporal chastisement as a father or guardian is allowed to inflict on his or her child or ward at common law: *Provided,* that in no case shall cruel or inhuman punishment be inflicted.

Sec. 4. . . . If any apprentice shall leave the employment of his or her master or mistress, without his or her consent, said master or mistress may pursue and recapture said apprentice, and bring him or her before any justice of the peace of the county, whose duty it shall be to remand said apprentice to the service of his or her master or mistress; and in the event of a refusal on the part of said apprentice so to return, then said justice shall commit said apprentice to the jail of said county, on failure to give bond, to the next term of the county court; . . . if the court shall believe that said apprentice had good cause to quit his said master or mistress, the court shall discharge said apprentice from said indenture, and also enter a judgment against the master or mistress for not more than one hundred dollars, for the use and benefit of said apprentice. . . .

III. Mississippi Vagrant Law

Sec. 2. . . . All freedmen, free negroes and mulattoes in this State, over the age of eighteen years, found on the second Monday in January, 1866, or thereafter, with no lawful employment or business, or found unlawfully assembling themselves together, either in the day or night time, and all white persons so assembling themselves with freedmen, free negroes or mulattoes, or usually associating with freedmen, free negroes or mulattoes, on terms of equality, or living in adultery or fornication with a freed woman, free negro or mulatto, shall be deemed vagrants, and on conviction thereof shall be fined in a sum not exceeding, in the case of a freedman, free negro or mulatto, fifty dollars, and a white man two hundred dollars, and imprisoned at the discretion of the court, the free negro not exceeding ten days, and the white man not exceeding six months. . . .

Sec. 7. . . . If any freedman, free negro, or mulatto shall fail or refuse to pay any tax levied according to the provisions of the sixth section of this act, it shall be *prima facie* evidence of vagrancy, and it shall be the duty of the sheriff to arrest such freedman, free negro, or mulatto or such person refusing or neglecting to pay such tax, and proceed at once to hire for the shortest time such delinquent tax-payer to any one who will pay the said tax, with accruing costs, giving preference to the employer, if there be one. . . .

IV. Penal Laws of Mississippi

Sec. 1. *Be it enacted,* . . . That no freedman, free negro or mulatto, not in the military service of the United States government, and not licensed so to do by the board of police of his or her county, shall keep or carry fire-arms of any kind, or any ammunition, dirk or bowie knife, and on conviction thereof in the county court shall be punished by fine, not exceeding ten dollars, and pay the costs of such proceedings. . . .

2. . . . Any freedman, free negro, or mulatto committing riots, routs, affrays, trespasses, malicious mischief, cruel treat-

ment to animals, seditious speeches, insulting gestures, language, or acts, or assaults on any person, disturbance of the peace, exercising the function of a minister of the Gospel without a license from some regularly organized church, vending spirituous or intoxicating liquors, or committing any other misdemeanor, the punishment of which is not specifically provided for by law, shall, upon conviction thereof in the county court, be fined not less than ten dollars, and not more than one hundred dollars, and may be imprisoned at the discretion of the court, not exceeding thirty days.

Sec. 3. . . . If any white person shall sell, lend, or give to any freedman, free negro, or mulatto any fire-arms, dirk or bowie knife, or ammunition, or any spirituous or intoxicating liquors, such person or persons so offending, upon conviction thereof in the county court of his or her county, shall be fined not exceeding fifty dollars, and may be imprisoned, at the discretion of the court, not exceeding thirty days. . . .

Sec. 5. . . . If any freedman, free negro, or mulatto, convicted of any of the misdemeanors provided against in this act, shall fail or refuse for the space of five days, after conviction, to pay the fine and costs imposed, such person shall be hired out by the sheriff or other officer, at public outcry, to any white person who will pay said fine and all costs, and take said convict for the shortest time.

4.2 An Ex-Slave Writes His Ex-Master

Hollywood has created the image, in films such as Birth of a Nation *and* Gone With the Wind, *of the faithful ex-slaves who, at the end of the Civil War, choose to stay and work for their old master and mistress. Obviously not all ex-slaves felt this way, as we can tell from Mississippi's vagrancy law (above) and from the following letter by Jourdon Anderson. Anderson was writing to his former owner, Col. H. P. Anderson of Big Spring, Tennessee.*

Questions

Why do you think Jourdon Anderson wrote the letter? Did he expect the terms to be met? Why do you think he made them?

In return for spending much of their lives building up the plantations of persons like Colonel Anderson, what did former slaves receive? What should they have received?

Dayton, Ohio, August 7, 1865
To My Old Master, Colonel
P. H. Anderson,
Big Spring, Tennessee

Sir: I got your letter and was glad to find you had not forgotten Jourdon, and that you wanted me to come back and live with you again, promising to do better for me than anybody else can. I have often felt uneasy about you. I thought the Yankees would have hung you long before this for harboring Rebs they found at your house. I suppose they never heard about your going to Col. Martin's to kill the Union soldier that was left by his company in their stable. Although you shot at me twice before I left you, I did not want to hear of your being hurt, and am glad you are still living. It would do me good to go back to the dear old home again and see Miss Mary and Miss Martha and Allen, Esther, Green, and Lee. Give my love to them all, and tell them I hope we will meet in the better world, if not in this. I would have gone back to see you all when I was working in the Nashville hospital, but one of the neighbors told me Henry intended to shoot me if he ever got a chance.

I want to know particularly what the good chance is you propose to give me. I am doing tolerably well here; I get $25 a month, with victuals and clothing: have a comfortable home for Mandy (the folks here call her Mrs. Anderson), and the children, Milly, Jane and Grundy, go to school and are learning well; the teacher says Grundy has a head for a preacher. They go to Sunday School, and Mandy and me attend church regularly. We are kindly treated; sometimes we overhear others saying, "Them colored people were slaves" down in Tennessee. The children feel hurt when they hear such remarks, but I tell them it was no disgrace in Tennessee to belong to Col. Anderson. Many darkies would have been proud, as I used to was, to call you master. Now, if you will write and say what wages you will give me, I will be better able to decide whether it would be to my advantage to move back again.

As to my freedom, which you say I can have, there is nothing to be gained on that score, as I got my free papers in 1864 from the Provost-Marshal General of the Department at Nashville. Mandy says she would be afraid to go back without some proof that you are sincerely disposed to treat us justly and kindly—and we have concluded to test your sincerity by asking you to send us our wages for the time we served you. This will make us forget and forgive old scores, and rely on your justice and friendship in the future. I served you faithfully for thirty-two years and Mandy twenty years. At $25 a month for me, and $2 a week for Mandy, our earnings would amount to $11,680. Add to this the interest for the time our wages has been kept back and deduct what you paid for our clothing and three doctor's visits to me, and pulling a tooth for Mandy, and the balance will show what we are in justice entitled to. Please send the money by Adams Express, in care of V. Winters, esq. Dayton, Ohio. If you fail to pay us for faithful labors in the past we can have little faith in your promises in the future. We trust the good Maker has opened your eyes to the wrongs which you and your fathers have done to me and my fathers, in making us toil for you for generations without recompense. Here I draw my wages every Saturday night, but in Tennessee there was never any pay day for the negroes any more than for the horses and cows. Surely there will be a day of reckoning for those who defraud the laborer of his hire.

In answering this letter please state if there would be any safety for my Milly and Jane, who are now grown up and both good-looking girls. You know how it was with poor Matilda and Catherine. I would rather stay here and starve and die if it comes to that than have my girls brought to shame by the violence and wickedness of their young masters. You will also please state if there has been any schools opened for the colored children in your neighbor-hood, the great desire of my life now is to give my children an education, and have them form virtuous habits.

P.S.—Say howdy to George Carter, and thank him for taking the pistol from you when you were shooting at me.

From your old servant,
Jourdon Anderson

4.3   On the Fate of the Indians

General William Tecumseh Sherman became notorious in the South during the Civil War when he ordered his 62,000 Union troops to live off the land in Georgia, methodically destroying the crops, public buildings, bridges, railroads and factories that lay in their path. As a result of his "March to the Sea," Sherman is considered "the first modern general."

As fate would have it, the white general named after the Shawnee Chieftain Tecumseh was assigned to pacify the western Indians. In a series of letters to his brother, Senator John Sherman, a powerful Ohio Republican (author of the Sherman Anti-Trust Act), he reveals prevailing attitudes and policies about Native Americans. He discusses the Sioux, Cheyenne and Navajo.

Questions

Does Sherman bring to the Indian wars any of the same military thinking he had used so successfully in the Civil War? Which racial stereotypes does he express? What does he mean by "extermination"? Does Sherman seem to welcome the chance to exterminate the Indians?

What is Sherman's attitude toward the white settlers—those who will force him to eliminate the Sioux and Cheyenne, as well as those who badly want the farms and property of the Mormons?

ST. LOUIS, SUNDAY, DEC. 30, 1866.
Dear Brother: I came up from New Orleans right through the country that I had been the means of raiding so thoroughly, and did not know but I should hear some things that would not be pleasant, but, on the contrary, many people met me all along the road in the most friendly spirit. . . .

I expect to have two Indian wars on my hands, and have no time for other things. The Sioux and Cheyennes are now so circumscribed that I suppose they must be exterminated, for they cannot and will not settle down, and our people will force us to it. It will also call for all possible prudence to keep us from war with the Mormons, for there are people that yearn for the farms and property the Mormons have created in the wilderness. . . .

Affectionately,

W. T. SHERMAN.

FORT UNION, NEW MEXICO,
June 11, 1868, Thursday.

Dear Brother: I have now been in New Mexico three weeks along with Col. Tappan, peace commissioner, for the purpose of seeing the Navajos, and making some permanent disposition of them. By a debate in the Senate I see you have a pretty good idea of their former history. These Indians seem to have acquired from the old Spaniards a pretty good knowledge of farming, rearing sheep, cattle, and goats, and of making their own clothing by weaving blankets and cloth. They were formerly a numerous tribe, occupying the vast region between New Mexico and the Colorado of the West, and had among them a class of warriors who made an easy living by stealing of the New Mexicans and occasionally killing. . . .

We found 7200 Indians there, seemingly abject and disheartened. They have been there four years. The first year they were maintained by the army at a cost of about $700,000, and made a small crop. The second year the cost was about $500,000, and the crop was small. Last year the crop was an utter failure, though all the officers say they labored hard and faithfully. This year they would not work because they said it was useless. The cost has been dimin-

ished to about 12 cents per head a day, which for 7000 Indians makes over $300,000, and this is as low as possible, being only a pound of corn, and a pound of beef with a little salt per day.

Now this was the state of facts, and we could see no time in the future when this could be amended. The scarcity of wood, the foul character of water, which is salty and full of alkali, and their utter despair, made it certain that we would have to move them or they would scatter and be a perfect nuisance. So of course we concluded to move them. After debating all the country at our option, we have chosen a small part of their old country, which is as far out of the way of the whites and of our future probable wants as possible, and have agreed to move them there forthwith, and have made a treaty which will save the heavy cost of their maintenance and give as much probability of their resuming their habits of industry as the case admits of. . . .

Yours affectionately,

W. T. SHERMAN.

. . . In our Indian matters I think we are making as much progress as could be expected. The great bulk of the Sioux have agreed to move to the Missouri where they will be too far away from the railroad to be provoked to do it damage, and where the appropriations for their benefit can be more economically and faithfully applied. Some small [bands] will always be warlike and mischievous, but the game of war will be simplified by their separation. The same as to the Cheyennes, etc., below the Arkansas. The commission for present peace had to concede a right to hunt buffaloes as long as they last, and this may lead to collisions, but it will not be long before all the buffaloes are extinct near and between the railroads, after which the Indians will have no reason to approach either railroad. . . .

Affectionately,

W. T. SHERMAN.

HEADQUARTERS MILITARY DIVISION
OF THE MISSOURI,
Sept. 23, 1868.

Dear Brother:

. . . The Indian War on the plains need simply amount to this. We have now selected and provided reservations for all, off the great roads. All who cling to their old hunting grounds are hostile and will remain so till killed off. We will have a sort of predatory war for years, every now and then be shocked by the indiscriminate murder of travellers and settlers, but the country is so large, and the advantage of the Indians so great, that we cannot make a single war and end it. From the nature of things we must take chances and clean out Indians as we encounter them.

Our troops are now scattered and have daily chases and skirmishes, sometimes getting the best and sometimes the worst, but the Indians have this great advantage,—they can steal fresh horses when they need them and drop the jaded ones. We must operate each man to his own horse, and cannot renew except by purchase in a distant and cheap market.

I will keep things thus, and when winter starves their ponies they will want a truce and shan't have it, unless the civil influence compels me again as it did last winter.

If Grant is elected, that old Indian system will be broken up, and then with the annuities which are ample expended in connection with and in subordination to military movements, will soon bring the whole matter within easy control. Then there are $134,000 appropriated for the Cheyennes and Arapahoes, all of whom are at war, and yet the Indian Bureau contend they are forced by law to invest it in shoes, stockings, blankets, and dry goods for these very Indians. They don't want any of these things, but if it could be put in corn, salt, and cattle, we could detach half the hostiles and get them down on the Canadian, two hundred miles south of the Kansas road. . . .

Yours affectionately,

W. T. SHERMAN.

4.4 Chief Joseph's Lament

In 1877, Chief Joseph, the revered leader of the Nez Percé ("Pierced Nose") Indians, refused to obey an order to move his people from Oregon to Idaho. Hoping instead to help them escape to Canada, he led most of his tribe on a tortuous 1,000-mile trek through the Rockies, with the U.S. Cavalry in hot pursuit. Despite his masterful generalship, the Nez Percé were forced to surrender in Montana, some 30 miles south of the Canadian border, on October 5, 1877. The surviving members of his tribe were forcibly removed to Indian Territory, where many died. Chief Joseph was taken first to Fort Leavenworth in Indian Territory, then to Washington, D.C., back to Indian Territory again, and finally to a reservation in the state of Washington, where he died in 1904.

In the speech excerpted below he pleads, successfully, for his people to be allowed to return to the Northwest. Chief Joseph voices his hope, fears and objectives.

Questions

What does Chief Joseph think of the whites? Are his overall goals reasonable? If so, why were they not achieved? Is the Chief's assessment of the future of his people realistic? Why does he say they will have to change?

I have heard talk and talk, but nothing is done. Good words do not last long unless they amount to something. Words do not pay for my dead people. They do not pay for my country, now overrun by white men. They do not protect my father's grave. They do not pay for my horses and cattle.

Good words do not give me back my children. Good words will not make good the promise of your war chief, General Miles. Good words will not give my people good health and stop them from dying. Good words will not get my people a home where they can live in peace and take care of themselves.

I am tired of talk that comes to nothing. It makes my heart sick when I remember all the good words and all the broken promises. There has been too much talking by men who had no right to talk. Too many misinterpretations have been made; too many misunderstandings have come up between the white men and the Indians.

If the white man wants to live in peace with the Indian, he can live in peace. There need be no trouble. Treat all men alike. Give them the same laws. Give them all an even chance to live and grow.

All men are made by the same Great Spirit Chief. They are all brothers. The earth is the mother of all people, and all people should have equal rights upon it. You might as well expect all rivers to run backward as that any man who was born a free man should be contented penned up and denied liberty to go where he pleases. If you tie a horse to a stake, do you expect he will grow fat? If you pen an Indian up on a small spot of earth and compel him to stay there, he will not be contented nor will he grow and prosper.

I have asked some of the Great White Chiefs where they get their authority to say to the Indian that he shall stay in one place, while he sees white men going where they please. They cannot tell me.

I only ask of the government to be treated as all other men are treated. If I cannot go to my own home, let me have a home in a country where my people will not die so fast. I would like to go to Bitter Root Valley [western Montana]. There my people would be healthy; where they are now, they are dying. Three have died since I left my camp to come to Washington. When I think of our condition, my heart is heavy. I see men of my own race treated as outlaws and driven from country to country, or shot down like animals.

I know that my race must change. We cannot hold our own with the white men as we are. We only ask an even chance to live as other men live. We ask to be recognized as men. We ask that the same law shall work alike on all men. If an Indian breaks the law, punish him by the law. If a white man breaks the law, punish him also.

Let me be a free man—free to travel, free to stop, free to work, free to trade where I choose, free to choose my own teachers, free to follow the religion of my fathers, free to think and talk and act for myself— and I will obey every law or submit to the penalty. . . .

4.5 A Reformer Favors "Citizenship" for Indians

At the end of the nineteenth century, white reformers worked to end the warfare with the Indians, to improve conditions on the reservations, and, finally, to end the reservation system. They thought the reservations isolated the Native Americans and allowed corrupt white officials and traders to cheat them. Many thought it best to try to turn the Indians into white farmers. The Dawes Severalty Act of 1886 was the reformers' major legislative effort along these lines. It provided for the distribution of communally owned reservation lands to individual Indian family heads.

Merrill E. Gates, the President of Amherst College, also served as the President of the Lake Mohonk Conference of the Friends of the Indians. He delivered these remarks to a gathering of fellow reformers in 1896. Similar ideas had been advanced in support of the Dawes Act a decade earlier.

Questions

How do these attitudes compare with those of General Sherman (Document 4.3)? What stereotypes does Gates express? What is meant by "citizenship"? How do his objectives for Native Americans compare with those expressed by Chief Joseph (4.4)? How successful was the Dawes Act in bringing about the objectives expressed by Gates?

We have, to begin with, the absolute need of awakening in the savage Indian broader desires and ampler wants. To bring him out of savagery into citizenship we must make the Indian more intelligently selfish before we can make him unselfishly intelligent. We need to *awaken in him wants.* In his dull savagery he must be touched by the wings of the divine angel of discontent. . . . Discontent with the teepee and the starving rations of the Indian camp in winter is needed to get the Indian out of the blanket and into trousers,—and trousers with a pocket in them, and with a *pocket that aches to be filled with dollars! . . .* There is an immense moral training that comes from the use of property. And the Indian has had all that to learn. Like a little child who learns the true delight of giving away only by first earning and possessing what it gives, the Indian must learn that he has no right to give until he has earned, and that he has no right to eat until he has worked for his bread. Our teachers upon the reservations know that frequently lessons in home-building, and providence for the future of the family which they are laboriously teaching, are effaced and counteracted by the old communal instincts and

customs which bring half a tribe of kinspeople to settle down at the door of the home when the grain is threshed or the beef is killed, and to live upon their enterprising kinsman so long as his property will suffice to feed the clan of his kinspeople. We have found it necessary, as one of the first steps in developing a stronger personality in the Indian, *to make him responsible for property.* Even if he learns its value only by losing it, and going without it until he works for more, the educational process has begun. To cease from pauperizing the Indian by feeding him through years of laziness,—to instruct him to use property which is legally his, and by protecting his title, to help him through the dangerous transition period into citizenship,—this is the first great step in the education of the race.

4.6 The Strategies of Black Leaders

Toward the end of the nineteenth century, the situation of black men and women in the United States was becoming increasingly grave. Throughout the South, state and local governments tightened and extended segregation laws. The U.S. Supreme Court in the case of Plessy *v.* Ferguson *decreed that racial segregation was constitutional if each race had equal facilities. White politicians developed methods, including poll taxes, literacy tests, and grandfather clauses, to strip power from blacks by denying them the chance to vote or participate in government. Thousands of blacks were intimidated or murdered by lynch mobs.*

In these circumstances, Booker T. Washington, a former slave and the founder and head of Tuskeegee Institute where black students acquired vocational skills, determined that the best way for blacks to survive was to accommodate themselves to the white power structure. He offered his solution in an address at an exposition in Atlanta in 1895 (excerpted below).

Washington's views made him immensely popular among whites. But other black leaders, including William E. B. Du Bois, a historian and one of the founders of the NAACP (National Association for the Advancement of Colored People), were more critical. Du Bois argued that Washington's methods would fail to meet the real needs of black people and would be harmful in the long run. Two selections from Du Bois set forth some of his views.

Questions

At which class of whites did Washington aim his appeal? What did he propose? What were Du Bois' criticisms of that proposal? How did Du Bois feel about the educational system that Washington had created? What was Du Bois' strategy for solving the problems that faced American blacks? Did he advocate violence?

If you were a black leader near the beginning of the twentieth century, which strategy would you have followed? Why? Could you have proposed yet another? Which events favored Du Bois' strategy, rather than Washington's?

Booker T. Washington, 1895 —

A ship lost at sea for many days suddenly sighted a friendly vessel. From the mast of the unfortunate vessel was sent the signal: "Water, water, we die of thirst." The answer from the friendly vessel at once came back, "Cast down your bucket where you are." A second time the signal, "Water, water, send us water," ran up from the distressed vessel and was answered, "Cast down your bucket where you are," and a third and fourth signal for water was answered, "Cast down your bucket where you are." The captain of the distressed vessel, at last heeding the injunction, cast down his bucket and it came up full of fresh, sparkling water from the mouth of the Amazon River.

To those of my race who depend on bettering their condition in a foreign land, or who underestimate the importance of cultivating friendly relations with the southern white man who is their next door neighbor, I would say, cast down your bucket where you are. Cast it down in

SOURCES: Booker T. Washington, *Up from Slavery* (New York: Doubleday and Co., 1903); W. E. B. Du Bois, *Souls of Black Folk* (Chicago: A. C. McClurg and Co., 1904), pp. 3–6, 50–53.

making friends, in every manly way, of the people of all races by whom you are surrounded. Cast it down in agriculture, in mechanics, in commerce, in domestic service, and in the professions. And in this connection it is well to bear in mind that, whatever other sins the South may be called upon to bear, when it comes to business pure and simple it is in the South that the Negro is given a man's chance in the commercial world; and in nothing is this Exposition more eloquent than in emphasizing this chance. Our greatest danger is that in the great leap from slavery to freedom, we may overlook the fact that the masses of us are to live by the production of our hands, and fail to keep in mind that we shall prosper in proportion as we learn to dignify and glorify common labor and put brains and skill into the common occupations of life; shall prosper in proportion as we learn to draw the line between the superficial and the substantial, the ornamental gewgaws of life and the useful. No race can prosper till it learns that there is as much dignity in tilling a field as in writing a poem. It is at the bottom of life we must begin and not at the top. Nor should we permit our grievances to overshadow our opportunities. . . .

To those of the white race who look to the incoming of those of foreign birth and strange tongue and habits for the prosperity of the South, were I permitted, I would repeat what I say to my own race, "Cast down your bucket where you are." Cast it down among the eight millions of Negroes whose habits you know, whose fidelity and love you have tested in days when to have proved treacherous meant the ruin of your firesides. Cast down your bucket among those people who have, without strikes and labor wars, tilled your fields, cleared your forests, builded your railroads and cities, and brought forth treasures from the bowels of the earth and helped make possible this magnificent representation of the progress of the South. Casting down your bucket among my people, helping and encouraging as you are doing on these grounds, and with education of head, hand, and heart, you will find that they will buy your surplus land, make blossom the waste places in your fields, and run your factories. While doing this you can be sure in the future, as you have been in the past, that you and your families will be surrounded by the most patient, faithful, law-abiding, and unresentful people that the world has seen.

As we have proved our loyalty to you in the past, in nursing your children, watching by the sickbeds of your mothers and fathers, and often following them with tear-dimmed eyes to their graves, so in the future, in our humble way, we shall stand by you with a devotion that no foreigner can approach, ready to lay down our lives, if need be, in defense of yours; interlacing our industrial, commercial, civil, and religious life with yours in a way that shall make the interests of both races one. In all things that are purely social we can be as separate as the fingers, yet one as the hand in all things essential to mutual progress.

Gentlemen of the Exposition: As we present to you our humble effort at an exhibition of our progress, you must not expect overmuch; starting thirty years ago with ownership here and there in a few quilts and pumpkins and chickens (gathered from miscellaneous sources), remember, the path that has led us from these to the invention and production of agricultural implements, buggies, steam engines, newspapers, books, statuary, carvings, paintings, the management of drug stores and banks, has not been trodden without contact with thorns and thistles. While we take pride in what we exhibit as a result of our independent efforts, we do not for a moment forget that our part in this exhibition would fall far short of your expectations but for the constant help that has come to our educational life, not only from the southern states, but especially from northern philanthropists who have made their gifts a constant stream of blessing and encouragement.

The wisest among my race understand that the agitation of questions of social equality is the extremest folly. . . . The opportunity to earn a dollar in a factory just now is worth infinitely more than the opportunity to spend a dollar in an opera house.

W. E. B. DuBois, 1904 —

Mr. Washington represents in Negro thought the old attitude of adjustment and submission: but adjustment at such a peculiar time as to make his programme unique. This is an age of unusual economic development, and Mr. Washington's programme naturally takes an economic cast, becoming a gospel of Work and Money to such an extent as apparently almost completely to overshadow the higher aims of life. Moreover, this is an age when the more advanced races are coming in closer contact with the less developed races, and the race-feeling is therefore intensified; and Mr. Washington's programme practically accepts the alleged inferiority of the Negro races. Again, in our own land, the reaction from the sentiment of war time has given impetus to race-prejudice against Negroes, and Mr. Washington withdraws many of the high demands of Negroes as men and American citizens. In other periods of intensified prejudice all the Negro's tendency to self-assertion has been called forth; at this period a policy of submission is advocated. In the history of nearly all other races and peoples the doctrine preached at such crises has been that manly self-respect is worth more than lands and houses, and that a people who voluntarily surrender such respect, or cease striving for it, are not worth civilizing.

In answer to this, it has been claimed that the Negro can survive only through submission. Mr. Washington distinctly asks that black people give up, at least for the present, three things—

First, political power,
Second, insistence on civil rights,
Third, higher education of Negro youth—

and concentrate all their energies on industrial education, the accumulation of wealth, and the conciliation of the South. This policy has been courageously and insistently advocated for over fifteen years, and has been triumphant for perhaps ten years. As a result of this tender of the palm-branch, what has been the return? In these years there have occurred:

1. The disfranchisement of the Negro.
2. The legal creation of a distinct status of civil inferiority for the Negro.
3. The steady withdrawal of aid from institutions for the higher training of the Negro.

These movements are not, to be sure, direct results of Mr. Washington's teachings; but his propaganda has, without a shadow of doubt, helped their speedier accomplishment. The question then comes: Is it possible, and probable, that nine millions of men can make effective progress in economic lines if they are deprived of political rights, made a servile caste, and allowed only the most meagre chance for developing their exceptional men? If history and reason give any distinct answer to these questions, it is an emphatic *No.* And Mr. Washington thus faces the triple paradox of his career:

1. He is striving nobly to make Negro artisans business men and property-owners; but it is utterly impossible, under modern competitive methods, for workingmen and property-owners to defend their rights and exist without the right of suffrage.
2. He insists on thrift and self-respect, but at the same time counsels a silent submission to civic inferiority such as is bound to sap the manhood of any race in the long run.
3. He advocates common-school and industrial training, and depreciates institutions of higher learning; but neither the Negro common-schools, nor Tuskegee itself, could remain open a day were it not for teachers trained in Negro colleges, or trained by their graduates.

This triple paradox in Mr. Washington's position is the object of criticism by two classes of colored Americans. One class is spiritually descended from Toussaint the Savior, through Gabriel, Vesey, and Turner, and they represent the attitude of revolt and revenge; they hate the white South blindly and distrust the white race generally, and so far as they agree on definite action, think that the Negro's only hope lies in emigration beyond the borders of the United States. And yet, by the irony of fate, nothing has more effectually made this programme seem hopeless than the recent course of the United States toward weaker and darker peoples in the West Indies, Hawaii, and the Philippines,—for where in the world may we go and be safe from lying and brute force?

The other class of Negroes who cannot agree with Mr. Washington has hitherto said little aloud. They deprecate the sight of scattered counsels, of internal disagreement; and especially they dislike making their just criticism of a useful and earnest man an excuse for a general discharge of venom from small-minded opponents. Nevertheless, the questions involved are so fundamental and serious that it is difficult to see how men like the Grimkes, Kelly Miller, J. W. E. Bowen, and other representatives of this group, can much longer be silent. Such men feel in conscience bound to ask of this nation three things:

1. The right to vote.
2. Civic equality.
3. The education of youth according to ability.

W. E. B. DuBois—

I am an earnest advocate of manual training and trade teaching for black boys, and for white boys, too. I believe that next to the founding of Negro colleges the most valuable addition to Negro education since the war has been industrial training for black boys. Nevertheless, I insist that the object of all true education is not to make men carpenters, it is to make carpenters men; there are two means of making the carpenter a man, each equally important: the first is to give the group and community in which he works liberally trained teachers and leaders to teach him and his family what life means; the second is to give him sufficient intelligence and technical skill to make him an efficient workman; the first object demands the Negro college and college-bred men—not a quantity of such colleges, but a few of excellent quality; not too many college-bred men, but enough to leaven the lump, to inspire the masses, to raise the Talented Tenth to leadership; the second object demands a good system of common schools, well-taught, conveniently located, and properly equipped. . . .

4.7 The "Mexican Race"

Racial bias against Mexicans has a history reaching back to the nineteenth century. This bigotry was strongly revived in the 1920s when Mexicans began entering the country in greater numbers than before. With European immigration sharply restricted by Congress, and the demand for labor rising, especially in the Southwest, 50,000 Mexicans came north from Mexico each year in the 1920s. They found jobs planting and chopping cotton, constructing and maintaining railroads, digging copper and plying other manual trades. Then congressional attention turned to restricting the flow of people from south of the border. (It is interesting to note that 75,000 Canadians came into the U.S. each year in the 1920s, with scarcely any protest.)

In the course of congressional debate, advocates of restriction used both economic and racial arguments. An outspoken supporter of restriction was Texas representative, James Slayden. Below, he presents his argument in a speech to the Academy of Social and Political Science in 1921.

Questions

What racial stereotypes does Slayden hold, and how do they compare with those used against blacks, Native Americans and other racial minorities? What class distinctions does the congressman make among different groups of Hispanics? What significance do you draw from the fact that this is presented to a scholarly organization?

At the end, Slayden ponders the future of immigration. What has changed since the 1920s? Are his concerns valid today?

James L. Slayden —

The importance of the question of immigration from Mexico can hardly be overestimated. It has a direct bearing on the general subject of immigration which Congress has been considering for years, and which has not yet been solved. It is tied up with the greatest of all of our problems, that of race mingling. . . .

This steady incoming of an alien race, not altogether white, is welcomed by some Americans, tolerated by others and utterly abhorred by those who look beyond the next cotton crop or the betterment of railway lines.

Large planters short of labor, because of the extraordinary hegira of Negroes in the last few years, know their value and wel-

come the Mexican immigrants as they would welcome fresh arrivals from the Congo, without a thought of the social and political embarrassment to their country. On the other hand, the small southern farmers (and they are the greater number) who cultivate their land with the help of their children, do not want the Mexicans, and would gladly see the movement of Negroes go on until the last one was settled in New England or Illinois or wherever they may be most happy, prosperous and welcome.

But both Negroes and Mexicans are here yet in large numbers, and close observers begin to detect a feeling of jealousy and dislike between them. In Texas and other southern states the Mexican is classed as white in public conveyances, hotels and places of amusement which does not make for good feeling between him and the Negro, and the Mexican, even of very low class, is not much inclined to social intimacy with the latter.

SOURCES: James L. Slayden, "Some Observations on Mexican Immigration,": *The Annals,* The American Academy of Political and Social Science, January, 1921, pp. 121–126.

That to substitute one for the other may be jumping from the frying-pan into the fire is a thought that will intrude itself. . . .

In Texas the word "Mexican" is used to indicate the race, not a citizen or subject of the country. There are probably 250,000 Mexicans in Texas who were born in the state but they are "Mexicans" just as all blacks are Negroes though they may have five generations of American ancestors.

Most Mexicans are Indians or Mestizos (mixed white and Indian blood) and between them and the other inhabitants of Mexico there is a sharply defined social distinction. The upper classes, of European ancestry, are frequently educated in Spain, France or the United States, and few of them become immigrants unless forced out by revolutions, when they go to San Antonio, El Paso or Los Angeles. At home they are the merchants, big planters, bankers and professional men.

With rare exceptions these people stay at home, look after their private affairs and do not meddle with politics. They would make good and useful citizens of any country. When one of them does go in for politics (or revolution, which is the same thing in Mexico) he does more mischief, because above his wicked heart is a cleverer head. He easily becomes the leader of the low-browed, poverty-stricken peon class, and by perfervid appeals to the prejudice of the thoughtless and uneducated mass of Indians and the promise of an impossible Utopia quickly converts them into murderous bandits. Resounding phrases about the Constitution, whether that of 1857 or that of Queretaro, makes no difference—and the rights of the Indians, mixed with contemptuous remarks about the "Gringoes" and the hated "Colossus of the North" soon can make fiends of otherwise quiet and useful men. . . .

These are the people, high and low, from whom thousands of immigrants are coming to the United States. What it may mean for Americans in the future no one can tell. Probably our safety and peace lie in the fact that as yet so few of them, comparatively are coming.

4.8 On the Internment of the Japanese Americans

The evacuation of all Japanese ethnics from the Pacific Coast in the spring of 1942 came in the wake of the disastrous attack on Pearl Harbor and was justified as military necessity. It was mandated by a presidential executive order in February, 1942, and involved 70,000 U.S. citizens and 40,000 aliens. No formal charges were made against the internees; they were merely accused of having Japanese ancestors. The U.S. Supreme Court upheld the internment. The 58,000 Italian and 23,000 German aliens living in the country during the war were not included in the evacuation order.

Two prominent officials urging the evacuation and detention were California Atty. Gen. Earl Warren, and Gen. John L. De Witt, the area military commander. The following excerpts are from testimony to congressional committees made by Warren in February, 1942, and by De Witt in April, 1943. Warren, who would serve as Chief Justice of the U.S. Supreme Court, later publicly recanted his earlier views of the internment.

Many of the Japanese ethnics who found themselves behind barbed wire in 1942 were native-born Americans or long-term U.S. residents. From the brief report by internee S. J. Oki, it is clear that the internees had very different views of themselves from those expressed by Warren and De Witt. In 1988 Congress and the President agreed to award a cash payment to the victims of the internment and their survivors.

Questions

What are the sources of such extreme anti-Japanese sentiment as those expressed by Warren and De Witt?

As the top military officer in the West, De Witt must have known that the Japanese represented no military threat; why therefore did he claim otherwise? How do you account for the fact that, although the U.S. territory of Hawaii was in the midst of the Pacific war, no such policies toward the Japanese were instituted there.

In justifying the internment, how does Warren rationalize the absence of sabotage?

According to Oki, how did the internees seem to define their ethnic identity? How did they feel about the physical conditions of the camps? What did they think of the legal basis of their imprisonment? If they had been out of the camps, what would they be doing?

In 1988, Congress authorized a cash settlement to be given to former evacuees for their internment. Do you believe that this was a proper action? If so, should other racial or ethnic groups be compensated for comparable wrongs?

Earl Warren —

ATTORNEY GENERAL WARREN. For some time I have been of the opinion that the solution of our alien enemy problem with

SOURCES: Testimony of Earl Warren, *Hearings before the Select Committee Investigating National Defense, Migration*, Part 29. "San Francisco Hearings," February 21 and February 23, 1942, U.S. House of Representatives, 77th Cong., 2nd sess., pp. 11009–11019; testimony of Gen. De Witt, *Investigation of Congested Areas, Hearing before a Subcommittee of the Committee on Naval Affairs*, House of Representatives, 78th Cong. 1st sess., April 13, 1943, pp. 739–740; S. J. Oki in the *Minidoka Irrigator*, n.d.

all its ramifications, which include the descendants of aliens, is not only a Federal problem but is a military problem. We believe that all of the decisions in that regard must be made by the military command that is charged with the security of this area. I am convinced that the fifth-column activities of our enemy call for the participation of people who are in fact American citizens, and that if we are to deal realistically with the problem we must realize that we will be obliged in time of stress to deal with subversive elements of our own citizenry. . . .

A wave of organized sabotage in California accompanied by an actual air raid or even by a prolonged black-out could not only be more destructive to life and property but could result in retarding the entire war effort of this Nation far more than the treacherous bombing of Pearl Harbor.

I hesitate to think what the result would be of the destruction of any of our big airplane factories in this State. It will interest you to know that some of our airplane factories in this State are entirely surrounded by Japanese land ownership or occupancy. It is a situation that is fraught with the greatest danger and under no circumstances should it ever be permitted to exist. . . .

Unfortunately, however, many of our people and some of our authorities and, I am afraid, many of our people in other parts of the country are of the opinion that because we have had no sabotage and no fifth column activities in this State since the beginning of the war, that means that none have been planned for us. But I take the view that that is the most ominous sign in our whole situation. It convinces me more than perhaps any other factor that the sabotage that we are to get, the fifth column activities that we are to get, are timed just like Pearl Harbor was timed and just like the invasion of France, and of Denmark, and of Norway, and all of those other countries. . . .

I want to say that the consensus of opinion among the law-enforcement officers of this State is that there is more potential danger among the group of Japanese who are born in this country than from the alien Japanese who were born in Japan. That might seem an anomaly to some people, but the fact is that, in the first place, there are twice as many of them. There are 33,000 aliens and there are 66,000 born in this country.

In the second place, most of the Japanese who were born in Japan are over 55 years of age. There has been practically no migration to this country since 1924. But in some instances the children of those people have been sent to Japan for their education, either in whole or in part, and while they are over there they are indoctrinated with the idea of Japanese imperialism. They receive their religious instruction which ties up their religion with their Emperor, and they come back here imbued with the ideas and the policies of Imperial Japan. . . .

We believe that when we are dealing with the Caucasian race we have methods that will test the loyalty of them, and we believe that we can, in dealing with the Germans and the Italians, arrive at some fairly sound conclusions because of our knowledge of the way they live in the community and have lived for many years. But when we deal with the Japanese we are in an entirely different field and we cannot form any opinion that we believe to be sound. . . .

MR. SPARKMAN. I have noticed suggestions in newspaper stories. I noticed a telegram this morning with reference to the civil rights of these people. What do you have to say about that?

ATTORNEY GENERAL WARREN. I believe, sir, that in time of war every citizen must give up some of his normal rights.

John L. DeWitt—

MR. MAAS. General, is there anything that you would like to suggest in connection with your problem? Have you any problem that you want to leave with the Congressmen? We are probably in a position to assist you.

GENERAL DE WITT. I haven't any except one—that is the development of a false sentiment on the part of certain individuals and some organizations to get the Japanese back on the West Coast. I don't want any of them here. They are a dangerous element. There is no way to determine their loyalty. The West Coast contains too many vital installations essential to the defense of the country to allow any Japanese on this coast. There is a feeling developing, I think, in certain sections of the country that the Japanese should be allowed to return. I am opposing it with every proper means at my disposal.

MR. ANDERSON. I wrote to the War Department when this policy was announced asking how come. There was strong protest from my district. I wrote the Secretary of War and inquired as to policy and they said it was a new policy that they intended to follow. The attitude in my district is that if you send any Japanese back here we will bury them. I think it is a mistake.

MR. MOTT. I received the same kind of an answer to my question but I doubt if it is a War Department policy. I believe it is a policy imposed upon the War Department by civilian agencies.

MR. BATES. I was going to ask—would you base your determined stand on experience as a result of sabotage or racial history or what is it?

GENERAL DE WITT. I first of all base it on my responsibility. I have the mission of defending this coast and securing vital installations. The danger of the Japanese was, and is now—if they are permitted to come back—espionage and sabotage. It makes no difference whether he is an American citizen, he is still a Japanese. American citizenship does not necessarily determine loyalty.

MR. BATES. You draw a distinction then between Japanese and Italians and Germans? We have a great number of Italians

and Germans and we think they are fine citizens. There may be exceptions.

GENERAL DE WITT. You needn't worry about the Italians at all except in certain cases. Also the same for the Germans except in individual cases. But we must worry about the Japanese all the time until he is wiped off the map. Sabotage and espionage will make problems as long as he is allowed in this area—problems which I don't want to have to worry about.

S. J. Oki —

Objectively, and on the whole, life in a relocation center is not unbearable. There are dust-storms and mud. Housing is inadequate, with families of six living in single rooms in many cases. Food is below the standard set for prisoners of war. In some of the camps hospitals are at times understaffed and supplies meager, as in many ordinary communities. . . .

What is not so bearable lies much deeper than the physical makeup of a center. It is seen in the face of Mr. Yokida, 65, a Montebello farmer. It is seen in the face of Mrs. Wata, 50, a grocer's widow from Long Beach. It is seen in the face of little John Zendo, 9, son of an Oakland restaurant owner. It is seen in the face of Mary Uchido, former sophomore from UCLA and the daughter of a Little Tokyo merchant. It is seen in the face of Sus Tana, young kibei who had been an employee in a vegetable stand in Hollywood.

Their faces look bewildered as they stare at the barbed-wire fences and sentry towers that surround the camp. Their eyes ask: Why? Why? What is all this?

Kats Ento, serious-looking ex-farmer from Norwalk, has made up his mind. He says: "I am an American citizen. I was born and brought up in California. I have never been outside the United States, and I don't know Japan or what Japan stands for. But because my parents weren't considerate enough to give me blue eyes, reddish hair, and a high nose, I am here, in camp, interned without the formality of a charge, to say nothing of a trial. Does the Constitution say that only white men are created equal? Put me down as disloyal, if you will, but I'm going where I won't have to live the rest of my life on the wrong side of the tracks just because my face is yellow. Keep me in camp for the duration. I will find my future in the Orient. . . ."

Mr. Yokida, technically an enemy alien after forty years' continuous residence in California, appears tired. "For forty years I worked in central and southern California. I can remember when Los Angeles was only a small town compared to San Francisco. This country never gave me citizenship, but I never went back to Japan and I have no interests there. The evacuation has worked a hardship on me and my family, but I suppose in time of war you have to stand for a lot of hardships. . . ."

"I have a son in the army," says Mrs. Wata. "Besides, my daughter has volunteered to join the WAACS. I am an alien, and being an alien I have nothing to say about evacuation or having to live in camp, although it would have been so nice to have spent the last winter in Long Beach. It was so cold here, and the stove in my apartment never gave out enough heat. I do wish, though, that they would let my children go back to California on furloughs. They have so many friends out there, and they miss them."

John Zendo, 9, is always talking about his friends, too, says his mother. "He was a pretty popular boy in the neighborhood," she smiles reminiscently as she speaks. "He talks about them all the time, and asks me when we can go back to them. . . ."

"I keep on thinking about Los Angeles and the people I know," says Mary Uchido. "My girl friend writes me and tells me all about the changes that have taken place since evacuation. How the Little Tokyo has been left unoccupied, how some of our Chinese and Korean friends are working in airplane factories, things like that. But I don't want to go back there any more, except perhaps for a visit. . . . Maybe I will try to get a domestic job or something, because I can't possibly hope to continue my education. I would join the WAACS if they would put us in an ordinary unit instead of an all-Japanese unit."

Sus Tana, 32, is a volunteer for the special Japanese-American combat team. He smiles broadly and seems jolly, but his dark eyebrows betray an uneasiness which is concealed somewhat behind his sunburned forehead. "I am a kibei and a Young Democrat. I lived and worked in Los Angeles nine years after my return from Japan. I never made over a hundred dollars a month, mostly seventy-five to eighty, and I could never save enough money to buy anything. So when evacuation came, I had nothing to lose. I do miss my friends among the Young Democrats, though. They were such a fine bunch. You forgot you were a Jap when you were with them; you were just an American fighting for the President and the New Deal. I do wish I could be back there now. Maybe I could get a defense job and do what I can. But I am glad that we are going to have a combat unit. Maybe I can show the reactionaries in California that a Japanese-American can be just as good a soldier as any American—if not better."

4.9 Letter from Birmingham Jail

From 1955, when he assumed the leadership of a boycott to desegregate the Montgomery, Alabama buses until 1968, when a gunman assassinated him, the Rev. Martin Luther King, Jr., was the chief advocate for black nonviolent resistance to oppression. King's strategy of civil disobedience was influenced by the teachings of Henry David Thoreau, Mahatma Gandhi, and Jesus Christ. The Southern Christian Leadership Conference that he helped found and led became a focal point for the struggle. King and his followers risked harassment, imprisonment and death in their pacifist campaign to desegregate the United States and won world-wide acclaim. In 1964 the Civil Rights Act was passed and King was awarded the Nobel Peace Prize.

The following excerpt, drawn from his "Letter from Birmingham Jail," written in 1963 while behind bars, is perhaps the most eloquent statement of King's philosophy. He had been arrested by Birmingham, Alabama Police Chief "Bull" Connor, a believer in force and a symbol of die-hard segregationism. It was scribbled in the margins of a newspaper and on scraps of paper supplied by a black prisoner and an attorney. It served as a reply to eight Christian and Jewish clergy from Alabama who questioned his tactics.

Questions

What did King mean by nonviolence? How was it supposed to work in practice? What was his answer to those who encouraged him to "be patient" and who pointed out that he was guilty of violating the law? What did King hope to achieve? Was his policy realistic, given the conditions blacks faced in America?

In the 1960s thousands of students from colleges all over the nation joined in civil-rights demonstrations. Had you been a student then, do you think you might have joined one of them?

How much of King's dream of an America where blacks and whites live peacefully together has been realized?

April 16, 1963

MY DEAR FELLOW CLERGYMEN:

While confined here in the Birmingham city jail, I came across your recent statement calling my present activities "unwise and untimely." Seldom do I pause to answer criticism of my work and ideas. . . . [But] I think I should indicate why I am here in Birmingham, since you have been influenced by the view which argues against "outsiders coming in." . . . I am in Birmingham because injustice is here. . . .

. . . We are caught in an inescapable network of mutuality, tied in a single garment of destiny. Whatever affects one directly, affects all indirectly. Never again can we afford to live with the narrow, provincial "outside agitator" idea. Anyone who lives inside the United States can never be considered an outsider anywhere within its bounds. . . .

In any nonviolent campaign there are four basic steps: collection of the facts to determine whether injustices exist; negotiation; self-purification; and direct action. We have gone through all these steps in Birmingham. There can be no gainsaying the fact that racial injustice engulfs this community. Birmingham is probably the most thoroughly segregated city in the United States. . . . On the basis of these conditions, Negro leaders sought to negotiate with the city fathers. But the latter consistently refused to engage in good-faith negotiation.

Then, last September, came the opportunity to talk with leaders of Birmingham's economic community. In the course

of the negotiations, certain promises were made by the merchants—for example, to remove the stores' humiliating racial signs. On the basis of these promises, the Reverend Fred Shuttlesworth and the leaders of the Alabama Christian Movement for Human Rights agreed to a moratorium on all demonstrations. As the weeks and months went by, we realized that we were the victims of a broken promise. A few signs, briefly removed, returned; the others remained.

As in so many past experiences, our hopes had been blasted, and the shadow of deep disappointment settled upon us. We had no alternative except to prepare for direct action, whereby we would present our very bodies as a means of laying our case before the conscience of the local and the national community. Mindful of the difficulties involved, we decided to undertake a process of self-purification. We began a series of workshops on nonviolence, and we repeatedly asked ourselves: "Are you able to accept blows without retaliating?" "Are you able to endure the ordeal of jail?" We decided to schedule our direct-action program for the Easter season, realizing that except for Christmas, this is the main shopping period of the year. Knowing that a strong economic-withdrawal program would be the byproduct of direct action, we felt that this would be the best time to bring pressure to bear on the merchants for the needed change. . . .

You may well ask: "Why direct action? Why sit-ins, marches and so forth? Isn't negotiation a better path?" You are quite right in calling for negotiation. . . . The purpose of our direct-action program is to create a situation so crisis-packed that it will inevitably open the door to negotiation. I therefore concur with you in your call for negotiation. Too long has our beloved Southland been bogged down in a tragic effort to live in monologue rather than dialogue.

One of the basic points in your statement is that the action that I and my associates have taken in Birmingham is untimely. Some have asked: "Why didn't you give the new city administration time to act?". . . We know through painful experience that freedom is never voluntarily given by the oppressor; it must be demanded by the oppressed. Frankly, I have yet to engage in a direct-action campaign that was "well timed" in the view of those who have not suffered unduly from the disease of segregation. For years now I have heard the word "Wait!" It rings in the ear of every Negro with piercing familiarity. This "Wait" has almost always meant "Never." We must come to see, with one of our distinguished jurists, that "justice too long delayed is justice denied."

We have waited for more than 340 years for our constitutional and God-given rights. . . . Perhaps it is easy for those who have never felt the stinging darts of segregation to say, "Wait." But when you have seen vicious mobs lynch your mothers and fathers at will and drown your sisters and brothers at whim; when you have seen hate-filled policemen curse, kick and even kill your black brothers and sisters; when you see the vast majority of your twenty million Negro brothers smothering in an airtight cage of poverty in the midst of an affluent society; when you suddenly find your tongue twisted and your speech stammering as you seek to explain to your six-year-old daughter why she can't go to the public amusement park that has just been advertised on television, and see tears welling up in her eyes when she is told that Funtown is closed to colored children, and

see ominous clouds of inferiority beginning to form in her little mental sky, . . . when you are harried by day and haunted by night by the fact that you are a Negro, living constantly at tiptoe stance, never quite knowing what to expect next, and are plagued with inner fears and outer resentments; when you are forever fighting a degenerating sense of "nobodiness"—then you will understand why we find it difficult to wait. . . .

You express a great deal of anxiety over our willingness to break laws. This is certainly a legitimate concern. Since we so diligently urge people to obey the Supreme Court's decision of 1954 outlawing segregation in the public schools, at first glance it may seem rather paradoxical for us consciously to break laws. One may well ask: "How can you advocate breaking some laws and obeying others?" The answer lies in the fact that there are two types of laws: just and unjust. . . . Any law that degrades human personality is unjust. All segregation statutes are unjust because segregation distorts the soul and damages the personality. It gives the segregator a false sense of superiority and the segregated a false sense of inferiority. . . . Thus it is that I can urge men to obey the 1954 decision of the Supreme Court, for it is morally right; and I can urge them to disobey segregation ordinances, for they are morally wrong. . . .

I hope you are able to see the distinction I am trying to point out. In no sense do I advocate evading or defying the law, as would the rabid segregationist. That would lead to anarchy. One who breaks an unjust law must do so openly, lovingly, and with a willingness to accept the penalty. I submit that an individual who breaks a law that conscience tells him is unjust, and who willingly accepts the penalty of imprisonment in order to arouse the conscience of the community over its injustice, is in reality expressing the highest respect for law.

Of course, there is nothing new about this kind of civil disobedience. It was evidenced sublimely in the refusal of Shadrach, Meshach and Abednego to obey the laws of Nebuchadnezzar, on the ground that a higher moral law was at stake. It was practiced superbly by the early Christians, who were willing to face hungry lions and the excruciating pain of chopping blocks rather than submit to certain unjust laws of the Roman Empire. To a degree, academic freedom is a reality today because Socrates practiced civil disobedience. In our own nation, the Boston Tea Party represented a massive act of civil disobedience. . . .

. . . I must confess that over the past few years I have been gravely disappointed with the white moderate. . . . Shallow understanding from people of good will is more frustrating than absolute misunderstanding from people of ill will. Lukewarm acceptance is much more bewildering than outright rejection.

I had hoped that the white moderate would understand that law and order exist for the purpose of establishing justice and that when they fail in this purpose they become the dangerously structured dams that block the flow of social progress. I had hoped that the white moderate would understand that the present tension in the South is a necessary phase of the transition from an obnoxious negative peace, in which the Negro passively accepted his unjust plight, to a substantive and positive peace, in which all men will respect the dignity and worth of human personality. Actually, we who engage in nonviolent direct action are not the creators of tension. . . .

In your statement you assert that our actions, even though peaceful, must be condemned because they precipitate violence. But is this a logical assertion? Isn't this like condemning a robbed man because his possession of money precipitated the evil act of robbery? Isn't this like condemning Socrates because his unswerving commitment to truth and his philosophical inquiries precipitated the act by the misguided populace in which they made him drink hemlock? Isn't this like condemning Jesus because his unique God-consciousness and never-ceasing devotion to God's will precipitated the evil act of crucifixion? We must come to see that, as the federal courts have consistently affirmed, it is wrong to urge an individual to cease his efforts to gain his basic constitutional rights because the quest may precipitate violence. Society must protect the robbed and punish the robber. . . .

. . . We will have to repent in this generation not merely for the hateful words and actions of the bad people but for the appalling silence of the good people. Human progress never rolls in on wheels of inevitability; it comes through the tireless efforts of men willing to be co-workers with God, and without this hard work, time itself becomes an ally of the forces of social stagnation. We must use time creatively, in the knowledge that the time is always ripe to do right. Now is the time to make real the promise of democracy and transform our pending national elegy into a creative psalm of brotherhood. Now is the time to lift our national policy from the quicksand of racial injustice to the solid rock of human dignity. . . .

. . . I stand in the middle of two opposing forces in the Negro community. One is a force of complacency, made up in part of Negroes who, as a result of long years of oppression, are so drained of self-respect and a sense of "somebodiness" that they have adjusted to segregation; and in part of a few middleclass Negroes who, because of a degree of academic and economic security and because in some ways they profit by segregation, have become insensitive to the problems of the masses. The other force is one of bitterness and hatred, and it comes perilously close to advocating violence. It is expressed in the various black nationalist groups that are springing up across the nation, the largest and best-known being Elijah Muhammad's Muslim movement. Nourished by the Negro's frustration over the continued existence of racial discrimination, this movement is made up of people who have lost faith in America, who have absolutely repudiated Christianty, and who have concluded that the white man is an incorrigible "devil."

I have tried to stand between these two forces, saying that we need emulate neither the "do-nothingism" of the complacent nor the hatred and despair of the black nationalist. For there is the more excellent way of love and nonviolent protest. I am grateful to God that, through the influence of the Negro church, the way of nonviolence became an integral part of our struggle.

If this philosophy had not emerged, by now many streets of the South would, I am convinced, be flowing with blood. And I am further convinced that if our white brothers dismiss as "rabble-rousers" and "outside agitators" those of us who employ nonviolent direct action, and if they refuse to support our nonviolent efforts, millions of Negroes will, out of frustration and despair, seek solace and security in black-nationalist ideologies—a development that would inevitably lead to a frightening racial nightmare.

Oppressed people cannot remain oppressed forever. The yearning for freedom eventually manifests itself, and that is what has happened to the American Negro. Something within has reminded him of his birthright of freedom, and something without has reminded him that it can be gained. Consciously or unconsciously, he has been caught up by the *Zeitgeist*, and with his black brothers of Africa and his brown and yellow brothers of Asia, South America and the Caribbean, the United States Negro is moving with a sense of great urgency toward the promised land of racial justice. If one recognizes this vital urge that has engulfed the Negro community, one should readily understand why public demonstrations are taking place. The Negro has many pent-up resentments and latent frustrations, and he must release them. So let him march; let him make prayer pilgrimages to the city hall; let him go on freedom rides—and try to understand why he must do so. If his repressed emotions are not released in nonviolent ways, they will seek expression through violence; this is not a threat but a fact of history. So I have not said to my people: "Get rid of your discontent." Rather, I have tried to say that this normal and healthy discontent can be channeled into the creative outlet of nonviolent direct action. And now this approach is being termed extremist. . . . Perhaps the South, the nation and the world are in dire need of creative extremists.

I had hoped that the white moderate would see this need. Perhaps I was too optimistic, perhaps I expected too much. I suppose I should have realized that few members of the oppressor race can understand the deep groans and passionate yearnings of the oppressed race, and still fewer have the vision to see that injustice must be rooted out by strong, persistent and determined action. I am thankful, however, that some of our white brothers in the South have grasped the meaning of this social revolution and committed themselves to it. They are still all too few in quantity, but they are big in quality. . . .

Let me take note of my other major disappointment. I have been so greatly disappointed with the white church and its leadership. Of course, there are some notable exceptions. . . . But despite these notable exceptions, I must honestly reiterate that I have been disappointed with the church. I do not say this as one of those negative critics who can always find something wrong with the church. I say this as a minister of the gospel, who loves the church; who was nurtured in its bosom; who has been sustained by its spiritual blessings and who will remain true to it as long as the cord of life shall lengthen. . . .

There was a time when the church was very powerful—in the time when the early Christians rejoiced at being deemed worthy to suffer for what they believed. In those days the church was not merely a thermometer that recorded the ideas and principles of popular opinion; it was a thermostat that transformed the mores of society. . . .

Things are different now. So often the contemporary church is a weak, ineffectual voice with an uncertain sound. So often it is an archdefender of the status quo. Far from being disturbed by the presence of the church, the power structure of the average community is consoled by the church's silent—and often even vocal—sanction of things as they are.

But the judgment of God is upon the church as never before. If today's church does not recapture the sacrificial spirit of the early church, it will lose its authenticity, forfeit the loyalty of millions, and be dismissed as an irrelevant social club with no meaning for the twentieth century. Every day I meet young people whose disappointment with the church has turned into outright disgust.

Perhaps I have once again been too optimistic. Is organized religion too inextricably bound to the status quo to save our nation and the world? . . .

I hope the church as a whole will meet the challenge of this decisive hour. But even if the church does not come to the aid of justice, I have no despair about the future. I have no fear about the outcome of our struggle in Birmingham, even if our motives are at present misunderstood. We will reach the goal of freedom in Birmingham and all over the nation, because the goal of America is freedom. Abused and scorned though we may be, our destiny is tied up with America's destiny. Before the pilgrims landed at Plymouth, we were here. Before the pen of Jefferson etched the majestic words of the Declaration of Independence across the pages of history, we were here. For more than two centuries our forebears labored in this country without wages; they made cotton king; they built the homes of their masters while suffering gross injustice and shameful humiliation—and yet out of a bottomless vitality they continued to thrive and develop. If the inexpressible cruelties of slavery could not stop us, the opposition we now face will surely fail. We will win our freedom because the sacred heritage of our nation and the eternal will of God are embodied in our echoing demands.

Before closing I feel impelled to mention one other point in your statement that has troubled me profoundly. You warmly commended the Birmingham police force for keeping "order" and "preventing violence." I doubt that you would have so warmly commended the police force if you had seen its dogs sinking their teeth into unarmed, nonviolent Negroes. I doubt that you would so quickly commend the policemen if you were to observe their ugly and inhumane treatment of Negroes here in the city jail; if you were to watch them push and curse old Negro women and young Negro girls; if you were to see them slap and kick old Negro men and young boys; if you were to observe them, as they did on two occasions, refuse to give us food because we wanted to sing our grace together. I cannot join you in your praise of the Birmingham police department. . . .

I wish you had commended the Negro sit-inners and demonstrators of Birmingham for their sublime courage, their willingness to suffer and their amazing discipline in the midst of great provocation. One day the South will recognize its real heroes. . . .

If I have said anything in this letter that overstates the truth and indicates an un-reasonable impatience, I beg you to forgive me. If I have said anything that understates the truth and indicates my having a patience that allows me to settle for anything less than brotherhood, I beg God to forgive me.

I hope this letter finds you strong in the faith. I also hope that circumstances will soon make it possible for me to meet each of you, not as an integrationist or a civil rights leader but as a fellow clergyman and a Christian brother. Let us all hope that the dark clouds of racial prejudice will soon pass away and the deep fog of misunderstanding will be lifted from our fear-drenched communities, and in some not too distant tomorrow the radiant stars of love and brotherhood will shine over our great nation with all their scintillating beauty.

Yours for the cause of Peace and Brotherhood,

MARTIN LUTHER KING, JR.

4.10 Black Nationalism

Like Martin Luther King, Jr., Malcolm X sought racial justice, but he felt that King's methods and objectives were inadequate and rejected King's integrationist vision. In Malcolm X's opinion, King's approach left power in the hands of whites and failed to deal adequately with the psychological needs of blacks. Living in white America, blacks underwent a sort of brainwashing which encouraged them to emulate whites, to reject their own heritage and to believe in the white racist's negative view of themselves. He would have none of this.

Born Malcolm Little in Omaha, Nebraska in 1925, he joined the Black Muslim movement while serving a prison term and took the name Malcolm X. Afterward, as a spokesperson for Elijah Muhammad, leader of America's Black Muslims, he urged blacks to free themselves from psychological, economic and political subjugation, and to form their own nation. As a black nationalist, Malcolm called for changes through legal means, such as voting. But he warned that if the ballot box did not work, blacks, like other oppressed peoples, must use the bullet. This terrified many whites.

After a pilgrimage to Mecca, he began to feel great kinship not only with Africans, but with all people of color struggling for national liberation, and, indeed, even with whites who were poor or subjugated. He began talking with King about the possibility of some joint undertakings. This side of his thinking was expanding when he was killed at the hands of an assassin in 1965.

Questions

Do you find the arguments Malcolm X uses here, particularly his criticism of King's approach, logical and reasonable? What about the methods he recommends? Do you have a better solution for the problems he talks about? How did his ideas change toward the end of his life? What areas of agreement do you think he could have found with King?

If violence is wrong in America, violence is wrong abroad. If it is wrong to be violent defending black women and black children and black babies and black men, then it is wrong for America to draft us and make us violent abroad in defense of her. And if it is right for America to draft us, and teach us how to be violent in defense of her, then it is right for you and me to do whatever is necessary to defend our own people right here in this country. . . .

. . . There's been a revolution, a black revolution, going on in Africa. In Kenya, the Mau Mau were revolutionary; they were the ones who brought the word "Uhuru" to the fore . . . they believed in scorched earth, they knocked everything aside that got in their way, and their revolution also was based on land, a desire for land. In Algeria, the northern part of Africa, a revolution took place. The Alge-

rians were revolutionists, they wanted land. France offered to let them be integrated into France. They told France, to hell with France, they wanted some land, not some France. And they engaged in a bloody battle.

So I cite these various revolutions, brothers and sisters, to show you that you don't have a peaceful revolution. You don't have a turn-the-other-cheek revolution. There's no such thing as a nonviolent revolution. The only kind of revolution that is nonviolent is the Negro revolution. The only revolution in which the goal is loving your enemy is the Negro revolution. It's the only revolution in which the goal is a desegregated lunch counter, a desegregated theater, a desegregated park, and a desegregated public toilet; you can sit down next to white folks on the toilet. That's no revolution. Revolution is based on land. Land is the basis of all independence. Land is the basis of freedom, justice, and equality. . . .

Revolution is bloody, revolution is hostile, revolution knows no compromise, revolution overturns and destroys every-

Source: Malcolm X, *Malcolm X Speaks*, George Breitman, ed. (New York: Grove Press, 1965); "The American Nightmare"; interview, Pierre Berton Show, Station CFTO-TV, Toronto, January 19, 1965.

thing that gets in its way. And you, sitting around here like a knot on the wall, saying, "I'm going to love these folks no matter how much they hate me." No, you need a revolution. Whoever heard of a revolution where they lock arms . . . singing "We Shall Overcome"? You don't do that in a revolution. You don't do any singing, you're too busy swinging. It's based on land. A revolutionary wants land so he can set up his own nation, an independent nation. These Negroes aren't asking for any nation—they're trying to crawl back on the plantation.

When you want a nation, that's called nationalism. When the white man became involved in a revolution in this country against England, what was it for? He wanted this land so he could set up another white nation. That's white nationalism. The American Revolution was white nationalism. The French Revolution was white nationalism. The Russian Revolution, too—yes, it was—white nationalism. You don't think so? Why do you think Khrushchev and Mao can't get their heads together? White nationalism. All the revolutions that are going on in Asia and Africa today are based on what?—black nationalism. A revolutionary is a black nationalist. He wants a nation. . . . If you're afraid of black nationalism, you're afraid of revolution. And if you love revolution, you love black nationalism. . . .

I am going to organize and head a new mosque in New York City, known as the Muslim Mosque, Inc. This gives us a religious base, and the spiritual force necessary to rid our people of the vices that destroy the moral fiber of our community.

Our political philosophy will be black nationalism. Our economic and social philosophy will be black nationalism. Our cultural emphasis will be black nationalism. . . .

The political philosophy of black nationalism means: we must control the politics and the politicians of our community. They must no longer take orders from outside forces. We will organize, and sweep out of office all Negro politicians who are puppets for the outside forces.

Our accent will be upon youth: we need new ideas, new methods, new approaches. We will call upon young students of political science throughout the nation to help us. We will encourage these young students to launch their own independent study, and then give us their analysis and their suggestions. We are completely disenchanted with the old, adult, established politicians. We want to see some new faces—more militant faces. . . .

Concerning nonviolence: it is criminal to teach a man not to defend himself when he is the constant victim of brutal attacks. It is legal and lawful to own a shotgun or a rifle. We believe in obeying the law.

In areas where our people are the constant victims of brutality, and the government seems unable or unwilling to protect them, we should form rifle clubs that can be used to defend our lives and our property in times of emergency, such as happened last year in Birmingham; Plaquemine, Louisiana; Cambridge, Maryland; and Danville, Virginia. When our people are being bitten by dogs, they are within their rights to kill those dogs.

We should be peaceful, law-abiding— but the time has come for the American Negro to fight back in self-defense whenever and wherever he is being unjustly and unlawfully attacked.

If the government thinks I am wrong for saying this, then let the government start doing its job.

I'm not a politician, not even a student of politics; in fact, I'm not a student of much of anything. I'm not a Democrat, I'm not a

Republican, and I don't even consider myself an American. If you and I were Americans, there'd be no problem. Those Hunkies that just got off the boat, they're already Americans; Polacks are already Americans; the Italian refugees are already Americans. Everything that came out of Europe, every blue-eyed thing, is already an American. And as long as you and I have been over here, we aren't Americans yet.

Well, I am one who doesn't believe in deluding myself. I'm not going to sit at your table and watch you eat, with nothing on my plate, and call myself a diner. Sitting at the table doesn't make you a diner, unless you eat some of what's on that plate. Being here in America doesn't make you an American. Being born here in America doesn't make you an American. Why, if birth made you American, you wouldn't need any legislation, you wouldn't need any amendments to the Constitution, you wouldn't be faced with civil-rights filibustering in Washington, D.C., right now. They don't have to pass civil-rights legislation to make a Polack an American.

No, I'm not an American. I'm one of the 22 million black people who are the victims of Americanism. One of the 22 million black people who are the victims of democracy, nothing but disguised hypocrisy. So, I'm not standing here speaking to you as an American, or a patriot, or a flag-saluter, or a flag-waver—no, not I. I'm speaking as a victim of this American system. And I see America through the eyes of the victim. I don't see any American dream: I see an American nightmare.

These 22 million victims are waking up. Their eyes are coming open. They're beginning to see what they used to only look at. . . .

If you don't take this kind of stand, your little children will grow up and look at you and think "shame." If you don't take an uncompromising stand—I don't mean go out and get violent; but at the same time you should never be nonviolent unless you run into some nonviolence. I'm nonviolent with those who are nonviolent with me. But when you drop that violence on me, then you've made me go insane, and I'm not responsible for what I do. And that's the way every Negro should get. Any time you know you're within the law, within your legal rights, within your moral rights, in accord with justice, then die for what you believe in. But don't die alone. Let your dying be reciprocal. This is what is meant by equality. What's good for the goose is good for the gander. . . .

A Con Man?

If I wanted to be just a con man, I wouldn't be fool enough to try it on these streets where people are looking for my life, where I can't walk around after dark. If I wanted power, I could have gone anywhere in the world. They offered me jobs in all the African countries.

Muhammad is the man, with his house in Phoenix, his $200 suits, and his harem. He didn't believe in the black state or in getting anything for the people. That's why I got out. . . .

On Racism

Usually the black racist has been produced by the white racist. In most cases where you see it, it is the reaction to white racism, and if you analyze it closely, it's not really black racism. I think black people have shown less racist tendencies than any people since the beginning of history. . . .

If we react to white racism with a violent reaction, to me that's not black racism. If you come to put a rope around my neck and I hang you for it, to me that's not racism. Yours is racism, but my reaction has nothing to do with racism. My reaction is the reaction of a human being, reacting to defend himself and protect himself. This is what our people haven't done, and some of them, at least at the high academic level, don't want to. But most of us aren't at that level. . . .

From Taped TV Show, 1965—

I believe in recognizing every human being as a human being—neither white, black, brown, or red; and when you are dealing with humanity as a family there's no question of integration or intermarriage. It's just one human being marrying another human being, or one human being living around and with another human being.

I may say, though, that I don't think it should ever be put upon a black man, I don't think the burden to defend any position should ever be put upon the black man, because it is the white man collectively who has shown that he is hostile toward integration and toward intermarriage and toward these other strides toward oneness.

So as a black man and especially as a black American, any stand that I formerly took, I don't think that I would have to defend it, because it's still a reaction to the society, and it's a reaction that was produced by the society; and I think that it is the society that produced this that should be attacked, not the reaction that develops among the people who are the victims of that negative society.

BERTON: But you no longer believe in a black state?

MALCOM: No.

BERTON: In North America?

MALCOLM: No, I believe in a society in which people can live like human beings on the basis of equality.

4.11 Letter from the Santa Fe Jail

In the 1960s, Reies Lopez Tijerina founded the Alianza de los Pueblos Libros (Alliance of Free City-States) to help the Indo-Hispanic people of New Mexico regain their ownership of the old Spanish and Mexican land grants. Tijerina was a Protestant clergyman who had several serious encounters with the law. In June, 1967, while making a citizen's arrest of the state district attorney, he was seized for kidnapping and assault. A jury found him innocent of wrongdoing in this "courthouse raid." But in June, 1969 he was tried for another assault on public officials, and convicted. While in jail awaiting trial, he wrote an open letter to his followers, a portion of which is included below.

Questions

What is Tijerina's perception of the Anglo world in which he lives? What are his goals, and do they seem realistic? How does he justify his rebellion? Does he take a leaf from the black civil rights movement? Is there justification in what he is saying? In your opinion, how should such conflicts be resolved?

From my cell block in this jail I am writing these reflections. I write them to my people, the Indo-Hispanos, to my friends among the Anglos, to the agents of the federal government, the state of New Mexico, the Southwest, and the entire Indo-Hispano world—"Latin America."

I write to you as one of the clearest victims of the madness and racism in the hearts of our present-day politicians and rulers.

At this time, August 17, I have been in jail for 65 days—since June 11, 1969, when my appeal bond from another case was revoked by a federal judge. . . .

What is my real crime? As I and the poor people see it, especially the Indo-Hispanos, my only crime is *upholding our rights as protected by the treaty of Guadalupe Hidalgo* which ended the so-called Mexican-American War of 1846–48. My only crime is demanding the respect and protection of our property, which has been confiscated illegally by the federal government. Ever since the treaty was signed in 1848, our people have been asking every elected president of the United States for a redress of grievances. Like the Black people, we too have been criminally ignored. Our right to the Spanish land grant pueblos is the real reason why I am in prison at this moment.

Our cause and our claim and our methods are legitimate. Yet even after a jury in a court of law acquitted me last December, they still call me a violent man. But the right to make a citizen's arrest, as I attempted to make that day on Evans, is not a violent right. On the contrary, it is law and order—unless the arrested person resists or flees to avoid prosecution. No honest citizen should avoid a citizen's arrest.

This truth is denied by the conspirators against the poor and by the press which they control. There are also the Silent Contributors. The Jewish people accused the Pope of Rome for keeping silent while Hilter and his machine persecuted the Jews in Germany and other countries. I support the Jews in their right to accuse those who contributed to Hitler's acts by their *silence.* By the same token, I denounce those in New Mexico who have never opened their mouths at any time to defend or support the thousands who have been killed, robbed, raped of their culture. I don't know of any church or Establishment organization or group of elite intellectuals that has stood up for the Treaty of Guadalupe-Hidalgo. We condemn the silence of these groups and individuals and I am sure that, like the Jewish people, the poor of New

Mexico are keeping a record of the Silence which contributes to the criminal conspiracy against the Indo-Hispano in New Mexico.

As I sit in my jail cell in Santa Fe, capitol of New Mexico, I pray that all the poor people will unite to bring justice to New Mexico. My cell block has no day light, no ventilation of any kind, no light of any kind. After 9 P.M., we are left in a dungeon of total darkness. Visiting rules allow only 15 minutes per week on Thursdays from 1 to 4 P.M. so that parents who work cannot visit their sons in jail. Yesterday a 22-year-old boy cut his throat. Today, Aug. 17, two young boys cut their wrists with razor blades and were taken unconscious to the hospital. My cell is dirty and there is nothing to clean it with. The whole cell block is hot and suffocating. All my prison mates complain and show a daily state of anger. But these uncomfortable conditions do not bother me, for I have a divine dream to give me strength: the happiness of my people.

I pray to God that all the Indo-Hispano people will awake to the need for unity, and to our heavenly and constitutional responsibility for fighting peacefully to win our rights. . . .

This government must show its good faith to the Indo-Hispano in respect to the Treaty of Guadalupe-Hidalgo and the land question by forming a presidential committee to investigate and hold open hearings on the land question in the northern part of New Mexico. We challenge our own government to bring forth and put all the facts on the conference table. We have the evidence to prove our claims to property as well as to the cultural rights of which we have been deprived. *We Are Right*—and therefore ready and willing to discuss our problems and rights under the Treaty with the Anglo federal government in New Mexico or Washington, D.C., directly or through agents.

This government must also reform the whole educational structure in the Southwest before it is too late. It should begin in the northern part of New Mexico, where 80% of the population are Indo-Hispanos, as a pilot center. If it works here, then a plan can be developed based on that experience in the rest of the state and wherever the Indo-Hispano population requires it.

Because I know *We Are Right*, I have no regrets as I sit in my jail cell. I feel very, very proud and happy to be in jail for the reason that I am. June 8 in Coyote could have been my last day on earth. My life was spared by God, and to be honored by that miracle at Coyote will keep me happy for many years to come. I am sure that not one of my prison days is lost. Not one day has been in vain. While others are free, building their personal empires, I am in jail for defending and fighting for the rights of my people. Only my Indo-Hispano people have influenced me to be what I am. I am what I am, for my brothers.

4.12 The State of Black America

In the two decades following the death of Martin Luther King, Jr. and the end of the civil rights movement, blacks and other racial minorities had made many strides in the United States. The Civil Rights Act of 1964 outlawing racial discrimination in public accommodations assured civil equality and dignity to millions of people, eliminating vestiges of the Jim Crow era such as segregated drinking fountains and "separate but equal" schools. The Voting Rights Act of 1965, by allowing federal examiners to register voters where necessary, had empowered hundreds of thousands of new voters and encouraged blacks to serve in public office. In 1988, some 6,000 black Americans held elective office nationwide, compared to only a handful in the 1950s, and black voters were playing a key role in both national and local elections. Political analysts announced that black voters had changed the composition of the U.S. Senate in the election of 1986.

But the struggle for social and economic equality for racial minorities was far from won. Public and private manifestations of racism continued to occur and economic conditions for most nonwhites had failed to keep pace with improvements in civil rights legislation. Certainly this was the case for blacks.

In 1989, the National Urban League, issued a report on **The State of Black America,** *declaring that during the eight-year administration of Ronald Reagan, the nation had experienced a marked regression in race relations. The League challenged the nations to regain its bearings and press forward the agenda of racial justice. Distinguished scholars writing for the League found serious disparities between whites and blacks in employment, income, housing, health and education. One third of all black people lived in poverty, half of whom were children under the age of six. The organization proposed major improvements in public policy regarding employment, schooling, family policy and aid to the cities. Their proclaimed goal was to erase the racial gulf by the year 2000.*

Since its founding in 1910, the National Urban League has been devoted to the advancement of social services and civil rights for blacks. Politically, it has been a voice for moderation. The following excerpts are from the report's introductory overview, written by League President and Chief Executive Officer, John E. Jacob.

Questions

What does Jacob believe were the causes for the high poverty and unemployment rates among blacks? What is his evaluation of the Reagan administration regarding racial matters? Do you believe he is right? If so, why did Reagan have such a high popularity rating?

What solutions does Jacob propose? How would the new public policies he proposes be funded? What must be done by the private businesses and by individual Americans to correct racial imbalances?

What do you imagine are the comparable conditions for other racial minorities, such as Native Americans, Mexican Americans and Asian Americans, and why?

. . . The legacy of the Reagan Era will leave its mark on our society for years to come. President Reagan is one of the few presidents to have largely achieved the goals he set for himself when he came to office—lower tax rates, a big defense buildup, federal withdrawal from social programs, and less government. . . .

Another legacy of the Reagan Era is deeper race and class divisions. The past eight years have seen the rich get richer and the poor get poorer. In effect, there has been a huge transfer of resources from the poor to the affluent. Inequality has always been a serious national problem, but in the past eight years, we have become a far more unequal society.

Racial divisions have also increased sharply. The Reagan administration's war on affirmative action, its refusal to allow access to decision-making by minorities, its fight against civil rights legislation, and its often demeaning acts and statements about the poor, have created bitterness among blacks and encouraged racists in the white community. . . .

History will make a final judgment on the Reagan Era, but from this vantage point it was a regressive period in our national life: a time when some Americans got richer, but our society as a whole got poorer, and blacks were driven further from the goal of equality.

That goal will be forever in the distance so long as black poverty remains so disproportionate. A third of all black people are poor—more if you use a measurement of poverty that is closer to the income needs required to meet minimally decent living standards than the current poverty index, which is based on a formula designed to

determine the minimum necessary for short-term survival.

Black—and white—poverty increased in the 1980s. Some eight million more people were poor in 1987 (the last year for which there are definitive figures) than a decade earlier. Two million of the new poor are black. Nearly half of all black children live in poverty. Blacks are three times as likely as whites to be poor.

But simply to state such shocking statistics is to understate the nature of black poverty. Ideologues and the callous say that it is the result of single female-headed families, or of the refusal to work, or of generous social benefits that discourage workforce participation.

The facts argue otherwise. Compared with a decade ago, when black poverty rates were lower, black unemployment rates are the same and the percentage of the black poor living in female-headed families is lower.

The rise in black poverty can be traced to two major factors—the shift in the economy that reduced opportunities for less-skilled workers and cuts in federal programs that provide opportunities to escape from poverty.

Over the past decade, poverty rates for intact black families have risen as fast as the rates for female-headed families. The region with the highest black poverty rate is the Midwest—the region hardest hit by deindustrialization and the decline in manufacturing jobs. The Center on Budget and Policy Priorities estimates that only one in every 12 black families with children that would have been poor without government benefits was lifted out of poverty by those benefits. A decade ago, the figure was one of every six. The Center says that Census Bureau data indicate that the reduced effectiveness of federal benefit programs account for almost 40 percent of

SOURCE: From John E. Jacob, "Black America, 1989: An Overview," *The State of Black America, 1989* (New York, The National Urban League, Inc., 1989).

the rise in black poverty over the past decade.

Another indicator of the economic deterioration among blacks is the decline in real black income. Among the poor, more are poorer—their incomes fell from over $5,000 in 1978 to under $4,000 in 1987, adjusted for inflation. Black men work ing full-time experienced an inflation-adjusted decline in earnings of 10 percent. Among younger black men—the under-30 group starting families—real income is half what it was in the early 1970s. A prime cause is the extraordinary high black unemployment rate—about two-and-a-half times that for whites, and trending higher.

The gap between blacks and whites extends beyond poverty and unemployment rates to include all the key indices of life, from infant mortality rates that are at Third World levels in some ghetto neighborhoods, to education, where a recent study has found blacks disproportionately shunted into slow learner classes and excluded from programs for the gifted, to housing, where a recent study found high levels of segregation in the suburbs, as well as in urban housing.

At year-end, the tragic dimensions of that gap was heightened by the report of the National Center for Health Statistics that revealed life expectancy for blacks declined for the second year in a row—the first back-to-back annual decline in this century—while white life expectancy continued to increase.

And it is ironic that in 1989, the 200th anniversary of the adoption of the U.S. Constitution that defined blacks as "three-fifths" of other persons, black income is well below 60 of percent of white income, and other indicators find blacks at an even greater disadvantage.

The black-white gap might be barely tolerable if it were narrowing, but in the 1980s it has widened. That is why the Commission on Minority Participation in Education and American Life, which included former Presidents Ford and Carter, issued a report in 1988 that charged America was "moving backward" in its efforts to secure equity for minority citizens. The Commission's report echoed the findings of the Kerner Commission two decades earlier that America was sliding into "two societies—separate and unequal." . . .

Chapter Five: Nationality and Religion

5.1 Science and Religion

The intellectual revolution started by the English naturalist Charles Darwin around 1860 spread throughout every field of thought for the next several generations. His theories of natural selection, supported by the findings of geologists, astronomers and biblical scholars, had an especially profound impact on religion. To people of rational belief, it was no longer clear whether humans were the product of divine intervention, as taught by religious teachers from time immemorial, or merely the descendants of creatures like apes. If the latter, then perhaps the Book of Genesis, and the Bible itself, was seriously flawed as a guide to creation, morality and to an understanding of the meaning of life.

Some ministers dug in their heels and offered refutations of evolutionary thinking; others decided to move with the tide and accommodate themselves to the new thinking. One religious leader who was able to reconcile Darwin with his Protestant beliefs was the Rev. Henry Ward Beecher, the dynamic and popular pastor of Plymouth Congregational Church in Brooklyn, New York. In this sermon, entitled "The Two Revelations," preached on May 31, 1885, Beecher explains how he unified his thinking.

Questions

How does Beecher explain Darwin and attempt to comfort his listeners as to the implications of evolution? How does Beecher reconcile divine law and faith with the new scientific discoveries? Summarize his main points in your own words.

What refutations would you expect from fundamentalists who took the Bible literally?

Does this debate still echo through American religious and intellectual circles today? Explain.

Does Darwin undermine the moral attitudes of Americans? Can you have morality based on a scientific view of nature, instead of on religion? Are they able to co-exist?

That the whole world and the universe were the creation of God is the testimony of the whole Bible, both Jewish and Christian; but how he made them—whether by

SOURCE: Henry Ward Beecher, *Evolution and Religion* (New York, 1885), pp. 44–55.

the direct force of a creative will or indirectly through a long series of gradual changes—the Scriptures do not declare. The grand truth is that this world was not a chance, a creative fermentation, a self-development, but that it was the product of an Intelligent Being, that the divine will in the continuance of this world manifests itself under the form of what are called natural laws, and that the operations of normal and legitimate laws are the results of divine will.

There are two records of God's creative energy. One is the record of the unfolding of *man* and of the race under the inspiration of God's nature: this is a mere sketch; of the ancient periods of man there is almost nothing known. The other of these records or revelations—if you choose to call them so—pertains to the physical globe, and reveals the divine thought through the unfolding history of *matter;* and this is the older. So we have two revelations: God's thought in the evolution of matter, and God's thought in the evolution of mind; and these are the Old Testament and the New—not in the usual sense of those terms, but in an appropriate scientific use of them. . . .

To be sure, the history of man in the Bible is more important than the history of the globe. The globe was created for man as a house is created to serve the family. But both are God's revelations; both are to be received with intelligent reverence; both are to be united and harmonized; both are to be employed in throwing light, the one upon the other. That noble body of investigators who are deciphering the hieroglyphics of God inscribed upon this temple of the earth are to be honored and encouraged. As it is now, vaguely bigoted theologists, ignorant priests, jealous churchmen, unintelligent men, whose very existence seems like a sarcasm upon creative wisdom, with leaden wit and stinging irony swarm about the adventurous surveyors who are searching God's handiwork and who have added to the realm of the knowledge of God the grandest treasures. Men pretending to be ministers of God, with all manner of grimace and shallow ridicule

and witless criticism and unproductive wisdom, enact the very feats of the monkey in the attempt to prove that the monkey was not their ancestor.

It is objected to all assertions of the validity of God's great record in matter, that certain is uncertain and unripe; that men are continually changing the lines of science, that it will not do to rest upon the results of scientific investigation. It will be time to consider science when it has ripened into a certainty, say men, but not now. . . . The whole Christian world for two thousand years, since the completion of the canons, has been divided up like the end of a broom into infinite splinters, quarreling with each other as to what the book did say, and what it did mean. Why then should men turn and say that scientific men are unsettled in their notions. . . .

It is said, or thought, that a layman should not meddle with that which can be judged by only scientific experts: that science demands a special training before one can discern correctly its facts, or judge wisely of the force of its conclusions. This is true; it is true both of those who accept and those who deny its results. But, when time and investigation have brought the scientific world to an agreement, and its discoveries pass into the hands of all men, there comes an important duty, which moral teachers, parents, and especially clergymen, are perhaps as well or better fitted to fulfill than mere scientists, viz., to determine what effect the discoveries of science will have upon questions of morality and religion. It is to this aspect that the best minds of the Christian ministry are now addressing themselves. . . .

A vague notion exists with multitudes that science is infidel, and that Evolution in particular is revolutionary—that is, revolutionary of the doctrines of the Church.

Men of such views often say, "I know that religion is true. I do not wish to hear anything that threatens to unsettle my faith." But faith can be unsettled by the access of light and knowledge had better be unsettled. The intensity of such men's faith in their own thoughts is deemed to be safer than a larger view of God's thoughts. Others speak of Evolution as a pseudo-science teaching that man descended from monkeys, or ascended as the case may be. They have no conception of it as the history of the divine process in the building of this world. They dismiss it with jests, mostly ancient jests; or, having a smattering of fragmentary knowledge, they address victorious ridicule to audiences as ignorant as they are themselves. . . .

First, then, what is Evolution, and what does it reveal? The theory of Evolution teaches that the creation of this earth was not accomplished in six days of twenty-four hours; that the divine method occupied ages and ages of immense duration; that nothing, of all the treasures of the globe as they now stand, was created at first in its present perfectness; that everything has grown through the lapse of ages into its present condition; that the whole earth, with their development in it, was, as it were, an egg, a germ, a seed; that the forests, the fields, the shrubs, the vineyards, all grasses and flowers, all insects, fishes, and birds, all mammals of every gradation, have had a long history, and that they have come to the position in which they now stand through ages and ages of gradual change and unfolding. Also that the earth itself went through a period of long preparation, passing from ether by condensation to a visible cloud form with increasing solidity, to such a condition as now prevails in the sun; that it condensed and became solid; that cold congealed its vapor;

that by chemical action and by mechanical grinding of its surface by ice a soil was prepared fit for vegetation, long before it was fit for animal life; that plants simple and coarse came first and developed through all stages of complexity to the present conditions of the vegetable kingdom; that aquatic, invertebrate animals were the earliest of animals, according to the testimony of fossils in the earth. Fishes came next in order, then amphibians, then reptiles. "All these tribes were represented by species before the earliest of the mammals appeared. The existence of birds before the earliest mammal is not proved, though believed by some paleontologists upon probable evidence. The early mammals were marsupial, like the opossum and the kangaroo, and lived in the same era called by Agassiz the reptilian period. True mammals came into geologic history in the tertiary era. Very long after the appearance of the first bird came man, the last and grandest of the series, it is doubtful whether in the tertiary period or immediately sequent. It is not established whether his bones or relics occur as far back as the tertiary era." . . .

Second.—As thus set forth, it may be said that Evolution is accepted as *the method* of creation by the whole scientific world, and that the period of controversy is passed and closed. A few venerable men yet live, with many doubts; but it may be said that ninety-nine per cent.—as has been declared by an eminent physicist—ninety-nine per cent. of scientific men and working scientists of the world are using this theory without any doubt of its validity. While the scientific world is at agreement upon this *order* of occurrence, it has been much divided as to the *causes* which have operated to bring about these results. There is a diversity of opinion still, but with every decade scientific men are drawing together to a common ground of belief.

Third.—The theory of Evolution is the *working* theory of every department of physical science all over the world. Withdraw this theory, and every department of physical research would fall back into heaps of hopelessly dislocated facts, with no more order or reason or philosophical coherence than exists in a basket of marbles or in the juxtaposition of the multitudinous sands of the seashore. We should go back into chaos if we took out of the laboratories, out of the dissecting-rooms, out of the fields of investigation, this great doctrine of Evolution.

Fourth.—This science of Evolution is taught in all advanced academies, in all colleges and universities, in all medical and surgical schools, and our children are receiving it as they are the elements of astronomy or botany or chemistry. That in another generation Evolution will be regarded as uncontradictable as the Copernican system of astronomy, or the Newtonian doctrine of gravitation, can scarcely be doubted. Each of these passed through the same contradiction by theologians. They were charged by the Church, as is Evolution now, with fostering materialism, infidelity, and atheism. . . .

Fifth.—Evolution is substantially held by men of profound Christian faith . . . by increasing numbers of Christian preachers in America; by Catholics like Mivart, in England . . . and finally, among hundreds of other soundly learned and Christian men, by the Bishop of London, Dr. Williams, whose Bampton Lectures for 1884 contain a bold, frank, and judicial estimate of Evolution, and its relations to Christianity.

Sixth.—To the fearful and the timid let me say, that while Evolution is certain to oblige theology to reconstruct its system, it will take nothing away from the grounds of true religion. . . . If you can change theology, you will emancipate religion; yet men are continually confounding the two terms, religion and theology. They are not alike. Religion is the condition of a man's nature as toward God and toward his fellowmen. That is religion—love that breeds truth, love that breeds justice, love that breeds harmonies of intimacy and intercommunication, love that breeds duty, love that breeds conscience, love that carries in its hand the scepter of pain, not to destroy and to torment, but to teach and to save. Religion is that state of mind in which a man is related by his emotions, and through his emotions by his will and conduct, to God and to the proper performance of duty in this world. Theology is the philosophy of God, of divine government, and of human nature. The philosophy of these may be one thing; the reality of them may be another and totally different one. Though intimately connected, they are not all the same. Theology is a science; religion, an art.

Evolution will multiply the motives and facilities of righteousness. . . . Not only will those great truths be unharmed, by which men work zealously for the reformation of their fellow-men, but they will be developed to a breadth and certainty not possible in their present philosophical condition. At present the sword of the spirit is in the sheath of a false theology. Evolution, applied to religion, will influence it only as the hidden temples are restored, by removing the sands which have drifted in from the arid deserts of scholastic and medieval theologies. It will change theology, but only to bring out the simple temple of God in clearer and more beautiful lines and proportions.

Seventh.—In every view of it, I think we are to expect great practical fruit from the application of the truths that flow now from the interpretation of Evolution. It will obliterate the distinction between natural and revealed religion, both of which are the testimony of God. . . . What is called morality will be no longer dissevered from religion. Morals bear to spirituality the same relation which the root bears to the blossom and the fruit. Hitherto a false and imperfect theology has set them in two different provinces. We have been taught that morality will not avail us, and that spirituality is the only saving element: whereas, there is no spirituality itself without morality; all true spirituality is an outgrowth, it is the blossom and fruit on the stem of morality. It is time that these distinctions were obliterated, as they will be, by the progress and application of the doctrine of Evolution.

In every view, then, it is the duty of the friends of simple and unadulterated Christianity to hail the rising light and to uncover every element of religious teaching to its wholesome beams. Old men may be charitably permitted to die in peace, but young men and men in their prime are by God's providence laid under the most solemn obligations to thus discern the signs of the times, and to make themselves acquainted with the knowledge which science is laying before them. And above all, those zealots of the pulpit—who make faces at a science which they do not understand, and who reason from prejudice to ignorance, who not only will not lead their people, but hold up to scorn those who strive to take off the burden of ignorance from their shoulders—these men are bound to open their eyes and see God's sun shining in the heavens.

That Evolution applied will greatly change the reading and the construction of the earlier periods of the Scripture history cannot be doubted. The Bible itself is one of the most remarkable monuments of the truth of the evolutionary process. . . .

The last years of my life I dedicate to this work of religion, to this purpose of God . . . and in no part of my life has my ministry seemed to me so solemn, so earnest, so fruitful, as this last decade will seem if I shall succeed in uncovering to the faith of this people the great truths of the two revelations—God's building revelation of the material globe, and God's building revelation in the unfolding of the human mind. May God direct me in your instruction!

5.2 Immigration to the United States, 1820–1951

The following tables summarize certain immigration trends in American history. The first presents statistics on immigration from 1820 to 1951, and the second indicates immigration quotas as of 1951. In evaluating the data, one should recall that the quota law was instituted in 1924.

Questions

What overall immigration patterns are revealed in the first chart? Why was there a sharp decline starting in 1931? How have wars affected immigration?

What ethnic, political or national biases are reflected in the 1951 quotas? Are these biases justified, or should immigration be more open, as it had been in the nineteenth century?

Conversely, as times change, do you believe immigration should be more restricted? And if so, on what basis? Should special consideration be given to people who have needed skills, are economically independent, are political refugees, are citizens of neighboring nations, have family relations in the U.S., etc.?

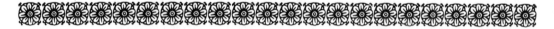

Immigration to the United States 1820–1951*

From 1820 to 1867 figures represent alien passengers arrived; 1868 to 1891 inclusive and 1895 to 1897 inclusive immigrant aliens arrived; 1892 to 1894 inclusive and from 1898 to the present time immigrant aliens admitted.

Year	Number of Persons	Year	Number of Persons	Year	Number of Persons	Year	Number of Persons
1820–1951	39,531,199	1849	297,024	1881–1890	5,246,613	1917	295,403
		1850	369,980	1881	669,431	1918	110,618
1820	8,385	1851–1860	2,598,214	1882	788,992	1919	141,132
		1851	379,466	1883	603,322	1920	430,001
1821–1830	143,439	1852	371,603	1884	518,592		
1821	9,127	1853	368,645	1885	395,346	1921–1930	4,107,209
1822	6,911	1854	427,833	1886	334,203	1921	805,228
1823	6,354	1855	200,877	1887	490,109	1922	309,556
1824	7,912	1856	200,436	1888	546,889	1923	522,919
1825	10,199	1857	251,306	1889	444,427	1924	706,896
1826	10,837	1858	123,126	1890	455,302	1925	294,314
1827	18,875	1859	121,282	1891–1900	3,687,564	1926	304,488
1828	27,382	1860	153,640	1891	560,319	1927	335,175
1829	22,520			1892	579,663	1928	307,255
1830	23,322	1861–1870	2,314,824	1893	439,730	1929	279,678
		1861	91,918	1894	285,631	1930	241,700
1831–1840	599,125	1862	91,985	1895	258,536		
1831	22,633	1863	176,282	1896	343,267	1931–1940	528,431
1832	60,482	1864	193,418	1897	230,832	1931	97,139
1833	58,640	1865	248,120	1898	229,299	1932	35,576
1834	65,365	1866	318,568	1899	311,715	1933	23,068
1835	45,374	1867	315,722	1900	448,572	1934	29,470
1836	76,242	1868	138,840			1935	34,956
1837	79,340	1869	352,768	1901–1910	8,795,386	1936	36,329
1838	38,914	1870	387,203	1901	487,918	1937	50,244
1839	68,069			1902	648,743	1938	67,895
1840	84,066	1871–1880	2,812,191	1903	857,046	1939	82,998
		1871	321,350	1904	812,870	1940	70,756
1841–1850	1,713,251	1872	404,806	1905	1,026,499		
1841	80,289	1873	459,803	1906	1,100,735	1941–1950	1,035,039
1842	104,565	1874	313,339	1907	1,285,349	1941	51,776
1843	52,496	1875	227,498	1908	782,870	1942	28,781
1844	78,615	1876	169,986	1909	751,786	1943	23,725
1845	114,371	1877	141,857	1910	1,041,570	1944	28,551
1846	154,416	1878	138,469			1945	38,119
1847	234,968	1879	177,826	1911–1920	5,735,811	1946	108,721
1848	226,527	1880	457,257	1911	878,587	1947	147,292
				1912	838,172	1948	170,570
				1913	1,197,892	1949	188,317
				1914	1,218,480	1950	249,187
				1915	326,700		
				1916	298,826	1951–1951	205,717

SOURCE: U.S. Department of Justice, Immigration and Naturalization Service. The quotas follow the rule established in President's Proclamation No. 2283 of April 1938.

*Data are for fiscal years ended June 30, except 1820 to 1831 inclusive and 1844 to 1849 inclusive fiscal years ended Sept. 30; 1833 to 1842 inclusive and 1851 to 1867 inclusive years ended Dec. 31; 1832 covers 15 months ended Dec. 31; 1843 nine months ended Sept. 30; 1850 15 months ended Dec. 31, and 1868 six months ended June 30.

Immigration Quotas
(As of 1951)

Country or Area	Quota	Country or Area	Quota
Afghanistan	100	Lithuania	386
Albania	100	Luxemburg	100
Andorra	100	Monaco	100
Arabian peninsula except Muscat, Aden Settlement and Protectorate, and Saudi Arabia	100	Morocco (French and Spanish zones and Tangier)	100
		Muscat (Oman)	100
Australia (including Tasmania, Papua, and all islands appertaining to Australia)	100	Nauru (British mandate)	100
		Nepal	100
Austria*	1,413	Netherlands	3,153
Belgium	1,304	New Guinea, Territory of (including appertaining islands) (Australian mandate)	100
Bhutan	100		
Bulgaria	100	New Zealand	100
Cameroons (British mandate)	100	Norway	2,377
Cameroun (French mandate)	100	Palestine (with Trans-Jordan) (British mandate)	100
China	100		
Chinese Race	105	Philippine Islands***	100
Czechoslovakia	2,874	Poland	6,524
Danzig, Free City of	100	Portugal	440
Denmark	1,181	Ruanda & Urundi (Belgium mandate)	100
Egypt	100	Rumania**	291
Estonia	116	Samoa, Western (mandate of New Zealand)	100
Ethiopia (Abyssinia)	100		
Finland	569	San Marino	100
France	3,086	Saudi Arabia	100
Germany*	25,957	Siam	100
Great Britain & Northern Ireland	65,721	South Africa, Union of	100
Greece**	310	South-West Africa (mandate of the Union of South Africa)	100
Hungary	869		
Iceland	100	Spain	252
India	100	Sweden	3,314
Iran	100	Switzerland	1,707
Iraq	100	Syria**	100
Ireland (Erie)	17,853	Tanganyika Territory (British mandate)	100
Israel**	100	Togoland (British mandate)	100
Italy**	5,677	Togoland (French mandate)	100
Japan	100	Trieste, Free Territory	100
Jordan (formerly Trans-Jordan)**	100	Turkey	226
Latvia	236	Union of Soviet Socialist Republics**	2,798
Lebanon**	100	Yap and other Pacific islands under Japanese mandate	100
Liberia	100		
Liechtenstein	100	Yugoslavia	938
		TOTAL	154,277

[1]President's Proclamation No. 2283 of April 28, 1938.

*Effective September 28, 1945
**Effective July 27, 1949
***Effective July 4, 1946

5.3   Strangers at the Gates

Two poems may be read to assess how some people felt about immigration in the late nineteenth century. The first is from the sonnet entitled, "The New Colossus," by the American poet, Emma Lazarus (1849–1887). Written around 1886 by the daughter of Jewish immigrants, it celebrates the generous and open policy of asylum that had long typified America's attitude toward immigration. The last lines, beginning "Give me your tired, . . ." are inscribed on the pedestal of the Statue of Liberty. The second poem is "Unguarded Gates," by the aristocratic Bostonian, Thomas Bailey Aldrich (1836–1907). Appearing in the Atlantic Monthly *magazine in 1892, the Aldrich poem was one of the first literary efforts to warn of the dangers of immigration. The author expressed the unease of Anglo-Saxons toward the newest immigrants then flooding the country from Eastern and Southern Europe.*

Questions

Why did Lazarus name her poem "The New Colossus"? Who was the "old" Colossus?

Compare the imagery in both poems for strength and emotional impact. Why does Lazarus succeed better than Aldrich?

The Lazarus poem remains the more famous and popular of the two, but the sentiment behind the poem by Aldrich is the one that soon prevailed. What brought about the change?

Emma Lazarus—

THE NEW COLOSSUS

Not like the brazen giant of Greek fame,
With conquering limbs astride from land to land;
Here at our sea-washed, sunset gates shall stand
A mighty woman with a torch, whose flame
Is the imprisoned lightning, and her name

Mother of Exiles. From her beacon-hand
Glows world-wide welcome; her mild eyes command
The air-bridged harbor that twin cities frame.
"Keep, ancient lands, your storied pomp!" cries she
With silent lips, "Give me your tired, your poor,
Your huddled masses yearning to breathe free,
The wretched refuse of your teeming shore.
Send these, the homeless, tempest-tost to me.
I lift my lamp beside the golden door!"

SOURCE: Thomas Bailey Aldrich, "Unguarded Gates," *Atlantic Monthly* (July 1892), p. 57; Emma Lazarus, *Poems* (1889).

Thomas Bailey Aldrich —

UNGUARDED GATES

Wide open and unguarded stand our gates,
Named of the four winds, North, South,
    East, and West;
Portals that lead to an enchanted land
Of cities, forests, fields of living gold,
Vast prairies, lordly summits touched with
    snow,
Majestic rivers sweeping proudly past

The Arab's date-palm and the Norseman's
    pine—
A realm wherein are fruits of every zone,
Airs of all climes, for lo! throughout the
    year
The red rose blossoms somewhere—a rich
    land,
A later Eden planted in the wilds,
With not an inch of earth within its bound

But if a slave's foot press it sets him free.
Here, it is written, Toil shall have its wage,
And Honor honor, and the humblest man
Stand level with the highest in the law.
Of such a land have men in dungeons
    dreamed,
And with the vision brightening in their
    eyes
Gone smiling to the fagot and the sword.

Wide open and unguarded stand our gates,
And through them presses a wild motley
    throng—
Men from the Volga and the Tartar steppes,
Featureless figures of the Hoang-Ho,
Malayan, Scythian, Teuton, Kelt, and Slav,
Flying the Old World's poverty and scorn;
These bringing with them unknown gods
    and rites,
Those, tiger passions, here to stretch their
    claws.
In street and alley what strange tongues are
    loud,
Accents of menace alien to our air,
Voices that once the Tower of Babel knew!

O Liberty, white Goddess! is it well
To leave the gates unguarded? On thy
    breast
Fold Sorrow's children, soothe the hurts of
    fate,
Lift the down-trodden, but with hand of
    steel
Stay those who to thy sacred portals come
To waste the gifts of freedom. Have a care
Lest from thy brow the clustered stars be
    torn
And trampled in the dust. For so of old
The thronging Goth and Vandal trampled
    Rome,
And where the temples of the Caesars stood
The lean wolf unmolested made her lair.

5.4   The Scientists and the "Hebrews"

   The "scientific" study of racial and ethnic matters became important at the end of the nineteenth and beginning of the twentieth centuries. Using what seemed like scientific methods of observation and investigation, academics in the fields of sociology, psychology and anthropology not only measured head sizes, skin colors and noses, but also classified and identified the social habits, manners and customs of various groups. In comparing one group with another they offered sweeping generalizations. These conclusions were not always intentionally ma-

licious, but they often ended up merely dressing old stereotypes in new clothes to give them a scientific look.

Below is a brief passage from a book published in 1904 by Nathaniel Shaler, Dean of Harvard University's Lawrence Scientific School, entitled, **The Neighbor: The Natural History of Human Contacts.** *It is especially concerned with the relationship of Jew and Gentile. He explains why the Jewish "race" is not as popular as it could be, why it comes off a poor second to Yankees, and why it also compares unfavorably with blacks in some respects.*

Questions

What characteristics does Shaler attribute to blacks, Jews and Anglo-Saxons? What sort of evidence does he rely on, and how valid is it for scientific inquiry?

Today, what do social scientists contribute to the discussion of ethnic and racial matters? What would they say about Shaler's use of the term "Hebrew" and "race?"

Does anti-Semitism remain a social reality? Is it increasing or diminishing? What factors keep it alive?

The greater number of the observers agree that there is a failure on the part of the Jews to respond in like temper to the greeting which they send them; they agree further that there is generally a sense of avidity, a sense of the presence of a seeking in the Jew for immediate profit, a desire to win at once some advantage from the situation such as is not immediately disclosed, however clear it might be in the mind of an interlocutor of his own race. Several have stated that the offense came from a feeling that the Jew neighbor was smarter than themselves, having keener wits and a mind more intent on gainful ends. Others state that the Israelitic spirit

makes a much swifter response to the greeting the stranger gives them than the Aryan, and that the acquaintance is forced in such an irritating manner as to breed dislike.

This last noted feature in the contact phenomena of Israelites and Aryans appears to me a matter of much importance, especially as it accords with my own experience and with observations formed long before I began to devise and criticise theories on this subject. As one of the Deans of Harvard University I have been for ten years in a position where I have to meet from year to year a number of young Hebrews. It has been evident to me from the first that these youths normally respond much more swiftly to my greeting than those of my own race, and that they divine and act on my state of mind with far greater celerity. They are, in fact, so quick that they

SOURCE: Nathaniel Southgate Shaler, *The Neighbor: The Natural History of Human Contacts* (Boston: Houghton Mifflin & Co., 1904), pp. 110–125.

are often where I am in my slower way about to be before I am really there; this would make them at times seem irritating, indeed presumptuous, were it not interesting to me from a racial point of view. To those who are in no wise concerned with such questions this alacrity is naturally exasperating, especially when the movement is not only of the wits but of the sympathies. We all know how disagreeable it is to have the neighbor call on us for some kind of affectionate response before we are ready to be moved, and how certain is such a summons to dry the springs which else might have yielded abundantly. In our slow Aryan way we demand an introductory process on the part of the fellow-man who would successfully appeal to our emotions. Our orators know this and provide ample exordiums for their moving passages; none ventures in the manner of the Hebrew prophet to assume that his hearers will awaken at a cry. . . .

It appears to me from my own observations, from those of the selected persons who have aided me, as well as from the history of the Jews, that their minds work in a somewhat different manner from our own. Our habit is to separate the fields of action so that we have a limited field for preliminary intercourse with men, another for business relations, yet another wherein the sympathies may enter. With the Hebrew all the man's work is done in one field and all together; he is at the same time friend, trader, and citizen, all of his parts working simultaneously. There is a basis for much friction in this diversity of mental habit. We are naturally offended to find the business motive mingled with affections, for the excellent reason that it is not our way to do this; therefore it appears out of the natural order; were we to change nature with the Jew the offense would be none the less. . . .

It is instructive to contrast the lack of a tendency to imitation in the Jews with the excess of it among the American Africans. Although I have watched Jews closely for many years, I have never seen in them the least disposition to adapt themselves to their neighbors as a Negro quickly and instinctively does. The black man at once becomes the mirror of his superior whether the man above him is his master or not. He so naturally imitates the tones, gestures, and even the superficial aspects of thought of our race, that those alone who have taken pains to search behind the sympathetic mask perceive that he is not a white man in a black skin, but that his deeper nature in many and most important regards is profoundly different from all the other peoples with whom we have intimate relations. This spontaneous imitative humor has stood the Negroes in good stead. It has enabled them to win past the original antipathy which their physical peculiarities tend to arouse in vastly greater measure than those of the Hebrews, and to make the whites who are accustomed to them their friends. This curious identification, the most complete that has ever taken place between two widely parted stocks, is clearly due to the unpremeditated and singularly well-accomplished adoption by the Negroes of the white man's ways.

5.5   Patriotism and Practical Politics

To assure their survival and success in America, immigrants developed several kinds of institutions. Their churches, synagogues and parochial schools helped preserve their old world customs and religions. Their saloons and restaurants were important as meeting places for socializing and conducting business. Each group established its own networks to find jobs, advance business connections and conduct charities, hospitals, theatres and sporting organizations. Immigrant theatres supported comedians who helped immigrant audiences laugh at themselves and at the outside world. The political party organizations took hold in immigrant neighborhoods as a means of securing jobs, wealth and power.

At the end of the nineteenth century, the New York County Democratic party organization known as Tammany Hall became a formidable center of immigrant power, especially for Irish Americans. Tammany kept its people in office by awarding city contracts to its friends and financial contributors, and by offering poor people jobs and favors in return for votes. Dominated after the Civil War by the Irish, but including other immigrant groups as well, Tammany's leaders helped themselves freely to New York City's wealth. Tammany's great enemy was the civil service system, which required office seekers to pass qualifying exams for municipal jobs rather than by obtaining appointments from party bosses for services rendered.

In 1905, Tammany leader George Washington Plunkitt explained Tammany's operations to the public in a series of "very plain talks on very practical politics." An example follows. Americans of older stock criticized the immigrants who supported Tammany for not being "American" enough. Yet as Plunkitt described it, "patriotism" was a vital part of Tammany's system. (See also Document 7.6.)

Questions

Do you believe that Plunkitt really woke up singing "The Star Spangled Banner"? If not, why did he make that claim? What do you suppose he means by investing in patriotism? Why does he defend Tammany's patriotism so strongly?

Would the Irish Americans who read his words interpret them the same way as Anglo-Saxon Protestants? If you were a recently arrived Irish immigrant, how would you respond when native-born Americans questioned your patriotism?

To which social class is Plunkitt speaking? What methods does he use to win its support?

I am for municipal ownership on one condition: that the civil service law be repealed. It's a grand idea—the city ownin' the railroads, the gas works and all that. Just see how many thousands of new places there would be for the workers in Tammany! Why, there would be almost enough to go around, if no civil service law stood in the way. My plan is this: first get rid of that infamous law, and then go ahead and by degrees get municipal ownership.

Some of the reformers are sayin' that municipal ownership won't do because it would give a lot of patronage to the politicians. How those fellows mix things up when they argue! They're givin' the strongest argument in favor of municipal ownership when they say that. Who is better fitted to run the railroads and the gas plants and the ferries than the men who make a business of lookin' after the interests of the city? Who is more anxious to serve the city? Who needs the job more?

Look at the Dock Department! The city owns the docks, and how beautiful Tammany manages them! I can't tell you how many places they provide for our workers. I know there is a lot of talk about dock graft, but that talk comes from the outs. When the Republicans had the docks under Low and Strong, you didn't hear them sayin' anything about graft, did you? No; they just went in and made hay while the sun shone. That's always the case. When the reformers are out they raise the yell that Tammany men should be sent to jail. When they get in, they're so busy keepin' out of jail themselves that they don't have no time to attack Tammany.

SOURCE: William L. Riordon, comp., *A Series of Very Plain Talks on Very Practical Politics, Delivered by Ex-Senator George Washington Plunkitt, the Tammany Philosopher, from His Rostrum—the New York County Court House Bootblack Stand* (New York, 1905).

All I want is that municipal ownership be postponed till I get my bill repealin' the civil service law before the next legislature. It would be all a mess if every man who wanted a job would have to run up against a civil service examination. For instance, if a man wanted a job as motorman on a surface car, it's ten to one that they would ask him: "Who wrote the Latin grammar, and, if so, why did he write it? How many years were you at college? Is there any part of the Greek language you don't know? State all you don't know, and why you don't know it. Give a list of all the sciences with full particulars about each one and how it came to be discovered. Write out word for word the last ten decisions of the United States Supreme Court and show if they conflict with the last ten decisions of the police courts of New York City."

Before the would-be motorman left the civil service room, the chances are he would be a raving lunatic. Anyhow I wouldn't like to ride on his car. Just here I want to say one last final word about civil service. In the last ten years I have made an investigation which I've kept quiet till this time. Now I have all the figures together, and I'm ready to announce the result. My investigation was to find out how many civil service reformers and how many politicians were in state prisons. I discovered that there was forty per cent more civil service reformers among the jailbirds. If any legislative committee wants the detailed figures, I'll prove what I say. I don't want to give the figures now, because I want to keep them to back me up when I go to Albany to get the civil service law repealed. Don't you think that when I've had my inning, the civil service law will go down, and the people will see that the politicians are all right, and that they ought to have the job of runnin' things when municipal ownership comes?

One thing more about municipal ownership. If the city owned the railroads, etc., salaries would be sure to go up. Higher salaries is the cryin' need of the day. Municipal ownership would increase them all along the line and would stir up such patriotism as New York City never knew before. You can't be patriotic on a salary that just keeps the wolf from the door. Any man who pretends he can will bear watchin'. Keep your hand on your watch and pocketbook when he's about. But, when a man has a good fat salary, he finds himself hummin' "Hail Columbia," all unconscious and he fancies, when he's ridin' in a trolley car, that the wheels are always sayin': "Yankee Doodle Came to Town." I know how it is myself. When I got my first good job from the city I bought up all the firecrackers in my district to salute this glorious country. I couldn't wait for the Fourth of July. I got the boys on the block to fire them off for me, and I felt proud of bein' an American. For a long time after

that I use to wake up nights singin' "The Star Spangled Banner." . . .

Now, a word about Tammany's love for the American flag. Did you ever see Tammany Hall decorated for a celebration? It's just a mass of flags. They even take down the window shades and put flags in place of them. There's flags everywhere except on the floors. We don't care for expense where the American flag is concerned, especially after we have won an election. In 1904 we originated the custom of givin' a small flag to each man as he entered Tammany Hall for the Fourth-of-July celebration. It took like wildfire. The men waved their flags whenever they cheered and the sight made me feel so patriotic that I forgot all about civil service for a while. And the good work of the flags didn't stop there. The men carried them home and gave them to the children, and the kids got patriotic, too. Of course, it all cost a pretty penny, but what of that? We had won at the polls the precedin' November, had the offices and could afford to make an extra investment in patriotism.

5.6 "The International Jew"

The pioneer auto manufacturer Henry Ford was a man of deep convictions, immense wealth and powerful social influence. From time to time he threw himself into controversial political and social issues. At one point he grew convinced that the world was gravely endangered by an immense international Jewish conspiracy, and he set about to destroy it. He published a document, an "exposé," in his weekly newspaper, The Dearborn Independent, *under the title of "The Jewish Peril."*

This document was a rehash of a forgery written early in the century by the Russian czarist secret police, originally published as Protocols of the Elders of Zion. *The Protocols alleged that the Jews had engineered a secret plot to take over the world by combining capitalism and communism. Ford swallowed the preposterous lie and could not be talked out of it. As he was a popular hero celebrated for his inventive genius, corporate success and personal wealth, Ford's anti-Semitism fueled a simmering hatred of Jews in this country and abroad. Numerous articles on the Jewish take-over conspiracy were published in his* Independent *after 1920.*

In 1927 the Ford paper published a four-volume book, The International Jew. *Portions of the preface are reprinted below. The book sparked a law suit and a commercial boycott campaign by the American Jewish community. Finally, Ford renounced his attacks on Jews and offered a sweeping public apology to American Jewry. Nevertheless, the popularity of* The International Jew *continued for years afterward. One avid reader was the future German dictator, Adolph Hitler, who incorporated some passages from it into his book,* Mein Kampf.

Questions

List the stereotypes about Jews that are presented here? Why would a man as creative and worldly as Ford accept anything as implausible as the Protocols? *To whom would such writings appeal?*

Are there any current beliefs which are comparable to the Protocols? *What are the most effective methods for combatting ethnic or racial bigotry?*

The motive of this work is simply a desire to make facts known to the people. Other motives have, of course, been ascribed to it. But the motive of prejudice or any form of antagonism is hardly strong enough to support such an investigation as this. Moreover, had an unworthy motive existed, some sign of it would inevitably appear in the work itself. We confidently call the reader to witness that the tone of these articles is all that it should be. The International Jew and his satellites, as the conscious enemies of all that Anglo-Saxons mean by civilization, are not spared, nor is that unthinking mass which defends anything that a Jew does, simply because it has been taught to believe that what Jewish

leaders do is Jewish. Neither do these articles proceed upon a false emotion of brotherhood and apology, as if this stream of doubtful tendency in the world were only accidentally Jewish. We give the facts as we find them; that of itself is sufficient protection against prejudice or passion. . . .

The single description which will include a larger percentage of Jews than members of any other race is this: he is in business. It may be only gathering rags and selling them, but he is in business. From the sale of old clothes to the control of international trade and finance, the Jew is supremely gifted for business. More than any other race he exhibits a decided aversion to industrial employment, which he balances by an equally decided adaptability to trade. The Gentile boy works his way up, taking employment in the pro-

SOURCE: *The International Jew*, Vol. 1, Preface (no author, publisher, or location of publication cited), pp. iii, 10, 17, 23, 39–40, 214; Vol. IV, pp. 50–51.

ductive or technical departments; but the Jewish boy prefers to begin as messenger, salesman or clerk—anything—so long as it is connected with the commercial side of business. . . .

Unfortunately the element of race, which so easily lends itself to misinterpretation as racial prejudice, is injected into the question by the mere fact that the chain of international finance as it is traced around the world discloses at every link a Jewish capitalist, financial family, or a Jewish-controlled banking system. . . .

The main source of the sickness of the German national body is charged to be the influence of the Jews, and although this was apparent to acute minds years ago, it is not said to have gone so far as to be apparent to the least observing. The eruption has broken out on the surface of the body politic, and no further concealment of this fact is possible. It is the belief of all classes of the German people that the collapse which has come since the armistice, and the revolution from which they are being prevented a recovery, are the result of Jewish intrigue and purpose. . . .

Jewish hands were in almost exclusive control of the engines of publicity by which public opinion concerning the German people was molded. The sole winners of the war were Jews. . . .

The American Jew does not assimilate. This is stated, not to blame him, but merely as a fact. The Jew could merge with the people of America if he desired, but he doesn't. If there is any prejudice existing against him in America, aside from the sense of injury which his colossal success engenders, it is because of his aloofness. The Jew is not objectionable in his person, creed, or race. His spiritual ideals are shared by the world. But still he does not

assimilate; he cultivates by his exclusiveness the feeling that he does not "belong." . . .

To make a list of the lines of business controlled by the Jews of the United States would be to touch most of the vital industries of the country—those which are really vital, and those which cultivated habit has made to seem vital. The theatrical business, of course, as everyone knows, is exclusively Jewish. Play-producing, booking, theater operation are all in the hands of Jews. This perhaps accounts for the fact that in almost every production today can be detected propaganda, sometimes glaringly commercial advertisement, which does not originate with playwrights, but with producers. The motion picture industry. The sugar industry. The tobacco industry. Fifty percent or more of the meat packing industry. Upward of 60 per cent of the shoe-making industry. Men and women's ready-made clothing. Most of the musical purveying done in the country. Jewelry. Grain. More recently cotton. The Colorado smelting industry. Magazine authorship. News distribution. The liquor business. The loan business. These, only to name the industries with national and international sweep, are in control of the Jews of the United States, either alone or in association with Jews overseas. . . .

The most persistent denials have been offered to the statement that Bolshevism everywhere, in Russia or the United States, is Jewish. In these denials we have perhaps one of the most brazen examples of the double intent referred to above. The denial of the Jewish character of Bolshevism is made to the Gentile; but in the confidence and secrecy of Jewish communication, or buried in the Yiddish dialect, or obscurely hidden in the Jewish national press, we find the proud assertion made—to their own people!—that Bolshevism is Jewish. . . .

The only absolute antidote to the Jewish influence is to call college students back to a pride of race. We often speak of the Fathers as if they were the few who happened to affix their signatures to a great document which marked a new era of liberty. The Fathers were the men of the Anglo-Saxon-Celtic race. The men who came across Europe with civilization in their blood and in their destiny; the men who crossed the Atlantic and set up civilization on a bleak and rock-bound coast;

the men who drove West to California and north to Alaska; the men who peopled Australia and seized the gates of the world at Suez, Gilbraltar and Panama; the men who opened the tropics and subdued the arctics—Anglo-Saxon men, who have given form to every government and a livelihood to every people and an ideal to every century. They got neither their God nor their religion from Judah, nor yet their speech nor their creative genius—they are the Ruling People, Chosen throughout the centuries to Master the world, by Building it ever better and better and not by breaking it down.

5.7 The Pledge of Allegiance and the First Amendment

In 1942 two West Virginia girls were expelled from public school for refusing to salute the flag and recite the Pledge of Allegiance. As members of the religious group known as Jehovah's Witnesses, Marie and Gatha Barnett had been taught that saying the Pledge would be swearing allegiance to a graven image and was thus a sin in God's eyes. In 1943 the U.S. Supreme Court reinstated the girls after they had been out of school for a year. They had made constitutional history, but they also created constitutional waves that have not yet subsided.

The U.S. is said to be the only nation in the world that pledges allegiance to itself. The ritual is of comparatively recent origin. The Pledge was written in 1892 by the editor of a youth magazine to mark the anniversary of Columbus's discovery of America and was made official by Congress in 1942. The words as originally penned were, "I plege allegiance to the Flag of the United States of America and to the Republic for which it stands; one Nation, indivisible, with liberty and justice for all." Since then the phrase "under God" has been added.

For standing mute in public school while the teacher and other students spoke the Pledge, some 200 Jehovah's Witness youngsters were expelled throughout the country beginning around 1935. Many of the them lived in the coal-mining region of Pennsylvania or in the South. During wartime the defiant Witnesses were lumped together with "Nazis," "Japs," and "traitors." They were jeered on the streets, had their churches burned, lost their jobs or businesses, were tarred-and-feathered, and otherwise tortured (a Nebraska man was castrated).

The U.S. Supreme Court in West Virginia State Department of Education *v.* Barnette *in 1943 ruled for the defendants (court records misspelled the name). Justice Jackson
wrote the majority opinion (see below). A few years earlier in the Gobitis Case, the Court had
upheld the expulsion of Witness youngsters from a Pennsylvania school. (The Gobitis boy said,
"I love my country, but I love God more, and must obey.") When the composition of the Court
changed, the Gobitis decision was overturned by Barnette. In the latter case, Justice Frankfurter wrote a vigorous dissent, upholding the principle of judicial restraint and the support
for local rights (see below).*

*In 1988 the Pledge issue surfaced once again when Republican presidential candidate
George Bush chided his Democratic counterpart, Michael Dukakis, for having refused to compel
the salute while governor of Massachusetts. Although Dukakis was upholding federal law,
the issue helped turn the public against him.*

Questions

*In your own words, summarize the arguments of the majority of the Court
and the dissent by Frankfurter in Barnette. What constitutional issues are involved?*

*Since Jehovah's Witnesses—as well as other religious minorities—constitute
only a small fraction of the population, why do we defer to them in such matters
as the Pledge?*

*What similar First Amendment issues are raised in related cases such as those
involving prayer in the public schools and the public celebration of religious holidays? What is your opinion in these matters?*

*As architects of the First Amendment, James Madison and Thomas Jefferson
hoped to erect an impenetrable "wall between church and state" in this country.
Has their ideal been realized?*

*Why do you think the words "under God" were added to the Pledge, and
what effect has it had, or should it have, on the constitutional issue?*

*What was there in our national development that has made us the only nation
in the world with a pledge of allegiance? In general, how do you assess the way
Americans handle patriotic rituals and symbols such as displaying the flag, saluting
honor guards, engraving slogans on currency and singing the national anthem at
baseball games?*

Justice Jackson, 1943 —

Appellees, citizens of the United States and of West virginia, brought suit in the United States District Court for themselves and others similarly situated asking its injunction to restrain enforcement of these laws and regulations against Jehovah's Witnesses. The Witnesses are an unincorporated body teaching that the obligation imposed by law of God is superior to that of laws enacted by temporal government. Their religious beliefs include a literal version of Exodus, Chapter 20, verses 4 and 5, which says: "Thou shalt not make unto thee any graven image, or any likeness of anything that is in heaven above, or that is in the earth beneath or that is in the water under the earth; thou shalt not bow down thyself to them, nor serve them." They consider that the flag is an "image" within this command. For this reason they refuse to salute it.

Children of this faith have been expelled from school and are threatened with exclusion for no other cause. Officials threaten to send them to reformatories maintained for criminally inclined juveniles. Parents of such children have been prosecuted and are threatened with prosecutions for causing delinquency. . . .

This case calls upon us to reconsider a precedent decision, as the Court throughout its history often has been required to do. Before turning to the Gobitis Case, however, it is desirable to notice certain characteristics by which this controversy is distinguished.

The freedom asserted by these appellees does not bring them into collision with rights asserted by any other individual. It is such conflicts which most frequently re-

Source: *West Virginia State Department of Education* v. *Barnette*, 319 U.S. 624; 63 Sup. Ct. 1178; 87 L. Ed. 1628 (1943).

quire intervention of the State to determine where the rights of one end and those of another begin. But the refusal of these persons to participate in the ceremony does not interfere with or deny rights of others to do so. Nor is there any question in this case that their behavior is peaceable and orderly. The sole conflict is between authority and rights of the individual. . . .

There is no doubt that, in connection with the pledges, the flag salute is a form of utterance. Symbolism is a primitive but effective way of communicating ideas. The use of an emblem or flag to symbolize some system, idea, institution, or personality, is a short cut from mind to mind. Causes and nations, political parties, lodges and ecclesiastical groups seek to knit the loyalty of their followings to a flag or banner, a color or design. The State announces rank, function, and authority through crowns and maces, uniforms and black robes; the church speaks through the Cross, the Crucifix, the altar and shrine, and clerical raiment. Symbols of State often convey political ideas just as religious symbols come to convey theological ones. Associated with many of these symbols are appropriate gestures of acceptance or respect: a salute, a bowed or bared head, a bended knee. A person gets from a symbol the meaning he puts into it, and what is one man's comfort and inspiration is another's jest and scorn. . . .

. . . It is now a commonplace that censorship or suppression of expression of opinion is tolerated by our Constitution only when the expression presents a clear and present danger of action of a kind the State is empowered to prevent and punish. It would seem that involuntary affirmation could be commanded only on even more immediate and urgent grounds than silence. But here the power of compulsion is invoked without any allegation that remaining passive during a flag salute ritual creates a clear and present danger that would justify an effort even to muffle expression. . . .

Whether the First Amendment to the Constitution will permit officials to order observance of ritual of this nature does not depend upon whether as a voluntary exercise we would think it to be good, bad or merely innocuous. Any credo of nationalism is likely to include what some disapprove or to omit what others think essential. . . .

Nor does the issue as we see it turn on one's possession of particular religious views or the sincerity with which they are held. . . . Many citizens who do not share these religious views hold such a compulsory rite to infringe constitutional liberty of the individual. . . .

The Gobitis decision, however, *assumed*, as did the argument in that case and in this, that power exists in the State to impose the flag salute discipline upon school children in general. The Court only examined and rejected a claim based on religious beliefs of immunity from an unquestioned general rule. The question which underlies the flag salute controversy is whether such a ceremony so touching matters of opinion and political attitude may be imposed upon the individual by official authority under powers committed to any political organization under our Constitution. . . .

Government of limited power need not be anemic government. Assurance that rights are secure tends to diminish fear and jealousy of strong government, and by making us feel safe to live under it makes for its better support. Without promise of a limiting Bill of Rights it is doubtful if our Constitution could have mustered enough strength to enable its ratification. To en-

force those rights today is not to choose weak government over strong government. It is only to adhere as a means of strength to individual freedom of mind in preference to officially disciplined uniformity for which history indicates a disappointing and disastrous end.

The subject now before us exemplifies this principle. Free public education, if faithful to the ideal of secular instruction and political neutrality, will not be partisan or enemy of any class, creed, party or faction. . . . Observance of the limitations of the Constitution will not weaken government in the field appropriate for its exercise.

It was also considered in the Gobitis Case that functions of educational officers in states, counties and school districts were such that to interfere with their authority "would in effect make us the school board for the country."

The Fourteenth Amendment, as now applied to the States, protects the citizen against the State itself and all of its creatures—Boards of Education not excepted. These have, of course, important, delicate, and highly discretionary functions, but none that they may not perform within the limits of the Bill of Rights. That they are educating the young for citizenship is reason for scrupulous protection of Constitutional freedoms of the individual, if we are not to strangle the free mind at its source and teach youth to discount important principles of our government as mere platitudes. . . .

The Gobitis opinion reasoned that this is a field "where courts possess no marked and certainly no controlling competence," that it is committed to the legislatures as well as the courts to guard cherished liberties and that it is constitutionally appropriate to "fight out the wise use of legislative authority in the forum of public opinion". . . .

The very purpose of a Bill of Rights was to withdraw certain subjects from the vicissitudes of political controversy, to place them beyond the reach of majorities and officials and to establish them as legal principles to be applied by the courts. One's rights to life, liberty, and property, to free speech, a free press, freedom of worship and assembly, and other fundamental rights may not be submitted to vote; they depend on the outcome of no elections.

In weighing arguments of the parties it is important to distinguish between the due process clause of the Fourteenth Amendment as an instrument for transmitting the principles of the First Amendment and those cases in which it is applied for its own sake. . . . Much of the vagueness of the due process clause disappears when the specific prohibitions of the First become its standard. . . . Freedoms of speech and of press, of assembly, and of worship may not be infringed on . . . slender grounds. They are susceptible of restriction only to prevent grave and immediate danger to interests which the state may lawfully protect. It is important to note that while it is the Fourteenth Amendment which bears directly upon the State it is the more specific limiting principles of the First Amendment that finally govern this case.

Nor does our duty to apply the Bill of Rights to assertions of official authority depend upon our possession of marked competence in the field where the invasion of rights occurs. True, the task of translating the majestic generalities of the Bill of Rights, conceived as part of the pattern of liberal government in the eighteenth century, into concrete restraints on officials dealing with the problems of the twentieth century, is one to disturb self-confidence. . . . But we act in these matters not by authority of our competence but by force of our commissions. We cannot, because of modest estimates of our competence in such specialities as public education, withhold the judgment that history authenticates as the function of this Court when liberty is infringed.

Lastly, and this is the very heart of the Gobitis opinion, it reasons that "national unity is the basis of national security," that the authorities have "the right to select appropriate means for its attainment," and hence reaches the conclusion that such compulsory measures toward "national unity" are constitutional. Upon the verity of this assumption depends our answer in this case. . . .

Struggles to coerce uniformity of sentiment in support of some end though essential to their time and country have been waged by many good as well as by evil men. Nationalism is a relatively recent phenomenon but at other times and places the ends have been racial or territorial security, support of a dynasty or regime, and particular plans for saving souls. As first and moderate methods to attain unity have failed, those bent on its accomplishment must resort to an ever increasing severity. As governmental pressure toward unity becomes greater, so strife becomes more bitter as to whose unity it shall be. Probably no deeper division of our people could proceed from any provocation than from finding it necessary to choose what doctrine and whose program public educational officials shall compel youth to unite in embracing. Ultimate futility of such attempts to compel coherence is the lesson of every such effort from the Roman drive to stamp out Christianity as a disturber to its pagan unity, the Inquisition, as a means to religious and dynastic unity, the Siberian exiles as a means to Russian unity, down to the fast failing efforts of our present totalitarian enemies. Those who begin coercive elimination of dissent soon find themselves exterminating dissenters. Compulsory unification of opinion achieves only the unanimity of the graveyard.

It seems trite but necessary to say that the First Amendment to our Constitution was designed to avoid these ends by avoiding these beginnings. There is no mysticism in the American concept of the State or of the nature or origin of its authority. We set up government by consent of the governed, and the Bill of Rights denies those in power any legal opportunity to coerce that consent. Authority here is to be controlled by public opinion, not public opinion by authority.

The case is made difficult not because the principles of its decision are obscure but because the flag involved is our own. Nevertheless, we apply the limitations of the Constitution with no fear that freedom to be intellectually and spiritually diverse or even contrary will disintegrate the social organization. To believe that patriotism will not flourish if patriotic ceremonies are voluntary and spontaneous instead of a compulsory routine is to make an unflattering estimate of the appeal of our institutions to free minds. We can have intellectual individualism and the rich cultural diversities that we owe to exceptional minds only at the price of occasional eccentricity and abnormal attitudes. When they are so harmless to others or to the State as those we deal with here, the price is not too great. But freedom to differ is not limited to things that do not matter much. That would be a mere shadow of freedom. The test of its substance is the right to differ as

to things that touch the heart of the existing order.

If there is any fixed star in our constitutional constellation, it is that no official, high or petty, can prescribe what shall be orthodox in politics, nationalism, religion, or other matters of opinion or force citizens to confess by word or act their faith therein. If there are any circumstances which permit an exception, they do not now occur to us.

We think the action of the local authorities in compelling the flag salute and pledge transcends constitutional limitations on their power and invades the sphere of intellect and spirit which it is the purpose of the First Amendment to our Constitution to reserve from all official control.

The decision of this Court in Minersville School District v. Gobitis . . . [is] overruled, and the judgment enjoining enforcement of the West Virginia Regulations is affirmed.

Justice Frankfurter, in dissent —

. . . As a member of this Court I am not justified in writing my private notions of policy into the Constitution, no matter how deeply I may cherish them or how mischievous I may deem their disregard. The duty of a judge who must decide which of two claims before the Court shall prevail, that of a State to enact and enforce laws within its general competence or that of an individual to refuse obedience because of the demands of his conscience, is not that of the ordinary person. It can never be emphasized too much that one's own opinion about the wisdom or evil of a law should be excluded altogether when one is doing one's duty on the bench. The only opinion of our own even looking in that direction that is material is our opinion whether legislators could in reason have enacted such a law. In the light of all the circumstances, including the history of this question in this Court, it would require more daring than I possess to deny that reasonable legislators could have taken the action which is before us for review. Most unwillingly, therefore, I must differ from my brethren with regard to legislation like this, I cannot bring my mind to believe that the 'liberty' secured by the Due Process Clause gives this Court authority to deny to the State of West Virginia the attainment of that which we all recognize as a legitimate legislative end, namely, the promotion of good citizenship, by employment of the means here chosen. . . .

5.8 The WASP as Endangered Species

The agitation of the civil rights movement in the 1960s sparked pride and self-awareness among blacks, Chicanos, Native Americans and other minorities. This, in turn, evoked resentment and political resistance from groups who had long ago either become part of the white Anglo-Saxon majority, or who regarded themselves as white ethnics. In some regions, Anglo-Saxons and white ethnics were a numerical minority who felt that their jobs, homes and schools were endangered by demands being made by racial minorities. In the rush to improve life for minorities, who would see to it that their rights were honored and their futures were assured? They felt angry and resentful.

Such was the mood expressed by a letter to the chair of the U.S. Civil Rights Commission meeting in Texas at the end of 1968 (below). Mrs. A. L. Pellegrin voiced the frustration over what she perceived to be the preferential treatment being given to Mexican Americans.

Questions

What is Pellegrin's complaint? How justified was she?

What rights do so-called WASPs have, and what rights should they have, under affirmative action legislation that protects job and college applicants from discrimination? How are "minorities" defined in America today; and who constitutes the "majority"?

Do you identify as a member of a minority, or of a majority group? Is it possible to be a member of both groups? Do you feel your status is threatened as a result of your ethnicity or race?

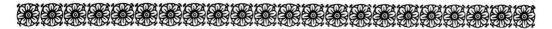

December 12, 1963

Dear Sir;

I have been following the current controversy on civil rights in the San Antonio area with a great deal of interest, and I sincerely hope you will read my letter, and perhaps return any comments you may have.

Let me preface my comments by stating that I hold no social or racial prejudices toward Mexican Americans. Quite the contrary; some of my dearest friends are Mexican American.

I sincerely believe in equality for all men and I am most willing to help those less fortunate than I in any way I can. It is my understanding that civil rights means equal opportunity for all without infringing on anyone's rights as guaranteed by the Constitution of the United States. That is to say, that all persons in minority groups deserve social, economic, and educational opportunities in equality with those in the majority. However, it is also my understanding that, in allowing these opportunities to the minority groups, it is the purpose and duty of civil rights to see that none of the rights of the majority are revoked or violated.

In my estimation, the true meaning of civil rights has been misinterpreted by the minority groups, as pertaining only to them, at the sacrifice of those of us in the majority. I submit that majority groups have civil rights as well, and when my rights are violated, in order to give a Mexican American, or anyone else preferential rights, I shall stand up for my rights, and call attention to the fact that I am not being treated fairly. . . .

SOURCE: Letter, Mrs. A. L. Pellegrin to Chairman, 12 December 1968, *Hearing before the United States Commission on Civil Rights, San Antonio, Texas, 9–14 December 1968*, pp. 1218–1219.

. . . The hearings have become a one-sided exercise in propaganda, which can only cause more disturbance and unrest in the Southwest, and indeed, throughout the country. It is no longer a sincere and realistic probe into the facts when only one side is heard, and there is no room for compromise. It is now left to the majority to do all the giving. This Civil Rights Committee has gone to the extreme with minority groups, and seems to be forgetting the majority. When this situation occurs, it is no longer civil rights. I do not believe that our entire social, economic, and educational structure should be done away with completely, in order to satisfy any minority group. This is precisely what the Mexican Americans are asking.

I would suggest that you focus a committee hearing on Eagle Pass, Texas, or any other Rio Grande border town, if you are interested in seeing discrimination in reverse. You are giving more and more to the minority groups, and neglecting to investigate what effect all this giving is having on the majority. The Anglo American is in fact, a minority group in these areas. That, in itself, means little or nothing to me, as I have lived most of my life in border towns, and have acclimated myself to such areas. I would hazard an estimate that better than 50% of the population of Eagle Pass, Texas does not speak English. In accordance with this estimated statistic, one is required to have a working knowledge of the Spanish language in order to secure employment, but as stated by a prominent figure in local politics, there is no requirement whatsoever regarding knowledge of English. Upon making application for employment here, one major deciding factor in acceptance is whether or not the applicant can speak Spanish. It has been the experience of several of my friends, as well as myself, that the applicant is refused employment despite his educational background, and or his job qualifications if he does not speak Spanish.

It is a common occurrence to be approached by non-English speaking clerks in the department stores, as well as restaurants, service establishments, and virtually every business concern in this area. In fact, it is more common than not.

The situations in these areas has always been a source of irritation and concern to me, as well as many others. But not until recently has this been a problem truly needy of bringing to the attention of your Committee. When an Anglo American cannot shop in his own country without benefit of a foreign language, and when he cannot secure employment for the same reason, I submit that the civil rights of the majority are being violated, and that it is time to take a look in the other direction.

When the Mexican Americans complain of discrimination because school classes are not taught in Spanish, and when they say that they are discriminated against in job opportunities, I submit to you, Mr. Chairman, that the Mexican American has a better chance than I, a native born American.

I am anxious for minority groups to have equal rights, as it should be, but I am most emphatic in stating that I am not willing to relinquish my rights as an American to satisfy a desire in them for preferential rights. America is rapidly becoming a country tailored to the wishes of minority groups, and a country where its native born must relinquish their rights to those who are in the minority. I ask you; is this a democracy, and am I being given equal opportunities? What has happened to my rights?

September 11, 1920

Price—15 Cents
Subscription Price $7.00 a ye

Leslie's

Illustrate   vaper

VOTING
BOOTH NO 1

The Mystery of 1920

Chapter Six: Women and the Family

6.1 Women's Fashions

Clothing inevitably reflects class and gender roles for both men and women. One need not be a feminist to realize this. But beginning in the Victorian era, fashion came under the critical eye of feminists, who alleged that clothing styles were deliberately intended to demean and restrict women.

Comments on woman's fashions follow below. First comes an exchange of letters between Gerrit Smith and his cousin, Elizabeth Cady Stanton. Smith (1797–1874) was a rich landowner and merchant from upstate New York who was interested in abolition and women's rights. He and Stanton (1815–1902), an outstanding feminist leader, debate whether women, in order to win equality with men, must reform dress styles first, or get the vote first.

This is followed by a comment from the controversial writer, Tennie C. (Tennessee) Claflin (1846–1923), who along with her even more controversial sister, Victoria Woodhull, published Woodhull & Claflin's Weekly *beginning in 1870. They advocated woman suffrage, a single standard of sexual morality, and free love.*

Finally, there is a comment from the economist Thorstein Veblen (1857–1929). Though not identified with feminism, Veblen was very interested in how personal customs reflected economics. He believed, for example, that ordinary Americans seldom spent their money rationally, but rather tried to ape the very rich, boastfully consuming and wasting goods as much as possible to prove their own worth. This is called "conspicuous consumption." His remarks are from his celebrated book, The Theory of the Leisure Class *(1899).*

Questions

Who makes better sense, Smith or Stanton—or is it all a trivial debate?

Would Claflin approve of today's women's fashions? Do you agree with her analysis?

Were he alive today, would Veblen still assert that women's clothing reflects "conspicuous consumption"? What else might fashion tell him about women's roles in contemporary society?

What kinds of statements have women made through dress in American history—or has someone else been making the statements for them? What statements do men make about their gender role through clothing?

Gerrit Smith —

. . . I admit that the dress of woman is not the primal cause of her helplessness and degradation. That cause is to be found in the false doctrines and sentiments of which the dress is the outgrowth and symbol. On the other hand, however, these doctrines and sentiments would never have become the huge bundle they now are, and they would probably have all languished, and perhaps all expired, but for the dress. For, as in many other instances, so in this, and emphatically so in this, the cause is made more efficient by the reflex influence of the effect. Let woman give up the irrational modes of clothing her person, and these doctrines and sentiments would be deprived of their most vital aliment by being deprived of their most natural expression. In no other practical forms of folly to which they might betake themselves, could they operate so vigorously and be so invigorated by their operation.

Were woman to throw off the dress, which, in the eye of chivalry and gallantry, is so well adapted to womanly gracefulness and womanly helplessness, and to put on a dress that would leave her free to work her own way through the world, I see not but that chivalry and gallantry would nearly or quite die out. No longer would she present herself to man, now in the bewitching character of a plaything, a doll, an idol, and now in the degraded character of his servant. But he would confess her transmutation into his equal; and, therefore, all occasion for the display of chivalry and gallantry toward her on the one hand, and tyranny on the other, would have passed away. . . .

Elizabeth Cady Stanton —

. . . I fully agree with you that woman is terribly cramped and crippled in her present style of dress. I have not one word to utter in its defense; but to me, it seems that if she would enjoy entire freedom, she should dress just like man. Why proclaim our sex on the house-tops, seeing that it is a badge of degradation, and deprives us of so many rights and privileges wherever we go? Disguised as a man, the distinguished French woman, "George Sand," has been able to see life in Paris, and has spoken in political meetings with great applause, as no woman could have done. In male attire, we could travel by land or sea; go through all the streets and lanes of our cities and towns by night and day, without a protector; get seven hundred dollars a year for teaching, instead of three, and ten dollars for making a coat, instead of two or three, as we now do. All this we could do without fear of insult, or the least sacrifice of decency or virtue. If nature has not made the sex so clearly defined as to be seen through any disguise, why should we make the difference so striking? Depend upon it, when men and women in their every-day life see and think less of sex and more of mind, we shall all lead far purer and higher lives. . . .

. . . Talk not to us of chivalry, that died long ago. . . . In social life, true, a man in love will jump to pick up a glove or bouquet for a silly girl of sixteen, whilst at home he will permit his aged mother to carry pails of water and armfuls of wood, or his wife to lug a twenty-pound baby, hour after hour, without ever offering to relieve her. . . . If a short dress is to make the men less gallant than they now are, I

SOURCES: Elizabeth Cady Stanton, Susan B. Anthony, and Matilda Joslyn Gage, eds., *History of Woman Suffrage* (New York, 1881), I, 836–42; Tennie C. Claflin, *Constitutional Equality a Right of Woman* (New York, 1871); and Thorstein Veblen, *The Theory of the Leisure Class* (1899).

beg the women at our next convention to add at least two yards more to every skirt they wear. . . .

Affectionately yours,
ELIZABETH CADY STANTON.

Tennie C. Claflin, 1871 —

. . . What sense is there in long skirts for business women at any time. 'Tis true that they are pretty nearly all the dressing or protection the lower limbs have; but what kind of protection? Sufficient, perhaps, when worn for nothing but to hide the limbs, but what against dampness, dust and the bleak wintry winds. Against these, clothing more nearly adjusted to the limbs is required; so that it comes down to this at last: that long skirts are worn, not for clothing, but for the purpose of hiding the limbs. Dress is either for the purpose of protection or for disguise. If for the last— and it is indelicate or revolting to the nature of woman to so dress her legs that they can be free to perform the functions of locomotion—why should it not be just as indelicate to go with arms naked to the shoulder, as thousands do who would scream if their leg to the knee were exposed? And why should it not be considered a hundred fold more indelicate to expose, virtually, their breasts to the waist, as thousands do, than it is to tastefully and reasonably dress their legs?

The fact of the case in this matter of female dress is, that a blind and foolish custom has decreed that women must wear skirts to hide their legs, while they may, almost *ad libitum*, expose their arms and breasts. For our part, we can see no more indelicacy in a properly clad leg than in a properly clad arm; but we can see a deal of sentimental and hypocritical mock modesty in the custom which demands skirts and allows bare arms, shoulders and breasts. It is time to call things by their right names, and to be honest enough to speak the truth about these things, which are fettering and diseasing women and producing a generation of sickly children. If those who affect a great deal more modesty and delicacy than they are willing to allow that those who are bold enough to discuss this question truthfully, vent their spleen and show their virtuous indignation, by calling us bad names, we simply assure them that our estimation of truth, and our desire to promote the true interests of our sex, rises far above all care for whatever they may say or think, and that we are perfectly willing to intrust the vindication of our course to the next ten years, when such unsightly and health-destroying things as our present system of dressing presents will be among the things which were. . . .

Thorstein Veblen —

. . . It has come about that obviously productive labor is in a peculiar degree derogatory to respectable women, and therefore special pains should be taken in the construction of women's dress, to impress upon the beholder the fact (often indeed a fiction) that the wearer does not and can not habitually engage in useful work. . . . Her sphere is within the household, which she should "beautify," and of which she should be the "chief ornament." The male head of the household is not currently spoken of as its ornament. . . .

[T]he high heel, the skirt, the impracticable bonnet, the corset, and the general disregard of the wearer's comfort which is an obvious feature of all civilized women's apparel, are so many items of evidence to the effect that in the modern civilized scheme of life the woman is still, in theory, the economic dependent of the man—that, perhaps in a highly idealized sense, she still is the man's chattel. The homely reason for all this conspicuous leisure and attire on the part of women lies in the fact that they are servants to whom, in the differentiation of economic functions, has been delegated the office of putting in evidence their master's ability to pay.

6.2   Women's Rights

After fifty years of struggle, how much had the woman's movement achieved, and how much more was there to do? In a magazine article in 1897, excerpted below, Susan B. Anthony (1820–1906), set about to answer this question.

Suffrage was her key concern. Twenty years earlier she had tested the right to vote under the Fourteenth Amendment by leading a group of women to the polls in Rochester, New York. She was arrested, tried and convicted for voting. A local judge imposed a small fine, but when she refused to pay, the case died.

Anthony then devoted her life to effecting changes in state laws and constitutions, and was partially successful. But the real prize, a federal Constitutional amendment, still eluded the suffragists. When the Nineteenth Amendment was finally approved in 1920 it was commonly known as the Anthony Amendment.

Questions

List the accomplishments in women's rights according to Anthony. How had the advances come about? What still remained to be done? Was suffrage an end in itself, or a means for achieving other goals? Why was it so important? How long did she think it would take to get the vote?

Athony cites the advances of women in the churches; what is the status of this issue today?

Compare this report with the conditions cited in the statement of the National Organization for Women in 1966 (Document 6.6).

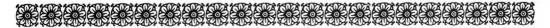

Fifty years ago woman in the United States was without a recognized individuality in any department of life. No provision was made in public or private schools for her education in anything beyond the rudimentary branches. An educated woman was a rarity and was gazed upon with something akin to awe. . . . Such was the helpless, dependent, fettered condition of woman when the first Woman's Rights Convention was called . . . by Elizabeth Cady Stanton and Lucretia Mott. While there had been individual demands, from time to time, the first organized body to formulate a declaration of the rights of women was the one which met at Seneca Falls, July 19–20, 1848, and adjourned to meet at Rochester two weeks later. In the Declaration of Sentiments and the Resolutions there framed, every point was covered that, down to the present day, has been contended for by the advocates of equal rights for women. . . .

Now, at the end of half a century, we find that with few exceptions, all of the demands formulated at this convention have been granted. The great exception is the yielding of political rights, and toward this one point are directed now all the batteries of scorn, of ridicule, of denunciation that formerly poured their fire all along the line. Although not one of the predicted calamities occurred upon the granting of the other demands, the world is asked to believe that all of them will happen if this last stronghold is surrendered. . . .

There is not one foot of advanced ground upon which women stand today that has not been obtained through the hard-fought battles of other women. The close of this 19th century finds every trade, vocation, and profession open to women, and every opportunity at their command

SOURCE: Susan B. Anthony, *The Arena*, May 1897.

for preparing themselves to follow these occupations.

The girls as well as the boys of a family now fit themselves for such careers as their tastes and abilities permit. A vast amount of the household drudgery that once monopolized the whole time and strength of the mother and daughters has been taken outside and turned over to machinery in vast establishments. A money value is placed upon the labor of women. The ban of social ostracism has been largely removed from the woman wage earner. She who can make for herself a place of distinction in any line of work receives commendation instead of condemnation. Woman is no longer compelled to marry for support, but may herself make her own home and earn her own financial independence.

With but few exceptions, the highest institutions of learning in the land are as freely opened to girls as to boys, and they may receive their degrees at legal, medical, and theological colleges, and practise their professions without hindrance. In the world of literature and art, women divide the honors with men; and our civil service rules have secured for them many thousands of remunerative positions under the government. . . .

The department of politics has been slowest to give admission to women. Suffrage is the pivotal right, and if it could have been secured in the beginning, women would not have been half a century in gaining the privileges enumerated above, for privileges they must be called so long as others may either give or take them away. If women could make the laws or elect those who make them, they would be in the position of sovereigns instead of subjects. Were they the political peers of man, they could command instead of having to beg, petition, and pray. Can it be possible it is for this reason that men have been so determined in their opposition to grant to women political power?

But even this stronghold is beginning to yield to the long and steady pressure. In twenty-five states women possess suffrage in school matters; in four states they have a limited suffrage in local affairs; in one state they have municipal suffrage; in four states they have full suffrage, local, state, and national. Women are becoming more and more interested in political questions and public affairs. Every campaign sees greater numbers in attendance at the meetings, and able woman speakers are now found upon the platforms of all parties. Especial efforts are made by politicians to obtain the support of women, and during the last campaign one of the presidential candidates held special meetings for women in the large cities throughout the country. . . .

There is no more striking illustration of the progress that has been made by woman than that afforded by her changed position in the church. Under the old regime the Quakers were the only sect who recognized the equality of women. Other denominations enforced the command of St. Paul, that women should keep silence in the churches. A few allowed the women to lift up their voices in class and prayer meetings, but they had no vote in matters of church government. Even the missionary and charity work was in the hands of men. Now the Unitarians, Universalists, Congregationalists, Wesleyan and Protestant Methodists, Christians, Free-Will Baptists, and possibly a few others, ordain women as ministers, and many parishes, in all parts of the country, are presided over by women preachers. The charitable and missionary work of the churches is practically turned over to women, who raise and disburse immense sums of money. While many of the great denominations still refuse to ordain women, to allow them a seat in their councils, or a vote in matters of church government, yet women themselves are, in a large measure, responsible for this state of affairs. Forming, as they do, from two-thirds to three-fourths of the membership, raising the greater part of the funds, and carrying on the active work of the church, when they unite their forces and assert their rights, the small minority of men, who have usurped the authority, will be obliged to yield to their just demands. The creeds of the churches will recognize woman's equality before God as the codes of the states have acknowledged it before man and the law. . . .

From that little convention of Seneca Falls, with a following of a handful of women scattered through half-a-dozen different states, we have now the great National Association, with headquarters in New York City, and auxiliaries in almost every state in the Union. These state bodies are effecting a thorough system of county and local organizations for the purpose of securing legislation favorable to women, and especially to obtain amendments to their state constitutions. As evidence of the progress of public opinion, more than half of the legislatures in session during the past winter have discussed and voted upon bills for the enfranchisement of women, and in most of them they were adopted by one branch and lost by a very small majority in the other. The legislatures of Washington and South Dakota have submitted woman-suffrage amendments to their electors for 1898, and vigorous campaigns will be made in those states during the next two years. . . . While the efforts of each state are concentrated upon its own legislature, all of the states combined in the national organization are directing their energies toward securing a Sixteenth Amendment to the Constitution of the United States. The demands of this body have been received with respectful and encouraging attention from Congress. Hearings have been granted by the committees of both houses, resulting, in a number of instances, in favorable reports. Upon one occasion the question was brought to a discussion in the Senate and received the affirmative vote of one-third of the members.

Until woman has obtained "that right protective of all other rights—the ballot," this agitation must still go on, absorbing the time and the energy of our best and strongest women. Who can measure the advantages that would result if the magnificent abilities of these women could be devoted to the needs of government, society, home, instead of being consumed in the struggle to obtain their birthright of individual freedom? Until this is gained we can never know, we cannot even prophesy, the capacity and power of woman for the uplifting of humanity.

It may be delayed longer than we think; it may be here sooner than we expect; but the day will come when man will recognize woman as his peer, not only at the fireside, but in the councils of the nation. Then, and not until then, will there be the perfect comradeship, the ideal union between the sexes that shall result in the highest development of the race. What this shall be we may not attempt to define, but this we know, that only good can come to the individual or to the nation through the rendering of exact justice.

6.3 The Woman's Bible

The way the Bible interpreted the role of women was a troublesome issue for feminists. The renowned feminist leader, Elizabeth Cady Stanton (1815–1902), believed that organized religion was the most serious obstacle to the woman's movement. She encouraged a group of scholars to evaluate fully how the Bible characterized women, publishing their commentaries in 1895 in a work entitled, The Woman's Bible. *The book appeared when the movement was trying to gain acceptance among the middle class. Some of it was so critical of the Bible that it caused a furor within the feminist movement. Younger, more moderate feminists rejected it flatly. At the 1896 convention of the National American Woman Suffrage Association (NAWSA) a resolution was presented renouncing any connection with Stanton's book. It passed by a vote of 53 to 41.*

A different interpretation of the Bible's view of women was held by Catherine Waugh McCulloch (1862–1945). A mother of four, a trained attorney, and the first American woman elected to a judicial office (Justice of the Peace in Illinois), McCulloch was also an official of NAWSA. Her pamphlet, The Bible on Women Voting, *issued in 1910 was far more typical of suffrage writings on the Bible. She argued vigorously that the Bible was not a male-supremacist work.*

There follow excerpts from the preface of The Woman's Bible, *from a letter by Stanton in 1896 defending the study, and from the pamphlet by McCulloch.*

Questions

How does Stanton believe religion affected women's lives? What are the main points made by the Woman's Bible?

How does McCulloch argue against the charge that the Bible is a sexist document?

How does religion impact on feminist issues today? Have there been any changes in religion lately regarding the status of women?

Elizabeth Cady Stanton, 1895 —

From the inauguration of the movement for woman's emancipation the Bible has been used to hold her in the "divinely ordained sphere," prescribed in the Old and New Testaments.

The canon and civil law; church and state; priests and legislators; all political parties and religious denominations have alike taught that woman was made after man, of man, and for man, an inferior being, subject to man. . . .

The Bible teaches that woman brought sin and death into the world, that she precipitated the fall of the race, that she was arraigned before the judgment seat of Heaven, tried, condemned and sentenced. Marriage for her was to be a condition of bondage, maternity a period of suffering and anguish, and in silence and subjection, she was to play the role of a dependent on

SOURCES: Elizabeth Cady Stanton and others, *The Woman's Bible* (1895), Part I; Stanton, letter to the editor of *The Critic*, March 28, 1896, pp. 218–19; and Catherine Waugh McCulloch, *The Bible on Women Voting* (Evanston, Ill., n.d., but by 1910).

man's bounty for all her material wants, and for all the information she might desire on the vital questions of the hour, she was commanded to ask her husband at home. Here is the Bible position of woman briefly summed up.

Those who have the divine insight to translate, transpose and transfigure this mournful object of pity into an exalted, dignified personage, worthy our worship as the mother of the race, are to be congratulated as having a share of the occult mystic power of the eastern Mahatmas.

The plain English to the ordinary mind admits of no such liberal interpretation. The unvarnished texts speak for themselves. The canon law, church ordinances and Scriptures, are homogeneous, and all reflect the same spirit and sentiments.

These familiar texts are quoted by clergymen in their pulpits, by statesmen in the halls of legislation, by lawyers in the courts, and are echoed by the press of all civilized nations, and accepted by woman herself as "The Word of God." So perverted is the religious element in her nature, that with faith and works she is the chief support of the church and clergy; the very powers that make her emancipation impossible. . . .

Listening to the varied opinions of women, I have long thought it would be interesting and profitable to get them clearly stated in book form. To this end six years ago I proposed to a committee of women to issue a Woman's Bible, that we might have women's commentaries on women's position in the Old and New Testaments. . . .

The large number of letters received, highly appreciative of the undertaking, is very encouraging. . . . But we have the usual array of objections to meet and answer. One correspondent conjures us to suspend the work, as it is "ridiculous" for "women to attempt the revision of the Scriptures." I wonder if any man wrote to the late revising committee of Divines to stop their work on the ground that it was ridiculous for men to revise the Bible. Why is it more ridiculous for woman to protest against her present status in the Old and New Testament, in the ordinances and discipline of the church, than in the statutes and constitutions of the state? . . . Why is it more audacious to review Moses than Blackstone, the Jewish code of laws, than the English system of jurisprudence? . . . Forty years ago it seemed as ridiculous to timid, time-serving and retrograde folk for women to demand an expurgated edition of the laws, as it now does to demand an expurgated edition of the Liturgies and the Scriptures. Come, come, my conservative friend, wipe the dew off your spectacles, and see that the world is moving. . . .

Elizabeth Cady Stanton, 1896 —

Reading the Book with our own unassisted common sense, we do not find that the Mother of the race is exalted and dignified in the Pentateuch. The female half of humanity rests under the ban of general uncleanness. Even a female kid is not fit for a burnt offering to the gods. Women are denied the consecrated bread and meat, and not allowed to enter the holy places in the temples. Woman is made the author of sin, cursed in her maternity, subordinated in marriage, and a mere afterthought in creation. It is very depressing to read such sentiments emanating from the brain of man, but to be told that the good Lord said and did all the monstrous things described in the Pentateuch, makes woman's position sorrowful and helpless. . . . The first step in the elevation of women under all systems of religion is to convince them that the great Spirit of the Universe is in no way responsible for any of these absurdities. If the Bible is a message from Heaven to Humanity, neither language nor meaning should be equivocal. If the salvation of our souls depends on obedience to its commands, it is rank injustice to make scholars and scientists the only medium of communication between God and the mass of the people. "The Woman's Bible" comes to the ordinary reader like a real benediction. It tells her the good Lord did not write the Book; that the garden scene is a fable; that she is in no way responsible for the laws of the Universe. The Christian scholars and scientists will not tell her this, for they see she is the key to the situation. Take the snake, the fruit-tree and the woman from the tableau, and we have no fall, nor frowning Judge, no Inferno, no everlasting punishment,—hence no need of a Savior. Thus the bottom falls out of the whole Christian theology. Here is the reason why in all the Biblical researches and higher criticisms, the scholars never touch the position of women.

Catherine Waugh McCulloch —

There are many modern problems to which no Bible Concordance can give us a clew. There are social questions today pressing for solution which Christ never named in words. He never said specifically that we should drag the little girl widows in India from the funeral pyre; that we should unbind the tortured feet of Chinese women; that we should make sanitary our prisons or do Red Cross work. Nor did Jesus say in so many words, "Let women vote."

But Christianity will solve these newer problems if we study the spirit of Christ's words and then apply the treatment most in accord with His life and teachings. . . .

The Jews to whom Christ came were better prepared than any other existing nation for a just recognition of women. They had learned in the books of Moses that men and women were made of the same flesh and blood, and that over the newly created world they had been given joint dominion.

They easily explained woman's subservient position as a punishment for sin, and every Jewish mother hoped her coming child might lift the curse from her sex. Perhaps some thought the Genesis statement, that woman should bring forth her children in sorrow and be subject to her husband, a divine command for all ages. Some early Christian teachers so construed it when they forbade the use of any anesthetic by a woman in childbirth, on the ground that God wanted women to suffer. Who could worship or love so cruel a God? Our God never wanted women to suffer, to be humiliated, to be degraded. Some one's sin, doubtless the sin and neglect of many, are responsible for women's physical suffering and social degradation. This statement in Genesis was not a law, but a prophecy of what the future held for women—a prophecy fulfilled by the sufferings of millions of wives and mothers through thousands of years. This prophecy should no more be called a command of God than the statement made at the same time to man, that he should eat his bread in the sweat of his face and that he should eat the herb of the field. If that also is a command to endure through countless generations, then any man who eats meat is wicked, for it was said that he would eat herbs, and any man who eats without perspiring is flying in the face of his Creator. This is no more absurd than to claim that God ordained women to suffer and to obey.

The scientists of today quite agree with the Genesis parable concerning creation; that creation was in the ascending scale, first the lower creatures, then the higher animals, then man, and last at the apex the more complex woman. The order of creation affords no argument why women should obey men, though Paul in I. Tim. 2:13 so seems to regard it. It might rather be a reason why men should obey women. The question as to joint government was foreshadowed in the Genesis statement, "to them," that is male and female humanity, "gave he dominion." . . .

Some have claimed that Paul wholly opposed women's preaching and recommended to them only humble tasks. But a careful reading of all his letters will show that he was only trying to conform somewhat to the customs of the day then prevalent among Eastern peoples, and was advising a line of conduct which might draw toward Christian women the least possible criticism. . . .

We must admit that Christianity has been the inspiration which has already partly lifted women out of the degradation of heathenism and the bondage of the dark ages. But it has not yet brought woman full freedom for self-development and helpfulness. It has not yet made her man's political equal throughout Christendom. There are more important matters before us today than whether a woman should speak veiled or unveiled, whether she should wear jewels or not, and whether her hair should be braided or not. . . .

6.4 Opposition to Suffrage

The prospect of female suffrage frightened many people, including some women. They voiced strong moral, political and social grounds for opposing suffrage. Following are two expressions of the anti-suffrage position.

The first selection was written by Amelia Barr in 1896, and concentrates on women's duties in the home. The second was authored by Henry T. Finck in 1901. He points out the inherent dangers in woman's suffrage, and its potential for destroying the social balance.

Questions

Why in Barr's view are women so unhappy? Where do the views of Finck and Barr coincide, and where do they differ? Do both writers view women in the same way?

Finck points out that if women had the vote, there would be dangers not only if too few voted but also if too many voted. What are those dangers? How does Finck equate voting with femininity? When would it be alright for women to leave their proper sphere and go to work?

Since male voters like Finck held the key to female suffrage, what arguments could you develop to persuade them to change their minds?

Amelia Barr—

. . . There has never been a time in the world's history, when female discontent has assumed so much, and demanded so much, as at the present day; and both the satisfied and the dissatisfied woman may well pause to consider, whether the fierce fever of unrest which has possessed so large a number of the sex is not rather a delirium than a conviction; whether indeed they are not just as foolishly impatient to get out of their Eden, as was the woman Eve six thousand years ago.

SOURCES: Henry T. Finck, "Are Womanly Women Doomed?" *The Independent*, 53 (January 1901), 269–70; Mrs. Amelia Barr, "Discontented Women," *North American Review*, 162 (1896), 202–3.

We may premise, in order to clear the way, that there is a noble discontent which has a great work to do in the world; a discontent which is the antidote to conceit and self-satisfaction, and which urges the worker of every kind continually to realize a higher ideal. . . .

Having acknowledged so much in favor of discontent, we may now consider some of the most objectionable forms in which it has attacked certain women of our own generation. In the van of these malcontents are the women dissatisfied with their home duties. One of the saddest domestic features of the day is the disrepute into which housekeeping has fallen; for that is a woman's first natural duty and answers to the needs of her best nature. It is by no means necessary that she should be a Cinderella among the ashes, . . . or a Penelope for ever at her needle, but all women of intelligence now understand that good cooking is a liberal science, and that there is a most intimate connection between food and virtue, and food and health, and food and thought. Indeed, many things are called crimes that are not as bad as the savagery of an Irish cook or the messes of a fourth-rate confectioner.

It must be noted that this revolt of certain women against housekeeping is not a revolt against their husbands; it is simply a revolt against their duties. They consider house-work hard and monotonous and inferior, and confess with a cynical frankness that they prefer to engross paper, or dabble in art, or embroider pillowshams, or sell goods, or in some way make money to pay servants who will cook their husband's dinner and nurse their babies for them. And they believe that in this way they show themselves to have superior minds, and ask credit for a deed which ought to cover them with shame. For ac-

tions speak louder than words, and what does such action say? In the first place, it asserts that any stranger—even a young uneducated peasant girl hired for a few dollars a month—is able to perform the duties of the house-mistress and the mother. In the second place, it substitutes a poor ambition for love, and hand service for heart service. In the third place, it is a visible abasement of the loftiest duties of womanhood to the capacity of the lowest paid service. A wife and mother can not thus absolve her own soul; she simply disgraces and traduces her holiest work. . . .

Fortunately, the vast majority of women have been loyal to their sex and their vocation. In every community the makers and keepers of homes are the dominant power; and these strictures can apply only to two classes—first, the married women who neglect husband, children and homes, for the foolish *eclât* of the club and the platform, or for any assumed obligation, social, intellectual or political, which conflicts with their domestic duties: secondly, the unmarried women who, having comfortable homes and loving protectors, are discontent with their happy secluded security and rush into weak art or feeble literature, or dubious singing and acting, because their vanity and restless immorality lead them into the market place, or on to the stage. Not one of such women has been driven afield by indisputable genius. Any work they have done would have been better done by some unprotected experienced woman already in the fields they have invaded. And the indifference of this class to the money value of their labor has made it difficult for the women working because they must work or starve, to get a fair price for their work. It is the baldest effrontery for this class of rich discontents to affect sympathy with Woman's Progress.

Nothing can excuse their intrusion into the labor market but unquestioned genius and super-excellence of work; and this has not yet been shown in any single case.

Henry Finck —

. . . But it is now obvious to impartial observers that these "rights" are in reality demanded by only a very small group of women—mostly mannish women, too, belonging to what has been aptly called "the third sex"; and that to grant them the "rights" demanded would in reality be to inflict a grievous *wrong* on the vast majority of women—the womanly women—as well as on children, on men, and on society in general. Here lies the gist of the whole matter.

A favorite question of the few women who want the suffrage is, "Why not let those of us vote who want to?" This very question shows their unfitness for the franchise. It puts them on a level with naughty children who want to do certain things regardless of consequences to themselves and others. All students of our political life know that its greatest danger lies in the difficulty of getting the better class of men to vote and attend to their civic duties, whereas the rabble, headed by demagogs and rascals, always votes. With refined women the difficulty of getting them to vote would be greater still. The rabble, which in both sexes has a majority, would therefore be doubled, while the educated—*including the woman suffragists themselves*—would be left in a helpless minority; wherefore it is the duty of legislators to protect these women against their own folly by refusing them the ballot.

If the danger of doubling the power of the ignorant and the vicious were not alone sufficient to condemn equal suffrage, there is another consideration which would give it the *coup de grâce*. With all their "blatant assumptions" and "wild vagaries" none of the female suffragists have ever gone quite so far as to demand that men should play *second* fiddle in politics. Yet this is what would inevitably happen if women were allowed to vote and took advantage of their privilege. For in most civilized countries there are more women than men, wherefore the men would be outvoted and the women might assume all the offices, from the presidency down. Then, truly, might the poet sing, "all the world's a stage"—and the play a topsy-turvy Gilbert and Sullivan operetta. Legislators are not likely to go into this burlesque business in a hurry.

Not only would woman's participation in political life take away man's supremacy in a field in which he has always, as a matter of course, played the leading part (except among a few barbarous tribes whose women were as masculine as the men), but it would involve the domestic calamity of a deserted home and the loss of the womanly qualities for which refined men adore women and marry them. "Motherhood," in the words of Bishop Doane, would be "replaced by mannishness," and "neglected homes" would "furnish candidates for mismanaged offices." To children the political activity demanded as a "right" would be a still greater wrong in often depriving them of a mother's care when most needed. Doctors tell us, too, that thousands of children would be harmed or killed before birth by the injurious effect of untimely political excitement on their mothers.

All these crimes, calamities and absurdities legislators are asked to countenance simply to please a handful of discontented women who clamor for "rights" which they have never been able to prove that they need in the least. Women were once the absolute slaves of men. Without any right to vote they have been gradually emancipated, until now, as Professor Goldwin Smith has remarked, "the attitude of men in the United States toward women is rather that of subjection than that of domination"; and in some states the pendulum has really swung too far. These concessions were made from a sense of gallantry and justice. Were women allowed to vote sex antagonism would be substituted for gallantry. "The arrogant assertion of demanded rights" would, to cite once more the happy phraseology of Bishop Doane, destroy "the instinctive chivalry of conceded courtesies." Of all the mistakes made by the equal suffragists, none is more ridiculous than their naive assumption that when women shall have become angry opponents in place of gentle companions and helpers, men will retain their chivalrous deference to them and refrain from using their brute force in an emergency.

If the suffragists alone were to be the sufferers one might teach them a lesson by giving them a trial of what they want; but it would be a great wrong to the womanly women to expose them to a loss of men's gallantry and at the same time to all the nastiness and villainy of political strife. It is indeed assumed that women would refine political life by imparting to it their gentleness, tenderness and delicacy; but as Goldwin Smith pertinently asks:

> Is it not because they have been kept out of politics and generally out of the contentious arena that they have remained gentle, tender, and delicate?

Politics in Colorado is, as Pastor Ryan testifies, "the same old dirty game" it was before women took part in it; and no worldly wise person endowed with an imagination can doubt that it would habitually degrade women instead of elevating men. It is infinitely easier to break a fine vase than to make one.

6.5 Locked Inside

Charlotte Perkins Gilman was one of the most original thinkers of the woman's movement. She wrote a major book, Women and Economics *(1898) analyzing the economic base and relationship of women, marriage and the home. She also wrote a short novel,* The Yellow Wallpaper *in 1891, a powerful depiction of a woman driven to madness.*

Gilman had rebuilt her own life after a disastrous marriage, followed by an emotional collapse. In her writings, she argued that society defined women as sexual creatures, rather than as complete human beings. The home, she argued, had become a prison for women, where they lived empty lives as consumers, always demanding more and manipulating and stunting the lives of their children. Women had to be liberated from "women's sphere" in order to exercise their full talents. To achieve this goal she proposed creating collective homemaking facilities such as communal kitchens and laundries.

In 1911, when the suffragists were campaigning to win votes for women in California, they reprinted the following poem, "Locked Inside," by Gilman.

Question

Why would suffragists use this poem? What emotional state does the poem describe? How could the opportunity to vote or to participate in government remedy the problem that afflicts the woman who is "locked inside"? Do you believe the poem still speaks to women today?

LOCKED INSIDE

She beats upon her bolted door,
   With faint weak hands;
Drearily walks the narrow floor
Suddenly sits, blank walls before;
   Despairing stands.

Life calls her, Duty, Pleasure, Gain—

Her dreams respond;
But the blank daylights wax and wane,
Dull peace, sharp agony, slow pain
   no hope beyond.

Then comes thought! She lifts her head.
   The world grows wide!
A voice—as if clear words were said—
"Your door, O long imprisoned,
   Is locked inside."

6.6 Unfinished Business: ERA

The Equal Rights Amendment has been the major unfinished business of the woman's movement since it was first introduced into Congress in 1923. Once suffrage had been achieved in 1920, an organization of young militant feminists, the National Woman's Party (NWP), began agitating in earnest for an ERA. Their constitutional proposal said, quite simply, "Men and women shall have equal rights throughout the United States and every place subject to its jurisdiction. Congress shall have power to enforce this article by appropriate legislation." The debate over ERA raged for decades. For much of the time even feminists could find no consensus, since some thought it might undo much of the special legislation that women's organizations had already won.

In the 1960s some feminists who originally opposed ERA changed their minds and withdrew their objections. A consensus of feminists was realized. Congress approved the ERA and sent it to the states for ratification. Even though the time limit for ratification was extended, the amendment narrowly failed to receive the necessary backing.

In 1931 the U.S. Senate held hearings on the ERA, from which the following pro and con testimony is taken. Burnita Shelton Matthews, a lawyer, was an official of the NWP and supporter of ERA; Rose Schneiderman, president of the National Women's Trade Union League, opposed ERA.

Question

Read the ERA proposal (above) carefully. What was it supposed to achieve and why did so many people find it so threatening?

Read the pros and cons carefully. What arguments for ERA did the advocates present? Why did the trade unionist leader oppose ERA?

What had occurred by the 1960s to unify feminist organizations in support of ERA? And what negative arguments still persisted?

Why did ERA fall short of ratification on the state level in 1982, when national polls showed that it was supported by a majority of Americans?

What do you predict will be the future of ERA? What do you consider to be the major arguments for and against ERA today?

Burnita Shelton Matthews—

There are many discriminations in the laws against women. The discriminations show the need for the proposed equal rights amendment.

The woman, even in the home—that place so often designated as her "appropriate sphere"—does not share equally in the husband's authority. The father is the sole natural guardian of minor children in Alabama and Georgia. Michigan, New York, and Massachusetts are among the States where the father alone is usually entitled to the services and earnings of a minor child. In Iowa and Montana the right to recover damages for loss of a child's services and earnings in case of injury to the child belongs primarily to the father.

SOURCE: From *Equal Rights*, Hearing before a Subcommittee of the Committee on the Judiciary, United States Senate, 71st Congress, 3d sess., S. J. Res. 52, January 6, 1931 (Washington, D.C., 1931).

The Louisiana Code provides that a child owes both parents obedience, "honor and respect," but in case of difference between the parents, "the authority of the father prevails." . . . In Arkansas and West Virginia, when a person dies, leaving a father and mother but no will and no descendants, the property of the decedent goes to the father to the exclusion of the mother. . . .

The double standard of morals is recognized in practically all States. In Maryland a man may divorce his wife for being unchaste before marriage, but a divorce is not available to a woman on that ground. In Minnesota a husband whose wife is guilty of infidelity may collect damages from her paramour. On the other hand, no wife whose husband is guilty of infidelity may claim compensation from his paramour.

Under the laws of Tennessee a woman divorced for adultery and living with the adulterer is rendered incapable of disposing of any of her lands, but no such incapacity is imposed upon a man guilty of similar conduct. . . .

Despite the adoption of the woman suffrage amendment to the National Constitution, the political rights of women are not equal to those of men.

Women are sometimes excluded from high public offices. . . .

Night work is open to men but closed to women in certain employments in 16 States. . . . Women workers are displaced by men as a result of minimum wage laws setting a standard below which their wages may not fall, but not regulating men's wages. . . .

Another method by which the industrial opportunities of women have been restricted is the limiting of the occupation[s] which women may enter. For instance, a law passed in Ohio in 1919 and still in force bars women from sixteen or more occupations.

The Woman's Party believes that labor legislation should be based on the occupation, not the sex of the worker. . . .

Throughout the country, at the present time, efforts are being made to solve the unemployment situation by throwing women out of work. The wool manufacturers, due to the pressure of the organized employees in the wool industry, consisting mostly of men, have ruled that women be excluded from night work in the wool manufacturing establishments. . . .

The Textile Institute has urged that women be excluded from night work in the textile establishments, and so after the first of March women are barred from night work, and that includes not only married women but single women as well who are dependent upon their jobs for their bread and butter.

As women go more and more into new occupations, competition becomes more keen, and efforts are made to have women come under further special restrictions in order that they may be rendered ineffective as competitors.

In the State of California, a few year ago, a bill was introduced providing that the 8-hour law in that State be extended to women physicians, women in real-estate offices, women in banks, women insurance agents; in fact, women in almost every activity under the sun in California. This was backed by the labor groups but was opposed by the women themselves who fortunately secured its defeat. . . .

. . . [I]t is not the effort of the Woman's Party at all to wipe out protective legislation but to try to see that the legislation is extended to both and that no handicap is placed on women.

One speaker has said that women can not stand up and say when they will work. Of course they can't. The laws in many States determine that for them but not for men. She speaks also of the prevention of work before and after childbirth. Well, no woman is going to work just before and after childbirth unless she has to. What is the use of saying she can't work when no provision is made for taking care of her during this period in case she is in need?

The attorney from Philadelphia stated that there are no discriminations against women in State constitutions except those with regard to jury service and public office. There are also discriminations pertaining to homesteads and other property rights, . . . I don't see why we should be so extremely afraid of the word "equality." We have it in a great many State constitutions. Moreover, we have "equal" protection guaranteed in the fourteenth amendment to the Federal Constitution.

Rose Schneiderman —

For the purpose of this hearing, I represent the 12 national organizations opposed to the equal rights amendment.

We are not against equality when we say we oppose the amendment, because most of the 12 organizations are working very diligently to bring about equality among men and women, the widest kind of equality, but we are opposed to this measure because we feel that it is an unwise measure, and that it would create a great deal of trouble everywhere; we would have a great deal of litigation as to what was equality in particular instances and so on, and we feel that equality can better be brought about by removing specific restrictions through specific laws. . . .

Our experience has shown us, especially in the industrial field, that this amendment would work havoc.

The National Women's Trade Union League, which I have the honor to represent, has for 27 years worked in the industrial field trying to organize, to educate, to bring about leadership among women, and we feel that the laws that have been built up through those 27 years would be wiped off the statute books with the enactment of this amendment. . . .

We hear a lot about girls and women having the right to work when and at what they will, and so on and so forth. As a matter of fact, we know that industry is so organized to-day that it is impossible for any woman to stand up and say, "I will work now. I prefer to work from midnight to 6 or 8 o'clock in the morning rather than work from 8 in the morning to 5 o'clock in the afternoon." We know that industry is become more and more mechanized; that employers are realizing the cost of overhead; that work must be done in specified hours, at specified times; and no factory, no

employer, will run his power because I decide that I want to stay home during the day and therefore I will work during the night. We know also that with the mechanization of industry work has become less skilled. . . .

We are absolutely committed to trade-unionism as the only way real equality can ever be attained, but nevertheless we know that the great majority of women in industry are outside of the trade-union movement. . . . The great bulk of our girls, the great bulk of women in industry, are between the ages of 16 and 25. Women still look upon marriage and home and children as their career. . . . You can not find a career in sewing on buttons or in testing bulbs or in canning peaches or anything of that kind. There is no career in that; and, whether rightly or wrongly, girls still look upon marriage as their right and their vocation. Because of this the plea for organization is not always responded to at the time and in the way that we would like to see it.

. . . The previous speakers here seem to feel that the best thing to bring about is competition between men and women. One of the speakers has said, "We are not concerned with men. We are concerned with our own class." Well, when that question comes to the working people, our answer is that we are concerned about both men and women, because we can not separate ourselves from our men folks. They are the men we are to marry. They are our fathers, brothers, and sweethearts, and we can not say that we prefer unlimited competition in the family, so to speak, because we know what competition does to workers. We are interested in eliminating competition because only then will the men and women in the working class be able to attain any kind of equality, and we say that protective labor laws go toward that step of bringing the women's standard up a little toward the standards of men.

For instance, the dressmakers of New York City have a 40-hour week. They enjoy the blessings of organization, but if we had no labor laws in the State of New York, a manufacturer could move up to Mount Vernon or Poughkeepsie and work women there 60 or 72 hours a week. The men in New York City who make dresses would very quickly come to the organized women there and say, "Now, see here, so and so is working 60 hours a week. I can't give you a 40-hour week. I am sorry." Then a great strike would take place and lots of employers would move out to Poughkeepsie and work the longer hours, and we would have quite a time bringing about better conditions. But in New York State the difference between the union standard of a 40-hour week and the legal standard of a 48-hour week for women is not as great as it would be if unlimited hours were permitted for employers to work, and the result is that the State law makes it easier to enforce the union standard.

Now, there is a great deal of talk of home responsibilities and the need for women to be able to work any hours and under any conditions to meet those responsibilities. There is no doubt that women have home responsibilities. . . . However, we must not forget that men have responsibilities, too. I do not feel that we can enter into a war between men and women, especially where working men and women are concerned. . . . What we want to do is bring women up to men's level rather than remove all safeguards that would tear that level down.

The ladies who are here advocating this amendment, I am afraid, have the grandiose idea of bringing about through the stroke of a pen this marvelous thing called equality. We know that equality is not brought about that way. Equality has to happen first within yourself. You have to regard yourself as a human being, and that can not be done by passing a law. That has to be a process of education and a process of growth, and it can only happen through the programs that these 12 organizations represented here to-day are pursuing. It can not be done quickly. . . .

6.7   A Statement of Purpose

Organized feminism started in this country over a century ago, at a meeting in Seneca Falls, New York in 1848. The Seneca Falls Declaration issued by that gathering remains the bench mark of all feminist statements. It listed the abuses that men inflicted upon women, including depriving women of the right to vote, rendering married women dead in the eyes of the law, depriving women of property and wages in marriage, framing divorce laws unfairly, denying women educational opportunities, subordinating women to men in religious institutions, maintaining a double standard of social conduct, and destroying women's self-confidence.

When the modern wave of feminism began in the 1960s, its leaders were quite aware of the 1848 declaration. Much had changed in the status of women, but some of the complaints still had a familiar ring. One sees this in the "Statement of Purpose" issued by the National Organization for Women (NOW) at its founding convention in 1966. NOW went on to become the most important civil rights pressure group for legislative and economic reforms to ensure equality for women. It has pressed for the ERA, equal employment opportunities, choice in abortions, day-care for working mothers, and reforms in divorce and alimony laws. Claiming a membership of 187,000, including men, NOW has had the greatest staying power of any feminist organization in modern times, and has achieved numerous reforms. Its original statement of purpose is printed in full below.

Questions

What had changed between 1848 and 1966, the years of the two feminist conventions? What had remained the same?

Compare and contrast the objectives stated in this statement of purpose with those stated by Susan B. Anthony in 1897 (Document 6.2). What had changed since Anthony had made her assessment?

To which social stratum of women did NOW appeal in 1966? Was the appeal too narrowly based? Is anything missing from NOW's list of grievances that would have made it more widely acceptable?

What main grievances did NOW identify and how did it propose to improve matters? How radical was this statement for its time?

What reforms has NOW achieved since 1966? What do you imagine it still wishes to achieve?

The feminist movement has changed life in America since the 1960s. Which changes do you believe have been positive and which do you believe have been negative?

WE, MEN AND WOMEN who hereby constitute ourselves as the National Organization for Women, believe that the time has come for a new movement toward true equality for all women in America, and toward a fully equal partner-ship of the sexes, as part of the world-wide revolution of human rights now taking place within and beyond our national borders.

The purpose of NOW is to take action to bring women into full participation in the mainstream of American society now, exercising all the privileges and respon-

SOURCE: National Organization for Women, "Statement of Purpose," adopted at the Organizing Conference in Washington, D.C., October 20, 1966.

sibilities thereof in truly equal partnership with men.

We believe the time has come to move beyond the abstract argument, discussion and symposia over the status and special nature of women which has raged in America in recent years; the time has come to confront, with concrete action, the conditions that now prevent women from enjoying the equality of opportunity and freedom of choice which is their right, as individual Americans, and as human beings.

NOW is dedicated to the proposition that women, first and foremost, are human beings, who, like all other people in our society, must have the chance to develop their fullest human potential. We believe that women can achieve such equality only by accepting to the full the challenges and responsibilities they share with all other people in our society, as part of the decision-making mainstream of American political, economic, and social life.

We organize to initiate or support action, nationally, or in any part of this nation, by individuals or organizations, to break through the silken curtain of prejudice and discrimination against women in government, industry, the professions, the churches, the political parties, the judiciary, the labor unions, in education, science, medicine, law, religion, and every other field of importance in American society.

Enormous changes taking place in our society make it both possible and urgently necessary to advance the unfinished revolution of women toward true equality, now. With a life-span lengthened to nearly 75 years it is no longer either necessary or possible for women to devote the greater part of their lives to childrearing; yet childbearing and rearing which continue to be a most important part of most women's lives—still is used to justify barring women from equal professional and economic participation and advance.

Today's technology has reduced most of the productive chores which women once performed in the home and in mass-production industries based upon routine unskilled labor. This same technology has virtually eliminated the quality of muscular strength as a criterion for filling most jobs, while intensifying American industry's need for creative intelligence. In view of this new industrial revolution created by automation in the mid-twentieth century, women can and must participate in old and new fields of society in full equality—or become permanent outsiders.

Despite all the talk about the status of American women in recent years, the actual position of women in the United States has declined, and is declining, to an alarming degree throughout the 1950's and 1960's. Although 46.4% of all American women between the ages of 18 and 65 now work outside the home, the overwhelming majority—75%—are in routine clerical, sales, or factory jobs, or they are household workers, cleaning women, hospital attendants. About two-thirds of Negro women workers are in the lowest paid service occupations. Working women are becoming increasingly—not less—concentrated on the bottom of the job ladder. As a consequence full-time women workers today earn on the average only 60% of what men earn, and that wage gap has been increasing over the past twenty-five years in every major industry group. In 1964, of all women with a yearly income, 89% earned under $5,000 a year; half of all full-time year round women workers earned less than $3,690; only 1.4% of full-time year round women workers had an annual income of $10,000 or more.

Further, with higher education increasingly essential in today's society, too few women are entering and finishing college or going on to graduate or professional school. Today, women earn only one in three of the B.A.'s and M.A.'s granted, and one in ten of the Ph.D's.

In all the professions considered of importance to society, and in the executive ranks of industry and government, women are losing ground. Where they are present it is only a token handful. Women comprise less than 1% of federal judges; less than 4% of all lawyers; 7% of doctors. Yet women represent 51% of the U.S. population. And, increasingly, men are replacing women in the top positions in secondary and elementary schools, in social work, and in libraries—once thought to be women's fields.

Official pronouncements of the advance in the status of women hide not only the reality of this dangerous decline, but the fact that nothing is being done to stop [it]. The excellent reports of the President's Commission of the Status of Women and of the State Commissions have not been fully implemented. Such Commissions have power only to advise. They have no power to enforce their recommendations; nor have they the freedom to organize American women and men to press for action on them. The reports of these commissions have, however, created a basis upon which it is now possible to build.

Discrimination in employment on the basis of sex is now prohibited by federal law, in Title VII of the Civil Rights Act of 1964. But although nearly one-third of the cases brought before the Equal Employment Opportunity Commission during the first year dealt with sex discrimination and the proportion is increasing dramatically, the Commission has not made clear its intention to enforce the law with the same seriousness on behalf of women as of other victims of discrimination. Many of these cases were Negro women, who are the victims of the double discrimination of race and sex. Until now, too few women's organizations and official spokesmen have been willing to speak out against these dangers facing women. Too many women have been restrained by the fear of being called "feminist."

There is no civil rights movement to speak for women, as there has been for Negroes and other victims of discrimination. The National Organization for Women must therefore begin to speak.

WE BELIEVE that the power of American law, and the protection guaranteed by the U.S. Constitution to the civil rights of all individuals, must be effectively applied and enforced to isolate and remove patterns of sex discrimination, to ensure equality of opportunity in employment and education, and equality of civil and political rights and responsibilities on behalf of women, as well as for Negroes and other deprived groups.

We realize that women's problems are linked to many broader questions of social justice; their solution will require concerted action by many groups. Therefore, convinced that human rights for all are indivisible, we expect to give active support to the common cause of equal rights for all those who suffer discrimination and deprivation, and we call upon other organizations committed to such goals to support our efforts toward equality for women.

WE DO NOT ACCEPT the token appointment of a few women to high-level positions in government and industry as a substitute for a serious continuing effort to recruit and advance women according to their individual abilities. To this end, we urge American government and industry to mobilize the same resources of ingenuity and command with which they have solved problems of far greater difficulty than those now impeding the progress of women.

WE BELIEVE that this nation has a capacity at least as great as other nations, to innovate new social institutions which will enable women to enjoy true equality of opportunity and responsibility in society, without conflict with their responsibilities as mothers and homemakers. In such innovations, America does not lead the Western world, but lags by decades behind many European countries. We do not accept the traditional assumption that a woman has to choose between marriage and motherhood, on the one hand, and serious participation in industry or the professions on the other. We question the present expectation that all normal women will retire from job or profession for 10 to 15 years, to devote their full time to raising children, only to re-enter the job market at a relatively minor level. This, in itself, is a deterrent to the aspirations of women, to their acceptance into management or professional training courses, and to the very possibility of equality of opportunity or real choice, for all but a few women. Above all, we reject the assumption that these problems are the unique responsibility of each individual woman, rather than a basic social dilemma which society must solve. True equality of opportunity and freedom of choice for women require such practical, and possible innovations as a nationwide network of child-care centers, which will make it unnecessary for women to retire completely from society until their

children are grown, and national programs to provide retraining for women who have chosen to care for their own children full-time.

WE BELIEVE that it is an essential for every girl to be educated to her full potential of human ability as it is for every boy—with the knowledge that such education is the key to effective participation in today's economy and that, for a girl as for a boy, education can only be serious where there is expectation that it will be used in society. We believe that American educators are capable of devising means of imparting such expectations to girl students. Moreover, we consider the decline in the proportion of women receiving higher and professional education to be evidence of discrimination. This discrimination may take the form of quotas against the admission of women to colleges and professional schools; lack of encouragement by parents, counselors, and educators; denial of loans or fellowships; or the traditional or arbitrary procedures in graduate and professional training geared in terms of men, which inadvertently discriminate against women. We believe that the same serious attention must be given to high school dropouts who are girls as to boys.

WE REJECT the current assumptions that a man must carry the sole burden of supporting himself, his wife, and family, and that a woman is automatically entitled to lifelong support by a man upon her marriage, or that marriage, home, and family are primarily woman's world and responsibility—hers to dominate—his to support. We believe that a true partnership between the sexes demands a different concept of marriage, an equitable sharing of the responsibilities of home and children and of the economic burdens of their support. We believe that proper recognition should be given to the economic and social value of homemaking and child care. To these ends, we will seek to open a re-examination of laws and mores governing marriage and divorce, for we believe that the current state of "half-equality" between the sexes discriminates against both men and women, and is the cause of much unnecessary hostility between the sexes.

WE BELIEVE that women must now exercise their political rights and responsibilities as American citizens. They must refuse to be segregated on the basis of sex into separate-and-not-equal ladies' auxiliaries in the political parties, and they must demand representation according to their numbers in the regularly constituted party committees—at local, state, and national levels—and in the informal power structure, participating fully in the selection of candidates and political decision-making, and running for office themselves.

IN THE INTERESTS OF THE HUMAN DIGNITY OF WOMEN, we will protest, and endeavor to change, the false image of women now prevalent in the mass media, and in the texts, ceremonies, laws, and practices of our major social institutions. Such images perpetuate contempt for women by society and by women for themselves. We are similarly opposed to all policies and practices—in church, state, college, factory, or office—which, in the guise of pro-tectiveness, not only deny opportunities but also foster in women self-denigration, dependence, and evasion of responsibility, undermine their confidence in their own abilities and foster contempt for women.

NOW WILL HOLD ITSELF INDEPENDENT OF ANY POLITICAL PARTY in order to mobilize the political power of all women and men intent on our goals. We will strive to ensure that no party, candidate, president, senator, governor, congressman, or any public official who betrays or ignores the principle of full equality between the sexes is elected or appointed to office. If it is necessary to mobilize the votes of men and women who believe in our cause, in order to win for women the final right to be fully free and equal human beings, we so commit ourselves.

WE BELIEVE THAT women will do most to create a new image of women by acting now, and by speaking out in behalf of their own equality, freedom, and human dignity—not in pleas for special privilege, nor in enmity toward men, who are also victims of the current, half-equality between the sexes—but in an active, self-respecting partnership with men. By so doing, women will develop confidence in their own ability to determine actively, in partnership with men, the conditions of their life, their choices, their future, and their society.

6.8   The Politics of Motherhood

Abortion is not about facts. It is about deeply felt principles, including concepts of personhood, of the role of women in society, and of sexuality, morality and religion. And lately it is about politics, as well.

Historically speaking, the act of abortion has been widely condemned and widely practiced. Also, the moral status of the embryo has always been ambiguous. No matter how far back one searches, one finds writers, philosophers, lawyers, physicians and clergy disagreeing among themselves and offering opposing views on abortion.

The open conflict between the "pro-choice" and "pro-life" camps is of very recent origin. There was a brief debate in the nineteenth century as to whether or not abortion was justified, but once doctors acquired the right to make the final decision, the issue quickly subsided. Abortion emerged publicly again in the 1960s as part of, or as a response to, the woman's movement. The Supreme Court in Roe v. Wade *in 1973 made an important but controversial ruling legalizing abortion, in a seven to two opinion. The fact that organized constituencies held divergent views about the proper role of women in society quickened the dispute.*

There is no more controversial social issue in American life. Richard A. McCormick, S.J., summed it up when he wrote, "abortion is a matter that is morally problematic, pastorally delicate, legislatively thorny, constitutionally insecure, ecumenically divisive, medically normless, humanly anguishing, racially provocative, journalistically abused, personally biased, and widely performed."

The following selections begin with an excerpt from the majority opinion in Roe v. Wade, *written by Justice Blackmun. The second is from Justice White's dissent in that case. Then come a variety of opinions, pro and con, on the subject of abortion: from Dr. Buchan (1797), Frederick Taussig (1936), Society for Humane Abortions (early 1960s), United Methodist Church (1972), Archbishop John Krol (1974), Mary Meehan (1983) and Malcolm Potts.*

Question

Summarize the legal situation stated in Roe v. Wade.

Succinctly state the positions of each side in the abortion dispute. Do they agree on anything? Do the pro-lifers want to impose their will on the nation, as charged? Do the pro-choice people condone abortion for birth control, as charged?

How do you predict the issue will develop or resolve itself in the next few years? What effect might new Supreme Court decisions, such as giving greater control to the states, have upon a woman's right to choose abortion? Will rapidly developing contraceptive technology influence the debate?

Justice Harry A. Blackmun —

. . . [A]t the time of the adoption of our Constitution, and throughout the major portion of the 19th century, abortion was viewed with less disfavor than under most American statutes currently in effect. Phrasing it another way, a woman enjoyed a substantially broader right to terminate a pregnancy than she does in most States today. At least with respect to the early stage of pregnancy, and very possibly without such a limitation, the opportunity to make this choice was present in this country well into the 19th century. Even later, the law continued for some time to treat less punitively an abortion procured in early pregnancy. . . .

Three reasons have been advanced to explain historically the enactment of criminal abortion laws in the 19th century and to justify their continued existence.

It has been argued occasionally that these laws were the product of a Victorian social concern to discourage illicit sexual conduct. . . .

A second reason is concerned with abortion as a medical procedure. When most criminal abortion laws were first enacted, the procedure was a hazardous one for the woman. . . . Abortion mortality was high. Even after 1900, and perhaps until as late as the development of antibiotics in the 1940's, standard modern techniques such as dilation and curettage

were not nearly so safe as they are today. Thus it has been argued that a State's real concern in enacting a criminal abortion law was to protect the pregnant woman. . . .

Modern medical techniques have altered this situation. Appellants and various *amici* refer to medical data indicating that abortion in early pregnancy, that is, prior to the end of first trimester, although not without its risk, is now relatively safe. Mortality rates for women undergoing early abortions, where the procedure is legal, appear to be as low as or lower than the rates for normal childbirth. . . .

The third reason is the State's interest— some phrase it in terms of duty—in protecting prenatal life. Some of the argument for this justification rests on the theory that a new human life is present from the moment of conception. . . .

Parties challenging state abortion laws have sharply disputed in some courts the contention that a purpose of these laws, when enacted, was to protect prenatal life. Pointing to the absence of legislative history to support the contention, they claim that most state laws were designed solely to protect the woman. Because medical advances have lessened this concern, at least with respect to abortion in early pregnancy, they argue that with respect to such abortions the laws can no longer be justified by any state interest. . . .

The Constitution does not explicitly mention any right of privacy. In a line of decisions, however, going back perhaps as far as *Union Pacific R. Co.* v. *Botsford*, 141 U.S. 250, 251 (1891), the Court has recognized that a right of personal privacy, or a guarantee of certain areas or zones of privacy, does exist under the Constitution. In varying contexts the Court or individual Justices have indeed found at least the roots of that right in the First Amendment, . . . in the Fourth and Fifth Amendments . . .

SOURCES: *Dr. Buchan's Domestic Medicine* (1797); Frederick Taussig, *Abortion: Spontaneous and Induced* (St. Louis, 1936); Malcom Potts, in, Ciba Foundation Symposium, *Abortion: Medical Progress and Social Implications* (London, 1985); Mary Meehan, *Aborted Women: Silent No More* (1983); excerpts of the views of Anthony Beilenson and an anonymous early member of the Society for Humane Abortions appeared in Kristin Luker, *Abortion and the Politics of Motherhood* (Berkeley and Los Angeles: University of California Press, 1984). Reprinted by permission of the publisher.

in the penumbras of the Bill of Rights . . . in the Ninth Amendment . . . or in the concept of liberty guaranteed by the first section of the Fourteenth Amendment, . . . These decisions make it clear that only personal rights that can be deemed "fundamental" or "implicit in the concept of ordered liberty," . . . are included in this guarantee of personal privacy. They also make it clear that the right has some extension to activities relating to marriage, . . . procreation, . . . contraception, . . . family relationships, . . . and child rearing and education, . . .

This right of privacy, whether it be founded in the Fourteenth Amendment's concept of personal liberty and restrictions upon state action, as we feel it is, or, as the District Court determined, in the Ninth Amendment's reservation of rights to the people, is broad enough to encompass a woman's decision whether or not to terminate her pregnancy. . . .

. . . appellants and some *amici* argue that the woman's right is absolute and that she is entitled to terminate her pregnancy at whatever time, in whatever way, and for whatever reason she alone chooses. With this we do not agree . . . a state may properly assert important interests in safeguarding health, in maintaining medical standards, and in protecting potential life. At some point in pregnancy, these respective interests become sufficiently compelling to sustain regulation of the factors that govern the abortion decision. The privacy right involved, therefore, cannot be said to be absolute. . . .

The appellee and certain *amici* argue that the fetus is a "person" within the language and meaning of the Fourteenth Amendment. In support of this they outline at length and in detail the well-known facts of fetal development. If this suggestion of personhood is established, the appellant's case, of course, collapses, for the fetus' right to life is then guaranteed specifically by the Amendment. The appellant conceded as much on reargument. On the other hand, the appellee conceded on reargument that no case could be cited that holds that a fetus is a person within the meaning of the Fourteenth Amendment.

All this, together with our observation, *supra,* that throughout the major portion of the 19th century prevailing legal abortion practices were far freer than they are today, persuades us that the word "person," as used in the Fourteenth Amendment, does not include the unborn. . . .

. . . We need not resolve the difficult question of when life begins. When those trained in the respective disciplines of medicine, philosophy, and theology are unable to arrive at any consensus, the judiciary, at this point in the development of man's knowledge, is not in a position to speculate as to the answer.

It should be sufficient to note briefly the wide divergence of thinking on this most sensitive and difficult question. There has always been strong support for the view that life does not begin until live birth. This was the belief of the Stoics. It appears to be the predominant, though not the unanimous, attitude of the Jewish faith. It may be taken to represent also the position of a large segment of the Protestant community, insofar as that can be ascertained; organized groups that have taken a formal position on the abortion issue have generally regarded abortion as a matter for the conscience of the individual and her family. As we have noted, the common law found greater significance in quickening. Physicians and their scientific colleagues have regarded that event with less interest and have tended to focus either upon conception or upon live birth or upon the interim point at which the fetus becomes "viable," that is, potentially able to live outside the mother's womb, albeit with artificial aid. Viability is usually placed at about seven months (28 weeks) but may occur earlier, even at 24 weeks. . . .

In areas other than criminal abortion the law has been reluctant to endorse any theory that life, as we recognize it, begins before live birth or to accord legal rights to the unborn except in narrowly defined situations and except when the rights are contingent upon live birth. . . . In short, the unborn have never been recognized in the law as persons in the whole sense.

In view of all this, we do not agree that, by adopting one theory of life, Texas may override the rights of the pregnant woman that are at stake. . . .

With respect to the State's important and legitimate interest in the health of the mother, the "compelling" point, in the light of present medical knowledge, is at approximately the end of the first trimester. This is so because of the now established medical fact . . . that until the end of the first trimester mortality in abortion is less than mortality in normal childbirth. . . .

This means, on the other hand, that, for the period of pregnancy prior to this "compelling" point, the attending physician, in consultation with his patient, is free to determine, without regulation by the State, that in his medical judgment the patient's pregnancy should be terminated. If that decision is reached, the judgment may be effectuated by an abortion free of interference by the State. . . .

To summarize and repeat:

1. A state criminal abortion statute of the current Texas type, that excepts from criminality only a *life saving* procedure on behalf of the mother, without regard to pregnancy stage and without recognition of the other interests involved, is violative of the Due Process Clause of the Fourteenth Amendment.
   a. For the stage prior to approximately the end of the first trimester, the abortion decision and its effectuation must be left to the medical judgment of the pregnant woman's attending physician.
   b. For the stage subsequent to approximately the end of the first trimester, the State, in promoting its interest in the health of the mother, may, if it chooses, regulate the abortion procedure in ways that are reasonably related to maternal health.
   c. For the stage subsequent to viability the State, in promoting its interest in the potentiality of human life, may, if it chooses, regulate, and even proscribe, abortion except where it is necessary, in appropriate medical judgment, for the preservation of the life or health of the mother.

2. The State may define the term "physician," as it has been employed in the preceding numbered paragraphs of this Part XI of this opinion, to mean only a physician currently licensed by the State, and may proscribe any abortion by a person who is not a physician as so defined.

. . . The decision leaves the State free to place increasing restrictions on abortion as the period of pregnancy lengthens, so long as those restrictions are tailored to the recognized state interests. The decision vindicates the right of the physician to administer medical treatment according to his professional judgment up to the points where important state interests provide compelling justifications for intervention. Up to those points the abortion decision in all its aspects is inherently, and primarily, a medical decision, and basic responsibility for it must rest with the physician. . . .

Justice White —

At the heart of the controversy in these cases are those recurring pregnancies that pose no danger whatsoever to the life or health of the mother but are nevertheless unwanted for any one or more of a variety of reasons—convenience, family planning, economics, dislike of children, the embarrassment of illegitimacy, etc. The common claim before us is that for any one of such reasons, or for no reason at all, and without asserting or claiming any threat to life or health, any woman is entitled to an abortion at her request if she is able to find a medical advisor willing to undertake the procedure.

The Court for the most part sustains this position: During the period prior to the time the fetus becomes viable, the Constitution of the United States values the convenience, whim or caprice of the putative mother more than the life or potential life of the fetus; the Constitution, therefore, guarantees the right to an abortion as against any state law or policy seeking to protect the fetus from an abortion not prompted by more compelling reasons of the mother.

With all due respect, I dissent. I find nothing in the language or history of the Constitution to support the Court's judgment. . . . As an exercise of raw judicial power, the Court perhaps has authority to do what it does today; but in my view its judgment is an improvident and extravagant exercise of the power of judicial

review which the Constitution extends to this Court.

The Court apparently values the convenience of the pregnant mother more than the continued existence and development of the life or potential life which she carries. . . .

It is my view, therefore, that the Texas statute is not constitutionally infirm because it denies abortions to those who seek to serve only their convenience rather than to protect their life or health. . . .

Dr. Buchan, 1797 —

Every woman who procures an abortion does it at the hazard of her life; yet there are not a few who run this risk, merely to prevent the trouble of bearing and bringing up children. It is surely a most unnatural crime, and cannot, even in the most abandoned, be viewed without horror, but in the decent matron it is still more unpardonable. Those wretches who daily advertise their assistance to women in this business, deserve, in my opinion, the most severe of all human punishments.

Frank Taussig, 1936 —

We are amazed at the frankness with which decent women discuss this matter [induced abortions] among themselves or with their physician. Every physician will testify that it is without any feeling of guilt that most women speak of induced abortions in the consultation room. The most striking evidence of the attitude of the public is the fact that, even when positive evidence of guilt is brought in the trial of an abortionist, he is rarely punished by the jury before whom the case is tried.

Member of Society for Humane Abortions, early 1960s —

When we talk about women's rights, we can get all the rights in the world—the right to vote, the right to go to school—and none of them means a doggone thing if we don't own the flesh we stand in, if we can't control what happens to us, if the whole course of our lives can be changed by somebody else that can get us pregnant by accident, or by deceit, or by force. So I consider the right to elective abortion, whether you dream of doing it or not, is the cornerstone of the women's movement. . . . It's been a common denominator of the women's movement because without that right, we'd have about as many rights as the cow in the pasture that's taken to the bull once a year. You could give her all those rights, too, but they wouldn't mean anything; if you can't control your own body you can't control your future, to the degree that any of us can control futures.

United Methodist Church, 1972 —

Because human life is distorted when it is unwanted and unloved, parents seriously violate their responsibility when they bring into the world children for whom they cannot provide love. . . . When, through contraceptive or human failure, an unacceptable pregnancy occurs, we believe that a profound regard for unborn human life must be weighed alongside an equally profound regard for fully formed personhood, particularly when the physical, mental and emotional health of the pregnant woman and her family show reason to be seriously threatened by the new life just forming. . . . Continuation of a pregnancy endangering the life of the mother is not a moral neces-sity. In such case, we believe the path of mature Christian judgment may indicate the advisability of abortion.

Archbishop John Cardinal Krol, 1974 —

. . . We reject any suggestion that we are attempting to impose "our" morality on others. First, it is not true. The right to life is not an invention of the Catholic Church or any other church. It is a basic human right which must undergird any civilized society. Second, either we all have the same right to speak out on public policy or no one does. We do not have to check our consciences at the door before we argue for what we think is best for society. . . . We dare not forget, however, that to separate political judgment from moral judgment leads to disorder and disaster.

Mary Meehan, 1983 —

It seems to me that honesty requires us to say that it is unjust that a woman must carry to term a child conceived through rape, *but that it is a far greater injustice to kill the child.* There is no way to avoid injustice in this situation; the best we can do is reduce it. The first injustice, which lasts for nine months of a life, can be relieved both financially and psychologically. But the second injustice ends a life, and there is no remedy for that.

Malcolm Potts —

When people with differing philosophies sit down and listen to one another . . . they learn that those who lean towards the right-to-life and those who lean towards the right-to-choice are both striving to create a situation with the minimum amount of artificially produced fetal wastage. With a subject as complex and intractable as [abortion], common goals about the welfare of individual women and respect for the awesome processes of human reproduction can still lead to different policies, but we should learn to respect one another's point of view.

Chapter Seven: Community

7.1 The Small Town Considered

"The country town," wrote Thorstein Veblen in 1923, "is one of the great American institutions; perhaps the greatest, in the sense that it has had . . . a greater part than any other in shaping public sentiment and giving character to American culture." Many Americans in the nineteenth and early twentieth century would have agreed with him. Small towns seemed to embody more "genuinely American" values and to offer a healthier, simpler, more pleasant way of life than the big cities that were then emerging.

The New England village and the Midwestern town were particular favorites. The first conjured up memories of town meetings in the colonial era, of patriots mustering on the village green to fight off Indians or redcoats, of religious worship in the small steepled white churches, and of people of unified background enjoying relative social equality. The Midwestern town, often established by New Englanders, also was held in high esteem. It reflected the life of the pioneer farmers on the Great Plains after the Civil War.

Three excerpts follow that express a range of opinions about small towns. The first is from the writer John Fiske, who in the 1880s developed an elaborate theory explaining the special meaning of the New England village. A Social Darwinist, Fiske theorized that this type of community had originated in the forests of Germany where the Anglo-Saxon race was born, had spread to England and then North America, and, with God's help, would continue to survive indefinitely. To him the New England village was not an accident of history or a momentary phenomenon, but the reflection of a long-term and deep-seated evolution.

The second selection is from the novelist Booth Tarkington, whose books often depicted middle-class Americans living in the small towns of the Middle West. This passage from his Pulitzer prize winning novel, **The Magnificent Ambersons** *(1918), describes the transformation of a community from small, peaceful town to a bustling metropolis. He may be describing Indianapolis, where he grew up.*

Finally, there is a small excerpt from Max Lerner's cultural history of the United States, published in 1957. It examines the reasons Americans seem to look back with such longing at the small town.

Questions

Which community values does Fiske seem to favor? To what extent might he have been influenced by ethnic, religious or racial considerations?

What is Tarkington's lament about the small town? The changes he describes took place in a single lifetime. How do you imagine they altered the lifestyles of those who lived through such changes?

What complaints have you heard about small-town life? What evidence can you cite to support Lerner's conclusion that the small town still holds a favored place in American culture?

What, in your opinion, is the best sort of community to live in, and how big or small should it be?

John Fiske —

In the outward aspect of a village in Massachusetts or Connecticut, the feature which would be most likely first to impress itself upon the mind of a visitor from England is the manner in which the village is laid out and built. Neither in England nor anywhere else in western Europe have I ever met with a village of the New England type. In English villages one finds small houses closely crowded together, sometimes in blocks of ten or a dozen, and inhabited by people belonging to the lower orders of society; while the fine houses of gentlemen stand quite apart in the country, perhaps out of sight of one another, and surrounded by very extensive grounds. The origin of the village, in a mere aggregation of tenants of the lord of the manor, is thus vividly suggested. In France one is still more impressed, I think, with this closely packed structure of the village. In the New England village, on the other hand, the finer and the poorer houses stand side by side along the road. There are wide straight streets overarched with spreading elms and maples, and on either

SOURCE: Thorstein Veblen, "The Country Town" (1923); John Fiske, *American Political Ideas Viewed from the Standpoint of Universal History* (New York, 1885), pp. 20–26; Booth Tarkington, *The Magnificent Ambersons* (1918); Max Lerner, *America as a Civilization* (1957), Vol. I.

side stand the houses, with little green lawns in front, called in rustic parlance "door-yards." The finer houses may stand a thousand feet apart from their neighbours on either side, while between the poorer ones there may be intervals of from twenty to one hundred feet, but they are never found crowded together in blocks. Built in this capacious fashion, a village of a thousand inhabitants may have a main street more than a mile in length, with half a dozen crossing streets losing themselves gradually in long stretches of country road. The finest houses are not ducal palaces, but may be compared with the ordinary country-houses of gentlemen in England. The poorest houses are never hovels, such as one sees in the Scotch Highlands. The picturesque and cosy cottage at Shottery, where Shakespeare used to do his courting, will serve very well as a sample of the humblest sort of old-fashioned New England farm-house. But most of the dwellings in the village come between these extremes. They are plain neat wooden houses, in capaciousness more like villas than cottages. A New England village street, laid out in this way, is usually very picturesque and beautiful, and it is highly characteristic. In comparing it with things in Europe, where one rarely finds anything at all like it, one must go to something very different from a village. As you stand in the Court of Heroes at Versailles

firewood has very likely a piano in his family sitting-room, with the *Atlantic Monthly* on the table and Milton and Tennyson, Gibbon and Macaulay on his shelves, while his daughter, who has baked bread in the morning, is perhaps ready to paint on china in the afternoon. In former times theological questions largely occupied the attention of the people; and there is probably no part of the world where the Bible has been more attentively read, or where the mysteries of Christian doctrine have to so great an extent been made the subject of earnest discussion in every household. Hence we find in the New England of to-day a deep religious sense combined with singular flexibility of mind and freedom of thought.

A state of society so completely democratic as that here described has not often been found in connection with a very high and complex civilization. In contemplating these old mountain villages of New England, one describes slow modifications in the structure of society which threaten somewhat to lessen its dignity. The immense productiveness of the soil in our western states, combined with cheapness of transportation, tends to affect seriously the agricultural interest of New England as well as those of our mother-country. There is a visible tendency for farms to pass into the hands of proprietors of an inferior type to that of the former owners,—men who are content with a lower standard of comfort and culture; while the sons of the old farmers go off to the universities to prepare for a professional career, and the daughters marry merchants or lawyers in the cities. The mountain-streams of New England, too, afford so much waterpower as to bring in ugly factories to disfigure the beautiful ravines, and to introduce into the community a class of people very different

from the landholding descendants of the Puritans. When once a factory is established near a village, one no longer feels free to sleep with doors unbolted.

It will be long, however, I trust, before the simple, earnest and independent type of character that has been nurtured on the Blue Hills of Massachusetts and the White Hills of New Hampshire shall cease to operate like a powerful leaven upon the whole of American society. . . .

Booth Tarkington, 1918—

New faces appeared at the dances of the winter; new faces had been appearing everywhere, for that matter, and familiar ones were disappearing, merged into the increasing crowd, or gone forever and missed a little and not long; for the town was growing and changing as it never had grown and changed before.

It was heaving up in the middle incredibly; it was spreading incredibly; and as it heaved and spread, it befouled itself and darkened its sky. It's boundary was mere shapelessness on the run; a raw, new house would appear on a country road; four or five others would presently be built at intervals between it and the outskirts of the town; the country road would turn into an asphalt street with a brick-faced drug-store and a frame grocery at a corner; then bungalows and six-room cottages would swiftly speckle the open green spaces—and a farm had become a suburb which would immediately shoot out other suburbs into the country, on one side, and, on the other, join itself solidly to the city. . . . But the great change was in the citizenry itself. What was left of the patriotic old-stock generation that had fought the Civil War, and subsequently controlled politics, had become venerable and little heeded . . . the old stock became less and less typical, and of the grown people who called the place home, less than a third had been born in it. There was a German quarter; there was a Jewish quarter; there was a negro quarter—square miles of it—called 'Bucktown'; there were many Irish neighborhoods; and there were large settlements of Italians, and of Hungarians, and of Rumanians. . . . But . . . the almost dominant type on the streets downtown . . . was the emigrant's prosperous offspring; descendant of the emigrations of the Seventies and Eighties and Nineties, those great folk-journeyings in search not so directly of freedom and democracy as of more money for the same labor. . . .

For as the town grew, it grew dirty, with an incredible completeness. The idealists put up magnificent business buildings and boasted of them, but the buildings were begrimed before they were finished. . . . They drew patriotic, optimistic breaths of the flying powdered filth of the streets, and took the foul and heavy smoke with gusto into the profundities of their lungs. "Boost! Don't knock!" they said. . . .

They were happiest when tearing down and building up were most riotous, and when new factory districts were thun-

dering into life. . . . They had one supreme theory; that the perfect beauty and happiness of cities and of human life was to be brought about by more factories; there was nothing they would not do to cajole a factory away from another city; and they were never more piteously embittered than when another city cajoled one away from them.

Max Lerner, 1957 —

"The phrase 'small town' has come itself to carry a double layer of meaning, at once sentimental and condescending. There is still a belief that democracy is more idyllic at the 'grass roots,' that the business spirit is purer, that the middle class is more intensely middling. There is also a feeling that by the fact of being small the small town somehow escapes the corruptions of life in the city and the dominant contagions that infest the more glittering places. History, geography, and economics gave each American town some distinctive traits of style that are imbedded in the mind, and the memory of this style is all the more marked because of the nostalgia felt, in a largely urban America, for what seems the lost serenity of small-town childhoods."

7.2   The Big City Considered

The nineteenth-century city had its detractors and its defenders. Two writers will exemplify the debate on the city that often flared in newspapers and magazines. They are Mark Twain (1835–1910), a correspondent for a San Francisco newspaper, and Frederick J. Kingsbury, a prominent Eastern banker and industrialist.

Writing in 1867, Twain regards New York, as a "splendid desert." Already the biggest city in the land, New York in 1860 had over 814,000 inhabitants, compared to San Francisco's 56,000. Twain writes at the time when many people were beginning to note the drift of pop-

ulation to the cities and the growing significance of cities in the nation's economic life. Later, as a resident of the town of Hartford, Connecticut, he would become the nation's most famous humorist, short-story writer and novelist.

Kingsbury, also a Connecticut resident, was president of the American Social Service Association. In his 1895 presidential address, "The Tendency of Men to Live in Cities," he explains particularly well the attractions of the city over the country.

Questions

What is Twain's major complaint about New York? Might he have had a more positive impression if he were a resident, instead of a stranger? Do you still hear echoes of his opinion about New York and other big cities?

What does Kingsbury see as the major attractions of city living? What was drawing people to cities? Do people still share his positive outlook?

As we have seen above (Document 7.1), great claims are made for the cultural values of the rural community. But what American values have come from the city?

Mark Twain—

The only trouble about this town is, that it is too large. You cannot accomplish anything in the way of business, you cannot even pay a friendly call, without devoting a whole day to it. . . . The distances are too great. . . . You cannot ride . . . unless you are willing to go in a packed omnibus that labors, and plunges, and struggles along at the rate of three miles in four hours and a half, always getting left behind by fast walkers, and always apparently hopelessly tangled up with vehicles that are trying to get to some place or other and can't. Or, if you can stomach it, you can ride in a horse-car and stand up for three-quarters of an hour, in the midst of a file of men that ex-

tends from front to rear (seats all crammed of course,)—or you can take one of the platforms, if you please, but they are so crowded you will have to hang on by your eye-lashes and your toe-nails. . . .

. . . I have at last, after several months' experience, made up my mind that . . . [New York] is a splendid desert—a domed and steepled solitude, where a stranger is lonely in the midst of a million of his race. A man walks his tedious miles through the same interminable street every day, elbowing his way through a buzzing multitude of men, yet never seeing a familiar face, and never seeing a strange one the second time. . . . Every man seems to feel that he has got the duties of two lifetimes to accomplish in one, and so he rushes, rushes, and never has time to be companionable—never has any time at his disposal to fool away on matters which do not involve dollars and duty and business.

All this has a tendency to make the city-bred man impatient of interruption, sus-

SOURCES: Franklin Walker and G. Ezra Dane, eds., *Mark Twain's Travels with Mr. Brown* (New York, 1940), 82–83, 259–61, 278; Frederick J. Kingsbury, "The Tendency of Men to Live in Cities," *Journal of Social Science*, XXXIII (1895), 8–11, 14–18.

picious of strangers, and fearful of being bored, and his business interfered with. The natural result is . . . the serene indifference of the New Yorker to everybody and everything without the pale of his private and individual circle.

There is something in this ceaseless buzz, and hurry, and bustle, that keeps a stranger in a state of unwholesome excitement all the time, and makes him restless and uneasy . . . a something which impels him to try to do everything, and yet permits him to do nothing. . . . A stranger feels unsatisfied, here, a good part of the time. He starts to a library; changes, and moves toward a theatre; changes again and thinks he will visit a friend; goes within a biscuit-toss of a picture-gallery, a billiard-room, a beer-cellar and a circus, in succession, and finally drifts home and to bed, without having really done anything or gone anywhere.

Frederick J. Kingsbury —

Aside from . . . industrial convenience, doubtless one of the very strongest of forces in the building of the city is the human instinct of gregariousness. . . . There is always a craving to get where there are more people. The countryman, boy or girl, longs for the village, the villager for the larger town, and the dweller in the larger town for the great city; and, having once gone, they are seldom satisfied to return to a place of less size. . . . As long ago as 1870 Mr. Frederick Law Olmsted, in a paper read before this Association, said, "There can be no doubt that in all our modern civilization . . . there is a strong drift townward"; and he quotes the language of an intelligent woman, whose early life had been spent in one of the most agreeable and convenient farming coun-

tries in the United States: "If I were offered a deed of the best farm I ever saw, on condition of going back to the country to live, I would not take it. I would rather face starvation in town." . . .

Doubtless one of the most potent factors in the modern growth of cities has been the immense improvement in the facilities for travel, which . . . make it as easy to get from city to country as from country to city; but the tide, except for temporary purposes, all sets one way. Nevertheless, there is no question that this ease of locomotion has been availed of to a surprising extent in transporting each year in the summer season a very large portion, not of the rich alone, but of nearly every class, not only from our great cities, but from our moderately large towns, to the woods and lakes and seashore for a time . . . and this fact is a great alleviation and antidote to some of the unfavorable influences of city life. . . .

If you will examine any city newspaper of fifty or sixty years ago, you will find frequent advertisements for boys as clerks in stores; and almost always they read "one from the country preferred." Now you never see this. Why is it? I think mainly because the class of boys which these advertisements were expected to attract from the country are no longer there. This was really a call for the well-educated boys of the well-to-do farmers of native stock, who thought they could better themselves by going to a city. They went, and did better themselves; and those who stayed behind fell behind. The country people deteriorated, and the country boy was no longer for business purposes the equal of the boy who had been trained in city ways. . . .

We must remember, too, that cities as places of human habitation have vastly improved within half a century. About fifty years ago neither New York nor Boston had public water, and very few of our cities had either water or gas, and horse railroads had not been thought of. When we stop to think what this really means in sanitary matters, it seems to me that the increase of cities is no longer a matter of surprise. . . . [Moreover], it must be noticed that it is always in cities that those who can afford it get the best food; and, if you are living in the country, you are largely dependent on the city for your supply. . . . It is also only in great cities, as a rule, that the best medical skill can be obtained. There we all go . . . to have our most serious diseases treated and our most critical surgical operations performed. It is almost wholly owing to the unsanitary condition among the children of the very poor that the city death-rate is so high. Mr. C. F. Wingate, in a paper read here in 1885, quotes Dr. Sargent as saying that "life in towns is, on the whole, more healthful than in the country." . . .

[The Reverend Dr. Greer said], "There is more . . . in common village life to lower and degrade and demoralize than in the city. Take the matter of amusements in the city. There are good ones, and we can make a choice. In the country one cannot make a choice. If a theatrical company comes to a village, it is a poor company. If a concert is given, it is a poor concert. . . . Then, again, there is a loneliness, an isolation, in the country life; and this tends to lower and depreciate that life. I believe statistics show that a large contingent of the insane in our asylums come from the farms. That hard drudgery of struggle with the clod and the soil from early morning to evening twilight is a lonely and bitter struggle." . . .

The country is a good place to rest in, especially if one can control his surroundings. . . . But the tranquil appearance of a country town, the apparent simplicity and serenity of rural life, the sweet idyllic harmony of rural surroundings, are, as every one must know who has much experience, very deceptive. . . . The small jealousies and rivalries, the ambitions, bickerings and strifes of a small rural community, are greatly intensified by the circumscribed area in which they find their vent, and compared with the same human frailties in a larger sphere have all the drawbacks of temper in a cart. . . .

7.3   The Greening of the City

The father of urban design and landscape architecture in America was Frederick Law Olmsted (1822–1903). He developed these arts not as a purely aesthetic exercise, but also out of a desire to humanize the urban environment for the masses.

Olmsted was born in rural Connecticut and educated at Yale University. He was the son of a wealthy merchant. For a while he devoted himself to farming, and then travelled widely throughout the country. In the course of his wanderings he developed an awareness of the growing ills of urban life—the crowded tenements, congested streets, foul-smelling air, shattered nerves and stunted lives. He decided to employ his aesthetic tastes and agricultural background to humanizing city life.

His proposed cure was to introduce nature into the city in the form of parks and parkways. In 1858 he (and a colleague) won a contest to design a park for New York City—Central Park, the first great city park in the United States. Because he battled the local politicians, private land developers, race track promoters and amusement park owners who had their own schemes for the park, he became a controversial figure. Olmsted was later hired to apply his design concepts for additional projects, including residential suburban communities and college campuses. The grounds of the University of California, Berkeley, and of Stanford University were laid out by him.

In 1870 Olmsted presented a comprehensive plan for the redesign of Boston, and gave a public address there on the work he had been doing to improve the quality of urban life. Excerpts from the speech follow.

Questions

Who is Olmsted trying to serve and what is he trying to achieve? Is he an avowed enemy of private enterprise? Was he right about the way to solve urban ills? Were his ideas practical?

Do city parks still act as a buffer against the evils of the city? Explain. What amount of city land should be given over to parks and parkways? How should college campuses—yours in particular—be designed to better serve the people who use them daily?

There can be no doubt . . . that, in all our modern civilization, . . . there is a strong drift townward. . . . It also appears to be nearly certain that the recent rapid enlargement of towns and withdrawal of people from rural conditions of living is the result mainly of circumstances of a permanent character. . . . Now, knowing that the average length of . . . life . . . in towns has been much less than in the country, and that the average amount of disease and misery and of vice and crime has been much greater in towns, this would be a very

SOURCE: F. L. Olmsted, *Public Parks and the Enlargement of Towns* (Cambridge, Mass.: Riverside Press, 1870), 4, 10–11, 15–18, 21–25.

dark prospect for civilization, if it were not that modern Science has beyond all question determined many of the causes of the special evils by which men are afflicted in towns. . . . It has shown . . . that . . . in the interior parts of large and closely built towns, a given quantity of air contains considerably less of the elements which we require to receive through the lungs than the air of the country . . . and that . . . it carries into the lungs highly corrupt and irritating matters, the action of which tends strongly to vitiate all our sources of vigor . . . and very seriously affect the mind and the moral strength. . . . People from the country are even conscious of the effect on their nerves and minds of the street contact—often complaining that they feel confused by it; and if we had no relief from it at all during our waking hours, we should all be conscious of suffering from it. It is upon our opportunities of relief from it, therefore, that not only our comfort in town life, but our ability to maintain a temperate, good-natured, and healthy state of mind, depends. . . .

Air is disinfected by sunlight and foliage. Foliage also acts mechanically to purify the air by screening it. Opportunity and inducement to escape at frequent intervals from the confined and vitiated air of the commercial quarter, and to supply the lungs with air screened and purified by trees, and recently acted upon by sunlight, together with opportunity and inducement to escape from conditions requiring vigilance, wariness, and activity toward other men—if these could be supplied economically, our problem would be solved. . . .

What I would ask is, whether we might not with economy make special provision in some of our streets—in a twentieth or a fiftieth part, if you please, of all—for trees to remain as a permanent furniture of the city? . . . If such [tree-lined] streets were made still broader in some parts, with spacious malls, the advantage would be increased. If each of them were . . . laid out with laterals and connections . . . to serve as a convenient trunkline of communication between two large districts of the town or the business centre and the suburbs, a very great number of people might thus be placed every day under influences counteracting those with which we desire to contend. . . .

We come then to the question: what accommodations for recreation can be provided which shall be so agreeable and so accessible as to be efficiently attractive to

the great body of citizens, and . . . also cause those who resort to them for pleasure to subject themselves . . . to conditions strongly counteractive to the special enervating conditions of the town? . . . If I ask myself where I have experienced the most complete gratification of [the gregarious and neighborly instinct] in public and out of doors, among trees, I find that it has been in the promenade of the Champs Elysées. As closely following it I should name other promenades of Europe, and our own . . . New York parks. . . . I have several times seen fifty thousand people participating in them; and the more I have seen of them, the more highly [do] I . . . estimate their value as means of counteracting the evils of town life. . . .

If the great city . . . is to be laid out little by little, and chiefly to suit the views of land-owners, acting only individually, and thinking only of how what they do is to affect the value in the next week or the next year of the few lots that each may hold at the time, the opportunities of so obeying this inclination as at the same time to give the lungs a bath of pure sunny air, to give the mind a suggestion of rest from the devouring eagerness and intellectual strife of town life, will always be few to any, to many will amount to nothing. . . . We want a ground to which people may easily go after their day's work is done, and where they may stroll for an hour, seeing, hearing, and feeling nothing of the bustle and jar of the streets. . . . Practically, what we most want is a simple, broad, open space of clean greensward . . . as a central feature. We want depth of wood enough about it . . . to completely shut out the city from our landscapes. The word *park*, in town nomenclature, should, I think, be reserved for grounds of the character and purpose thus described. . . .

A park fairly well managed near a large town, will surely become a new centre of that town. With the determination of location, size, and boundaries should therefore be associated the duty of arranging new trunk routes of communication between it and the distant parts of the town existing and forecasted. . . . I hope you will agree with me that . . . reserves of ground for the purposes I have referred to should be fixed upon as soon as possible, before the difficulty of arranging them, which arises from private building, shall be greatly more formidable than now . . . for want of a little comprehensive and business-like foresight and study.

7.4   How the Other Half Lived

The dream of providing decent, low-cost housing for all city dwellers has been an elusive one in the United States. Despite the best intentions of enlightened individuals and reform administrations, the lower classes have usually lived in substandard dwellings. Waves of incoming native farmers and poor foreign immigrants have repeatedly overwhelmed the city's capacity to provide adequate housing. In the nineteenth century they crowded into deteriorated row houses, private residences, boarding houses and into the barracks-like apartment buildings that were known as tenements. Even today, in an age of affluence, the neighborhoods of the urban poor are generally crowded, unsafe, unsanitary and crime-ridden.

Each generation has tried to identify the source of the slum problem and has proposed ways of eliminating it. Among the many reforms proposed have been: enforcing building codes to improve the housing stock; improving existing housing stock; designing entirely new communities ("garden cities"); subsidizing rents for the poor; providing low-interest loans to the builders of low income housing; providing tax incentives for builders or owners; constructing public housing; and improving public transportation so that the poor can get to and from work.

The slum housing problem first came to prominent public attention around the turn of the century. The earliest writer on the subject was Jacob August Riis, a Danish immigrant and journalist who in 1890 issued a report on New York's slums entitled How the Other Half Lives. *Riis' perceptions were shaped by his boyhood experiences in the small towns of rural Denmark, but also by his work as a police reporter for the* New York Tribune. *He became the chief propagandist for housing reform.*

A second person identified with cleaning up the slums was an upcoming politician named Theodore Roosevelt. He was installed as a police commissioner by a New York reform administration that had dedicated itself to cleaning up the slums of lower Manhattan. A political progressive, Roosevelt was enormously optimistic about housing reform.

Yet a third individual interested in the housing issue was Lawrence Veiller, founder of the National Housing Association and author of the New York Tenement Act of 1901. Veiller was the technician of housing reform, and a political moderate. He advocated dealing with the problem chiefly through improved building codes.

Excerpts from the writings of these men follow. Riis is represented by selections from How the Other Half Lives: *a vivid description of a slum neighborhood and tenement, and a cool assessment of the problem. The next selection, written by Roosevelt in 1911, compares old and new tenement buildings and discusses reform. The last item is by Veiller, written in 1913, and deals with the need for regulatory legislation. (A "privy vault" was a public toilet in a back alley next to a tenement.)*

Questions

According to Riis, what causes the slum conditions he describes, and how should they be remedied?

Why was Roosevelt so optimistic? On what remedies was he relying to solve the problem?

Which housing reforms did Veiller like, and which did he dislike?

If these three men were alive today what might they say went wrong with housing reform? What reforms would they be most likely to prefer now?

How does "the other half" live today, and what has changed or remained the same since the first decade of the century? What are the most promising housing remedies today, and what do you think will come of them?

Jacob Riis—

Where Mulberry Street crooks like an elbow within hail of the old depravity of the Five Points, is "the Bend," foul core of New York's slums. . . . Around "the Bend" cluster the bulk of the tenements that are stamped as altogether bad, even by the optimists of the Health Department. Incessant raids cannot keep down the crowds that make them their home. . . .

SOURCES: Jacob Riis, *How the Other Half Lives: Studies Among the Tenements of New York* (1890); Theodore Roosevelt, "The American Worker in Country and Town: I—A Visit to the Tenements," *The Outlook,* XCVII (April, 1911), 934–37; Lawrence Veiller, "Housing Reform through Legislation,": *Housing and Town Planning,* The American Academy of Political and Social Science, *The Annals,* LI (January, 1914), 70–74, 76–77.

The whole district is a maze of narrow, often unsuspected passageways—necessarily, for there is scarce a lot that has not two, three, or four tenements upon it, swarming with unwholesome crowds. . . .

In the street, where the city wields the broom, there is at least an effort at cleaning up. There has to be, or it would be swamped in filth overrunning from the courts and alleys. . . . It requires more than ordinary courage to explore these on a hot day. The undertaker has to do it then, the police always. . . . In . . ."the Bend" proper, the late Tenement House Commission counted 155 deaths of children [under 5] in a specimen year (1882). Their percentage of the total mortality in the block was 68.28, while for the whole city the proportion was only 46.20. . . .

What if I were to tell you that this alley, and more tenement property in "the Bend," all of it notorious for years as the vilest and worst to be found anywhere, stood associated on the tax-books . . . with the name of an honored family, one of the "oldest and best," rich in possessions and in influence, and high in the councils of the city's government? It would be but the plain truth. . . .

Look into any of these houses. . . . Here is a "flat" of "parlor" and two pitch-dark coops called bedrooms. Truly, the bed is all there is room for. The family tea-kettle is on the stove, doing duty for the time being as a wash-boiler. By night it will have returned to its proper use again, a practical illustration of how poverty in "the Bend" makes both ends meet. One, two, three beds are there, if the old boxes and heaps of foul straw can be called by that name; a broken stove with crazy pipe from which the smoke leaks at every joint, a table of rough boards propped up on boxes. . . . The closeness and smell are appalling. How many people sleep here? The woman with the red bandanna shakes her head sullenly, but the bare-legged girl with the bright face counts on her fingers—five, six! . . .

Well do I recollect the visit of a health inspector to one of these tenements on a July day when the thermometer outside was climbing high in the nineties; but inside, in that awful room, with half a dozen persons washing, cooking, and sorting rags, lay the dying baby alongside the stove, where the doctor's thermometer ran up to 115°. . . . What squalor and degredation inhabit these dens the health officers know. . . . From midnight till far into the small hours of the morning the policeman's thundering rap on closed doors is heard . . . on his rounds gathering evidence of illegal overcrowding.

The doors are opened unwillingly enough . . . upon such scenes. . . . In a room not thirteen feet either way slept twelve men and women, two or three in bunks set in a sort of alcove, the rest on the floor. A kerosene lamp burned dimly in the fearful atmosphere, probably to guide other and later arrivals to their "beds," for it was only just past midnight. . . . The "apartment" was one of three in two adjoining buildings we had found, within half an hour, similarly crowded. Most of the men were lodgers, who slept there for five cents a spot. . . .

What, then, are the bald facts with which we have to deal in New York?

I. That we have a tremendous, ever-swelling crowd of wage earners which it is our business to house decently.

II. That it is not housed decently.

III. That it must be so housed *here* for the present, and for a long time to come, all schemes of suburban relief being as yet utopian, impracticable.

IV. That it pays high enough rents to entitle it to be so housed, as a right.

V. That nothing but our own slothfulness is in the way of so housing it, since "the condition of the tenants is in advance of the condition of the houses which they occupy" (Report of Tenement-House Commission).

VI. That the security of the one no less than of the other half demands, on sanitary, moral, and economic grounds, that it be decently housed.

VII. That it will pay to do it. As an investment, I mean, and in hard cash. This I shall immediately proceed to prove.

VIII. That the tenement has come to stay, and must itself be the solution of the problem with which it confronts us.

This is the fact from which we cannot get away, however we may deplore it. Doubtless the best would be to get rid of it altogether; but as we cannot, all argument on that score may at this time be dismissed as idle. The practical question is what to do with the tenement. I watched a Mott Street landlord, the owner of a row of barracks that have made no end of trouble for the health authorities for twenty years, solve that question for himself the other day. His way was to give the wretched pile a coat of paint, and put a gorgeous tin cornice on with the year 1890 in letters a yard long. From where I stood watching the operation, I looked down upon the same dirty crowds camping on the roof, foremost among them an Italian mother with two stark-naked children who had apparently never made the acquaintance of a wash tub. That was a landlord's way, and will not get us out of the mire.

The "flat" is another way that does not solve the problem. Rather, it extends it. The flat is not a model, though it is a modern, tenement. It gets rid of some of the nuisances of the low tenement, and of the worst of them, the overcrowding—if it gets rid of them at all—at a cost that takes it at once out of the catalogue of "homes for the poor," while imposing some of the evils from which they suffer upon those who ought to escape from them.

There are three effective ways of dealing with the tenements in New York:

I. By law.

II. By remodeling and making the most out of the old houses.

III. By building new, model tenements. . . .

Theodore Roosevelt —

On February 13 I spent the afternoon . . . visiting a number of tenement-houses in Brooklyn, our purpose being to see the difference between the old tenement-

houses and the new. . . . Thirty years ago, when I was a member of the Albany Legislature, hardly so much as a beginning in the movement for tenement-house reform had taken place. At that time, with considerable difficulty, we passed . . . a bill to do away with the tenement-house cigar factories, but neither public opinion nor judicial opinion had been educated up to the proper point . . . thereby delaying for twenty years the cure of the festering misery which it in part sought to prevent.

Fortunately, year by year we have grown away from the destructive system of social philosophy which found expression in this decision. What I saw on my brief trip through the tenement-houses that afternoon was enough to show the really extraordinary good that had been done by legislative interference with the conditions of tenement-house life. The struggle has been hard, because the owners of the property involved have fought the improvement laws at almost every step. . . .

We first visited a number of old tenement-houses, built before there was any thought of meeting hygiene requirements. . . . Mr. Murphy [Tenement-House Commissioner] does not have an adequate force of inspectors, but he is doing all that can be done with the force he has. His aim is to do all that the law permits in making these old tenements more habitable, by giving better opportunities for light and air, preventing overcrowding, and providing for the cutting of windows; and gradually, as from natural causes the old tenement-houses are pulled down, the new tenements, built under the new law and representing an immense improvement, will take their places.

Some of the tenement-houses we first visited showed very bad conditions. . . . In one ground floor below the level of the street we found a rear room in which thirteen people had been sleeping, in addition to a baby. . . . The authorities were already working an improvement in this room. They had cut a window through one wall and had forced a reduction by over a half of the number of people who slept there. . . . It is hard to arouse the public on a matter like this to the need of law. Without law only a few exceptional men will act. The owners of tenement-house property include some hard men who care nothing for the welfare of poor people; others are themselves unaware of how bad the conditions are; while there are small owners, themselves brought up in tenement-houses, who do not understand that the conditions really are bad. All of these fight bitterly against any legislative change which would reduce, and perhaps even do away with, their profits. Mr. Murphy mentioned also the difficulty he had with some of the magistrates in securing the punishment of offenders guilty of overcrowding and the like. . . .

Having finished our tour of the older tenement-houses, we then visited several of the newer tenement-houses. The first series . . . which we saw . . . were built by Mr. [Alfred T.] White, who . . . without any compulsion, built his tenements practically along the lines now demanded by enlightened legislation. They were so constructed that it was an easy matter for the persons who dwelt there to keep them clean and to lead healthy and self-respecting lives. Each set of rooms was isolated from every other set of rooms, and each room was lighted by a window opening on to the outer air. Moreover, each group of buildings opened on to a large yard. . . .

My next visit was to a row of tenement houses . . . built, not by philanthropists, but by business men who wished in good faith to meet the requirements of the new tenement-house law and at the same time to get as good a return as was possible upon their investments. . . . The first suite of rooms we entered was typical of all the rest. It was on the ground floor, and consisted of a kitchen, a living-room, two bedrooms, and a bath-room. The family included a father, mother, and, I believe, five or six children. Everything was as neat as possible, and it was a really attractive apartment; the older people prosperous and contented, the children growing up under good conditions, which represented an immeasurable advance over those in which their ancestors had lived for untold generations, and an almost equally great advance over the conditions of tenement-house life in New York a generation ago. As elsewhere, I looked carefully into the bath-room. Like every one else, I had heard many stories told to the discredit of the inmates of the new tenements by those worthy persons who always object to any effort to better conditions; and chief among these stories was the statement that wherever bath-rooms were put in, the tenants used the bath-tubs for storage of coal and other goods. In each case I found the bath-room well cared for, the bath-tub used for its normal purpose, and, as I was assured by every one, regularly used, too. Inquiry developed the fact that when bath-tubs were first put in tenement-houses a score of years ago or so the inmates at first knew nothing about them, did not use them for their legitimate purposes, and did often use them as receptacles for coal and other things. But . . . a short visit among and look down the broad and noble avenue that leads to Paris, the effect of the vista is much like that of a New England village street. As American villages grow into cities, the increase in the value of land usually tends to crowd the houses together into blocks as in a European city. But in some of our western cities founded and settled by people from New England, this spacious fashion of building has been retained for streets occupied by dwelling-houses. In Cleveland—a city on the southern shore of Lake Erie, with a population about equal to that of Edinburgh—there is a street some five or six miles in length and five hundred feet in width, bordered on each side with a double row of arching trees, and with handsome stone houses, of sufficient variety and freedom in architectural design, standing at intervals of from one to two hundred feet along the entire length of the street. The effect, it is needless to add, is very noble indeed. The vistas remind one of the nave and aisles of a huge cathedral.

Now this generous way in which a New England village is built is very closely associated with the historical origin of the village and with the peculiar kind of political and social life by which it is characterized. First of all, it implies abundance of land. As a rule the head of each family owns the house in which he lives and the ground on which it is built. The relation of landlord and tenant, though not unknown, is not commonly met with. No sort of social distinction or political privilege is associated with the ownership of land; and the legal differences between real and personal property, especially as regards ease of transfer, have been reduced to the smallest minimum that practical convenience will allow. Each householder, therefore, though an absolute proprietor,

cannot be called a miniature lord of the manor, because there exists no permanent dependent class such as is implied in the use of such a phrase. Each larger proprietor attends in person to the cultivation of his own land, assisted perhaps by his own sons or by neighbours working for hire in the leisure left over from the care of their own smaller estates. So in the interior of the house there is usually no domestic service that is not performed by the mother of the family and the daughters. Yet in spite of this universality of manual labour, the people are as far as possible from presenting the appearance of peasants. Poor or shabbily-dressed people are rarely seen, and there is no one in the village whom it would be proper to address in a patronizing tone, or who would not consider it a gross insult to be offered a shilling. As with poverty, so with dram-drinking and with crime; all alike are conspicuous by their absence. In a village of one thousand inhabitants there will be a poor-house where five or six decrepit old people are supported at the common charge; and there will be one tavern where it is not easy to find anything stronger to drink than light beer or cider. The danger from thieves is so slight that it is not always thought necessary to fasten the outer doors of the house at night. The universality of literary culture is as remarkable as the freedom with which all persons engage in manual labour. The village of a thousand inhabitants will be very likely to have a public circulating library, in which you may find Professor Huxley's "Lay Sermons" or Sir Henry Maine's "Ancient Law": it will surely have a high-school and half a dozen schools for small children. A person unable to read and write is as great a rarity as an albino or a person with six fingers. The farmer who threshes his own corn and cuts his own tenement-houses of the new type shows that the movement for them has been more than abundantly justified.

Lawrence Veiller—

There is a great variety of opinions on [the subject of housing reform]. . . . Some of our friends seem to believe that the housing problem is essentially the problem of cheap houses. . . . Another group believe that . . . if cheap and effective rapid transit could be once provided the housing problem would be solved. . . . Still another element believes that . . . anything which tends to encourage the building of more houses will solve the housing problem, the assumption being that there is a dearth of housing accommodations and that people live under bad conditions simply because there are not enough houses to go around. . . . The assumption that thousands of people live under conditions such as are found in our large cities throughout America because there are no other places in which they can live is . . . not borne out by the facts. . . . We may as well frankly admit that there is a considerable portion of our population who will live in any kind of abode that they can get irrespective of how unhygienic it may be.

If housing reform is not to be achieved through legislation . . . how are we . . . to remedy the main housing evils which we find in America today? Take the evil of the privy vault, for example, . . . certainly the greatest evil from a sanitary point of view. I can think of a hundred cities where privy vaults exist literally by the thousands. Each one of these . . . is a potent source of infection to the community. . . . Do [the proponents of garden cities] really believe that in a city of 500,000 people where there are 12,000 of these vaults . . . the estab-

lishment of a garden city or suburb on the outskirts in which possibly a thousand people might be housed, will get rid of the vaults?

If the establishment of garden cities would not rid the city of this plague of privy vaults, I am puzzled to see in just what way the development of better transit facilities would accomplish this result. . . . Improved transit . . . might move many of the population to the more sparsely settled sections of the city, but it is also equally true that in such sections privies are apt to exist to a far greater extent than they do in the older sections. . . . The tendency of better transit then would be . . . to increase the total number of such vaults within the community.

Let us take another housing evil—the evil of cellar dwellings. . . . I am here puzzled also as to how the establishment of garden cities or improvement in our systems of transit or changes in methods of taxation or government subsidies to builders of homes will drive these people from their dismal cellars. So long as these cellar rooms stay there, so long as there are landlords to derive a profit from renting them and so long as there are people poor enough . . . to live in them, they will be occupied. There is no city in America in which it is not a common experience to find such rooms occupied in considerable number and to find in the same town a very large quantity of vacant apartments of a much more adequate and sanitary type. The only method I know of by which the occupancy of these unfit habitations can be stopped is to forbid people to live in them. This can be done only through legislation; but even then people will live there, unless the laws are enforced.

In housing reform we need especially to beware of importations from across the sea

. . . because the conditions which exist in the old-world countries are so totally different from those which prevail in America. . . . The methods which have been successful in Europe have been so because they have been suited to the conditions which exist there. To be successful here we should have to engraft upon our civilization the governmental bureaucracy which we find in Europe. . . . That legislation alone will solve the housing problem is of course absurd. . . . But the point . . . is that in most cases the largest results have come from legislative action and that until certain fundamental evils have been remedied it is futile, or worse, to adopt the methods of housing reform which may be said to belong to the post-graduate period rather than to the kindergarten stage of a community's development. In other words, we must get rid of our slums before we establish garden cities. We must stop people living in cellars before we concern ourselves with changes in methods of taxation. We must make it impossible for builders to build dark rooms in new houses before we urge the government to subsidize the building of houses. We must abolish privy vaults before we build model tenements. When these things have been done there is no question but that effort can be profitably expended in the other directions mentioned.

7.5 The Shame of the Cities

Lincoln Steffens was a reform-minded journalist whose specialty was uncovering political corruption. As managing editor of McClure's Magazine *from 1902 to 1906, Steffens (1866–1936) became widely known as a "muckraker," that is, one who exposes wrong-doing. His book,* The Shame of the Cities *(1904), originally appeared in* McClure's. *It caused a sensation by tracking political corruption to the doorsteps of the most respectable business and political leaders of urban America. His reports were partly responsible for encouraging the city-manager system of government and civil-service reforms. In the following selection from* The Shame of the Cities *he describes the political corruption in Philadelphia.*

Questions

Describe how the political machine operated in Philadelphia. How could the city rid itself of the machine? What criticisms does Steffens level against urban reformers?

Does anything like this still happen, or have politics changed too drastically? Do corrupt city political machines still exist, or have tougher laws made such systems unfeasible in recent years?

Other American cities, no matter how bad their own condition may be, all point with scorn to Philadelphia as worse—"the worst-governed city in the country." . . .

This is not fair. Philadelphia is, indeed, corrupt; but it is not without significance. Every city and town in the country can learn something from the typical experience of this great representative city. New York is excused for many of its ills because it is the metropolis, Chicago because of its forced development; Philadelphia is our "third largest" city and its growth has been gradual and natural. Immigration has been blamed for our municipal conditions; Philadelphia, with 47 per cent of its population native-born of native-born parents, is the most American of our greater cities. It is "good," too, and intelligent. I don't know just how to measure the intelligence of a community, but a Pennsylvania college professor who declared to me his belief in education for the masses as a way out of political corruption, himself justified the "rake-off" of preferred contractors on public works on the ground of a "fair business profit." Another plea we have made is that we are too busy to attend to public business, and we have promised, when we come to wealth and leisure, to do better. Philadelphia has long enjoyed great and widely distributed prosperity; it is the city of homes; there is a dwelling house for every five persons—men, women, and children,—of the population; and the people give one a sense of more leisure and repose than any community I have ever dwelt in. Some Philadelphians account for their political state on the ground of their ease and comfort. There is another class of optimists whose hope is in an "aristocracy" that is to come by and by; Philadel-

phia is surer that it has a "real aristocracy" than any other place in the world, but its aristocrats, with few exceptions, are in the ring, with it, or of no political use. Then we hear that we are a young people and that when we are older and "have traditions," like some of the old countries, we also will be honest. Philadelphia is one of the oldest of our cities and treasures for us scenes and relics of some of the noblest traditions of "our fair land." Yet I was told once, "for a joke," a party of boodlers counted out the "divvy" of their graft in unison with the ancient chime of Independence Hall.

Philadelphia is representative. This very "joke," told, as it was, with a laugh, is typical. All our municipal governments are more or less bad, and all our people are optimists. Philadelphia is simply the most corrupt and the most contented. Minneapolis has cleaned up, Pittsburgh has tried to, New York fights every other election, Chicago fights all the time. Even St. Louis has begun to stir (since the elections are over), and at its worst was only shameless. Philadelphia is proud; good people there defend corruption and boast of their machine. My college professor, with his philosophic view of "rake-offs," is one Philadelphia type. Another is the man, who, driven to bay with his local pride, says: "At least you must admit that our machine is the best you have ever seen."

Disgraceful? Other cities say so. But I say that if Philadelphia is a disgrace, it is a disgrace not to itself alone, nor to Pennsylvania, but to the United States and to American character. For this great city, so highly representative in other respects, is not behind in political experience, but ahead, with New York. Philadelphia is a city that has had its reforms. Having passed through all the typical stages of corruption, Philadelphia reached the period of

SOURCE: Lincoln Steffens, *The Shame of the Cities* (1904).

miscellaneous loot with a boss for chief thief, under James McManes and the Gas Ring 'way back in the late sixties and seventies. This is the Tweed stage of corruption from which St. Louis, for example, is just emerging. Philadelphia, in two inspiring popular revolts, attacked the Gas Ring, broke it, and in 1885 achieved that dream of American cities—a good charter. The present condition of Philadelphia, therefore, is not that which precedes, but that which follows reform, and in this distinction lies its startling general significance. What has happened since the Bullitt Law or charter went into effect in Philadelphia may happen in any American city "after reform is over."

For reform with us is usually revolt, not government, and is soon over. Our people do not seek, they avoid self-rule, and "reforms" are spasmodic efforts to punish bad rulers and get somebody that will give us good government or something that will make it. A self-acting form of government is an ancient superstition. We are an inventive people, and we think that we shall devise some day a legal machine that will turn out good government automatically. The Philadelphians have treasured this belief longer than the rest of us and have tried it more often. Throughout their history they have sought this wonderful charter and they thought they had it when they got the Bullitt Law, which concentrates in the mayor ample power, executive and political, and complete responsibility. Morever, it calls for very little thought and action on the part of the people. All they expected to have to do when the Bullitt Law went into effect was to elect as mayor a good business man, who, with his probity and common sense, would give them that good business administration which is the ideal of many reformers.

The Bullitt Law went into effect in 1887. A committee of twelve—four men from the Union League, four from business organizations, and four from the bosses—picked out the first man to run under it on the Republican ticket, Edwin H. Fitler, an able, upright business man, and he was elected. Strange to say, his administration was satisfactory to the citizens, who speak well of it to this day, and . . . also the next business mayor, Edwin S. Stuart, likewise a most estimable gentleman. Under these two administrations the foundation was laid for the present government of Philadelphia, the corruption to which the Philadelphians seem so reconciled, and the machine which is "at least the best you have ever seen."

The Philadelphia machine isn't the best. It isn't sound, and I doubt if it would stand in New York or Chicago. The enduring strength of the typical American political machine is that it is a natural growth—a sucker, but deep-rooted in the people. The New Yorkers vote for Tammany Hall. The Philadelphians do not vote; they are disfranchised, and their disfranchisement is one anchor of the foundation of the Philadelphia organization.

This is no figure of speech. The honest citizens of Philadelphia have no more rights at the polls than the negroes down South. . . .

The machine controls the whole process of voting, and practices fraud at every stage. The assessor's list is the voting list, and the assessor is the machine's man. "The assessor of a division kept a disorderly house; he padded his list with fraudulent names registered from his house; two of these names were used by election officers. . . . The constable of the division kept a disreputable house; a policeman was assessed as living there. . . . The election was held in the disorderly house maintained by the assessor. . . . The man named as judge had a criminal charge for a life offense pending against him. . . . Two hundred and fifty-two votes were returned in a division that had less than one hundred legal votes within its boundaries." These extracts from a report of the Municipal League suggest the election methods. The assessor pads the list with the names of dead dogs, children, and nonexistent persons. One newspaper printed the picture of a dog, another that of a little four-year-old negro boy, down on such a list. A ring orator in a speech resenting sneers at his ward as "low down" reminded his hearers that that was the ward of Independence Hall, and, naming the signers of the Declaration of Independence, he closed his highest flight of eloquence with the statement that "these men, the fathers of American liberty, voted down here once. And," he added, with a catching grin, "they vote here yet." Rudolph Blankenburg, a persistent fighter for the right and the use of the right to vote (and, by the way, an immigrant), sent out just before one election a registered letter to each voter on the rolls of a certain selected division. Sixty-three per cent were returned marked "not at," "removed," "deceased," etc. From one four-story house where forty-four voters were addressed, eighteen letters came back undelivered; from another of forty-eight voters, came back forty-one letters; from another sixty-one out of sixty-two; from another forty-four out of forty-seven. Six houses in one

division were assessed at one hundred and seventy-two voters, more than the votes cast in the previous election in any one of two hundred entire divisions.

The repeating is done boldly, for the machine controls the election officers, often choosing them from among the fraudulent names; and when no one appears to serve, assigning the heeler ready for the expected vacancy. The police are forbidden by law to stand within thirty feet of the polls, but they are at the box and they are there to see that the machine's orders are obeyed and that repeaters whom they help to furnish are permitted to vote without "intimidation" on the names they, the police, have supplied. The editor of an anti-machine paper who was looking about for himself once told me that a ward leader who knew him well asked him into a polling place. "I'll show you how it's done," he said, and he had the repeaters go round and round voting again and again on the names handed them on slips. "But," as the editor said, "that isn't the way it's done." The repeaters go from one polling place to another, voting on slips, and on their return rounds change coats, hats, etc. The business proceeds with very few hitches; there is more jesting than fighting. Violence in the past has had its effect; and is not often necessary nowadays, but if it is needed the police are there to apply it. Several citizens told me that they had seen the police help to beat citizens or election officers who were trying to do their duty, then arrest the victims. . . .

7.6 A Party Boss Defends the Boss System

At the turn of the century, political boss George Washington Plunkitt would occasionally hand down bits of wisdom about machine politics while having his shoes shined in the lobby of the Manhattan courthouse. He would describe how, with backing from the immigrant poor and the business community, the Tammany Hall political machine ran the Democratic party and therefore the City of New York. (Plunkitt was born in a poor neighborhood in Manhattan to Scottish parents.)

A word of caution is in order. Even if the political bosses who ran the cities were dishonest, it is important to remember that the voters elected them time and again. Despite the corruption inherent in the political process, voter participation was high. At least eighty percent of the eligible electorate came out to vote in those days—compared to only about fifty percent today.

Some of Plunkitt's brief lectures were written up and published by journalist William Riordan as Very Plain Talks on Very Practical Politics *(1905). Some excerpts follow. The first and longest is a reply to Lincoln Steffens and includes an explanation of the difference between honest graft and dishonest graft. (See Document 5.5, above.) The next two short excerpts offer a taste of his attitudes on civil service and on the "spoils" system. The final selection describes his activities during a typical day.*

Questions

From Plunkitt's point of view, what was **right** *about the political machine? How did the party leader maintain his position? How did he earn his rewards?*

How does the life of today's city politician differ from that of his counterpart in the 1890s or early twentieth century? What has changed since the heyday of party machines? Who takes the place of the Plunkitts; who performs the social services and provides the relief that used to be handled by the city bosses?

Recalling the high voter participation in elections in the Gilded Age, is it possible that the old political system had something positive about it that has since been lost? Should there be more of the old-style politics, rather than less?

On *The Shame of the Cities*—

I've been readin' a book by Lincoln Steffens on *The Shame of the Cities.* Steffens means well but, like all reformers, he don't know how to make distinctions. He can't see no difference between honest graft and dishonest graft and, consequent, he gets things all mixed up. There's the biggest kind of a difference between political looters and politicians who make a fortune out of politics by keepin' their eyes wide open. The looter goes in for himself alone without considerin' his organization or his city. The politician looks after his own interests, the organization's interests, and the city's interests all at the same time. See the distinction? For instance, I ain't no looter. The looter hogs it. I never hogged. I made my pile in politics, but, at the same time, I served the organization and got more big improvements for New York City than any other livin' man. And I never monkeyed with the penal code.

The difference between a looter and a practical politician is the difference between the Philadelphia Republican gang and Tammany Hall. Steffens seems to think they're both about the same; but he's all wrong. The Philadelphia crowd runs up against the penal code. Tammany don't. The Philadelphians ain't satisfied with robbin' the bank of all its gold and paper money. They stay to pick up the nickels and pennies and the cop comes and nabs them. Tammany ain't no such fool. Why, I remember, about fifteen or twenty years ago, a Republican superintendent of the Philadelphia almshouse stole the zinc roof off the buildin' and sold it for junk. . . . Any man who undertakes to write political

books should never for a moment lose sight of the distinction between honest graft and dishonest graft, which I explained in full in another talk. If he puts all kinds of graft on the same level, he'll make the fatal mistake that Steffens made and spoil his book.

Steffens made one good point in his book. He said he found that Philadelphia, ruled almost entirely by Americans, was more corrupt than New York, where the Irish do almost all the governin'. I could have told him that before he did any investigatin' if he had come to me. The Irish was born to rule, and they're the honestest people in the world. Show me the Irishman who would steal a roof off an almhouse! He don't exist. Of course, if an Irishman had the political pull and the roof was much worn, he might get the city authorities to put on a new one and get the contract for it himself, and buy the old roof at a bargain—but that's honest graft. It's goin' about the thing like a gentleman, and there's more money in it than in tearin' down an old roof and cartin' it to the junkman's—more money and no penal code.

One reason why the Irishman is more honest in politics than many Sons of the Revolution is that he is grateful to the country and the city that gave him protection and prosperity when he was driven by oppression from the Emerald Isle. Say, that sentence is fine, ain't it? I'm goin' to get some literary feller to work it over into poetry for next St. Patrick's Day dinner.

Yes, the Irishman is grateful. His one thought is to serve the city which gave him a home. He has this thought even before he lands in New York, for his friends here often have a good place in one of the city departments picked out for him while he is still in the old country. Is it any wonder that he has a tender spot in his heart for old New York when he is on its salary list the mornin' after he lands?

Source: *A Series of Very Plain Talks on Very Practical Politics, Delivered by Ex-Senator George Washington Plunkitt . . .*, William L. Riordon, comp. (New York: McClure, Phillips & Co., 1905).

Now, a few words on the general subject of the so-called shame of cities. I don't believe that the government of our cities is any worse, in proportion to opportunities, than it was fifty years ago. I'll explain what I mean by "in proportion to opportunities." A half a century ago, our cities were small and poor. There wasn't many temptations lyin' around for politicians. There was hardy anything to steal, and hardly any opportunities for even honest graft. A city could count its money every night before goin' to bed, and if three cents was missin', all the fire bells would be rung. What credit was there in bein' honest under them circumstances? . . .

Understand, I ain't defendin' politicians of today who steal. The politician who steals is worse than a thief. He is a fool. With the grand opportunities all around for the man with a political pull, there's no excuse for stealin' a cent. The point I want to make is that if there is some stealin' in politics, it don't mean that the politicians of 1905 are, as a class, worse than them of 1835. It just means that the old-timers had nothin' to steal, while the politicians now are surrounded by all kinds of temptation and some of them naturally—the fool ones—buck up against the penal code. . . .

I'm gettin' richer every day, but I've not gone in for dishonest graft—blackmailin' gamblers, saloonkeepers, disorderly people, etc.—and neither has any of the men who have made big fortunes in politics.

There's an honest graft, and I'm an example of how it works. I might sum up the whole thing by sayin': "I seen my opportunities and I took 'em."

Just let me explain by examples. My party's in power in the city, and it's goin' to undertake a lot of public improvements.

Well, I'm tipped off, say, that they're going to lay out a new park at a certain place.

I see my opportunity and I take it. I go to that place and I buy up all the land I can in the neighborhood. Then the board of this or that makes its plan public, and there is a rush to get my land, which nobody cared particular for before.

Ain't it perfectly honest to charge a good price and make a profit on my investment and foresight? Of course, it is. Well, that's honest graft.

Or supposin' it's a new bridge they're goin' to build. I get tipped off and I buy as much property as I can that has to be taken for approaches. I sell at my own price later on and drop some more money in the bank.

Wouldn't you? It's just like lookin' ahead in Wall Street or in the coffee or cotton market. It's honest graft, and I'm lookin' for it every day in the year. I will tell you frankly that I've got a good lot of it, too.

I'll tell you of one case. They were goin' to fix up a big park, no matter where. I got on to it, and went lookin' about for land in that neighborhood.

I could get nothin' at a bargain but a big piece of swamp, but I took it fast enough and held on to it. What turned out was just what I counted on. They couldn't make the park complete without Plunkitt's swamp, and they had to pay a good price for it. Anything dishonest in that? . . .

Another kind of honest graft. Tammany has raised a good many salaries. There was an awful howl by the reformers, but don't you know that Tammany gains ten votes for every one it lost by salary raisin'?

The Wall Street banker thinks it shameful to raise a department clerk's salary from $1500 to $1800 a year, but every man who draws a salary himself says: "That's all right. I wish it was me." And he feels very much like votin' the Tammany ticket on election day, just out of sympathy. . . .

Now, in conclusion, I want to say that I don't own a dishonest dollar. If my worst enemy was given the job of writin' my epitaph when I'm gone, he couldn't do more than write:

"George W. Plunkitt. He Seen His Opportunities, and He Took 'Em."

The Curse of Civil Service Reform —

This civil service law is the biggest fraud of the age. It is the curse of the nation. There can't be no real patriotism while it lasts. How are you goin' to interest our young men in their country if you have no offices to give them when they work for their party? . . . They say: "What's the use of workin' for your country anyhow? There's nothin' in the game." And what can they do? I don't know, but I'll tell you what I do know. I know more than one young man in past years who worked for the ticket and was just overflowin' with patriotism, but when he was knocked out by the civil service humbug he got to hate his country and became an Anarchist. . . .

The Spoils System —

When the people elected Tammany, they knew just what they were doin'. We didn't put up any false pretenses. We didn't go in for humbug civil service and all that rot. We stood as we have always stood, for rewardin' the men that won the victory. They call that the spoils system. All right; Tammany is for the spoils system, and when we go in we fire every anti-Tammany man from office that can be fired under the law. It's an elastic sort of law and you can bet it will be stretched to the limit.

Strenuous Life of the Tammany District Leader —

The life of the Tammany district leader is strenuous. . . .

This a record of a day's work by Plunkitt:

2 A.M.: Aroused from sleep by the ringing of his doorbell; went to the door and found a bartender, who asked him to go to the police station and bail out a saloonkeeper who had been arrested for violating the excise law. Furnished bail and returned to bed at three o'clock.

6 A.M.: Awakened by fire engines passing his house. Hastened to the scene of the fire, according to the custom of the Tammany district leaders, to give assistance to the fire sufferers, if needed. Met several of his election district captains who are always under orders to look out for fires, which are considered great vote-getters. Found several tenants who had been burned out, took them to a hotel, supplied them with clothes, fed them, and arranged temporary quarters for them until they could rent and furnish new apartments.

8:30 A.M.: Went to the police court to look after his constituents. Found six "drunks." Secured the discharge of four by a timely word with the judge, and paid the fines of two.

9 A.M.: Appeared in the Municipal District Court. Directed one of his district captains to act as counsel for a widow against whom dispossess proceedings had been instituted and obtained an extension of time. Paid the rent of a poor family about to be dispossessed and gave them a dollar for food.

11 A.M.: At home again. Found four men waiting for him. One had been discharged by the Metropolitan Railway Company for neglect of duty, and wanted the district leader to fix things. Another wanted a job on the road. The third sought a place on

the Subway and the fourth, a plumber, was looking for work with the Consolidated Gas Company. The district leader spent nearly three hours fixing things for the four men, and succeeded in each case.

3 P.M.: Attended the funeral of an Italian as far as the ferry. Hurried back to make his appearance at the funeral of a Hebrew constituent. Went conspicuously to the front both in the Catholic church and the synagogue, and later attended the Hebrew confirmation ceremonies in the synagogue.

7 P.M.: Went to district headquarters and presided over a meeting of election district captains. Each captain submitted a list of all the voters in his district, reported on their attitude toward Tammany, suggested who might be won over and how they could be won, told who were in need, and who were in trouble of any kind and the best way to reach them. District leader took notes and gave orders.

8 P.M.: Went to a church fair. Took chances on everything, bought ice cream for the young girls and the children. Kissed the little ones, flattered their mothers and took their fathers out for something down at the corner.

9 P.M.: At the clubhouse again. Spent $10 on tickets for a church excursion and promised a subscription for a new church bell. Bought tickets for a baseball game to be played by two nines from his district. Listened to the complaints of a dozen pushcart peddlers who said they were persecuted by the police and assured them he would go to Police Headquarters in the morning and see about it.

10:30 P.M.: Attended a Hebrew wedding reception and dance. Had previously sent a handsome wedding present to the bride.

12 P.M.: In bed. . . .

7.7   The Regional City

For a major portion of their history, most Americans lived first on farms and small towns, and later in big cities. But the suburbs have mushroomed in the last half century, and it is in the suburbs where, increasingly, most Americans now live.

Not everyone has favored the suburbs. Lewis Mumford, social philosopher, architectural critic, and one of the most influential writers on the history of cities, disliked both the big cities and the suburbs that began to surround them in the early twentieth century. He had in mind another alternative—the planned regional city. This type of community was realized in several places, such as the greenbelt cities of the New Deal era, but it never became a major trend. Yet it is worth knowing about, if only because it helps cast a sharper light on the suburban lifestyle most of us live today.

Mumford has been a prolific writer. His massive study, The City in History *(1961) won the National Book Award. The following excerpt is from his 1926 magazine article entitled "The Intolerable City."*

Questions

What faults did Mumford find with the big city and with the suburbs? Describe his alternative plan? If he had his way as a regional planner in the 1920s, would we be better or worse off today? Would it have made a difference? Consider what might have been the impact on today's transportation, housing, recreation, and ecological concerns.

Manifestly, the suburb is a public acknowledgment of the fact that congestion and bad housing and blank vistas and lack of recreational opportunity and endless subway rides are not humanly endurable. . . . The suburb is an attempt to recapture the environment which the big city, in its blind and heedless growth, has wiped out within its own borders. With the aid of the suburb, business and living are divided into two compartments, intermittently connected by a strip of railroad. . . . The sort of life the suburb aims at is of course only partial: inevitably the suburbanite loses many of the cultural advantages and contacts of a complete city; but even its limited effort to obtain two essential things—a decent home for children and a comely setting for life—is thin and ephemeral in its results. The suburb is not a solution. It is merely a halting place. So long as the big city continues to grow, the suburb cannot remain suburban. . . . Sooner or later it will be swallowed up and lost in the maw of the great city. . . .

Our technicians usually accept the fact of unregulated and unbounded urban growth as "given." So instead of attempting to remove the causes that create our mangled urban environments, they attempt only to relieve a few of the intolerable effects. They exhaust the devices of mechanical engineering and finance to provide palliatives for expanding cities and expanding populations, and they flinch, most of them, from asking the one question which promises any permanent and effectual answer—how can we provide a stable environment for a stable population? . . . How are we to obtain the physical foundations of a good life in our cities?

The problem would be utterly discouraging were it not for two conditions. One is that the growth of modern invention has diminished the necessity for urban concentration. The other is . . . that the more intelligent and sensitive part of the population is becoming a little bored by "greatness," and they are beginning to feel towards their skyscrapers the way an Egyptian slave perhaps felt toward the Pyramids. . . . During the railroad era the favored urban spots were at the terminals of trunk lines. . . . The result was vast urban agglomerations . . . at points where the traffic ended, coalesced, or crossed. Modern motor transportation and modern airplane traffic do not abet this tendency: They favor a more even distribution of population . . . ; for the net of motor roads makes it possible to serve any point in a

SOURCE: Lewis Mumford, "The Intolerable City," *Harper's Magazine*, February 1926.

whole area by car or truck, instead of simply those points "on the line." Economically, this works towards regional rather than metropolitan development; towards industrial decentralization rather than toward further congestion. . . .

The alternative to super-congestion is not "back to the farm" or "let things go." The real alternative to unlimited metropolitan growth is limited growth, and, along with it, the deliberate planning and building up of new communities. . . . Any effective effort to provide good living conditions within our existing cities rests upon achieving a fairly stable population: this can be accomplished only by building up new communities in the hinterland, which will hold back the flood . . . but also drain off some of the surplus from existing centers. What we need is a policy of "community afforestation." . . . Our present small towns and villages are unable to retain their young people because so many of them are scrub communities. . . . If we are to prevent congestion, we must deliberately create communities which will be fully equipped for work, play, study, and "living" . . . ; in other words, they must be, in English usage, complete garden cities.

How would these new communities differ from existing cities? First, in placement; they would be established in relation to the best remaining water and power resources, and in country districts where land values were still low. They would be surrounded by a permanent belt of agricultural land, to provide a continuous local food supply of green vegetables, and to preserve open spaces without taking them altogether out of productive use. Second, provisions for all the institutions necessary for a community of a given size, say ten thousand or fifty thousand, would be

made from the beginning. That is, the land needed for schools, churches, libraries, theaters, hospitals, municipal buildings, associations, playgrounds, and parks would be calculated, platted, and reserved; at the same time, the land needed for shops, factories, and offices would be allocated, with due respect to convenient access, to amenity, and—in the factory district—to prevailing winds and outlooks. The residential parts of the city, instead of being intersected by innumerable streets, would be planned for quiet, safety, and beauty. . . . In general, no houses higher than three stories, and no offices higher than five, would be permitted; but that would not prevent the erection of a single tall building, or a small group, as high as, say, ten stories if the height served some direct purpose, such as the grouping of municipal departments, or medical services. The high building would not, however, be permitted as a mere rent barracks. . . .

The provision of gardens and playgrounds would likewise be made on the initial plan; and since the population would be definitely limited, their adequacy would be permanently insured. The time now wasted in subway travel would, since the area of the city is limited, be available for sport, rest, education, or entertainment. Land values increase in the business district of such a city; but the increase is kept for communal purposes. . . . If some potent institution, like an expanding industry or a great center of learning, caused such a city to attract more people than originally provided for, the further extension of the city, once it had filled its sites, would be taken care of by founding another city, similarly restricted in area and population, similarly surrounded by a rural belt. . . .

Here then is the choice—between growth by the "mechanical extension" of existing urban areas, and growth by the foundation of new communities, fully equipped for working, learning, and living. In the growth by mechanical extension we move inertly towards the intolerable city. . . . With a tithe of the constructive power we now spend on palliatives, we might found a hundred fresh centers in which life would really be enjoyable, in which the full benefit of modern civilization and culture might be had.

7.8 The Los Angeles Riot of 1965

The cities of the 1960s were plagued by urban riots from coast to coast. One of the ugliest riots occurred in the Watts area of Los Angeles in 1965. For six days in August, some ten thousand black residents roamed the streets of the South Central area of the city torching their ghetto. Spectators sat glued to their television screens watching the unprecedented looting, burning and killing that resulted in thirty-four deaths, over one thousand injured, some four thousand arrests, and $40 million in property damage.

Everyone seemed to have an explanation for the riot. California's Senator George Murphy implied it was a leftist rebellion, or an offshoot of the civil rights movement. Ghetto residents charged that a breakdown in police-community relations was a major factor. The indifference of a mayoral administration to the needs of the black community and its refusal to accept federal programs was assigned a measure of blame. Others called it a "commodity riot," that is, a disturbance expressed by the pillage of retail goods.

California Governor Edmund G. "Pat" Brown established a blue-ribbon commission to discover what had caused the disaster and to recommend ways to prevent a recurrence. The nine-member body, headed by former CIA chief John McCone, heard the testimony of hundreds of people, including representatives of public agencies involved with employment, education, health, transportation, social welfare, and police and community services.

Twenty years later, in 1985, the human rights commissions of the City and the County of Los Angeles joined forces and returned to Watts to see what changes had taken place. They were not encouraged by what they found. Some improvements had been made, but the overall condition of the area remained unchanged.

Questions

What caused the Watts Riot of 1965? Why has so little been done since then to improve the conditions that brought on the disturbance?

What are the underlying problems of the ghettos and barrios of the U.S.? How do drugs, street violence, racism, unemployment owing to the decline of industrial production, and the impoverishment of women affect the quality of life in those areas of the cities?

Do you expect another round of rioting in the U.S. in the near future? Explain.

The McCone Report, 1965 —

The Dull Devastating Spirit of Failure

In examining the sickness in the center of our city, what has depressed and stunned us most is the dull, devastating spiral of failure that awaits the average disadvantaged child in the urban core. His home life all too often fails to give him the incentive and the elementary experience with words and ideas which prepares most children for school. Unprepared and unready, he may not learn to read or write at all; and because he shares his problem with 30 or more in the same classroom, even the efforts of the most dedicated teachers are unavailing. . . .

Frustrated and disillusioned, the child becomes a discipline problem. Often he leaves school, sometimes before the end of junior high school. (About two-thirds of those who enter the three high schools in the center of the curfew area do not graduate.) He slips into the ranks of the per-

SOURCES: State of California, Governor's Commission on the Los Angeles Riots, "Violence in the City— An End or a Beginning?" (Los Angeles, 1965); and, Los Angeles County Commission on Human Relations, and Los Angeles City Human Relations Commission, "McCone Revisited: A Focus on Solutions to Continuing Problems in South Central Los Angeles. Report on a Public Hearing . . ." (Los Angeles, January 1985), 11–16.

manent jobless, illiterate and untrained, unemployed and unemployable. . . .

Reflecting this spiral of failure, unemployment in the disadvantaged areas runs two to three times the county average, and the employment available is too often intermittent. A family whose breadwinner is chronically out of work is almost invariably a disintegrating family. Crime rates soar and welfare rolls increase, even faster than the population. . . .

From our study, we are persuaded that there is a reasonable possibility that raising the achievement levels of the disadvantaged Negro child will materially lessen the tendency towards de facto segregation in education, and that this might possibly also make a substantial contribution to ending all de facto segregation.

All Segments of Society

What can be done to prevent a recurrence of the nightmare of August? It stands to reason that what we and other cities have been doing, costly as it all has been, is not enough. Improving the conditions of Negro life will demand adjustments on a large scale unknown to any great society. The programs that we are recommending will be expensive and burdensome. . . .

The consequences of inaction, indifference, and inadequacy, we can all be sure now, would be far costlier in the long run than the cost of correction. If the city were to elect to stand aside, the walls of segregation would rise even higher. The disadvantaged community would become more and more estranged and the risk of violence would rise. The cost of police protection would increase, and yet would never be adequate. Unemployment would climb; welfare costs would mount apace. And the preachers of division and demagoguery would have a matchless opportunity to tear our nation asunder. . . .

The Problem—Deep and Serious

The conduct of law enforcement agencies, most particularly the Los Angeles Police Department, has been subject to severe criticism by many Negroes who have appeared before the Commission as witnesses. . . . "Police brutality" has been the recurring charge. One witness after another has recounted instances in which, in their opinion, the police have used excessive force or have been disrespectful and abusive in their language or manner. . . .

The reasons for the feeling that law enforcment officers are the enemy of the Negro are manifold and it is well to reflect on them before they are accepted. An examination of seven riots in northern cities of the United States in 1964 reveals that each one was started over a police incident, just as the Los Angeles riot started with the arrest of Marquette Frye. . . .

Our society is held together by respect for law. A group of officers who represent a tiny fraction of one percent of the population is the thin thread that enforces observance of law by those few who would do otherwise. . . . So, while we must examine carefully the claim of police brutality and must see that justice is done to

all groups within our society, we must, at the same time, be sure that law enforcement agencies, upon which so much depends, are not rendered impotent. . . .

More Negroes and Mexican-Americans Must Enter Careers in Law Enforcement

We believe it essential that the number of sworn officers of each minority group should be increased substantially. . . .

Employment—Key to Independence

. . . Unemployment and the consequent idleness are at the root of many of the problems we discuss in this report. Many witnesses have described to us, dramatically and we believe honestly, the overwhelming hopelessness that comes when a man's efforts to find a job come to naught. Inevitably, there is despair and a deep resentment of a society which he feels has turned its back upon him. Welfare does not change this. It provides the necessities of life, but adds nothing to a man's stature, nor relieves the frustrations that grow. In short, the price for public assistance is loss of human dignity.

The welfare program that provides for his children is administered so that it injures his position as the head of his household, because aid is supplied with less restraint to a family headed by a woman, married or unmarried. Thus, the unemployed male often finds it to his family's advantage to drift away and leave the family to fend for itself. Once he goes, the family unit is broken and is seldom restored. . . . The despair and disillusionment of the unemployed parent is passed down to the children. The example of failure is vividly present and the parent's frustrations and habits become the children's. ("Go to school for what?" one youngster said to us.). . . .

Government Job Efforts

Government authorities have recognized the problem and have moved to solve it. City, county, state and federal governments have helped to siphon off some of the distress by hiring high proportions of Negroes. For example, 25% of all new Los Angeles county employees in 1964 were Negro. . . .

In making this recommendation, we believe that if the maximum degree of cooperation from employers and labor unions is to be achieved, FEPC and other agencies dealing with discriminatory employment practices must continue to rely heavily on persuasion and education in the affirmative action programs. These are the techniques that have been most successful in the past. . . .

Education—Our Fundamental Resource

. . . [W]e launched an in-depth study to determine the quality of education offered in the public schools in the riot area and in other areas of the city. . . .

It is our belief that raising the level of scholastic achievement will lessen the trend towards *de facto* segregation in the schools in the areas into which the Negroes are expanding and, indeed, will tend to reduce all *de facto* segregation. . . .

Accordingly, our major recommendations are:

1. Elementary and junior high schools in the disadvantaged areas which have achievement levels substantially below the city average should be designated as "Emergency Schools." In each of

these schools, an "Emergency Literacy Program" should be established consisting of a drastic reduction in class size to a maximum of 22 students and additional supportive personnel to provide special services. It is estimated that this program will cost at least $250 per year per student in addition to present per student costs and exclusive of capital expenditures, and that it must be continued for a minimum of six years for the elementary schools and three years for the junior high schools.

2. A permanent pre-school program should be established throughout the school year to provide education beginning at age three. Efforts should be focused on the development of language skills essential to prepare children to learn to read and write.

A recent survey indicates that 90% of the AFDC [Aid to Families with Dependent Children] families are Negro. In nine out of 10 of these homes, the father is absent. Over 70% of the parents involved were born in the South or Southwest. Seven out of 10 families on AFDC receive aid for one or more illegitimate children.

In Los Angeles County as a whole, expenditures for the AFDC program have been increasing dramatically, far outrunning the population trends. . . . A portion of the rapid increase may be explained by the fact that the Negro and Mexican-American population in Los Angeles is estimated to have increased approximately 40% in the last five years, compared with the general population increase of 13 percent in the same period. Moreover, the high unemployment in this area, referred to early in this report, no doubt has contributed to the increase. However, the increase in AFDC expenditures, coupled with the increase in population, raises a question in the minds of some whether the generosity of the California welfare program compared with those in the southern and southwestern states is not one of the factors causing the heavy immigration of disadvantaged people to Los Angeles. . . .

. . . [A] truly successful welfare program must, wherever feasible, create an initiative and an incentive on the part of the recipients to become independent of state assistance. Otherwise, the welfare program promotes an attitude of hopelessness and permanent dependence.´ . . .

Similarly, welfare agencies should be cognizant of the many available training programs. From our study of the matter, we believe that there is much room for improvement here. We also believe that the use of child care centers to free heads of families for employment or training should be emphasized. . . .

Health Problems

Statistics indicate that health conditions of the residents of south central Los Angeles are relatively poor and facilities to provide medical care are insufficient. Infant mortality, for example, is about one and one-half times greater than the city-wide average. Life expectancies are considerably shorter. A far lower percentage of the children are immunized against diphtheria, whooping cough, tetanus, smallpox, and poliomyelitis than in the rest of the county.

As established by the comprehensive reports of consultants to the Commission, the number of doctors in the southeastern part of Los Angeles is grossly inadequate as compared with other parts of the city. It is reported that there are 106 physicians for some 252,000 people, whereas the county ratio is three times higher. The hospitals

readily accessible to the citizens in southeastern Los Angeles are also grossly inadequate in quality and in numbers of beds. Of the eight proprietary hospitals, which have a total capacity of 454 beds, only two meet minimum standards of professional quality. The two large public hospitals, County General and Harbor General, are both distant and difficult to reach. . . .

In light of the information presented to it, the Commission believes that immediate and favorable consideration should be given to a new, comprehensively-equipped hopsital in this area, which is now under study by various public agencies. . . .

The Commission recognizes that much of what it has to say about causes and remedies is not new, although it is backed up by fresh additional evidence coming out of the investigation of the Los Angeles riots. . . . Among the many steps which should be taken to improve the present situation, the commission affirms again that the three fundamental issues in the urban problems of disadvantaged minorities are: employment, education and police-community relations. Accordingly, the Commission looks upon its recommendations in these three areas as at the heart of its plea and the City's best hope. . . .

The Human Relations Report, 1985—

Findings

The following finding of the Los Angeles County and Los Angeles City Human Relations Commissions are based on the testimony presented at this hearing and in supporting documents. . . .

1. We find that the greatest progress since 1965 has been made in Transportation. . . .

2. We find that significant progress has been made in Health, although many critical problems remain.

   A. . . . The Martin Luther King Jr. Hospital and Drew Post-Graduate Medical School were completed in 1972. . . .

   C. Despite the progress noted, South Central Los Angeles still has the highest infant mortality rate, the lowest rate of immunization, the highest incidence of communicable disease, an alarming rate of drug abuse, and the fewest doctors per capita in the County. The area leads the County in morbidity and mortality rates. The number of Black teenage pregnancies increases each year. Homicide is the primary cause of mortality among Black males in South Central Los Angeles.

3. We find that despite substantial progress Police-Community Relations and the issue of equitable law enforcement continues to be one of the most contentious and serious problems for residents of South Central Los Angeles. . . .

   C. The Department has made a serious effort to recruit Black and Latino sworn personnel, and there has been a significant increase since 1965 . . . however . . . the allocation formula fails to make a sufficient distinction between crimes against property and crimes against people, to the detriment of South Central Los Angeles. . . .

4. We find that problems of Employment in South Central Los Angeles remain critical.

   A. . . . There now appears to be no comprehensive job training and placement center or program in the area, and coordination of existing programs is described as poor.

   B. Plant closures and the disappearance of jobs in heavy manufacturing have made a major impact on South Central Los Angeles. . . .

5. We find that problems of Welfare and Social Services remain critical.

   Poverty is becoming increasingly feminized: nearly one-third of all households with children in South Central Los Angeles are headed by women. . . . Reduction in Federal funds for welfare and social services has had a disproportionate negative impact on the level and quality of life in the South Central area.

6. We find that problems of Education remain critical and may be growing worse.

   A. The McCone Commission recommended that elementary and junior high schools with achievement levels below the average for the Los Angeles Unified School District be designated "Emergency Schools," but this was not done. The Commission recommended establishment of a permanent pre-school program beginning at age three to focus on development of language skills, but this was not done.

   B. Schools in South Central Los Angeles are as racially isolated today as in 1965, perhaps more so. . . .

7. We find that Housing remains one of the most critical problems in South Central Los Angeles.

   A. The McCone Commission urged implementation of a continuing urban rehabilitation and renewal program for South Central Los Angeles. This has not been done. . . .

Recommendations

Some problems reported 19 years ago by the McCone Commission have been resolved. Many have not. . . . While realizing that involvement of other agencies is critical, we have focused on one key agency in each problem area.

The Los Angeles County Human Relations Commission and the Los Angeles City Human Relations Commission recommend:

1. In each area where the Commissions have found serious problems in South Central Los Angeles, a key agency should be designated by the appropriate authority to review the McCone Commission Report, the Report of the Joint Task Force on South Central Los Angeles, and this hearing report on McCone Revisited in order to develop specific solutions to the problems identified, ways to implement those solutions, resources required, and a timetable for implementation, however long-range. These agencies should be designated as quickly as possible and should report back to the appointing authority by July 1985.

   a. The Los Angeles County Board of Supervisors should direct the County Health Department to develop a plan to reduce infant mortality, increase the rate of immunization, reduce communicable disease, reduce drug abuse, increase the number of physicians, and otherwise address the health problems of South Central Los Angeles.

   b. The Mayor of Los Angeles and the Los Angeles City Council should request the Board of Police Commissioners to develop a plan, in cooperation with the Chief of Police, to improve police-community relations, police-community communication, and the current allocation or deployment formula in South Central Los Angeles. The plan should also address the issues of drug traffic and homicide in South Central Los Angeles.

   c. The Board of Supervisors, Mayor, and City Council should request the Governor . . . to address the critical employment problems of South Central Los Angeles.

   d. The Board of Supervisors should direct the County Department of Public Social Services to develop a plan, including legislation if necessary, to address the critical welfare and social services problems of South Central Los Angeles.

   e. The Los Angeles Unified School District Board of Education should direct the Superintendent of Schools to develop a plan to decrease racial isolation, increase achievement scores, increase parent participation, reduce teacher shortages, improve year-round schools, and otherwise address the education problems of South Central Los Angeles.

   f. The Mayor and City Council should request the City Planning Commission to develop a plan, including legislation if necessary, to address the critical housing problems of South Central Los Angeles.

2. A Blue Ribbon Task Force composed of elected officials and leaders from private industry, religious institutions, and the community, should be appointed by the Governor by January 1986. This Task Force, acting with the same sense of responsibility and urgency as the McCone Commission, would evaluate responses to the preceding recommendations and the effectiveness of solutions offered, making a report to the Governor and the public. . . .

Chapter Eight:
Environment

8.1 "Save Hetch Hetchy!"

The naturalist John Muir wanted wild nature protected for aesthetic and religious reasons. Wilderness, he believed, was a "window opening into heaven, a mirror reflecting the Creator." Born in Scotland in 1838 and reared on the Wisconsin frontier, Muir was a poet, essayist, geologist, ornithologist and botanist. He spent much of his life exploring the deserts, forests and mountains of the West. In California he founded the Sierra Club in 1892, and served as its leader for some years.

Muir conducted several successful political campaigns in behalf of the natural environment. The most successful was an effort to establish Yosemite as a national park. But he also suffered disappointments. His most bitter defeat was the lost battle to preserve the Hetch Hetchy Valley, a beautiful remote part of the Yosemite area. It was here that San Francisco proposed building a dam to supply itself with drinking water and electricity. Muir asserted that the city could achieve its purposes through other, less destructive means. A prominent opponent to Muir in this contest was fellow naturalist and sometime colleague, Gifford Pinchot, who held an entirely different outlook on the natural environment (see Document 8.2).

After long debate, aesthetics lost out to practical considerations. The hydro-electric system was built and the valley flooded. Muir died heart-broken in 1914, though the Hetch Hetchy defeat helped call attention to the movement for the preservation of wilderness. Seven decades later, the administration of President Reagan suggested that Hetch Hetchy could be restored to its original natural state. The Sierra Club, invoking the memory of Muir, said it might be worth considering.

Questions

What, according to Muir, are the benefits of preserving wilderness generally and Hetch Hetchy in particular? Who did Muir believe were the greatest enemies of wilderness? Contrast his views with those of Pinchot, below.

If every beautiful wild place were preserved along the lines suggested by Muir, would the cause of progress and civilization be helped or hindered?

The tendency nowadays to wander in wildnerness is delightful to see. Thousands of tired, nerve-shaken, over-civilized people are beginning to find out that going to the mountains is going home; that wildness is a necessity; and that mountain parks and reservations are useful not only as fountains of timber and irrigating rivers, but as fountains of life. Awakening from the stupefying effects of the vice of over-industry and the deadly apathy of luxury, they are trying as best they can to mix and enrich their own little ongoings with those of Nature, and to get rid of rust and disease. Briskly venturing and roaming, some are washing off sins and cobweb cares of the devil's spinning in all-day storms on mountains; sauntering in rosiny pinewoods or in gentian meadows, brushing through chaparral, bending down and parting sweet, flowery sprays; tracing rivers to their sources, getting in touch with the nerves of Mother Earth; jumping from rock to rock, feeling the life of them, learning the songs of them, panting in whole-souled exercise, and rejoicing in deep, long-drawn breaths of pure wildness. This is fine and natural and full of promise. So also is the growing interest in the care and preservation of forests and wild places in general, and in the half wild parks and gardens of towns. Even the scenery habit in its most artificial forms, mixed with spectacles, silliness, and kodaks; its devotees arrayed more gorgeously than scarlet tanagers, frightening the wild game with red umbrellas,—even this is encouraging, and may well be regarded as a hopeful sign of the times.

SOURCE: The general statement is from John Muir, "The Wild Parks and Forest Reservations of the West," in the *Atlantic Monthly*, Vol. LXXXI, No. 483 (January 1898). The statement on Hetch Hetchy is from John Muir, *The Yosemite* (New York: Century Publishing Co., 1912), 255–257, 260–262.

All the Western mountains are still rich in wildness, and by means of good roads are being brought nearer civilization every year. To the sane and free it will hardly seem necessary to cross the continent in search of wild beauty, however easy the way, for they find it in abundance wherever they chance to be. Like Thoreau they see forests in orchards and patches of huckleberry brush, and oceans in ponds and drops of dew. Few in these hot, dim, strenuous times are quite sane or free; choked with care like clocks full of dust, laboriously doing so much good and making so much money,—or so little,—they are no longer good for themselves. . . .

. . . As in Yosemite, the sublime rocks of [Hetch Hetchy's] walls seem to glow with life, whether leaning back in repose or standing erect in thoughtful attitudes, giving welcome to storms and calms alike, their brows in the sky, their feet set in the groves and gay flowery meadows, while birds, bees, and butterflies help the river and waterfalls to stir all the air into music— things frail and fleeting and types of permanence meeting here and blending, just as they do in Yosemite, to draw her lovers into close and confiding communion with her.

Sad to say, this most precious and sublime feature of the Yosemite National Park, one of the greatest of all our natural resources for the uplifting joy and peace and health of the people, is in danger of being dammed and made into a reservoir to help supply San Francisco with water and light, thus flooding it from wall to wall and burying its gardens and groves one or two hundred feet deep. This grossly destructive commercial scheme has long been planned and urged (though water as pure and abundant can be got from sources outside of the people's park, in a dozen different places), because of the comparative cheapness of the dam and of the territory which it is sought to divert from the great uses to which it was dedicated in the Act of 1890 establishing the Yosemite National Park.

The making of gardens and parks goes on with civilization all over the world, and they increase both in size and number as their value is recognized. Everybody needs beauty as well as bread, places to play in and pray in, where Nature may heal and cheer and give strength to body and soul alike. This natural beauty-hunger is made manifest in the little window-sill gardens of the poor, though perhaps only a geranium slip in a broken cup, as well as in the carefully tended rose and lily gardens of the rich, the thousands of spacious city parks and botanical gardens, and in our magnificent National parks—the Yellowstone, Yosemite, Sequoia, etc.—Nature's sublime wonderlands, the admiration and joy of the world. Nevertheless, like anything else worth while, from the very beginning, however well guarded, they have always been subject to attack by despoiling gain-seekers and mischief-makers of every degree from Satan to Senators, eagerly trying to make everything immediately and selfishly commercial, with schemes disguised in smug-smiling philanthropy, industriously shampiously crying, "Conservation, conservation, panutilization," that man and beast may be fed and the dear Nation made great. Thus long ago a few

enterprising merchants utilized the Jerusalem temple as a place of business instead of a place of prayer, changing money, buying and selling cattle and sheep and doves; and earlier still, the first forest reservation, including only one tree, was likewise despoiled. Ever since the establishment of the Yosemite National Park, strife has been going on around its borders and I suppose this will go on as part of the universal battle between right and wrong, however much its boundaries may be shorn, or its wild beauty destroyed. . . .

That any one would try to destroy [Hetch Hetchy Valley] seems incredible; but sad experience shows that there are people good enough and bad enough for anything. The proponents of the dam scheme bring forward a lot of bad arguments to prove that the only righteous thing to do with the people's parks is to destroy them bit by bit as they are able. Their arguments are curiously like those of the devil, devised for the destruction of the first garden. . . .

These temple destroyers, devotees of ravaging commercialism, seem to have a perfect contempt for Nature, and, instead of lifting their eyes to the God of the mountains, lift them to the Almighty Dollar.

Dam Hetch Hetchy! As well dam for water-tanks the people's cathedrals and churches, for no holier temple has ever been consecrated by the heart of man.

8.2 The Conservation of Natural Resources

The man credited with inventing the term "conservation" was the naturalist Gifford Pinchot (1865–1946). As the nation's first professionally trained forester, he headed the new forestry division of the Department of Agriculture. Pinchot believed in managing forests not for aesthetic, but for practical reasons, for "maximum sustained yield." "Wise use" was his main criterion; essentially, forests should be handled like farms.

Pinchot was an important mover and shaker in the progressive moement, and a co-founder of the Progressive Party. Theodore Roosevelt regarded him as the key figure in the conservation movement and helped further his career. One reason was that Pinchot was genuinely interested in preventing monopolies from controlling natural resources.

As Pinchot saw it, the Hetch Hetchy project was not only soundly planned, but could supply enough water to keep San Francisco from being strangled by greedy private utilities. The case seemed so clear cut that Pinchot broke with his friend and co-worker John Muir over Hetch Hetchy (Document 8.1).

When Roosevelt's successor, Pres. William Howard Taft, turned a blind eye to conservation, Pinchot presented his case to the people. His plea took the form of a book, The Fight for Conservation, *published in 1910. Brief passages are reprinted below.*

Questions

List Pinchot's main principles of conservation. What are the philosophical bases of his ideas of conservatism? Contrast these ideas with those of Muir, above.

If Pinchot's idea were to prevail, and all wild places could be exploited for "efficiency" and "wise use," would we be better or worse off as a nation?

Are you most in sympathy with the views of Muir or Pinchot? Is there room for compromise? What form could such compromise take?

. . . The principles which govern the conservation movement, like all great and effective things, are simple and easily understood. . . .

SOURCE: Gifford Pinchot, *The Fight for Conservation* (Garden City, New York: Doubleday, Page and Company, 1910), 42–50.

The first great fact about conservation is that is stands for development. There has been a fundamental misconception that conservation means nothing but the husbanding of resources for future generations. There could be no more serious mistake. Conservation does mean provision for the future, but it means also and first of all the recognition of the right of the present generation to the fullest necessary use of all the resources with which this country is so abundantly blessed. Conservation demands the welfare of this generation first, and afterward the welfare of the generations to follow.

The first principle of conservation is development, the use of the natural resources now existing on this continent for the benefit of the people who live here now. There may be just as much waste in neglecting the development and use of certain natural resources as there is in their destruction. We have a limited supply of coal, and only a limited supply. Whether it is to last for a hundred or a hundred and fifty or a thousand years, the coal is limited in amount, unless through geological changes which we shall not live to see, there will never be any more of it than there is now. But coal is in a sense the vital essence of our civilization. If it can be preserved, if the life of the mines can be extended, if by preventing waste there can be more coal left in this country after we of this generation have made every needed use of this source of power, then we shall have deserved well of our descendants.

Conservation stands emphatically for the development and use of water-power now, without delay. It stands for the immediate construction of navigable waterways under a broad and comprehensive plan as assistants to the railroads. More coal and more iron are required to move a ton of freight by rail than by water, three to one. In every case and in every direction the conservation movement has development for its first principle, and at the very beginning of its work. The development of our natural resources and the fullest use of them for the present generation is the first duty of this generation. . . .

In the second place conservation stands for the prevention of waste. There has come gradually in this country an understanding that waste is not a good thing and that the attack on waste is an industrial necessity. I recall very well indeed how, in the early days of forest fires, they were considered simply and solely as acts of God, against which any opposition was hopeless and any attempt to control them not merely hopeless but childish. It was assumed that they came in the natural order of things, as inevitably as the seasons or the rising and setting of the sun. Today we understand that forest fires are wholly within the control of men. So we are coming in like manner to understand that the prevention of waste in all other directions is a simple matter of good business. The first duty of the human race is to control the earth it lives upon.

We are in a position more and more completely to say how far the waste and destruction of natural resources are to be allowed to go on and where they are to stop. It is curious that the effort to stop waste, like the effort to stop forest fires, has often been considered as a matter controlled wholly by economic law. I think there could be no greater mistake. Forest fires were allowed to burn long after the people had means to stop them. The idea that men were helpless in the face of them held long after the time had passed when the means of control were fully within our reach. It was the old story that "as a man thinketh, so is he"; we came to see that we could stop forest fires, and we found that the means had long been at hand. When at length we came to see that the control of logging in certain directions was profitable, we found it had long been possible. In all these matters of waste of natural resources, the education of the people to understand that they can stop the leakage comes before the actual stopping and after the means of stopping it have long been ready at our hands.

In addition to the principles of development and preservation of our resources there is a third principle. It is this: The natural resources must be developed and preserved for the benefit of the many, and not merely for the profit of a few. We are coming to understand in this country that public action for public benefit has a very much wider field to cover and a much larger part to play than was the case when there were resources enough for every one, and before certain constitutional provisions had given so tremendously strong a position to vested rights and property in general.

. . . [B]y reason of the XIVth amendment to the Constitution, property rights in the United States occupy a stronger position than in any other country in the civilized world. It becomes then a matter of multiplied importance, since property rights once granted are so strongly entrenched, to see that they shall be so granted that the people shall get their fair share of the benefit which comes from the development of the resources which belong to us all. The time to do that is now. By so doing we shall avoid the difficulties and conflicts which will surely arise if we allow vested rights to accrue outside the possibility of governmental and popular control.

The conservation idea covers a wider range than the field of natural resources alone. Conservation means the greatest good to the greatest number for the longest time. One of its great contributions is just this, that it has added to the worn and well-known phrase, "the greatest good to the greatest number," the additional words "for the longest time," thus recognizing that this nation of ours must be made to endure as the best possible home for all its people.

Conservation advocates the use of foresight, prudence, thrift, and intelligence in dealing with public matters, for the same reasons and in the same way that we each use foresight, prudence, thrift, and intelligence in dealing with our own private affairs. It proclaims the right and duty of the people to act for the benefit of the people. Conservation demands the application of common sense to the common problems for the common good.

The principles of conservation thus described—development, preservation, the common good—have a general application which is growing rapidly wider. The development of resources and the prevention of waste and loss, the protection of the public interests, by foresight, prudence, and the ordinary business and home-making virtues, all these apply to other things as well as to the natural resources. There is, in fact, no interest of the people to which the principles of conservation do not apply.

The conservation point of view is valuable in the education of our people as well as in forestry; it applies to the body politic as well as to the earth and its minerals. A municipal franchise is as properly within its sphere as a franchise for water-power. The same point of view governs in both. It applies as much to the subject of good roads as to waterways, and the training of our people in citizenship is as germane to it as the productiveness of the earth. The application of commonsense to any problem for the Nation's good will lead directly to national efficiency wherever applied. In other words, and that is the burden of the message, we are coming to see the logical and inevitable outcome that these princi- ples, which arose in forestry and have their bloom in the conservation of natural re- sources, will have their fruit in the in- crease and promotion of national efficiency along other lines of national life.

The outgrowth of conservation, the in- evitable result, is national efficiency. In the great commercial struggle between na- tions which is eventually to determine the welfare of all, national efficiency will be the deciding factor. So from every point of view conservation is a good thing for the American people.

8.3 A New Ethic

As we have seen, John Muir advanced aesthetic and religious considerations for pre- serving wilderness, while Gifford Pinchot urged practical ones. But both men considered human benefit the first and last objective in dealing with the environment. The naturalist Aldo Leo- pold (1887–1948) came from a completely different perspective. When considering the envi- ronment, he held that human and animal welfare had to be viewed together, along with the soil and the water. He raised the issue of "ecology."

Aldo Leopold began his professional career by joining the U.S. forest service in 1909, soon after that agency was founded. He served in the Southwest as a naturalist, pioneering in the study of wildlife management and wilderness preservation. Starting in 1933, he taught biology at the University of Wisconsin, with a specialty in game management. Shortly after becoming an advisor on conservation to the United Nations in 1948, he died while fighting a brush fire on a neighbor's farm on the banks of the Wisconsin River.

While Leopold's was basically a scientific view of the environment, it raised ethical and philosophical issues. He believed it was necessary to study philosophical texts as well as con- duct scientific experiments. He questioned whether the main objective of managing the en- vironment should be human economic profit. The world was made up not only of humans but of complex communities of soils, waters, plants, insects and animals. All of these interdepen- dent, elements—or the natural community that they comprised—needed protection. He ex- plained that the existing policies of conservation lacked an ethical content, and proposed that a new "man-land" ethic be devised that would give greater consideration to wild nature.

Leopold's collected essays, A Sand County Almanac, *prepared largely from his lec- tures in the 1930s at Wisconsin University, explore these issues. They are considered a major source of ideas for today's ecology movement. A brief selection appears next.*

Questions

Summarize Leopold's implied criticism of today's conservation policies, and his reasons for suggesting that a "man-land" ethic must be created. Compare Leopold's ideas with those of Muir and Pinchot, above. With which man is he most in sympathy? Why hasn't the proposed ethic developed further or achieved greater support? What is the status of the preservation of wildlife today? How do the views of these three men differ? In what areas do they agree?

One basic weakness in a conservation system based wholly on economic motives is that most members of the land community have no economic value. Wildflowers and songbirds are examples. Of the 22,000 higher plants and animals native to Wisconsin, it is doubtful whether more than 5 per cent can be sold, fed, eaten, or otherwise put to economic use. Yet these creatures are members of the biotic community, and if (as I believe) its stability depends on its integrity, they are entitled to continuance.

When one of these non-economic categories is threatened, and if we happen to love it, we invent subterfuges to give it economic importance. At the beginning of the century song-birds were supposed to be disappearing. Ornithologists jumped to the rescue with some distinctly shaky evidence to the effect that insects would eat us up if birds failed to control them. The evidence had to be economic in order to be valid.

It is painful to read these circumlocutions today. We have no land ethic yet, but

SOURCE: Aldo Leopold, *A Sand County Almanac and Sketches Here and There* (New York: Oxford University Press, Inc., 1949). Reprinted by permission of the publisher.

we have at least drawn nearer the point of admitting that birds should continue as a matter of biotic right, regardless of the presence or absence of economic advantage to us.

A parallel situation exists in respect of predatory mammals, raptorial birds, and fish-eating birds. Time was when biologists somewhat overworked the evidence that these creatures preserve the health of game by killing weaklings, or that they control rodents for the farmer, or that they prey only on 'worthless' species. Here again, the evidence had to be economic in order to be valid. It is only in recent years that we hear the more honest argument that predators are members of the community, and that no special interest has the right to exterminate them for the sake of a benefit, real or fancied, to itself. Unfortunately this enlightened view is still in the talk stage. In the field the extermination of predators goes merrily on: witness the impending erasure of the timber wolf by fiat of Congress, the Conservation Bureaus, and many state legislatures.

Some species of trees have been 'read out of the party' by economics-minded foresters because they grow too slowly, or have too low a sale value to pay as timber crops: white cedar, tamarack, cypress, beech, and hemlock are examples. In Europe, where forestry is ecologically more advanced, the non-commercial tree species are recognized as members of the native forest community, to be preserved as such, within reason. Moreover some (like beech) have been found to have a valuable function in building up soil fertility. The interdependence of the forest and its constituent tree species, ground flora, and fauna is taken for granted.

Lack of economic value is sometimes a character not only of species or groups, but of entire biotic communities: marshes, bogs, dunes, and 'deserts' are examples. Our formula in such cases is to relegate their conservation to government as refuges, monuments, or parks. The difficulty is that these communities are usually interspersed with more valuable private lands; the government cannot possibly own or control such scattered parcels. The net effect is that we have relegated some of them to ultimate extinction over large areas. If the private owner were ecologically minded, he would be proud to be the custodian of a reasonable proportion of such areas, which add diversity and beauty to his farm and to his community.

In some instances, the assumed lack of profit in these 'waste' areas has proved to be wrong, but only after most of them had been done away with. The present scramble to reflood muskrat marshes is a case in point.

There is a clear tendency in American conservation to relegate to government all necessary jobs that private landowners fail to perform. Government ownership, operation, subsidy, or regulation is now widely prevalent in forestry, range management, soil and watershed management, park and wilderness conservation, fisheries management, and migratory bird

management, with more to come. Most of this growth in governmental conservation is proper and logical, some of it is inevitable. That I imply no disapproval of it is implicit in the fact that I have spent most of my life working for it. Nevertheless the question arises: What is the ultimate magnitude of the enterprise? Will the tax base carry its eventual ramifications? At what point will governmental conservation, like the mastodon, become handicapped by its own dimensions? The answer, if there is any, seems to be in a land ethic, or some other force which assigns more obligation to the private landowner.

Industrial landowners and users, especially lumbermen and stockmen, are inclined to wail long and loudly about the extension of government ownership and regulation to land, but (with notable exceptions) they show little disposition to develop the only visible alternative: the voluntary practice of conservation on their own lands.

When the private landowner is asked to perform some unprofitable act for the good of the community, he today assents only with outstretched palm. If the act costs him cash this is fair and proper, but when it costs only forethought, open-mindedness, or time, the issue is at least debatable. The overwhelming growth of land-use subsidies in recent years must be ascribed, in large part, to the government's own agencies for conservation education: the land bureaus, the agricultural colleges, and the extension services. As far as I can detect, no ethical obligation toward land is taught in these institutions.

To sum up: a system of conservation based solely on economic self-interest is hopelessly lopsided. It tends to ignore, and thus eventually to eliminate, many elements in the land community that lack commercial value, but that are (as far as we know) essential to its healthy functioning. It assumes, falsely, I think, that the economic parts of the biotic clock will function without the uneconomic parts. It tends to relegate to government many functions eventually too large, too complex, or too widely dispersed to be performed by government.

An ethical obligation on the part of the private owner is the only visible remedy for these situations. . . .

It is inconceivable to me that an ethical relation to land can exist without love, respect, and admiration for land, and a high regard for its value. By value, I of course mean something far broader than mere economic value; I mean value in the philosophical sense.

Perhaps the most serious obstacle impeding the evolution of a land ethic is the fact that our educational and economic system is headed away from, rather than toward, an intense consciousness of land. Your true modern is separated from the land by many middlemen, and by innumerable physical gadgets. He has no vital relation to it; to him it is the space between cities on which crops grow. Turn him loose for a day on the land, and if the spot does not happen to be a golf links or a 'scenic' area, he is bored stiff. If crops could be raised by hydroponics instead of farming, it would suit him very well. Synthetic substitutes for wood, leather, wool, and other natural land products suit him better than the originals. In short, land is something he has 'outgrown'.

Almost equally serious as an obstacle to a land ethic is the attitude of the farmer for whom the land is still an adversary, or a taskmaster that keeps him in slavery. Theoretically, the mechanization of farming ought to cut the farmer's chains, but whether it really does is debatable.

One of the requisites for an ecological comprehension of land is an understanding of ecology, and this is by no means co-extensive with 'education'; in fact, much higher education seems deliberately to avoid ecological concepts. An understanding of ecology does not necessarily originate in courses bearing ecological labels; it is quite as likely to be labeled geography, botany, agronomy, history, or economics. This is as it should be, but whatever the label, ecological training is scarce.

The case for a land ethic would appear hopeless but for the minority which is in obvious revolt against these 'modern' trends.

The 'key-log' which must be moved to release the evolutionary process for an ethic is simply this: quit thinking about decent land-use as solely an economic problem. Examine each question in terms of what is ethically and esthetically right, as well as what is economically expedient. A thing is right when it tends to preserve the integrity, stability, and beauty of the biotic community. It is wrong when it tends otherwise.

It of course goes without saying that economic feasibility limits the tether of what can or cannot be done for land. It always has and it always will. The fallacy the economic determinists have tied around our collective neck, and which we now need to cast off, is the belief that economics determines *all* land-use. This is simply not true. An innumerable host of actions and attitudes, comprising perhaps the bulk of all land relations, is determined by the land-users' tastes and predilections, rather than by his purse. The bulk of all land relations hinges on investments of time, forethought, skill, and faith rather than on investments of cash. As a land-user thinketh, so is he.

8.4 The Grand Canyon and the Sistine Chapel

The history of the physical environment in the United States is marked by constant tradeoffs, the sacrifice of one value to gain another. The problem is that it is much easier to estimate the number of houses that could be built with redwood logs, the number of workers who could be paid to cut down the forest, and the amount of money the logging company could make, than to put a value on the untouched grandeur of a standing forest of ancient redwood trees.

A classic instance of such a trade-off was a plan developed in the 1960s to dam the Grand Canyon of the Colorado River. This proposal, part of the Central Arizona Project, would destroy a great natural wonder but would generate hydro-electric power, and provide swimming and waterskiing recreation on the newly developed lakes. It would also create jobs, irrigate farms, and increase real estate values in cities like Phoenix and Tucson who would receive irrigation water. It would produce measurable wealth.

The proposal to dam the Grand Canyon caused an uproar from environmentalists and others who opposed the project. Senator Barry Goldwater of Arizona, a conservative opponent of big government, answered these critics in a newspaper column from his home in Phoenix in June, 1966.

A few months later, the Sierra Club placed an ad in the New York Times *attacking plans to flood the Canyon. It compared that act with flooding the Sistine Chapel in Rome, whose ceiling is covered with Michelangelo's priceless and irreplaceable painting of the Creation. Goldwater's column, and a portion of the Sierra Club ad, follows.*

Questions

Senator Goldwater and the Sierra Club suggest a number of questions about environmental trade-offs. For example, is the Grand Canyon less worth preserving in its current form than the Sistine Chapel? Does it matter if parts of the Canyon are flooded if most tourists can't see them anyway? Should we alter the Grand Canyon to expand such centers of industry and population as Phoenix? What values enable us to decide if we want to preserve or change treasures such as the Grand Canyon and the Sistine Chapel?

Do current educational practices help us understand the value of things that cannot be quantified? How do we decide when a trade-off is desirable. What elements should be taken into consideration when making such a decision?

Barry Goldwater —

I want to put some of my news colleagues straight on the Central Arizona Project and what we are trying to do in the arid Southwest about water, our major problem. . . . To put it bluntly, we who have made our homes in this beautiful desert do not want to become the sixth generation to leave because the water ran out.

We had looked to the transportation of Colorado River water to central Arizona originally for agricultural uses. But our population explosion has been so great that the water will have to be used for essential domestic purposes.

We propose to do this under the U.S. Reclamation Act, by which vast projects have been constructed in the arid sections of the West.

Because I have stood for confining the extensions of Washington's power, my advocacy of the Central Arizona Project has drawn snide and decisive comments from uninformed writers.

For their particular information, many of the West's reclamation projects already have been paid for—not by U.S. taxpayers, but by the people who use the water in the affected areas. This financing arrangement is being applied to all such projects.

For CAP, the initial outlays would be provided by congressional authorization. But under the Reclamation Act the users are obligated to repay every cent of federal money except that used for functions specifically allocated to the federal government under the Constitution.

This is a lot different from the picture painted by some eastern columnists. Arizona is NOT asking for something for nothing from Washington.

Those who believe Arizona is asking for a giant handout should look into the history of the Theodore Roosevelt dam completed in 1911. The users were charged with the repayment of 85% of all funds used. The other 15% was charged to the federal government for its constitutionally ordered responsibilities. The money has now been repaid.

Because of the foresight of the founders of the dam project, the valley that I see from my study window is the fastest-growing industrial area and one of the fastest-growing population areas in the nation.

As with all projects of this nature there is opposition to the CAP from people who believe the construction of two dams at the bottom of the Grand Canyon would turn one of nature's great wonders into a huge bathtub. I don't claim to be the world's leading expert on the Grand Canyon, but I have spent much time traveling and studying it, and I say this argument is utter nonsense.

The dams would be built in one of the least attractive parts of the entire canyon system, and the resulting lake could not even be seen by visitors on either rim, with the exception of a couple of points not now accessible to the average tourist.

A major argument from the standpoint of those who want to preserve the canyon for its awe-inspiring effect is that one of the dams, the Bridge Canyon Dam, would provide a view of some of the world's most spectacular scenery. At present only those few who can afford to spend between $500 and $1,000 on a boat trip get the view.

The Sierra Club —

Supporters of the dams suggest that building them in the Grand Canyon is only good sense.

They point out that the new 'recreational lakes' will benefit tourists in power boats who will enjoy viewing the upper canyon walls more closely.

Should we flood the Sistine Chapel, so tourists can get nearer the ceiling?

8.5 Getting Better and Worse at the Same Time

For the past two decades the National Wildlife Federation has issued an "Environmental Quality Index," an annual report card on the progress and regression of environmental issues. Appearing in the organization's publication, National Wildlife, *the EQ Index measures the status of wildlife, air, water, energy, forests and soil. In 1988 the Index concluded that "things are getting better and worse at the same time."*

The EQ Index is ambiguous because the techniques of analysis are becoming more sophisticated. Some progress is being made, but every time scientists dig deeper they find the problems more complicated and more difficult to treat. For this reason, some aspects, like air quality, appear better to the naked eye, but upon closer examination are seriously deficient. Meanwhile, public support for environmental quality and public expectations for a cleaner, better environment remain high. "This then is the fundamental pattern that emerges from 20 years of EQ Indexes: the problems besetting America's environment have proved far tougher than anyone predicted—but the same thing is true of the resolve of the American people."

Questions

Summarize the pros and cons of the Environmental Quality Index in the basic categories of wildlife, air, water, energy and forests. Since most people want better environmental quality, why isn't there a greater public outcry about environmental issues? Why is there backsliding? Is the problem one of low consciousness, political inertia, organized opposition, or something else?

What changes would make the biggest environmental difference? How should the U.S. deal with international and global issues, such as the greenhouse effect and acid rain? What kind of leadership do you expect from the White House?

Many Americans assume that science and technology will automatically solve the most important environmental problems; others say that science and technology are part of the problem, not the solution. What is your opinion?

. . . Two decades of EQ Indexes . . . offer a glimpse into the changing face of the environmental movement. In the beginning, Americans were slow and reluctant to wake from their long daydream of endless growth, limitless consumption and irresponsible waste. The call to awareness was the strenuous work of a few visionaries who struggled to persuade their dubious countrymen, as the prophets of the Old Testament once did, to repent and reform.

Then came an orgy of revelations and alarms about the fragility of the environment and the incompatibility of limitless appetites with limited resources. The indifference of the 1960s gave way to shock, determination and then action. All of this was celebrated in a grim but exuberant national town meeting called Earth Day in 1970. More importantly, the rush of feeling was translated into a flood of federal legislation aimed at cleansing our water and air and protecting wildlife. . . .

Not only were the problems more difficult than expected, but as the 1970s gave way to the 1980s, public interest lagged. There were no more Earth Days, no charismatic national leaders calling us to environmental awareness. The environmental movement, it was said, was moribund.

Yet something else was happening. The protesters and writers and speakers of the early days had been replaced by the lawyers and scientists of the Environmental Protection Agency, the Council on Environmental Quality and a number of highly organized national organizations supported by steadily growing memberships.

SOURCE: "Environmental Quality Index," *National Wildlife*, February–March 1988, pp. 38–45, published by the National Wildlife Federation.

As a result, environmental concerns have been made part of the fabric of our institutions. In the words of Jay D. Hair, president of the National Wildlife Federation, "the greatest accomplishment of the environmental movement since Earth Day has been putting our strong desire for environmental protection at the heart of the quality of life in our society."

Thus the success stories charted by these 20 years of EQ Indexes include not only hard-fought victories against pollution, but the steadily growing, increasingly steadfast acceptance by the American people of the necessity of the fight.

In fact, since the early days of environmentalism Americans have consistently expressed, in public opinion polls and political contests, their determination to clean up the environment and to pay the costs.

This then is the fundamental pattern that emerges from 20 years of EQ Indexes: the problems besetting America's environment have proved far tougher than anyone predicted—but the same thing is true of the resolve of the American people.

Wildlife —

. . . [T]he plight of four individual birds symbolized the ambiguous state of America's wildlife in general. Each gained brief notoriety in 1987.

One, the last wild California condor, moved to center stage in April when he was captured and joined with the other 26 surviving members of his species. The birds are part of a controversial captive breeding program designed to aid condor survival. . . .

Two months later, newspapers across the country announced the death of another bird, Orange Band, the last known dusky seaside sparrow. . . .

Just five days later, scientists from the Maryland Department of Natural Resources spotted something in suburban Baltimore that had not been seen there for more than 50 years: a nesting pair of bald eagles. . . .

In the same month that the dusky seaside sparrow became extinct, 12 other species of animals and plants were added to the federal Endangered Species List. Another, the American alligator, was removed from that list and declared "biologically secure" by the U.S. Fish and Wildlife Service (FWS). . . .

. . . Currently, there are about 1,000 species that the agency has determined should be added to the Endangered Species List, but most will have to wait years to gain protection.

While continued attention to the plight of wildlife is producing results, the pressures exerted on habitat by encroaching humans continue to increase. National parks and wildlife refuges are reporting mounting pollution problems and threats from nearby development; last year, authorities noted some alarming decreases in resident animal populations in the reserves. One study of western national parks found some species of mammals have vanished from nearly all of them.

Another survey reported that more people than ever went hunting and fishing in 1987—many of them finding shorter seasons and reduced bag limits. Yet the more people who encounter directly the results of pollution and development on the natural world, the more pressure that may be brought to bear on behalf of wildlife.

Air—

The quality of the nation's air can be seen either as improving or getting worse, depending on where you live. Some cities, such as Charleston, West Virginia, and Grand Rapids, Michigan, met the federal standards for the cleanliness of their air before the 1987 deadline for compliance. Many others, however, still have a long way to go.

Consider, for instance, the case of Denver, Colorado. Once a haven for people with such lung afflictions as tuberculosis, the Mile High City now has a death rate for lung disease that is 30 percent higher than the national average. The noxious cloud of pollutants over Denver much of the time threatens not only the physical health of its residents, but also the economic health of the entire area. . . .

Denver had plenty of company, however. More than 60 American cities found it impossible to comply with the law, even though the standards had been eased and the deadlines extended repeatedly in the 17 years since they were first promulgated under the Clean Air Act.

Even so, significant progress has been made in the past two decades, and that progress continued in the latest year for which detailed figures are available: 1985. After a worrisome increase in 1984 levels of particulates, sulfur dioxide and nitrogen oxide, 1985 figures continued their ten-year downward trend. Despite the trend, however, certain air-pollution problems remain unsolved.

What's more, there are new categories of problems to be dealt with. Scientists and doctors told a Senate committee in April that, in many instances, indoor air pollution may now pose a greater threat to public health than the familiar outdoor variety. In some buildings, pollution from radon, household chemicals and other products can reach levels five times worse than the grimiest air outside.

Although startling, indoor air pollution problems generally are not difficult to relieve. The same cannot be said for one of the country's most uncontrolled dilemmas: the long-distance transport of pollution through the air. "It's a tougher problem than we thought," said EPA Administrator Lee M. Thomas last year.

As a result, a visitor to the Grand Canyon or Shenandoah National Park will find the view obscured by pollution more than 90 percent of the time, according to an Interior Department study released last year. EPA regulations were designed to eliminate specific, identifiable sources of pollution from national parks and wilderness areas. But the Interior Department found that regional haze, a mix of air pollutants from sources far away, has cut visibility in much of the eastern United States by more than 50 percent in the last 40 years. In July, six northeastern states and five environmental groups sued EPA for failing to control such haze.

The suit was added to a long list of similar actions brought against the EPA, many claiming the agency has failed to solve the similarly intractable problem of acid rain. Unlike regional haze, the sources of acid rain have been documented. The sulphur and nitrogen emissions that can make rainwater more acidic than vinegar are put into the atmosphere by fossil-fuel burners such as electric utilities and cars in states far from where the acid is deposited.

Last year, a Congressional committee was told by representatives of several public health groups of strong evidence that acid rain not only poses a serious threat to lakes and buildings, but also to the health of children and the elderly. . . .

Water —

CONSERVATIONISTS were heartened early in 1987 by the enactment, over President Reagan's veto, of an eight-year extension of the federal Clean Water Act. The move not only provided $20 billion for fighting water pollution, it also signaled a stronger Congressional commitment to the cause and a change in the nature of the country's clean-up battle. . . .

. . . The goal of the original Clean Water Act—to make the country's freshwater "swimmable and fishable" once more—has been met in many of the nation's waterways. In New York, for instance, 78 percent of the state's 70,000 miles of rivers and streams have reportedly met federal standards. "It was easy to build the sewage treatment plants," observed EPA official Peter Wise. "It will be harder to clean up the sediments and the pollution transported in by air."

Wise was speaking in particular about the Great Lakes, which contain 95 percent of the country's fresh water and thus showcase the nature of the country's problems. Fish generally are thriving in the lakes now, where once they were struggling—and failing—to survive. But they remain dangerous to the health of humans who consume them.

It is a situation not restricted to the Great Lakes alone. Despite their clean-up successes, for example, authorities in New York last year warned consumers not to eat more than one meal a week of any fish taken from any waters in the state.

The problem is high levels of toxic chemicals and poisonous metals—pesticide residues such as DDT and dieldrin, along with industrial emissions including heavy metals and polychlorinated biphenyls (PCBs)—that are still finding their way into many water bodies and the fish that live in them.

Researchers in Iowa discovered in 1986 that water from 25 percent of the state's private wells (70 percent in some counties) contained unsafe levels of nitrates, an ingredient in agricultural fertilizers. One-third of the wells tested were contaminated by pesticides. Last year, the state took action.

As a result of a new law, Iowa became one of the first farm states to target agricultural pollution of groundwater, and the first to propose that the polluters pay for their regulation. The state legislature approved a bill providing not only for better disposal of hazardous wastes, but for a vigorous campaign to reduce the amount of fertilizer and pesticides applied in Iowa fields. The money for the program is to come from a tax on agricultural chemicals and such toxic household materials as wax and paint thinner.

Energy —

. . . [A] rising chorus of voices warned in 1987 of a larger problem—that the U.S. and the world are running out of oil. As *The New York Times* reported in February, "Few experts quarrel seriously with estimates that economically recoverable domestic supplies will be all but depleted by 2020." The same experts agree that by 2000, OPEC production will begin an irreversible decline.

The Reagan Administration's major response to the problem was to press for the exploration and development of virtually every known potential oil field in or near the United States. In a highly controversial decison, the Interior Department proposed opening for exploratory drilling not only millions of acres of the outer continental shelf, but the 1.5-million-acre coastal plain of the Arctic National Wildlife Refuge in Alaska. . . .

Meanwhile, uncertainty over future oil supplies and prices made coal seem more attractive. . . . Coal burning, some scientists believe, is one of the main causes of acid rain. . . .

A far better alternative to drilling for oil or using coal, environmentalists argued, was conservation. As *Business Week* magazine pointed out, "Saving a barrel of oil is far cheaper than producing it." But neither the public nor the administration showed much interest. Americans bought more large cars and drove farther in 1987 than the previous year. Additionally, U.S. requirements for improving auto gasoline mileage remained slackened at an average of 26 miles per gallon.

There was, however, one conservation success in 1987. The President signed a bill (which he had rejected in 1986) setting new efficiency targets for home appliances. Refrigerators, water heaters, air conditioners and the like consume one-quarter of the country's electricity, and have long been notorious energy wasters. The efficiency standards mandated by the bill will reduce the nation's estimated power consumption in the year 2000 by 21,000 megawatts, the output of 21 power plants. And over the next 15 years, the average household should save 300 dollar's worth of electricity.

Still, the events of 1987 showed that the nation's energy future is uncertain. "We are driving into a 'tunnel of the future' and our headlights are off," said Jay Hair of the National Wildlife Federation. "The children of the 21st century will pay the price if we do not start to deal with this critical issue now."

Forests—

IT WAS an exception that proved a rule. The exception: everyone is happy with the way the 50-year plan for Vermont's Green Mountain National Forest turned out. The rule: virtually no one is happy with the plans for the other 155 national forests.

Over the last six years, the U.S. Forest Service has been releasing future plans for the national forests that envisage doubling the amount of timber harvested and building thousands of miles of roads in order to facilitate the harvest. Upon their release in draft form, these long-range plans are subjected to public review.

In Vermont, the public response was loud and clear: the draft plan that called for tripling the timber cut in the Green Mountains was unacceptable. People wanted the forest preserved for wildlife and recreation. In the final plan, local Forest Service planners struck an admirable compromise last year, assigning a lower priority to logging but assuring the harvest of higher quality timber. Most of the 325,000-acre forest was reserved for the use of wildlife and people.

The level of satisfaction with the plan was remarkable. The timber industry swallowed hard, then pronounced the compromise acceptable. Conservationists said the plan should be a model for the Forest Service.

More typical, however, was the situation with California's Shasta-Trinity National Forest, where the final 50-year plan

has been delayed indefinitely by strife. The draft plan presented in 1986 called for a 73 percent increase in the timber harvest. Even some timber industry people said the plan was excessive; "They're asking us to use a meat cleaver," said one logger, "where a sharp knife would be better." Outraged conservation organizations, including the National Wildlife Federation, argued against the plan and it was thrown out. A new plan is being developed.

Particularly in the South and Far West, source of most of the country's wood products, the Forest Service is under heavy pressure and embroiled in unrelieved controversy. One reason is that the amount of privately owned timberland continues to decline while demand for forest products is growing. A Forest Service study released in July forecast the loss of as much as 18.8 million acres of southern timberland by 1995. Conversion to agriculture is a serious problem, but another factor is the failure of the individuals who own more than half the South's forests to replant cutover land. As a result, pressure is on the Forest Service to open more publicly-owned land to heavier timber cutting.

As the economic pressures increase, the prospects for protecting wildlife habitat become more precarious. The Forest Service is supposed to maintain its forests in perpetuity, but according to many conservationists, it is being forced to approve overcutting to keep up with demand. It is also charged with maintaining biological diversity, yet its reliance on monocultures—seeding large stands with a single type of tree and killing off competing vegetation with herbicides—and its eagerness to build roads into undisturbed areas to get at the timber are seen as potentially devastating to wildlife populations.

The offsetting benefits of these Forest Service policies are hard to find. According to the Wilderness Society, for every dollar the federal government spent on road construction and timber-sale administration, it received less than one cent in income; a $600 million dollar loss in 1985 alone, according to a recent analysis.

In addition to increasing encroachment from road construction, U.S. forests continue to be afflicted by a nameless malaise that is slowing growth rates and increasing tree mortality. Acid rain is thought to be a cause, but the connection has yet to be fully proven. And evidence uncovered in 1987 was ambiguous.

Last February, scientists reported that fog samples taken in California and Maryland contained high concentrations of toxic chemicals. The water droplets in the fog studied had absorbed thousands of times more pesticide and other chemicals than was thought possible according to a long-accepted law of chemistry. Investigation is under way into whether toxic fog is connected with the forest decline. . . .

The same month, however, forest biologist Dudley Raynal was reporting that the slow tree growth in Adironack Mountain forests can be attributed largely to recent weather extremes—the severe drought of the 1960s followed by the unusually cold winters in the 1970s and 1980s. "We have not eliminated acid rain as a factor" in forest decline, Raynal said. "Rather, we have pointed out that climatic factors play a role in tree growth."